AN INTRODUCTION TO A

HISTORY OF WOODCUT

WITH A DETAILED SURVEY OF WORK DONE IN

THE FIFTEENTH CENTURY

BY

ARTHUR M. HIND

Late Keeper of Prints and Drawings in the British Museum

WITH FRONTISPIECE AND 483 ILLUSTRATIONS IN THE TEXT

IN TWO VOLUMES

VOL. II

DOVER PUBLICATIONS, INC. NEW YORK

Published in Canada by General Publishing Company, Ltd., 30 Lesmill Road, Don Mills, Toronto, Ontario.

Published in the United Kingdom by Constable and Company, Ltd., 10 Orange Street, London WC 2.

This Dover edition, first published in 1963, is an unabridged and unaltered republication of the work first published by the Houghton Mifflin Company in 1935. In the original edition the frontispiece of the first volume was reproduced in collotype.

International Standard Book Number: 0-486-20953-9
Library of Congress Catalog Card Number: 63-5621

Manufactured in the United States of America

Dover Publications, Inc.
180 Varick Street
New York 14, N. Y.

*This Dover Edition is dedicated
to the memory of*
ARTHUR MAYGER HIND
(1880–1957)

CONTENTS

Bibliographies come at the end of each chapter or section, while references to special books are given in the footnotes. Additions and Corrections to Vols. I. and II. are given in Vol. I. at p. 265, and space is left for further notes

VOL. I

CHAPTER I

v

CHAPTER V

VOL. II

CHAPTER VI

CHAPTER VII

BOOK-ILLUSTRATION AND CONTEMPORARY SINGLE CUTS IN THE
NETHERLANDS 559

CHAPTER VIII

BOOK-ILLUSTRATION AND CONTEMPORARY SINGLE CUTS IN FRANCE
AND FRENCH SWITZERLAND 597

CHAPTER IX

CHAPTER X

AN
INTRODUCTION TO A
HISTORY OF WOODCUT

CHAPTER VI

BOOK-ILLUSTRATION AND CONTEMPORARY SINGLE CUTS IN ITALY

WE have already noted how the Venetian woodcutters and playing-card makers in 1441 essayed to protect their trade against foreign competition; and how in consequence regulations were made forbidding the import of every kind of print.[1] But this does not seem to have interfered with the continued influence of the foreign craftsman, which became even more marked in the early years of book-printing in Italy. The pupils of the earliest German printers soon realised the extensive field that lay before them, and many turned South, preferring the places where they would be pioneers rather than remaining among many competitors in their own country. It is probable also that they took with them their own cutters, or they may even have ventured to undertake block-cutting themselves when free from the restrictions imposed by the guilds in their own country.

ROME

The earliest series of illustrations known with Italian printed text seems to be that of the dotted prints, the so-called *Stoeger Passion*, which has been described in an earlier chapter.[2] This was a set of German metal-cuts, probably issued in Italy by some travelling printer from Mainz or Bamberg. But the first book-illustrations, cut on wood, in Italy, appeared in the edition of Turrecremata's *Meditationes*,[3] printed at Rome by ULRICH HAN in 1467 (H. 15722), i.e. two years after the first dated book printed in Italy (the *Lactantius*, printed by SWEYNHEYM and PANNARTZ at Subiaco). They were thoroughly German in linear character, though they were certainly derived from Italian designs. According to the text the cuts, chiefly illustrations from the Old and New Testaments, were based on a series of frescoes (no longer extant) in St. Maria sopra Minerva, Rome, and the dignified character of the design, poorly seconded by the crudeness of the cutting, entirely supports the claim.

[1] See pp. 82-83.   [2] See p. 192.

[3] Cardinal Turrecremata (Torquemada), the Abbot of the Benedictine Monastery of St. Scholastica of Subiaco, was no doubt partly responsible for the introduction of printing in Italy, for it was in his convent that Sweynheym and Pannartz set up their first press.

There are thirty-one cuts in the first edition, of 1467 (e.g. Manchester, Vienna and Nuremberg), the extra three cuts in the Nuremberg copy being inserted later. The second edition, of 1473 (H. 15724, e.g. Manchester, Vienna), contains thirty-three cuts, three subjects being added, i.e. the *Fall* (f. 3, verso), the *Flight into Egypt* (f. 8, verso), the *Trinity* (f. 25), and one omitted, i.e. the *Last Judgment* (which occurred on f. 33, verso of the first edition). The same cuts appeared in Han's third edition,

Fig. 183. Procession of the Eucharist, from Turrecremata, *Meditationes*, Rome 1467.

1478 (H. 15725, Pierpont Morgan Library, lacking f. 26 with the cut of the *Dominican Tree*), and in that of 1484 printed by his successor Stephan Planck (Reithling 1100, Dyson Perrins No. 34). Stephan Planck also issued an edition in 1498 (H. 15728) with small copies of somewhat delicate cutting (about $2\frac{3}{4} \times 3$ inches), in which the first cut is surrounded by a border (white scroll on black ground with a *putto* at the foot) similar in style to the ornament of the Naples *Aesop* of 1485.

Adaptations of the same subjects printed by J. Neumeister at Mainz in 1479 have already been described.[1]

[1] See p. 194.

Fig. 184. Initial G, from Barberiis, *Opuscula,* Rome, about 1481–83.

Sweynheym and Pannartz used no woodcut decoration in their books printed at Subiaco (1465–67), but used a woodcut bar and capitals in occasional copies of Suetonius, *Vitae Caesarum,* printed at Rome in 1470 (e.g. in the Pierpont Morgan copy, Catalogue, vol. ii. No. 245). These capitals were used later at Rome by the printers GEORGIUS TEUTONICUS and SIXTUS RIESSINGER (1481–83) and OLIVERIUS SERVIUS (1484).[1] The bar, like the capitals, is in outline branch-work on a black ground, printed by hand after the text, probably in the rubricator's shop, and intended as a basis for hand colouring.[2] The same practice of using outline woodcut as a basis for rubrication is also seen in certain books printed by JOHANNES and VINDELINUS DE SPIRA, NICOLAUS JENSON and BARTHOLOMAEUS CREMONENSIS at Venice between 1469 and 1472.[3]

[1] Very close replicas of the same capitals were used in books printed by Johann Müller (Regiomontanus) at Nuremberg, about 1474 (see p. 369). Careful comparison of the capitals in Teutonicus and Riessinger's with those in Müller's books leads me to conclude that Müller's were probably for the most part (if not all) metal casts from the original blocks. In the cases where the original capital lacked its left border (intended for use against a border), this is repeated in Müller's version. If they had been woodcut copies it is more likely that the capital would have been completed with its four borders. Moreover, the Müller versions combine a very exact relation to the originals with small flaws which appear like faulty casting. On the other hand, occasional dots in the background differing in position suggest copies, made perhaps from tracings or from prints.

The following letters can be compared in Italian and German versions in the British Museum:

S (*a*) Teutonicus and Riessinger. *Ad Peccatorem Sodomitam,* n.d. IB. 19245.

   (*b*) Müller. Marcus Manilius, *Astronomica,* n.d. (H. 10703). C. 16. h. 6.

I (*a*) Teutonicus and Riessinger. *Decisiones Novae Rotae Romanae,* n.d. (H. 604). IB. 19237.

   (*b*) Müller. Manilius, *Astronomica,* n.d. (H. 10703). C. 16. h. 6.

P (*a*) Teutonicus and Riessinger. Philippus de Barberiis, *Opuscula,* n.d. IA. 19241.

   (*b*) Müller. J. Müller, *Tractatus contra Cremonensia,* n.d. (H. 13805). IB. 7885.

E (*a*) Oliverius Servius. Boethius, *Topica,* 1484 (H. 3429). IB. 19259.

   (*b*) Müller. Basilius, *Opusculum ad Juvenes,* n.d. IA. 7883.

On the question of metal casts cf. Index of Subjects (under *Casts*).

[2] See p. 534, for a certain Francesco Rosselli, described as *miniatore e stampatore* (illuminator and printer), who, judging from his son's inventory, was no doubt the owner of a large stock of copper plates and wood blocks.

[3] See A. W. Pollard, *Woodcut Designs for Illuminators in Venetian Books,* 1469–73, Bibliographica, iii., 1897, 122. Nothing is known of the famous printer Jenson, apart from his activity at Venice, except that he was French and a native of Sommevoire (Aube). Tradition makes him

The design is generally more in the nature of a 'branch' pattern in the 'white vine' style, as it is usually termed in regard to contemporary manuscript illuminations. The borders are for the most part composed of several blocks arranged in various ways, for two, three or four sides; and small pieces of pattern could be adapted by repetition to whatever spaces they were required to fill.

The chief books noted by Essling and elsewhere as containing such borders are as follows:

(a) Printed by JOHANNES DE SPIRA (d. 1470) and VINDELINUS DE SPIRA:

Pliny, *Historia Naturalis*, 1469. H. 13087, E. 2.

Augustinus, *De Civitate Dei*, 1470. H. 2048, E. 72.

Virgil, *Opera*, 1470. E. 52.

Livy, *Decades*, 1470. H. 10130, E. 32.

Petrarch, *Sonetti*, etc., 1470. H. 12753, E. 74.

Sallust, *Opera*, 1470. H. 14197, E. 43.

Cicero, *De Officiis*, 1470 and 1472. H. 5257-8, E. 7 and 8.

Cicero, *Epistolae ad Familiares*, 1470 and 1471. H. 5166-7, E. 20 and 22.

Appianus, *De Bellis Civilibus Romanis*, 1472. H. 1306, E. 220.

Georgius Trapesuntius, *Rhetorica*, 1470. H. 7608, E. 118.

Curtius, *Historia Alexandri Magni*, c. 1470. E. 119.

Valerius Maximus, *De factis dictisque mirabilibus*, 1471. H. 15775, E. 211.

(b) Printed by NICOLAUS JENSON:

Eusebius, *De Evangelica Preparatione*, 1470. H. 6699, E. 71.

Quintilian, *Institutiones Oratoriae*, 1471. H. 13647, E. 130.

Cicero, *Epistolae ad Familiares*, 1471. H. 5168, E. 21.

Leonardus Bruni (Aretinus), *De Bello adversus Gothos*, 1471. H. 1559, E. 219.

Suetonius, *Vitae Caesarum*, 1471. H. 15117, E. 207.

Pliny, *Historia Naturalis*, 1472. H. 13089, E. 3.

(c) Printed by CHRISTOPHORUS VALDARFER:

Cicero, *Orationes*, 1471. H. 5122, E. 218.

(d) Printed by BARTHOLOMAEUS CREMONENSIS:

Virgil, *Opera*, 1472. E. 53.

St. Jerome, *Vita et Transita*, 1473. H. 8637, E. 122.

at some period Master of the Mint at Troyes or Paris, and sends him at the behest of Louis XI. on a secret mission to Mainz to find out about the newly discovered methods of printing.

(*e*) Printed by JACOBUS RUBEUS (JACQUES LE ROUGE):
Ovid, *Metamorphoses*, 1474. H. 12138, E. 222.
(*f*) Printer unknown:
Cicero, *De Oratore* (V. de Spira?), *c.* 1470. H. 5096, E. 115.
Petrarch, *Sonetti*, etc. (N. Jenson?), n.d. H. 12757, E. 75.

The Grenville copy of the Virgil (British Museum), of which a reproduction is here given (fig. 185), is of particular interest as it shows the
woodcut uncoloured, but with the remains of an outside border-line of
yellowish paste, probably the ground work (adhesive material) for a gold
border to the illumination. The paste border has set off on the opposite
page, and a fragment of a simple black-leaf border prepared for the top
and left side of the page also shows clearly in the offset, though it has
almost disappeared on the original page.

That Sweynheym and Pannartz intended to use woodcut illustration is
shown by the spaces left in Nicolaus de Lyra, *Postilla super Bibliam*, 1471–72
(H. 10363), with headings *hic figura, sequitur figura*, etc. No copies are
known with cuts, but a few contain drawings.[1]

After Turrecremata's *Meditationes* no subject illustrations are known in
Roman books until those in the various editions of Philippus de Barberiis,
Opuscula, printed in and about 1481, with illustrations chiefly of *Sibyls* and
Prophets.

There is an edition printed by J. P. DE LIGNAMINE and dated 1st December
1481 (British Museum, from the Malcolm Collection) in which thirteen
subjects, i.e. the twelve *Sibyls* and the figure of *Proba*, are printed from
five blocks. They are rudely cut, in strong outline and little shading, within
a thick border-line, and measure about $4\frac{1}{4} \times 2\frac{7}{8}$ inches in size.

A second edition printed by Lignamine, n.d. (H. 2455), includes twenty-
nine illustrations printed from twenty-three blocks, all being newly cut
except the *Proba*. To distinguish them from the earlier edition, many of
the figures stand under round arches; they are as crudely cut, and even
broader in line. The subjects added to the *Sibyls* and *Proba* were twelve
Prophets, Plato, the *Man of Sorrows,* a *Nativity*[2] and *St. John the Baptist.*
Despite the rudeness of the cutting, there is something attractive in the
designs of both these editions.

A rough and angular title-block to Horace, *Carmen Saeculare,* n.d.,
about 1484 (issued by the printer of Manilius, *Astronomicum*), is certainly

---

[1] See p. 282.
[2] The *Man of Sorrows* and the *Nativity* based on engravings by the German Master E.S.

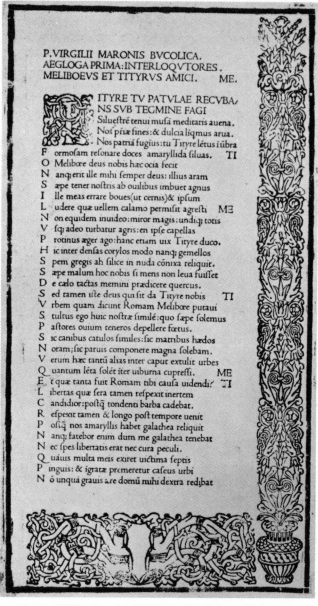

P. VIRGILII MARONIS BVCOLICA.
AEGLOGA PRIMA: INTERLOQVTORES.
MELIBOEVS ET TITYRVS AMICI.   ME.

ITYRE TV PATVLAE RECVBA,
NS SVB TEGMINE FAGI
Siluestré tenui musa meditaris auena.
Nos priæ fines: & dulcia liqmus arua.
Nos patriä fugius: tu Tityre létus i ûbra
F ormosam resonare doces amaryllida siluas.   TI
O Melibœe deus nobis hæc ocia fecit
N anq; erit ille mihi semper deus: illius aram
S æpe tener nostris ab ouilibus imbuet agnus
I lle meas errare boues (ut cernis) & ipsum
L udere quæ uellem calamo permisit agresti   ME
N on equidem inuideo: miror magis: undiq; totis
V scq; adeo turbatur agris: en ipse capellas
P rotinus æger ago: hanc etiam uix Tityre duco.
H ic inter densas corylos modo nanq; gemellos
S pem gregis ah silice in nuda cönixa reliquit.
S æpe malum hoc nobis si mens non leua fuisset
D e cælo tactas memini prædicere quercus.
S ed tamen iste deus qui sit da Tityre nobis   TI
V rbem quam dicunt Romam Melibœe putaui
S tultus ego huic nostræ similé: quo sæpe solemus
P astores ouium teneros depellere fœtus.
S ic canibus catulos similes: sic matribus hædos
N oram; sic paruis componere magna solebam.
V erum hæc tantü alias inter caput extulit urbes
Q uantum léta solét iter uiburna cupressi.   ME
E t quæ tanta fuit Romam tibi causa uidendi?   TI
L ibertas quæ sera tamen respexit inertem
C andidior: postq tondenti barba cadebat.
R espexit tamen & longo post tempore uenit
P ostq nos amaryllis habet galathea reliquit
N anq; fatebor enim dum me galathea tenebat
N ec spes libertatis erat nec cura peculi.
Q uäuis multa meis exiret uictima septis
P inguis: & igratæ premeretur caseus urbi
N ö unquä grauis ære domü mihi dextra redjbat

Fig. 185. Half-border and Initial T, from Virgil, *Opera*, Venice 1472.

by the same cutter as the second edition of Lignamine's *Opuscula* of
Barberiis.

Better known in design though still weak and angular (and also
probably German) in cutting, are the blocks in the edition printed by
GEORGIUS TEUTONICUS and
SIXTUS RIESSINGER, between
1481 and 1483 (H. 2453).

Here the subjects are limited
to the twelve *Sibyls* and *Proba*,
and there is no economy in
using blocks for more than one
subject. There is considerable
grace in several of the *Sibyls*
and a certain classical dignity
in the *Proba*, which is here
reproduced (fig. 186). The
beautiful capitals in strap-work
on black ground, used in this
and other books by Teutonicus
and Riessinger, came from
the stock of Sweynheym and
Pannartz.

Another book printed by
J. P. de Lignamine, the
Herbarius of Lucius Apuleius,
n.d., about 1483–84 (H. 1322),
is certainly one of the earliest,
if not actually the first, among
printed herbals.[1] It contains a
hundred and thirty-one illus-

Fig. 186. Proba, from Barberiis, *Opuscula,* Rome, about
1481–83.

trations of plants, about 4 × 3 inches, simply designed and cut, making
good use of broad black lines and spaces.

Two other Italian herbals printed in the xv century may be mentioned

---

[1] Schreiber dates it about 1493 in his facsimile edition of Schoeffer's *Gart der Gesuntheit,*
1485 (*Hortus Sanitatis Deutsch,* Munich 1924), but the dedication of one issue to Cardinal
Gonzaga, who died 21st October 1483, is witness to the earlier date. The British Museum
copy is dedicated to Giuliano della Rovere, and is probably after the Cardinal's death. See
A. C. Klebs, Papers, Bibliographical Society of America, Chicago, xi., 1917, p. 82, and see
above, p. 348.

here as their simple cutting of plants shows little individuality of style, and does not call for special reference in our local sections, i.e. the *Herbolarium*, printed by Leonardus Achates and Gulielmus of Pavia, at Vicenza, 1491 (H.8451), and *De Virtutibus Herbarum* printed by Bevilaqua at Venice in 1499 (H.1807). Both of these books may be found variously described under the title of *Aggregator*, or the name of Arnoldus de Villa Nova. They each contain 150 woodcuts of plants and derive from the Mainz *Herbarius Latinus* of 1484.

By the same draughtsman and cutter as the illustrations in Planck's edition of Turrecremata, *Meditationes*, of 1498,[1] are the little cuts in Thomas Ochsenbrunner, *Priscorum Heroum Stemmata*, printed by JOHANN BESICKEN,[2] 1494 (H.11934), and the frontispiece to Bernardus Granollachs, *Lunarium*, printed by Planck, about 1497 (H.7863). The latter subject is freely adapted from the frontispiece to the Florentine editions of the *Lunarium* printed by Morgiani, 1496, with suggestions from the cut of the *Astrologer in his Study* at the end of the Florentine edition.

The subjects in the *Priscorum Heroum Stemmata* (mostly about $1\frac{3}{8} \times 1\frac{7}{8}$ inches; one or two $2\frac{3}{8} \times 1\frac{7}{8}$ inches) represent for the most part Roman and later heroes issuing half-length from decorative stems. Whether by a German or Italian cutter, these little blocks and the other works by the same hand are far more delicately cut than any of the other Roman blocks hitherto mentioned.

The Florentine frontispiece is in its turn closely related to the title cut of Anianus, *Compotus*, printed by ANDREAS FREITAG at Rome 1493 (H.5596) and might be copied from it (unless there is a lost earlier edition of the Florentine version, which would give it the priority). The *Compotus* block is surrounded with a black-ground *passe-partout* border, with children tilting on pigs, which is copied from one used by Morgiani and Petri at Florence.[3] The first suggestion of the *Compotus* and *Lunarium* subjects was the frontispiece in B. Granollachs, *Sommario dell' arte di astrologia*, Naples, about 1485 (F.-B.65).

The only other illustrated book printed in Rome during the xv century that demands our attention is the *Mirabilia Romae* (or, in its German editions, *Wie Rom gepauet ward*). We have already described these popular guide-books to the Papal city, for its first edition was a block-book.[4]

Of the very numerous type-printed editions in the last fifteen years of

[1] See p. 397.
[2] For another book recently attributed to Besicken, see my Additions in vol. i., p. 265.
[3] See No. 6 in my list of Florentine *passe-partout* borders, p. 533.   [4] See p. 258.

the xv century there are two distinct classes: (1) those with black-line cuts, based more or less closely on the block-book illustrations; (2) those with cuts within black-ground borders, with additional subjects of the Virgin and Child, the Crucifixion and various saints.

Of the first class the German edition of STEPHAN PLANCK, 20th November 1489, reproduced by the Wiegendruckgesellschaft, Berlin, 1925 (ed. C. Hülsen), is a good example; the Latin edition of Andreas Freitag, 1492, contains much cruder copies of the original cuts.

Of the second class Planck's Latin issue of about 1497 (H. 11177) is perhaps the best in quality, while much poorer copies of Planck's illustrations occur in the editions printed by Johann Besicken (e.g. that of 29th January 1500 in Latin, H. 11203).

It has already been noted that one of the earliest type-printed editions, formerly attributed to Planck, contains illustrations cut from the blocks of the original block-book. The British Museum Catalogue of xv-Century Printed Books (part iv. p. 144) describes it as by an unknown printer, not before 1485, remarking on the similarity of the type to that used at Gaeta in 1487 by Andreas Freitag, who, as we have seen, printed an edition with crude copies at Rome in 1492.

NAPLES

The leading spirit in the production of illustrated books at Naples[1] was the humanist FRANCESCO DEL TUPPO. It has only been recently established that SIXTUS RIESSINGER, the earliest of printers at Naples, and certain 'Germani fidelissimi', JOHANN TRESSER, MARTINUS DE AMSTERDAM, and CHRISTIAN PRELLER, used Tuppo's own press in various books. Tuppo was evidently the publisher, and after the printers mentioned had severed connection with him, it is known that works were still issuing from his press in 1498.

The earliest of these illustrated books was the Boccaccio, *Filocolo* (*Florio e Biancofiore*), printed by Sixtus Riessinger, 8th March 1478 (H. 3299, F.-B. 46). The illustrations, very simply cut in outline with little shading, are German in style, and though considerably inferior to the average of contemporary German work, possess a certain naïve charm. Sixtus Riessinger's own device, which appears at the end of the volume, is probably by the same designer and cutter, and displays greater refinement of execution than the illustrations (fig. 187).

[1] Mariano Fava and Giovanni Bresciano, *La stampa a Napoli nel XV secolo*, Leipzig 1911–13 (Hefte 32-34 of C. Dziatzko and C. Haebler, Sammlung Bibliothekswissenschaftlicher Arbeiten).

It may be noted in passing that ARNALDUS DE BRUXELLA had evidently intended using woodcuts in his edition of Lucianus, *Vera Historia*, 6th March 1475/76 (H. 10259, F.-B. 91), as there are spaces left for illustrations: but these were never filled up.

Another interesting early Naples book is Franchinus Gafurius, *Theorica Musicae*, printed by FRANCESCO DI DINO, 8th October 1480 (H. 7404, F.-B. 170). It contains two subject illustrations, *Figures at an anvil* (*Tubal Cain*), and an *Organist playing*. The block of the organist was reprinted in the Milan edition of 1492, and as Gafurius was a Lombard, and the style of the design Milanese or Brescian in character, it is almost certain that he had the block cut in Lombardy.[1]

Fig. 187. The Mark of the printer Sixtus Riessinger, Naples.

But by far the most important Naples book is the Aesop, *Vita et Fabulae*, with Tuppo's Italian paraphrase.[2] It was printed in 1485 on Tuppo's press by the 'Germani fidelissimi' already mentioned. The illustrations are framed in richly decorated *passe-partout* borders, of which there are several varieties. These borders show a combination of black line and white on black ground, and are characteristic of Neapolitan tendencies in the Oriental richness of their design.[3] The border at the beginning of the Fables is a handsome design on a black ground, scroll work with a cupid attacking a lion's head with a lance in the right border, and with two cupids at the foot flanking a wreathed circular space left blank for the insertion of arms.[4] The same border was used at Soncino by the publisher Joshua Solomon in his *Hebrew Bible* of 1488, and later the same block, cut up and

[1] See p. 516 and fig. 281.

[2] For a recent study of the illustrator of this Aesop, see Lamberti Donati, *Di Alcune ignote zilografie del XV secolo nella Bibl. Vaticana*, Gutenberg-Jahrbuch, Mainz, 1934, p. 86. Donati derives the designer's origin from the Netherlands.

[3] If there are actually any Islamic elements in the design (which is not beyond question), they would probably have come to Naples through Sicily, just as Spain derived similar elements through Moorish channels (Hispano-Mauresque).

[4] A modified version of the same design in which a cow's head is added in the upper border, and in which the cupid on the right armed with sword and buckler attacks a large lion rampant, appears in Hebrew books printed at Naples by ISAAC BEN JUDAH (Moses ben Nachman, *Commentarius in Pentateuchum*, 1490, H. 11671, F.-B. 268; and David Kimchi, *Liber Radicum*, 1491, H. 6034, F.-B. 272). It is somewhat coarser in cutting than the *Aesop* version.

rearranged with the side-pieces on the reverse sides to fit the reversed order of the Hebrew book, was printed in his edition of Jacob ben Ascher, *Arba Turim*, 1490 (H. 1880).

A fairly close copy of the 1485 *Aesop* border appeared in the Aesop, *Vita et Fabulae*, printed at Aquila by Eusanius de Stella, Johannes Picardus de Hamel and Louis de Masson, 1493 (H. 355, Paris and Pierpont Morgan). This Aquila edition contains eighty-eight copies of the original illustrations, and a cut of *Master and Pupils* on the title page, of which I have not identified an earlier version.

Fig. 188. Aesop's introduction to the house of Xanthus, from his *Vita et Fabulae*, Naples 1485.

The subject designs of the 1485 *Aesop* were very probably cut, if not designed, by an artist from Northern Europe; they are angular in style, exhibit strong emphasis on the inner contours of the face, and are characterised by the use of a very regular system of short lines in parallel series, and ribbons of close parallel shading against the outlines of drapery. The borders are more possibly the design of an Italian artist. The illustrations of the Life of Aesop are on the whole more clumsy in design than those of the Fables; they certainly show the northern craftsman in his more independent vein, as he had no Italian models for this part of the work. He probably knew the cuts to Johann Zainer's Ulm edition of about 1475-76, which included a Life, but he did not follow them in his designs. In the Fables he borrowed largely from the inventions of the Verona *Aesop* of 1479,

Fig. 189. The Ox and the Frog, from Aesop, *Vita et Fabulae*, Naples 1485.

though he modified his originals with great freedom, and occasionally showed entirely independent designs. Further notes about *Aesop* illustrations in general will be added in relation to the Italian *editio princeps* of Verona.

Kristeller very rightly compared the style of the Naples *Aesop* cuts with illustrations signed I.D. in books published at Lyon,[1] and with certain cuts in Spanish books. It is necessary, however, to specify more definitely the incidence of the comparison. The subject cuts in the *Aesop*, on the one hand, are certainly near in character of design and cutting to I.D.'s signed work at Lyon, Toulouse, and in Spain.[2] On the other hand, the border at the beginning of the Fables is undoubtedly related in style to such Spanish borders as that first used by the printer Spindeler in his 1490 edition of *Tirant lo Blanch* (Kurz 252, Haebler 639), and to the woodcut of *King in Council* in the *Usatges de Barcelona e Constitucións de Cataluña*, printed by Pere Miguel and Diego de Gumiel, Barcelona, 28th February 1495 (K. 98, H. 652, Olschki, *Le Livre illustré*, 1926, No. 89).[3] But I would nevertheless hesitate to go so far as to identify the woodcuts of the *Aesop* with the Master I.D., and even less to assume his later activity in Spain. But neither conjecture is unreasonable, as the Naples cutter, who was probably a wandering craftsman from the North, whose style shows much kinship with Netherlandish woodcut, might well have continued his wanderings in Spain and France. But there was later work at Naples comparable with that of the *Aesop*, e.g. another fine border with scroll work, children and stags,[4] which was used by the publisher Joshua Solomon in his *Hebrew Bible*, n.d., about 1490-91 (H. 3028, F.-B. 270; fig. 190), and in his *Pentateuch* which is dated 1491 (H. 12574, F.-B. 271), and in a reversed copy by Ayolfo de Cantono in his edition of Leonardo Bruni (Aretino), *L'Aquila*, 1492 (H. 1577, F.-B. 188);[5] and the illustrations in Marino Gionata (Angionese), *Il Giardino*, 28th June 1490 (F.-B. 178), and in the Aesop, *Fabulae*, n.d., about 1495 (F.-B. 179 *bis*), both printed by Christian Preller, who was one of Tuppo's 'Germani fidelissimi', show a continuation of a similar style of subject design, less skilfully cut. So that an alibi might be urged against the identification of the Aesop Master with I.D.

---

[1] See pp. 614-616.   [2] See p. 754.   [3] See p. 746.

[4] The animals in the scroll-work of this border, somewhat heraldic in character, may possibly derive from Islamic designs.

[5] The title cut of *L'Aquila* (an eagle within a border) is in the manner of various heraldic cuts in Spanish books, another slight link with Spain in Naples woodcuts.

Fig. 190. Border, from the *Hebrew Bible*, Naples, about 1490–91.

We have already referred to the frontispiece to Granollachs, *Sommario dell' arte di astrologia*, (n.d., issued by Tuppo, about 1485), in relation to its adaptation in a Roman book of 1493, and two other cuts worthy of note are the *Magister cum Discipulis* subject in Sinulphius, *Institutiones Grammaticae*, printed by AYOLFO DE CANTONO, 13th November 1491 (H. 14792, F.-B. 186), and the border in another of Ayolfo's books, Zacharias Lilius, *Orbis Breviarium*, 9th November 1496 (F.-B. 190). But more attractive are several series of small woodcuts which occur in certain devotional books issued by various Naples printers. They are for the most part in delicate outline, with little shading, within scroll or floral borders, and unfortunately seldom found except illuminated, as was no doubt the intention of the printer. The most delicate are the miniature cuts, within scroll and floral borders, in the *Officium B.V. Mariae* printed by MATHIAS MORAVUS (of Olmütz), 30th June 1486 (F.-B. 134),[1] the last subject, the *Service for the Dead*, being an excellently drawn record of contemporary custom. Others that may be mentioned are the *Officium B.V. Mariae*, printed by Christian Preller, 15th November 1487 (F.-B. 172, H. 11990, and later editions) and by Ayolfo de Cantono, 20th March 1496 (F.-B. 189), with five and six cuts respectively. The cuts in Preller's edition, within floral borders, are Netherlandish in character, those of Cantono are near the classic Venetian style, and seem to have been partly based on the *Officium* of Hieronymus de Sanctis, Venice 1494 (E. 457). These editions are among the earliest books printed in Italy, corresponding with the French *Hours of the Virgin*, but they do not yet show the bordered page initiated in the *Horae* printed by Dupré at Paris 1488-89, and followed soon after by various printers at Venice.[2]

VERONA

The earliest subject illustrations in an Italian printed book occur at Verona in Robertus Valturius, *De Re Militari*, 1472 (H. 15847). The JOANNES NICOLAI DE VERONA who printed this book may be identical with the GIOVANNI ALVISE, who shared with ALBERTO ALVISE in printing the Verona *Aesop* of 1479.[3] The illustrations are of great technical interest in relation to contemporary engines of war, but little attempt was made to give them any harmonious setting in the page. They are almost entirely

---

[1] Later edition, 1488 (F.-B. 138), contains five cuts. There are only four of these cuts in the only copy known of the 1486 edition (British Museum), but it lacks two leaves, one of which no doubt contained the extra cut.

[2] See pp. 499, 500.

[3] And perhaps also with Joannes Alvisius of Venice (or with one or the other).

outline cuts, and to judge from their irregular placing on the page, they must have been printed by hand after the printing of the type. Several of the subjects show figures, and the designs were evidently done by an artist of considerable talent, though their quality may in many cases have been blunted by careless cutting. Both design and cutting have been attributed to

Fig. 191. From Valturius, *De Re Militari*, Verona 1472.

MATTEO DE' PASTI,[1] an artist of many crafts (architect, painter, sculptor, and illuminator) chiefly remembered for his medals and for his architectural and other work under the direction of L. B. Alberti in St. Francesco at Rimini. But in spite of the plausibility of the suggestion that he was the designer of the cuts (it is highly unlikely that an artist of his standing would cut the blocks) from his close relation with Sigismondo Malatesta and

---

[1] See W. Y. Ottley, *Inquiry into the Origins and Early History of Engraving*, 1816, p. 257. He refers back to F. M. Maffei (*Verona Illustrata*, Verona 1732, fol., parte terza, col. 195), who in his turn quotes a letter transcribed in Étienne Baluze, *Miscellanea*, Paris 1678–83, liber quartus, p. 524. The letter in question was one written by Valturius in the name of Sigismondo Malatesta (about 1461) introducing the bearer, Matteo de' Pasti, to the Sultan Mahomet II., whose portrait he was travelling to paint. But there is no direct reference in the letter to the specific arts practised by Pasti, much less any reference to his having been an engraver or designer of woodcuts. He was taking with him for presentation a MS. copy of Valturius, *De Re Militari*. But he was arrested by the Venetian authorities at Candia on suspicion of taking a map to the enemy, and never reached his destination.

Valturius (who was on Sigismondo's council), there is no documentary evidence in its support. Though Matteo de' Pasti is known to have painted the *Triumphs of Petrarch* for Piero di Cosimo de' Medici at Venice in 1441,

and to have worked with Giorgio Tedesco and others on a Breviary for Lionello d' Este (between 1441 and 1446), these works are either lost or perished, so that comparison with painted work is not available.[1] Moreover, Valturius himself, who designed engines of war, must have invented his own illustrations, and may well have been capable of embellishing his designs with figures. We have already noted early adaptations of Valturius's designs in Vegetius Renatus, *Von der Ritterschaft*, printed at Augsburg by J. Wiener about 1475. Two later Verona editions with reduced copies of the original woodcuts were printed by BONINUS DE BONINIS in 1483

Fig. 192. The Youth and Thais, from *Aesop*, Verona 1479.

(H. 15848, 13th February 1483, in Latin; H. 15849, 17th February 1483, in Italian). They contain (in book XI.) an interesting new subject representing *Three Soldiers in a Tent*, which appeared later in Antonio Cornazano, *Opera Bellissima del Arte Militar*, Venice (C. de Pensis) 1493 (E. 723).

In very much the same style of cutting as the Valturius are the illustrations to the first edition printed in Italy of Aesop's *Fables* (in Latin and

[1] Essling and Müntz (*Pétrarque*, Paris 1902, p. 136) identified Matteo's *Triumphs of Petrarch* with the paintings (*Fame, Religion, Love* and *Death*) on a circular box preserved in the Uffizi. Their identification is not, however, generally accepted, as the paintings appear to be Florentine, and Matteo's *Triumphs* are more likely to have been miniatures (see P. Schubring, *Cassoni*, Leipzig 1915, p. 271, Nos. 208-11, and pl. xlvi for description and reproduction).

Italian verse) issued by Giovanni and Alberto Alvise, 26th June 1479 (H. 345, GW. 428). And the figures are sufficiently similar in character to render it possible that if Valturius had been helped by a figure draughtsman, it was the same man who designed the *Aesop* cuts. They are charming and lively inventions, and the cutter, though hardly precise as a craftsman, sufficed to support the simple linear style of design, made even simpler by a frequent and fitting use of black spaces. The printer used a variety of small blocks of decorative designs, technically known as 'printer's flowers', with which he made up his border decoration, the various designs being no doubt multiplied by casting. The same 'flowers' are also used decoratively at various places throughout the text, at the beginning and end of sections and lines, etc., in this and other books from the same press, e.g. in Capranica, *Arte di bene morire*, 28th April 1478 (H. 4398) and Hieronymus Manfredi, *Prognosticon Anni 1479* (H. 15848). Reference has already been made to the Naples *Aesop* as largely dependent on the present edition for its designs. Regarding the Verona *Aesop* as the *editio princeps* of the Fables in Italy, I would add some further comparative notes on *Aesop* illustrations. In the first place the designer of the Verona cuts must have known those of Johann Zainer's Ulm edition (of about 1476–77), but his illustrations seldom show more than general points of comparison, and even in the examples of closer resemblance show originality of rendering.

The Brescia edition of 1487, printed by Boninus de Boninis (H. 348, GW. 430), is very closely modelled on the Verona edition. There is variety in the *passe-partout* borders, but the frontispece and the subjects themselves are for the most part copies in reverse, far inferior to the originals in draughtsmanship and cutting. The Venice editions, which are of two families, printed respectively by BERNARDINUS BENALIUS and MANFREDUS DE BONELLIS, deserve more attention. They are two distinct series of cuts, deriving from both Verona and Naples editions, but more from that of Naples.

The subjects of the edition printed by Benalius in 1487 (E. 358, GW. 431) are framed within *passe-partout* borders on a black ground with three variant designs in the arch above. The cuts themselves are variable in quality, rather heavy and unsensitive in line, and considerably inferior to either the Verona or the Naples edition.

The series first printed by Manfredus de Bonellis, 31st January 1491 (E. 360, GW. 432), are of finer quality. Their author, who is nearly related to (if not identical with) the designer of the Malermi Bible of

1493, has a fine classic sense, and is well served by the delicate draughts-manship of his cutter. The frontispiece with *Aesop and his Commentators* is an

independent design, and the illustrations of the fables are framed within a variety of attractive scroll and figure borders in black line. In the later issue of 1497 (E. 363, H. 351) the original frontispiece is replaced by a poorer cut of the same design with parallel shading within a border repeated from Lucan's *Pharsalia* (1495), but the other blocks are reprinted with slight differences in the borders. Bonellis also issued editions of the *Life of Aesop* in 1492 (E. 611, H. 354, GW. 445) and 1493 (E. 612,

Fig. 193. The Rat and the Frog, from *Aesop*, Venice 1491.

GW. 612) with cuts derived from those of Naples, and repeating the frontispiece from his 1491 edition of the Fables.

POJANO

The only book printed at Pojano (*Rure Polliano Verona ad lapidem jacente quartum*, i.e. four miles from Verona, as it appears in the colophon) is an Italian translation of Petrarch, *Libro degli Uomini Famosi*, issued from the press of FELICIANUS (ANTIQUARIUS) and INNOCENS ZILETUS in 1476 (H. 12808). It contains two outline strap-work borders of attractive design, of which one or the other is repeated at the beginning of each section (see fig. 194).

There are two copies of the book in the British Museum, one in which the borders (which never surround any text) are left uncoloured, the other in which the borders are covered in opaque colours and the blank centre filled with drawings of the various heroes in pen and light washes of water-colour. The drawings are evidently by a hack draughtsman, who found especial difficulty with his mounted figures. It is probable that the printer intended the whole edition to be illuminated in this way, as the borders served no other purpose.

VENICE [1]

ITS EARLIEST BOOK-ILLUSTRATION
AND THE SO-CALLED BLOCK-BOOK PASSION

Like the borders already noted, the earliest subject illustrations in Venetian books were cut chiefly in outline, and no doubt in the first place intended as bases for illumination. An isolated example is the series of six small cuts to the *Days of Creation* in the *Italian Bible* printed by ADAM DE AMBERGAU on 1st October 1471 (E. 131, H. 3148), but it is curious that the only copy in which the cuts are noted (and in that case illuminated) is the Spencer copy in the John Rylands Library, Manchester. In other copies, such as that of the British Museum, the spaces are left blank.

---

[1] For Venetian books the indispensable work of reference is Prince d'Essling (Victor Masséna, Duc de Rivoli), *Études sur l'art de la gravure sur bois à Venise, Les Missels imprimés à Venise de 1481 à 1600*, Paris [1895] 1896; *Les Livres à figures vénitiens de la fin du XVe siècle et du commencement du XVI*. I^e Partie: *Ouvrages imprimés de 1450 à 1490 et leurs éditions successives jusqu'en 1525*, tome i. Nos. 1-530 (1469–90), Florence, Paris 1907; tome ii. Nos. 531-1255 (1491–1500), Florence, Paris 1908; IIe Partie: *Ouvrages imprimés de 1501 à 1525*, (1) Nos. 1256-1950 (1501–17); (2) Nos. 1960-2307 (1517–25); Nos. 2308-2585 (n.d., early XVI century), Florence, Paris 1909. IIIe Partie: *Les Origines et le développement de la xylographie à Venise*, Revision; Appendix; Tables, Florence, Paris 1914. It should be noted that successive editions of each work are given after its first edition. The work entirely supersedes the same author's *Bibliographie des livres à figures vénitiens* (1469–1525), Paris 1892. See also Prince d'Essling, *Études sur l'art de la gravure sur bois à Venise, Les Missels imprimés à Venise de 1481 à 1600*. Paris [1895]–1896; Paul Kristeller, *La xylografia veneziana (a proposito dell' opera del Duca di Rivoli*, Archivio Storico dell' Arte, v., 1892, 95; P. Kristeller, Review of Essling, I^e Partie, tom i., in *Mitteilungen der Gesellsch. für vervielfältigende Kunst*, 1907, p. 12; C. Castellani, *L' arte della stampa del rinascimento italiano, Venezia*, Venice 1894; also works specifically on the Venetian Block-book, footnote to p. 416.

After this apparently abortive experiment no subject cuts appear in Venetian books until the *Crucifixion* subject (the Canon cut) in certain Missals, again in outline, and mostly found coloured by hand. Such are the several blocks of different sizes, each in the same style, in the Missals printed by Octavianus Scotus, i.e. the *Missale Romanum*, in quarto, 29th December 1481 (E. 18), and in folio, 31st August 1482 (E. 21), and the *Missale Ordinis Praedicatorum*, in quarto, 24th December 1482 (E. 248, H. 11289). The large cut in the folio Missal is by far the finest of the three blocks (fig. 195).

Fig. 194. Border, from Petrarch, *Libro degli Uomini Famosi*, Pojano 1476.

Apart from these early illustrations in Bibles and Missals, Venetian woodcuts are seldom coloured, even though their style is predominantly outline. This devotion to purity of line in woodcut was more marked, and persisted longer, in Venice than elsewhere, only yielding to a fuller system of shading in the early XVI century.

Some orientation in regard to the earliest work of Italian block-printed illustration, the so-called *Block-book Passion* at Berlin[1] (S. iv. p. 325), is offered by the appearance of later impressions from the same blocks in a Venetian book, i.e. Bonaventura, *Meditazioni sopra la Passione*, printed in

[1] Paul Kristeller, *Ein venezianisches Blockbuch in Berlin*, Pr. Jahrbuch, xxii., 1901, 132; Victor Masséna, Prince d'Essling, *Le Premier Livre xylographique imprimé à Venise vers 1450*, Paris

1487 by HIERONYMUS DE SANCTIS and his partner CORNELIO. Though examples of the loan and transfer of blocks from one locality to another are recognised,[1] nevertheless it is more natural to assume that the blocks remained in the place of their origin, and comparison of their style with early Venetian art in general, with its Gothic architecture and sculpture in particular, a comparison which has been developed in detail by Kristeller, fully supports the assumption.

In spite of its usual designation, the *Passion* series is not a block-book in the strict sense of the word, though it might have originally been issued as one. As preserved in the unique set at Berlin it includes eighteen subjects (each about $8\frac{5}{8} \times 5\frac{5}{8}$ inches) printed in black ink, probably in an ordinary printing-press, on both sides of nine sheets. Three lines of Latin text from the Bible, cut in Gothic letters, appear

Fig. 195. Christ on the Cross, from *Missale Romanum*, Venice 1482.

below each subject on a scroll held by two angels. The prints are heavily illuminated, and no watermark can be deciphered.

1903 (in shorter form in Gazette des Beaux-Arts, 3ᵉ pér., xxx., 1903, pp. 89, 243); Paul Kristeller, *Eine Folge venezianischer Holzschnitte aus dem XV^{ten} Jahrhundert im Besitze der Stadt Nürnberg*, Graphische Gesellschaft, ix., Berlin 1909 (a series of Venetian copies from the Block-book series); Paul Kristeller, *Das italienische Blockbuch des Kupferstichkabinetts zu Berlin*, Monatshefte für Bücherfreunde und Graphiker, i., 1925, 331.

[1] See Index of Subjects (*Blocks, Transfer of*).

Fig. 196. Christ before Pilate, from the Venetian *Block-book Passion*.

A series of early Venetian copies in the Germanic Museum, Nuremberg, came from a miscellaneous collection of early cuts pasted on an altarpiece in the Church of St. Catherine, in the same town.[1] It is equally possible that the original set might have been intended for church decoration rather than for issue in book form, but there is no evidence on one side or the other.

Fig. 197. The Raising of Lazarus, from Bonaventura, *Meditazioni*, Venice 1487.

That the Berlin set was early in Germany or in German hands is proved by the German manuscript inscriptions above and below each subject, which appear to be nearly contemporary with the prints. But this does not in any way invalidate the attribution of the designs or the cutting to Venice.

As issued in Bonaventura's *Meditazioni sopra la Passione*, the blocks were cut down to about $6\frac{1}{2} \times 5\frac{1}{4}$ inches, taking away the lettered scrolls, and leaving the supporting angels' heads in meaningless isolation. This rare

---

[1] The prints related to the Berlin block-book were described and reproduced by P. Kristeller, Graphische Gesellschaft (see Bibliography in footnote to p. 416). These copies were made from the lettered blocks, but as preserved are cut down like the later state of the originals. There is a second copy of the *Entombment*, with Cross added behind the tomb and buildings in the background, in Paris (S. 516, Bouchot 51, Lemoisne, xxxi.; about $10\frac{1}{2} \times 7\frac{1}{2}$ inches).

An early notice of the Nuremberg altar-piece is in Passavant, i. p. 33, No. 24, where it is stated that it was removed from the Church of St. Catherine to the Burg in 1811. Further description and reproduction of miscellaneous cuts apart from the Venetian series are given by W. Stengel,

book, of which copies are known in the British Museum (from the Huth Collection), Rome (Bibl. Casanatense), Ferrara and Modena, contains eleven cuts, ten from the Berlin series, and an additional subject, the *Raising of Lazarus*, which is used as the frontispiece (fig. 197). This additional cut is in precisely the same style and shows the isolated angels, so that it evidently belonged to the original series.

Fig. 198. The Martyrdom of St. Sebastian. Miniature from the *Mariegola dell' Arte dei Verrieri di Venezia.*

The series of copies at Nuremberg, to which reference has already been made, includes twenty-five subjects in all, but lacks the *Christ washing the Disciples' Feet* (Berlin) and the Bonaventura *Raising of Lazarus*. The additional subjects are six scenes from the *Life of Christ* (the *Annunciation*, *Nativity*, *Circumcision*, *Adoration of the Magi*, *Massacre of the Innocents*, and *Christ disputing with the Doctors*), and two scenes after the Resurrection, *Christ appearing to the Magdalene*

Unedirte Holzschnitte im Nürnberger Kupferstichkabinett, Strassburg (Heitz, *Einbl.*, 37) 1913. Stengel states that the watermark on three of the Venetian series is Briquet 13618, noted about 1426–1446 and chiefly in North Italy, so that Stengel appears to regard these 'copies' as earlier than the Berlin block-book. Most of the miscellaneous cuts are crude work rather in the style of the German block-books, *Decalogus* and *Septimia Poenalis*, and can hardly be much later than 1450. Stengel suggests that they were cut in the Katharinenkloster.

and the *Incredulity of S. Thomas*. It is probable, therefore, that the original series was a *Passion*, preceded by a select number of scenes from the *Life of Christ*, certainly including twenty-seven subjects, and possibly a few more.

The copies [1] at Nuremberg show greater refinement than the originals in both cutting and draughtsmanship, and Kristeller has rightly compared them with the allegorical woodcut in Sacro Busto, *Sphaera Mundi* of 1488, which is known from the colophon verses to have been cut by Hieronymus de Sanctis after the invention or design by JOHANNES SANTRITTER.[2] As de Sanctis was in possession of the blocks of the original series (for it was he who published the *Meditazioni*), it is reasonable to suppose that as a woodcutter himself he may also have been responsible for the copies. It is curious, however, that they are not known in any of his publications.

The Berlin series is vigorous and crude in character, with strong plastic qualities, and from its style probably dates about 1450. It is not far removed in general character from painted work by Michele Giambono (e.g. panels illustrating the story of St. Mamas, Exhibition of Italian Art, Royal Academy, London, 1930, No. 23-27).

Another link with Venice is offered by the close kinship in style to a miniature of the *Martyrdom of St. Sebastian* in the *Mariegola dell' Arte dei Verrieri di Venezia* (Members' List of the Guild of Glass Makers) of 1436, discovered by Kristeller in the Archivio di Stato, Venice (fig. 198).[3]

The relationship is equally marked in various single cuts of the period, of which the largest collection is preserved in the Biblioteca Classense, Ravenna,[4] which now demand our attention.

---

[1] For contention that they are too early to be the copies, see p. 420, footnote.

[2] See p. 463 for other work attributed to De Sanctis.

[3] See Essling, Gazette des Beaux-Arts, 3ᵉ pér., xxx., 1903, 255.

[4] For reproduction of the Ravenna cuts see W. L. Schreiber, *Einzel-Formschnitte des xv^{ten} Jahrhunderts in der Bibl. Classense, Ravenna*, Einbl., Band 68, Strassburg (Heitz) 1929. For other notes on the series see (1) the articles by Kristeller on the Berlin block-book; (2) Essling, *Les Livres à figures vénitiens*, 3ᵉ partie, 1914; (3) Kristeller, *Holzschnitte des Meisters des Abendmahls in Ravenna*, Festschrift für Max Friedländer, Leipzig 1927, p. 3 (which gives a careful classification of the prints).

All the Ravenna cuts except one occur in a xv-century Codex (No. 485, *Consilia Jurisconsultorum*). Until recently it appeared to contain forty impressions from thirty-eight blocks, a few of which may be German, including a criblée print of *St. Roch* (S. 2722); but Heitz has noted in his introduction to Schreiber's volume that two new subjects have been found concealed behind S. 1414 and 1248, which have still not been reproduced. An additional subject (the *Trinity with the Virgin and Child and Saints*, S. 749 f) came from a different source, the Abbazia di Porto, and the Archivio Communale.

Fig. 199. The Martyrdom of St. Sebastian. S. 1676.

The most striking comparison with the Venetian *Mariegola* miniature is afforded by the woodcut of the *Martyrdom of St. Sebastian* at Ravenna (S. 1676). There is the same type for the Christ, and the same costume and character in the other figures. And similar analogies in style of design and cutting are manifest in the Berlin block-book.

Unfortunately most of the woodcuts pasted in the Ravenna Codex have been much mutilated or obscured. In some, the figures have been cut round like silhouettes and mounted; in nearly all, the backgrounds have been so darkly coloured that practically nothing can be seen of this part of the design. Happily, certain photographs have been taken by transparency, rendering the background visible. One of these, and the

Fig. 200. St. Anthony of Padua. S. 1233.

finest cut of the whole collection, the *St. Anthony of Padua* (S. 1233; fig. 200), shows buildings in the background based on the Santo at Padua, and I am glad to have Prince d'Essling's permission to give a reproduction from a photograph, obtained by transparency, first used in his father's *Livres à figures vénitiens*, 3ᵉ partie, 1914.

Like most of the others, it shows great simplicity in the linear design, which is left, as in the Verona *Valturius* and *Aesop* cuts, without any shading, but it surpasses the rest in the structural quality of draughts-manship displayed, e.g. in the rendering of head and hands. The only direct evidence in regard to the dating of any of the series is offered by the *Martyrdom of St. Simon of Trent* (S. 1970), which cannot be before 1475, the date of the event, and can hardly be much later.[1]

From the manuscript inscription *Sktarina* on S. 1316, Schreiber sur-mises that the original owner was a German. One at least of the prints in the collection is German, i.e. the criblée *St. Roch* (S. 2722), and it is possible that others are either German or cut by German craftsmen in Italy, e.g. the *Last Supper* (S. 169) and *St. Martin* (S. 1619), which Kristeller regarded as Ulm work of about 1450–70, christening the author of a series of cuts which he grouped round these as the 'Master of the Ravenna Last Supper'.[2] He was certainly right in regarding the *Death of the Virgin* (S. 710, British Museum) as by the same hand, and possibly so in his attri-bution of the *St. Nicholas of Tolentino* (S. 1637, Vienna), but less near the mark in placing the *St. Christopher* at Weimar (S. 1348) in the same group.

German characteristics appear also in the *Stigmatisation of St. Francis* (S. 1423), and the *St. Bernardino of Siena* (S. 1279),[3] both of which show the slight shading and angular drawing of the *Last Supper*, but here Kristeller was justified in comparing the style with Brescian illustration, and accepting them as Italian. I incline to the same conclusion in regard to the supposed Ulm group. *St. Martin* in particular seems to me to be unlike German work, and it should be noted that the *St. Nicholas of Tolentino* at Vienna (S. 1637)[4] corresponds in its presentation of the title along a strip across the centre with another certainly Italian example from the Ravenna group, the *St. Joseph* (S. 1575).

In most, the design is in outline, and the drapery drawn in a simple system of parallel lines tending to break into curves rather than angles, and the general style of several of the somewhat static figures of saints

---

[1] Two other Italian woodcuts of this subject, which must be nearly contemporary with the event, are preserved in the Vatican (S. 1969, and 1969 a). They are both crudely cut in outline, the one allegorical, the other naturalistic in treatment.

[2] See p. 421, note 4, and W. Cohn, *Untersuchungen zur Geschichte des Deutschen Einblattholzschnitts*. Strassburg 1934, p. 29.

[3] A transparency (Essling, iii., 1914, p. 39) shows the saint standing in a garden before a battlemented wall, essentially Italian in conception.

[4] Its date (1446) refers to the canonisation of the saint.

Fig. 201. St. Clara. S. 1380.

reminiscent of Antonio Vivarini and the school of Murano, and of the years 1450–70. A further link with Venice is provided by the ogival form of arch in the Gothic niche in front of which stands *St. Bartholomew* (S. 1267). Essling, whose reproduction, made by transparency, shows up this niche in the woodcut (*Les Livres à figures vénitiens*, 3ᵉ partie, 1914, p. 37) rightly compares it with the Porta della Carta, in the Ducal Palace at Venice.

A *St. John the Baptist* (S. 1511) is among the more sensitive in design, and the most beautiful perhaps is the *St. Clara* (S. 1380; fig. 201), which, with the *Meeting of St. Dominic and St. Francis* (S. 1391), is gentler and more harmonious in its line than most of the other figures of saints. Something of the more mature dignity of the Venetian style of the last two decades of the century, under the influence of Giovanni Bellini, may be noted in the *Group of Four Saints: Dominic, Sebastian, Peter Martyr and Roch* (S. 1770). Perhaps further transparent photographs may lead in other examples to definite links, and perhaps with schools outside Venice.[1]

Leaving the Ravenna series, another woodcut closely related in style to the *Passion*, and one of the largest and most important Italian cuts of the period, is the *Calvary* at Prato (S. 470 k; fig. 202).[2] The treatment of the drapery in the group of the Virgin supported by the Holy Women exhibits striking analogies to that of Christ's robe in the *Mocking of Christ* and to other details that might be cited from the *Passion*. The outline style, in thin and flowing line, is also comparable with the Veronese work in the *Valturius* of 1472 and the *Aesop* of 1479. The print, which is pasted on panel, is coloured apparently by the use of stencils.[3]

Apart from its unusually large dimensions for woodcut (about 22 × 16 inches) the design is monumental in character, and far more probably the work of a painter than the original design of a craftsman cutter.

Among the single cuts probably belonging to North Italy, a similar outline style may be mentioned in *St. Nicholas of Tolentino*, only known in modern impressions, of which the original block is in the Royal Gallery at

---

[1] In relation to the Ravenna cuts I would mention a *Profile Head of S. Bernardino* in the collection of Mrs. Rayner Wood, at Old Colwall, Malvern. It appears to be an outline woodcut coloured by hand, but its condition renders it difficult to be certain that it is not merely a drawing. If woodcut, its style would place it in North Italy near the outline work exemplified in the Ravenna cuts. Mrs. Rayner Wood's collection, chiefly drawings, was made by John Skippe in Venice in the xviii century.

[2] Kristeller, *Le gallerie nazionali italiane*, ii., 1896, 184.

[3] See p. 171.

Fig. 202. Calvary. S. 470 k.

Venice [1] and a *Madonna di Loreto* (Virgin and Child and Angels under a small domed building) in the collection of Baron Edmond de Rothschild, Paris (S. 1104) [2]. A cut of similar design to the latter occurs in the *Miracoli della Gloriosa Maria*, printed by BAPTISTA DE FARFENGO, at Brescia, 1490 (Reichling 630, Naples), [3] and the same motive appears in a line-engraving of about the same date in the Liechtenstein Collection (P. v. 15, 9).

The leaf border of the *St. Nicholas of Tolentino* is found in several of the illuminated borders used by Venetian printers, e.g. Vindelinus de Spira, Jenson, and Bartholomaeus Cremonensis, between 1469 and 1473, [4] and occurs also in a North Italian line-engraving, representing the *Month of March* at Vienna (P. V. 116, 84), and in the large *Virgin and Child with the Infant St. John* at Hamburg (S. 1137) which is more probably Florentine (see p. 448 and fig. 211).

A woodcut of *St. Albert of Trapani* (S. 1184 a, Berlin), which is pasted inside a box, is of the same style as several of the figures of saints at Ravenna (e.g. the *St. Philip of Florence*, S. 1651), and certainly Italian of about 1470. Of other cuts of similar character two may be noted, which, if not Italian, are at least based on Italian originals, i.e. a *St. Bernardino of Siena* once at Maihingen (S. 1278 a), [5] and a *St. Benedict and two seated Monks* (S. 1268) at Vienna. [6]

One of the most beautiful of Italian cuts of the period, probably produced in North Italy between 1490 and 1500, is the *Annunciation* (S. 29 m, Oxford, and Rothschild). Its inscription *Annuntiata Fratrum Carmelitarum Conventus Bgomi* connects it with Bergamo, though the block might of course have been commissioned elsewhere (fig. 203).

By some designer influenced by the Paduan school or Carlo Crivelli, is a *Virgin and Child* preserved in fragmentary condition at Berlin (S. 1041, fig. 204). It is characterised by the hanging festoons, and by the border of geometrical patterns, such as are seen in the decorative cuts of the same

---

[1] Paul Kristeller, *Un blocco d' una silografia antica italiana*, Bollettino d' Arte, iii., 1909, 429.

[2] *Xilografia italiana inedita posseduta e descritta da Luigi Arrigoni*, Milan 1884. See p. 448 for possibility of identification of the *St. Nicholas* and *Madonna di Loreto* with Florentine blocks.

[3] The cut occurred in a copy in the possession of E. P. Goldschmidt & Co., London 1928.

[4] See p. 399. It occurs on the Virgil border reproduced, in the part which is clearly seen only in the offset.

[5] Karl and Faber, Auction xi, Munich, May 7, 1935, No. 24. Cf. a similar, but much inferior, cut on the reverse of the title of S. Bernardinus, *Sermones de Evangelio*, Basle (N. Kesler), about 1494 (S. 3428, H. 2828).

[6] For the motive of the seated monk in the background cf. a cut of *St. Bernardino and two monks* in St. Bernardino, *Confessiones*, Venice (B. Benalius), n.d., about 1493 (Essling 730).

Fig. 203. The Annunciation. S. 29 m.

period preserved on a Cassone at Berlin.[1] There is another *Virgin and Child* by the same hand in Berlin, again only a fragment (S. 1042), and on the reverse another rough proof of S. 1042, with a second proof of S. 1041 superimposed.

A larger *Virgin and Child* at Berlin (S. 1020), likewise fragmentary, also shows a border of geometrical figures; but the types of the Virgin and Child are more reminiscent of northern design, comparable with Dierick Bouts, and the features preserved in the woodcut inscribed *Bernhardinus Milnet*, and its peers.[2]

Again under the influence of Crivelli, or Mantegna, is a *Christ on the Cross between the Virgin and St. John* (S. 948, Berlin). These last two cuts, like many others at Berlin, and another in the British Museum,[3] came from a house at Bassano, apparently pasted as decoration on door-panel or wall.

The other prints at Berlin from the Bassano house, which are mostly fragments of impressions, are chiefly later in style, with the parallel shading which developed in Venice from about 1500. Several are near in character to the work of Jacob of Strassburg. Of these may be mentioned a large *Virgin and Child* (S. 1045), of which the two original blocks are at Modena, the *Last Supper* (S. 166, and 167), a *Passion* (S. 23), *Christ bearing the Cross* (S. 338), the *Virgin and Child in a Roundel* (S. 1127), a *Salvator Mundi* (S. 832) and a *Death of the Virgin* (S. 636). They are powerfully cut, but entirely lacking in sensitive quality.

One of the fragments in this style, showing *Solomon seated, l., and David playing a harp, r.* (possibly part of a *Tree of Jesse*), is signed *fiorio di vavasori fecit al p̄ote di fuseri in Venetia* (Berlin, Inv. 867-301; inv. 869-301, being another figure from the same subject). This FLORIO VAVASSORE was no doubt a kinsman of GIOVANNI (ZOAN) ANDREA VAVASSORE (detto Guadagnino), who issued the block-book *Opera Nova Contemplativa*, printed at Venice in the earlier half of the xvi century, not before 1510 (Essling 206).[4] He is probably the cutter who uses the initials F.V., and Essling attributes to him the cutting of Zoan Andrea's block-book. It is still uncertain whether this Zoan Andrea Vavassore[5] is identical with the Zoan Andrea who signed the woodcut copies of Dürer's *Apocalypse* published at Venice by Alex. Paganino in 1515, and with the cutter indicated by the Z.A. which appears on many Venetian blocks of the earlier xvi century; still more

---

[1] See p. 77.   [2] See p. 183.   [3] See p. 162.   [4] See p. 239.
[5] There is a large woodcut of the Battle of Marignano (555 × 1525 mm.) now in the Zentral-bibliothek, Zurich, with his imprint, and this is not likely to be much after 1515, the date of the battle.

Fig. 204. The Virgin and Child. S. 1041.

uncertain whether the latter is also identical with the line-engraver Zoan Andrea of the Mantegna school, who appears to have worked later at Milan.[1] Another cutter who has sometimes been confused with one or other of the Zoan Andreas is the author of the signature **1 a**.[2]

Better is a large *Virgin and Child on a Crescent* (S. 1047), of which only the lower half is preserved (11 × 15 inches, so that the entire composition would be about 22 × 15 inches) The Virgin holds a circle containing the view of a church by a lake. The block of this subject appears to be among those now in the Galleria Estense at Modena. The style of cutting, in which considerable use is made of the white line, is rather like that of the copy of Pollaiuolo's *Battle of Naked Men* by Johannes of Frankfurt,[3] and probably dates about 1500–10. The complete subject of S. 1047 occurs in a copy of about half the size, which may be of about 1520, also in the Berlin Print Room.

The large collection of original blocks at Modena, acquired about 1890, had long belonged to the Soliani, a family which had been active as printers in Modena between about 1645 and 1870.[4] They range in date from about 1500 to about 1800; some, as we have seen, known in old impressions; the majority poor in quality; a few of known designers of the xvi century, such as FRANCESCO DI NANTO; others with genuine monograms; an occasional date of the xvi or xvii century; many bearing monograms or signatures which appear to have been added with fraudulent intent in the xix century.

A *Last Judgment* (S. 598), generally found in late impressions with the signature **MF**, preserves a dignified design under the influence of Mantegna or Giovanni Bellini, and is probably North Italian about 1500. There is a still later state, with a border added, in the Museo Civico, Pavia, where the block itself is also preserved. An early state before the monogram was once noted by Kristeller in the collection of G. B. Venturi at Reggio.

An ill-drawn but naïvely attractive *St. George* in the collection of the late Mr. Henry Oppenheimer[5] is very definitely established as Venetian by the orthography of its title ·S·ZORZO·CHAVALIERO· With its white-line background, influenced by Florentine work, like many examples of Venetian book-illustration in the early xvi century, it probably dates near 1500. Another cut by the same hand (similar in style of drawing and in the design

---

[1] See A. M. Hind, *Catalogue of Early Italian Engravings in the British Museum*, 1910, p. 382.

[2] See pp. 433, 469, 489, 500, and 502.   [3] See p. 450.

[4] See Achille Bertarelli, *Di alcune falsificazioni moderne eseguite cogli antichi legni della tipografia Soliani di Modena*, Il Libro e la Stampa, Bolletino Ufficiale della Società Bibliografica Italiana, ii., Milan 1909, p. 64.   [5] Now belonging to Mr. W. M. Ivins, Jr., New York.

of border and background) is the *Christ on the Cross between the Virgin and St. John* (inscribed CHROCIFISO·DE·FRA·MINORI·DI·VINEZIA·) in the Guildhall, London (S. 417 m; C. Dodgson, Graphische Gesellschaft, xx., 1914, No. 11, pl. x.). And the fragment of a third, *St. Barbara with Christ Child*, is at Berlin (S. 1264).

L' Hora Passa, an allegory on the transitoriness of life, with hour-glass and a naked child leaning on a skull (Paris, S. 1896, Hirth and Muther, 31), is another example which appears to be Venetian in design, though evidently related to the Florentine manner in its white scheme on black ground.

One of the few known woodcutters working in Venice about 1500 is JACOB OF STRASSBURG (JACOBUS ARGENTORATENSIS). His developed manner of cutting with clear outline, and shading in close parallels, achieving qualities of tone which imitate line-engraving, undoubtedly originated in the school of woodcutters who worked for Johann Grüninger at Strassburg, in the style first seen fully developed in the *Terence* of 1496.

Jacob's only dated work, the *Triumph of Caesar* (P. 1. 113, 1), signed at Venice *MDIII Idibus Februarii* (i.e. probably 1504 in present calendar), is shaded in fairly open parallels, as if at that time he had not developed the 'Grüninger' style, and with its angular drawing and crude cutting, appears to be an early work. The design forms a procession made up of twelve sheets, and is evidently inspired by Mantegna's famous paintings, now at Hampton Court. It is not altogether outside the grounds of possibility that he is identical with the cutter I a who signed numerous blocks in Venetian books, from 1497 onwards, chiefly in the 'shaded' style, for the letters of the signature are never divided by stops and very probably refer to some Jacobus.[1] The fact that some of the earliest of these (in the Ovid of 1497) are in the outline style does not preclude the possibility, as a cutter would in most cases merely follow his designer.

His other cuts are much nearer to the Grüninger style, and more developed in their tonal qualities. The *Istoria Romana*, a large oblong cut signed *opus · iacobi* (P. 1. 133, 3), may be derived from some Roman sarcophagus relief, but it is entirely Mantegnesque in treatment, and probably due to some designer of Mantegna's school such as Giovanni Antonio da Brescia.[2]

Jacob of Strassburg was also responsible for a series of roundels illustrating the *Passion*, which has already been noted for its decorative use in St. Damiano, Assisi.[3] The series is incompletely represented at Berlin and in the British Museum, and one original is preserved in the Museo Civico, Padua. The designs show considerable dependence on other artists (e.g.

---

[1] See p. 469.   [2] See p. 438.   [3] See p. 76.

Schongauer in *Pilate washing his Hands*, and Mantegna in details of the *Descent from the Cross*), and Jacob himself may have been capable of designing as well as cutting so derivative a work.

But his most important woodcut, in which the signatures specifically assign him the rôle of cutter, is the large *Virgin and Child with St. Sebastian and St. Roch*, after BENEDETTO MONTAGNA (Paris, and British Museum; P. v. 159, 53, P. 1. 133, 2). Nevertheless, as the inscription is *Benedetto Pinxit Jacobus Fecit*, it is possible that Jacob made the design in his own convention after a painting, a work of no mean skill in so ambitious a subject. Possibly details, such as the thirteen little panels of the *Passion*, above the throne and on its base, may have been added to a simpler composition by Montagna, which unfortunately is not identified.[1]

Another contemporary woodcut gives the same composition in simpler and modified form (S. 1147), which occurs in Berlin with a border, only partially preserved, containing portraits of the Jewish kings, and in an impression once at Dresden (Sammlung Friedrich August II.),[2] with the imprint in type *In Verona Per Bortolamio Merlo*. Benedetto Montagna, the son of the better known painter Bartolommeo Montagna of Vicenza, is chiefly known as a line-engraver, and his work dates from about 1500 (or a little earlier) until after 1540.

Another North Italian painter and line-engraver who designed woodcuts is the Venetian JACOPO DE' BARBARI,[3] whose work interested Dürer on his first visit to Venice about 1494. He was born at Venice about 1450 (if not before, as he is referred to in a document of 1511 as 'old and infirm'); worked in Germany between about 1500 and 1508, and was later in the service of the Archduchess Margaret in the Netherlands, where he died before 1516.

The three large woodcuts attributed to Barbari are not actually signed, but have all the marks of his style. Jacopo de' Barbari frequently added the *caduceus* (Mercury's wand) to his signature, and this mark alone serves as signature on most of his line-engravings. Its occurrence in actual elements of the design in the woodcuts may have appeared to Barbari sufficient indication of his authorship. The most important is a large *Bird's-eye View*

---

[1] A painting by Benedetto Montagna of a *Virgin and Child with St. Sebastian and St. Roch* is recorded as signed and dated 1533 and once on an altar in St. Rocco, Vicenza. It was later in the Academy, Venice, but it cannot now be traced (see Tancred Borenius, *The Painters of Vicenza*, London 1909, p. 120).

[2] Boerner Sale, 4th–6th May 1927, No. 52 (with reproduction).

[3] See Paul Kristeller, *Engravings and Woodcuts by Jacopo de' Barbari*, International Chalcographical Society, 1896; A. M. Hind, *Catalogue of Early Italian Engravings in the British Museum*, 1910, p. 442.

Fig. 205. Jacob of Strassburg, after Benedetto Montagna. The Virgin and Child with
St. Sebastian and St. Roch.

of Venice (P. III. 142, 33) dated 1500. It is printed from six blocks, the four outside portions measuring about $26\frac{1}{2} \times 35\frac{3}{4}$ inches, the two inner portions about $26\frac{1}{2} \times 39\frac{1}{4}$ inches, making when complete a surface of about 4 ft. $4\frac{1}{2}$ in. $\times$ 9 ft. $\frac{1}{2}$ in. (see fig. 206).

The head-piece of the upper central block is formed by a figure of Mercury with the *caduceus*, the inscription *Mercurius preceteris huic fauste emporiis illustro*, and *VENETIE MD.*

A fine impression in the British Museum, from the Mitchell Collection, has the six parts complete with separate border-lines; it is in the first state, dated 1500, and shows the flat temporary roof placed on the Campanile after a fire in 1489. In the second state, which is also represented in the British Museum, the date is removed, and the Campanile is shown with the restored pyramidical roof, which was done between 1511 and 1514. There is a third state in which the original date and temporary roof are replaced, and the original blocks still exist in the Correr Museum, Venice.

There is documentary evidence, in the four years' copyright granted him by the Signoria in October 1500, that the plan was published at the expense of Anton Kolb, a Nuremberg merchant (and friend of Dürer) resident at Venice, but no mention is made therein of Barbari by name.

The figures (the Mercury, Neptune, and the faces of the Winds) are entirely in Barbari's manner, so that this part at least was probably cut in facsimile after his design on the block. The actual view itself is a remarkable achievement, with many side-issues of interest in addition to the excellently drawn buildings, notably in the representation of ships and a regatta. It is conceivable that the topographical details were provided by another hand, but if not by Barbari himself, it must have required an artist of great talent to fuse them into this splendid sheet.

The other cuts attributed to Barbari actually form one subject, the *Battle between Men and Satyrs* and the *Triumph of Men over Satyrs* (P. III. 141, 31 and 32), the former on a large block about $15\frac{1}{4} \times 21\frac{1}{4}$ inches, the latter from three blocks each about $11\frac{1}{2} \times 16\frac{7}{8}$ inches. Two figures in the left portion of P. 32 carry tall Mercury wands. The motto on a banner in the central portion of P. 32 (*Virtus excelsa cupidinem ere regnantem domat*) shows that the subject is an allegory on the Triumph of Virtue over Lust, or of Civilisation over Barbarism. Here too the style of drawing the figures with their sinuous outlines and shading is so characteristic of Barbari that the cutter might be translating in facsimile the master's design. There is no clue to the identity of the cutter, who was almost certainly not Barbari himself.

Among North Italian artists of the earlier XVI century to whom woodcuts

Fig. 206. Jacopo de' Barbari. Part of the Bird's-eye View of Venice.

have been attributed is GIOVANNI ANTONIO DA BRESCIA, well known as a line-engraver, educated in the school of Mantegna.[1] One of these cuts, an *ornament panel*, bearing his signature (B. XIII. 330, 22), is merely a woodcut copy of a line-engraving by G. A. da Brescia.[2] The other woodcut bearing a signature corresponding to his, 10 · AN · BO, and dated 1538, a large *Ecce Homo*, is partially in a white-line manner resembling that of GIUSEPPE SCOLARI. But the signature might apply to another Giovanni da Brescia who was working as a painter in Venice about 1512–31, or it might even be a later falsification (like many of the names on the blocks at Modena).[3]

The majority of the larger Venetian woodcuts of 'pageant' and miscellaneous subjects belong to the XVI century, but one exceedingly fine example, recently acquired by the British Museum from the collection at Gotha,[4] probably falls just within the XV century, as it represents a fight between Turkish and Venetian ships which took place in 1499, the *Battle of Zonchio*. The Turkish ship was commanded by a famous corsair, Kemal Ali; the Venetians were defeated; one commander, Andrea Loredano, fell on his burning ship; the other, Albano Armer, was taken prisoner and put to death in Constantinople. The decorative character of the woodcut is heightened by the brilliance of the contemporary colouring (see fig. 207).

In regard to several of the artists just noticed we have exceeded the strict limits of our study, i.e. the XV century. But it is impossible and perhaps inconvenient to preserve perfect consistency, as certain of these artists who worked before the influence of the greater masters of the XVI century might escape notice in a survey of woodcut of the High Renaissance.

Another designer of woodcut who might be mentioned, as he is generally studied as a line-engraver in company with XV-century artists, is DOMENICO CAMPAGNOLA.[5] But as a designer of woodcuts he is so essentially a representative of the Titian influence that he is best left for study in this later phase.

More appropriately considered here is the artist who uses the signature ·I·B·⚘.[6] Zani stated[7] that he had reason to identify the monogrammist with

---

[1] Cf. above, p. 433.

[2] A. M. Hind, *Catalogue of Early Italian Engravings in the British Museum*, 1910, p. 362.

[3] See G. Ludwig, Pr. Jahrbuch, 1905, Beiheft, pp. 112-17.

[4] Boerner Sale, Leipzig, 2nd and 3rd May 1932, No. 187. The only known impression, measuring 21½ × 31⅝ inches. See British Museum Quarterly, vii. p. 32 (Sept. 1932).

[5] A. M. Hind, *Catalogue of Early Italian Engravings in the British Museum*, 1910, p. 501.

[6] See F. Lippmann, *The Woodcuts of the Master I B with the Bird*, International Chalcographical Society, 1894; A. M. Hind, *Early Italian Engravings in the British Museum*, 1910, p. 535; J. Byam Shaw, Print Collector's Quarterly, xix. (1932), 273; xx. (1933), 9, 169.

[7] *Materiali*, 1802, p. 134, note 56.

Fig. 207. The Battle of Zonchio. British Museum.

a Modenese engraver Giovanni Battista del Porto, who is mentioned in Vedriani's *Raccolta de' Pittori Modonesi*, 1662 (p. 45). There was nothing improbable in the conjecture, and it might have been supported by various points of contact in his style with the work of the line-engraver Nicoletto da Modena,[1] but later research has failed to add anything along the lines of Zani's theory, beyond noting the activity of a certain goldsmith and die-cutter Battista del Porto at Modena about 1529–39.

Far more probable, and indeed practically convincing, is the suggested identity, recently advanced by J. Byam Shaw, with JACOPO RIPANDA of Bologna. He was known as Jacopo Bolognese, and as *ripanda* is Italian for a water-bird, the signature ·I·B·℞ is aptly explained. He is mentioned in the XVII and XVIII centuries as *intagliatore in legno*,[2] and his documented work in fresco, notably the series of the *Punic Wars* in the Palazzo dei Conservatori, Rome, harmonises with the monogrammist's prints.

·I·B·℞ is known as line-engraver as well as designer of woodcuts, and one of his copper plates is dated 1503.

In style of design he is something of an eclectic, his work reminding one now of Mantegna, now of Nicoletto da Modena, now of Sodoma, now of Baldassare Peruzzi, now of Francesco Francia. Landscape and accessories are marked by Bolognese character, and it is in Bologna that Kristeller was inclined to place him.

As in the case of the young Marcantonio and many of the Italian engravers of the early XVI century, there is constant borrowing from Dürer, particularly in motives of landscape background.

This description of his style, made before Byam Shaw's identification, falls into line with what is known of Ripanda's life and work.[3] He is said to have been born at Bologna, and to have worked between 1490 and 1530. Philotheo Achillini, a Bolognese poet, associates him with Marcantonio in his *Viridario* of 1504 (published in 1513).[4] By 1507 he was settled in Rome, and probably painted his Capitol frescoes within the next six years. Apart from the frescoes, there are several drawings of a similar character, one in the Louvre, possibly an *Allegory of the Third Punic War*, having been engraved by Marcantonio (B. XIV. 173, 213, as 'Triumph of Titus'). And finally some sheets of a small sketch-book at Lille, signed by a

---

[1] Whose signature actually occurs on a reworked state of the line-engraving of *Leda* by ·I·B·℞ (Hind, *loc. cit.* p. 538, No. 2).

[2] A. Masini, *Bologna perlustrata*, 1666; M. Oretti, *Notizie di professori del disegno*, XVIII-century MS. at Bologna.   [3] See Giuseppe Fiocco, L' Arte, xxiii., 1920, 27.

[4] See A. M. Hind, *History of Engraving*, 1923, p. 92.

Fig. 208. The Master ·I·B·☙ (Jacopo Ripanda?). Apollo and Daphne.

Jac. pictor da Bollogna at Sulmona, 1516, with numerous small designs which show remarkable resemblance to Bolognese nielli, clearly indicating another side of the artist's activity.

To come to the woodcut work of our monogrammist, ten blocks are known bearing his signature, and an eleventh at Berlin (*Apollo and Daphne*, L. 11) is unsigned but certainly his work (fig. 208). Two of his cuts, *St. Jerome* (L. 4) and the *Three Graces* (L. 7), bear a second monogram ⋀⋀ (AAM?), and there are also two woodcut versions of the *Venus, Mars and Vulcan* (L. 9) in the British Museum, one of which (from the Mitchell Collection) appears to have a second obscure signature near the lower left corner, which looks like *cynthio* or *cynebio*. In any case these further signatures almost certainly indicate ·IB· cutters, himself being in all probability only a designer of woodcuts.

There is a superficial relation between his *St. Jerome* and the *St. Jerome* in Vivaldus, *De Veritate Contricionis*, printed by the brothers Le Signerre, Saluzzo 1503, and a resemblance was noted by Lippmann between the style of ·IB·'s *Calvary* and the new cuts in the same printers' *Tesauro Spirituale*, Milan 1499. Kristeller stated[1] that the St. Jerome appeared in a Venetian Missal, but I am unable to confirm his statement. A copy of the *Christ on the Cross with the Virgin, St. John, and the Magdalene* (L. 3, Correr Museum, Venice) occurs in the *Graduale* issued by L. A. Giunta, 1513–15 (E. 1209), and later in the same publisher's Roman Missal of 1523 (Essling, Missals, 96), so that it is not unlikely that he worked at some time in Venice.

One of his cuts, the *St. Sebastian* (L. 5, Berlin), is printed as a chiaroscuro from two blocks (line, and one colour), and it is hardly probable that this dates before 1516, when Ugo da Carpi obtained a *privilegium* from the Signoria at Venice for the practice of his new method. But it must be remembered that Lucantonio degli Uberti signed and dated in 1516 a chiaroscuro copy of Baldung's *Witches* (P. v. 64, 9, after B. vii. 319, 55) entirely in the German manner, with line-block complete in itself supported by a single tone-block. ·IB·'s chiaroscuro also follows German models rather than Ugo da Carpi's characteristic style,[2] so that even if done before

---

[1] *Kupferstich und Holzschnitt*, 1922, p. 152. The impression of the *St. Jerome* at Venice has text printed above with instructions about the celebration of the Mass, and the *Christ on the Cross* (L. 3) printed on the reverse; another impression (British Museum) has an anonymous *Christ on the Cross* on the reverse, with Latin verses printed below. Possibly Kristeller based his statement on the Venice impression, as if it were a leaf from a Missal. But it looks as if both impressions might have been pulled on printer's waste leaves.   [2] See p. 51.

1516, Ugo might still have had some claim to the invention of a method of his own.

Nearest to Mantegna in style, and perhaps the earliest of ·I·B·⚘·'s woodcuts, is the *Calvary* (L. 2); it is certainly less skilful and structural than the rest in quality, thinner and somewhat more angular in line, characteristics which probably depend as much on the design as on the cutting.

Apart from the prints already mentioned, all the other cuts by ·I·B·⚘· are of classical themes, except the *David with the Head of Goliath* (L. 1), which is as classical in its conception as the purely mythological subjects. It is of the type of composition, isolated figure standing before a fragment of ancient architecture

Fig. 209. Head of a Man in Profile. S. 2013.

in a landscape, which was constantly used by Nicoletto da Modena. This print and the *Three Graces* show qualities of graceful design which are related to Francesco Francia and the young Raphael.

The *Ganymede* (L. 8) and the *Meleager and Atalanta* (L. 6) are somewhat stiffer in drawing, and rather lacking in unity of composition. As successful as any in their own genre are the *Diana and Actaeon* (L. 10) and *Apollo and Daphne* (L. 11).

Continuing the survey of anonymous single woodcuts of North Italy, I would mention the *St. John the Evangelist under an Arch* (S. 1519,

Berlin), which was tentatively assigned by Kristeller to the Lombard school.[1] I am more inclined to regard it as Ferrarese under the influence of Francesco Cossa, and would compare the style of a line-engraving at Bologna of *St. John the Evangelist seated.*[2]

More probably Milanese is the fine cut of *St. Martin and the Beggar in a Tiled Courtyard*, now in the Masson Collection at the École des Beaux-Arts, Paris.[3]

Harder in linear style, and even more characteristic of the Milanese school of the last quarter of the xv century, especially in the profile portraits of the kneeling figures, is the *St. Nicholas of Tolentino*, once in the Schreiber Collection (S. 1636).

Similarly characteristic is the *Head of a Man in Profile* at Berlin, S. 2013 (fig. 209). Schreiber compares with Florentine profile drawings such as one attributed to Paolo Uccello in the Uffizi (Berenson, *Florentine Drawings*, No. 2766, and pl. xii.), but the outline drawing seems less subtle than one would expect from a Florentine, and finds closer analogies in a North Italian drawing from the Wauters Collection (reproduced F. Lees, *Art of the Great Masters*, London 1913, frontispiece, and Sale Catalogue, Muller, Amsterdam, 15th and 16th July 1926, No. 109). It is unique in its technical style among prints of the period, and in its appearance anticipates chiaroscuro woodcut, though it is only printed from a single block. Lippmann[4] expressed the opinion that its effect was entirely achieved in the press. I am on the whole inclined to think that the background silhouetting the contour of the head is printed, but that the delicate modelling of the face was largely done with delicate touches of the brush in a greyish bistre, possibly also with slight use of chalk. The background is nearly black, but the general appearance is brownish, partly from the tone of the paper.

A Miracle of St. Martha in the collection of Baron Edmond de Rothschild (S. 1618; Lippmann, p. 196 and reprod. p. 163) has been rightly compared by Lippmann with Milanese illustrations such as that printed by the brothers Le Signerre (*Specchio dell' Anima*, 1498, *Tesauro Spirituale*, 1499) and with the *St. Jerome* in Vivaldus, *De Veritate Contricionis*, issued by the same printers at Saluzzo, 1503. The style of the border decoration, which is nearly related to the *St. Jerome*, emanates from the school of Mantegna, and is represented at Milan by ornament panels such as are seen in the

[1] P. Kristeller, *Die Lombardische Graphik*, Berlin 1913, p. 28 and pl. xi.

[2] Kristeller, *Le gallerie nazionali ital.*, ii., 1896, 166.

[3] Kristeller, *Die Lombardische Graphik*, pp. 27-28 and pl. x.

[4] *Italian Wood-Engraving*, p. 170.

Fig. 210. Christ bearing the Cross. S. 919.

line-engravings of Zoan Andrea and the Master of the *Sforza Book of Hours*.[1] The motive of *putti* with signs of the Passion in the border is similar to that found in the panels above the throne in the large cut by Jacob of Strassburg after Benedetto Montagna.

Near to Solario, as Lippmann suggested, are a *Man of Sorrows* (S. 855; reproduced, Lippmann, p. 167) and a *Christ bearing the Cross* (S. 919, fig. 210), both within decorative borders on black ground. The latter, powerfully designed and cleanly cut with little shading, can only be rightly estimated in the contemporary impression at Berlin. Modern impressions are known, without the border, in which the line is considerably altered, but they appear to be from the re-cut block which is still preserved at Modena. The *Man of Sorrows*, of which the block is also at Modena, is only known to me in modern impressions at Berlin and Hamburg, and its inferiority in quality of line to the other subject might depend to some extent on deterioration and partial re-cutting. In subject, the *Man of Sorrows* finds a near relation in the picture of Andrea Solario in the Poldi-Pezzoli Gallery, Milan, and the painter might have actually designed the woodcut. The *Christ bearing the Cross* may also be compared with Solario's pictures at the Borghese Gallery, Rome, and at Berlin, but it is even more closely related to pictures by Giovanni Francesco Maineri of Parma (who was working at Ferrara after 1489) at Florence, Modena and Rome (Venturi, *Storia della pittura italiana*, VII. iii. p. 1104).

A *Virgin and Child standing with St. Sebastian and St. Roch* (S. 1148, Berlin, fragment) is described as Milanese by Kristeller, who compares its decorative elements with the *St. Martin and the Beggar* and with cuts in Milanese books. It is certainly a work of about 1480–90, but I am doubtful as to whether it is North Italian or Florentine. If the latter, it might be identical with *Una Vergine Maria e San Rocho e San Bastiano in dua pezi di lengno*[2] cited in the Rosselli Inventory of the year 1528.

This inventory[3] of the stock-in-trade of a certain Alessandro di Francesco Rosselli, known as Matassa, a mercer (*d.* 1525) and son of Francesco Rosselli, described as an illuminator and printer, who was brother of the

---

[1] See A. M. Hind, *Catalogue of Early Italian Engravings in the British Museum*, 1910, p. 397.

[2] The size of the Berlin fragment is about 10 × 7 inches, so that the whole cut might easily have been on two blocks.

[3] See I. del Badia, *Miscellanea fiorentina*, ii. No. 14, p. 25 (Florence 1894); and A. M. Hind, *Catalogue of Early Italian Engravings in the British Museum*, 1910, p. xxix.

Fig. 211. The Virgin and Child with the Infant St. John. S. 1137.

well-known Florentine painter, Cosimo Rosselli, contains record of a large assortment of miscellaneous goods, including numerous books, volumes of maps and views drawn and engraved, playing-cards, miscellaneous prints, as well as original copper plates and wood blocks. A certain number of the original plates can be identified with Florentine line-engravings of the xv century, but the majority of references are not sufficiently specific for identification. In addition to the entry already quoted, here are a few others definitely referring to wood blocks:

1º *Giuoco d' Apostoli chol Nostro Singnore, in sette pezze, di lengno.*

1ª *Santa Maria di Loreto, in due pezi di lengno.*

1º *Vergine Maria* (as quoted above).

1º *Giuoco di sete virtù in 5 pezi, di lengno.*

4º *Forme da roste in 2 pezi, di lengno.*

1ª *Vergine Maria d' un foglio qumane, di lengno.*

10 *Pezzi di forme di lengno d' uomini famossi, cioè pezi dopi e uno cienpio.*

1ª *Stampa di San Nicholo da Talentino in dua fogli chomuni.*

1º *Cenacholo di foglio chomune, la Nostra Donna da l'altra banda, di lengno.*

1º *San Gristofano e uno uomo famoso, di lengno.*

1º *San Michele, e San Nicholo da Talentino di lengno.*

It is probable that *foglio comune* is a small size, possibly the same as the *ordinary* paper noted by Briquet (*Dictionnaire des filigranes*, 1907) from standard Arabian sizes, i.e. 142 × 213 mm. = about $5\frac{1}{2}$ × $8\frac{1}{2}$ inches. To judge from one of the identified line-engravings (the *Deluge* in the Broad Manner, B. XIII. 71, 3) a *foglio reale* is 268 × 400 mm., i.e. about $10\frac{1}{2}$ × $15\frac{1}{2}$ inches.

On this scale it should be noted that the *San Nicholo di Talentino in due fogli chomuni* would fit well with the dimensions of the print already noted as probably North Italian, about $11\frac{3}{4}$ × $8\frac{1}{4}$ inches (see p. 426), while the *Santa Maria di Loreto* would probably be too large (being on two blocks) to be identified with the cut also noted in the same place. But such subjects must have been sufficiently common to render conjectural identifications dangerous.

It is of interest, however, to note that the *Virgin and Child with the Infant St. John* at Hamburg (S. 1137; fig. 211), which is generally regarded as Florentine, has the same border design as the *St. Nicholas of Tolentino*, though this actual design seems more usual in North Italy. This print is one of the most beautiful of early Italian woodcuts, and is undoubtedly

Fig. 212. The Flagellation.

the design of some more than ordinary painter, and it is strange that his identity should elude the student. Lippmann's suggestion of the influence of Raffaellino del Garbo does not appear to me entirely satisfactory.

Recently discovered by Dr. Ugo Procacci [1] inside the binding of a xv-century Venetian book in the *Biblioteca dell' Accademia Etrusca* at Cortona is an interesting woodcut of the *Flagellation*, within a border with white scroll decoration on a black ground, and with white line, characteristic of Florentine work, in the rendering of the ground with its grass and plants. The design reflects the influence of Filippino Lippi, and is comparable with a smaller *Flagellation* woodcut in Bonaventura, *Meditazioni sopra la Passione*, printed by Miscomini, Florence, about 1494.[2]

Somewhat later is a *Nativity and Annunciation to the Shepherds* (S. 86, Paris; Hirth and Muther, pl. 42), rather in the manner of Lorenzo di Credi. From its technical character, with close parallel shading related to the conventions of line-engraving, it may confidently be dated in the early years of the xvi century.

A *Tobias and the Angel* (S. 1702, Paris)[3] derives its design from some good Florentine painter of about 1480, and should be compared with such pictures as those in Turin (Venturi, *Storia dell' arte italiana*, vii. i. p. 566, A. and P. Pollaiuolo) and in the National Gallery (No. 781, Tuscan School). But the woodcut in its coarsely shaded manner might be as late as 1500. Similarly crude, but without shading, is a *St. Jerome* (S. 1555, and VI, pl. 26; Paris); and here again a good Florentine design of about 1480 is the source. Both cuts are only known in the late impressions at Paris (both inscribed 1562 in MS.), which probably do injustice to the cuts in their original condition.

A roughly cut *Nativity*, preserved at Bremen (S. 85), may also be placed somewhat in the same category.

JOHANNES OF FRANKFURT may be mentioned here as he is only known for an early woodcut copy of Pollaiuolo's famous line-engraving of the *Battle of Naked Men*.[4] The copy (P. 1. p. 132), which is signed *Johānes de franc-*

---

[1] See Ugo Procacci, *Due incisioni fiorentine del' 400*, Rivista d' Arte, xvi., 1934, No. 3 (July-September). The book in which it was found is Robertus Caracciolus, *Specchio della Fede*, Venice (Jo. Rubeus) 1495 (H. 4494, E. 833).

[2] See p. 539.

[3] Reproduced, Delaborde, *La Gravure en Italie avant Marcantoine*, p. 206.

[4] For the original engraving, which probably dates about 1470, see A. M. Hind, *Catalogue of Early Italian Engravings in the British Museum*, 1910, p. 192, No. 1. Dr. Panofsky has recently suggested that the subject represents *Titus Manlius Torquatus in combat with a Gaul*.

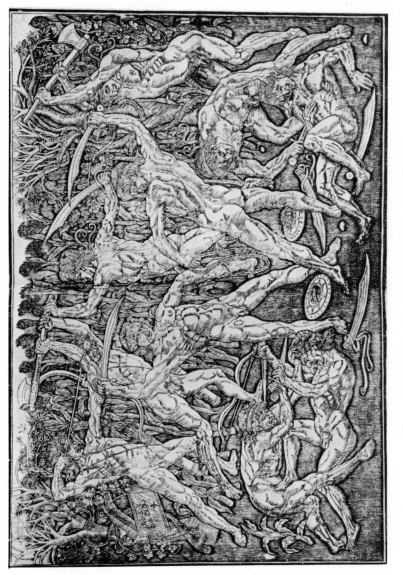

Fig. 213. Johannes of Frankfurt. Battle of Naked Men, after Pollaiuolo.

fordia, and is practically of the original size (about 16¾ × 24 inches), follows the engraving in its contours and shading of the figures, but renders the dark background in its own convention, a series of white perpendicular lines and of dots on a black ground. The resemblance of this convention to Florentine woodcut makes it probable that the cutter worked at Florence. A certain *Hans von Frankfurt* is mentioned in documents at Würzburg, where he painted a crucifix in 1470, and his activity extended to 1501, and other painters of the same name are recorded in the later xv and early xvi centuries at Strassburg, but there is no clue to identify any of them with the woodcutter.

A true Florentine, on the other hand, is LUCANTONIO DEGLI UBERTI,[1] but his work falls largely in the xvi century, though its beginnings may come within the last years of the xv century. The description of his work has been obscured by Passavant, who added to it somewhat promiscuously from cuts in books issued by his Florentine namesake, Lucantonio Giunta, who was the most prolific publisher in Venice between about 1490 and 1510. As Uberti occasionally appeared himself as a printer of books the confusion was an easy pitfall.

His signature occurs in most explicit form on one of the five series of woodcuts of the *Triumph of Faith*, of which Titian did the designs, according to Vasari, in the year 1508.[2] It is signed *Opus Luce Antonii ubertii i venetiis ipreso* (early impressions at Florence and Gotha; late impressions in the British Museum and at Bassano). A large cut of *St. George and St. Catherine* at Copenhagen (P. v. 64, 7) is signed *Opus . Luce . Atonii . v . f.*, and a full-size copy of Pollaiuolo's *Battle of Naked Men*, OPVS LVCE M FLORENTINI ED INPLESA IN STRAGVA (P. v. 64, 8). Both these cuts from their style are certainly by Uberti, but I cannot explain the *v.* in the former, nor the M or IN STRAGVA in the latter. INPLESA is probably in error for *impreso*.

Explicit again as to printer and cutter is the *Opus lucha ātonio de uberti fe i vinetia* on the last block of the *Libro d' Abacco*, a popular ready-reckoner, first issued at Venice in 1520. He is also probably the *Lucantonius Florentinus* who printed a few books at Verona in 1503 and 1504.

In addition to these more fully signed works, a considerable number of line-engravings and cuts signed LA, LA*, LAF (in various forms) may be

---

[1] See Kristeller, *Early Florentine Woodcuts*, London 1897, p. xli; A. M. Hind, *Catalogue of Early Italian Engravings in the British Museum*, 1910, p. 209.

[2] See P. Kristeller, *Il Trionfo della Fede*, Graphische Gesellschaft, i., 1906, Berlin (the version D).

Fig. 214. Attributed to Lucantonio degli Uberti. Part of a View of Florence.

attributed to him with fair certainty on the basis of their style. Of single cuts may be mentioned:

(1) The series of four blocks after designs by Domenico Campagnola (*Procession and Adoration of the Magi* and the *Massacre of the Innocents*), of which the *Adoration of the Magi* bears the signature LA*, and the *Massacre of the Innocents* the date 1517 and imprint of the publisher, *In Venetia Il Vieceri* (P. v. 63, 5, and D. Campagnola, P. 4, a and b, and Galichon, 1-4).

(2) A copy of Baldung's *Witches*, dated 1516, printed as a chiaroscuro in the German manner, with key-block and a single tone-block (P. v. 64, 9, after B. vii. 319, 55); signed LA*.

(3) *A woman seated in meditation, with a Child*, based on motives from Marcantonio after Raphael (P. v. 64, 10; Gotha).

Another very large woodcut subject which bears the same imprint as No. (1), *In Venetia Il Vieceri*, i.e. the *Martyrdom of the Ten Thousand Christians* (British Museum), is signed L*, and might well be another work of Uberti, the differences in style being easily accounted for by difference of designer.

On the other hand, caution is necessary even with cuts signed LA*, for the *Virgin and Child with St. John the Baptist and St. Gregory* (P. v. 63, 6), which bears the imprint and date *Gregorius de Gregoriis MDXVII*, would appear to be by the same hand as one of the versions of Titian's *Triumph of Faith* (Kristeller, version B) which is inscribed *Gregorius de Gregoriis excussit MDXVII*. As we have already seen, another version of the same subject bears Uberti's full signature, so that the unsigned version B is hardly likely to be his.

Essling attributes to Uberti a great variety of monograms occurring on cuts in Venetian books, chiefly in the early half of the xvi century, L, LA, LA*, LF (in various forms), and Kristeller has noted certain cuts signed LA in Florentine books (e.g. a *St. Anthony and St. Stephen* in the *Historia di S. Antonio di Padova*, 1557, P. K., 'Early Florentine Woodcuts', No. 32, and cut 193). From its condition the Florentine cut was probably only in a late issue in 1557, but it seems likely that Uberti returned to Florence after a prolonged stay at Venice.

A series of six large upright sheets in the Bibliothèque Nationale, Paris, representing the *Ages of the World* (Courboin, 'Catalogue de la Réserve', 416; with inscriptions *Vis Imaginaria, Humana Christi Genealogia*), is unsigned but might reasonably be attributed to Lucantonio as cutter. The procession is shown in five of the sheets against an architectural background with angels playing musical instruments above: the last subject has a landscape background with river in hilly country of distinctly Tuscan character.

Finally there is the large woodcut *View of Florence*, only known in the impression at Berlin, which has been attributed by Kristeller to Lucantonio.[1] Measuring in all about 23 × 52 inches, it appears to be printed from eight blocks, two on the left being narrower than the rest. The whole is surrounded by a border composed of chain and padlock, such as one might imagine the border which Vasari had in mind in describing Pollaiuolo's line-engraving of the *Battle of Naked Men* (though the latter is not known in that form).[2] Lippmann dated the view before 1489, as it does not show the Palazzo Strozzi, whose building was begun in that year. It has been found that the woodcutter merely copied an earlier line-engraving, of which only the upper left portion is preserved in an impression belonging to the Società della Columbaria at Florence. Though the original portion which might include the Strozzi Palace is not known, it may be assumed from the closeness of the copy of the one part that the Strozzi Palace was not shown on its section, and that the argument for dating must apply to the original and not to the woodcut, which can hardly be before 1500. The line-engraving is undoubtedly the *Firenze di sei fogli reali* which occurs in the Rosselli inventory which we have already mentioned.[3]

In technical character the woodcut is in the Venetian manner typified by Jacob of Strassburg, if not actually introduced by him from the North. Comparison of its figures with subjects such as Jacob's *Istoria Romana*, with its strong outline and close parallel shading, shows the resemblance most clearly. The by-play of the subject (the ferry-boat, the naked fishermen with drag-net, and workmen driving piles into the weir) adds human interest to a view of great topographical importance.

In line-engraving it may perhaps be assumed that Lucantonio's work was in part at least original,[4] and on that score the poverty of his achievement is evident. As a woodcutter he no doubt worked chiefly after the designs of

---

[1] See F. Lippmann, *Italian Wood-Engraving*, London 1888, p. 30, for description and re-production; see also P. N. Ferri, Rivista d' Arte, viii., 1912, 103; and C. Hulsen, Pr. Jahrbuch, 1914, p. 90, for a discussion of the original line-engraving.

[2] Vasari, ed. Milanesi, vol. iii. p. 295, *ignudi . . . e di quelli tutti, cinti d' una catena, intagliò in rame una battaglia.*

[3] And it was probably this line-engraving which was the source of the woodcut views in the *Supplementum Chronicarum*, Venice (Rizus) 1490, and the *Nuremberg Chronicle* of 1493.

[4] Though his most important plate reproduces the fresco of the *Last Supper* in St. Onofrio, Florence.

others, and as a craftsman he was respectable, perhaps the best word that can be said for his productions.

With a passing reference to an earlier section in which we described certain Italian woodcuts of more purely decorative character,[1] we will retrace our steps, and continue the survey of book-illustration in Venice.

VENICE

(continuation)

While the discussion of the large *View of Florence* is fresh in our minds, I would mention the two books which are chiefly noteworthy in our study for their topographical cuts, i.e. Werner Rolewinck, *Fasciculus Temporum*,

Fig. 215. The Ducal Palace, Venice, from the *Fasciculus Temporum*, Venice 1480.

and Jacobus Philippus Foresti (Bergomensis), *Supplementum Chronicarum*. The general scheme of illustration of the Italian editions of the *Fasciculus* corresponds with that of the German editions on which they were based,[2] including woodcuts of *Noah's Ark*, the *Tower of Babel* and of the *Redeemer*, and various views of towns. In the first two Italian editions, that of Georgius Walch (evidently a Northern craftsman) of 1479 (H. 6924, E. 276), and Erhard Ratdolt of 1480 (H. 6926, E. 277), the cuts are German in character and crude in execution. In the 1480 edition the cuts are somewhat the better, and the little *View of Venice with the Ducal Palace* (at f. 37, verso) is decorative in quality (fig. 215), while a few further views added in Ratdolt's edition of 1481 (H. 6928, E. 278) show an attractive simplicity in landscape design.

A distinct advance in topographical study is made in the 1486 edition of the *Supplementum Chronicarum*, printed by BERNARDINUS BENALIUS (H. 2807, E. 342). Here the *Genoa*, at f. 50, and certain other views look as if based on drawings from nature, but that does not hinder the printer using the same block again as a *View of Rome*, on f. 79. The cuts are also more Italian in character than those published by Walch and Ratdolt, and the same character, as well as a continued improvement in topography, may be

---

[1] See pp. 73-77.   [2] See p. 357.

noted in the editions printed by BERNARDINUS RIZUS in 1490 (H. 2808, E. 343) and subsequent years. The *View of Rome* is of particular interest, and is certainly one of the earliest printed views of the city of any claim to accuracy; while that of *Venice* is pictorially even more attractive. In the various editions the views always occur at particular dates in the history of the world, and as an aid to finding those I have mentioned in other editions, I would add that *Genoa* illustrates the year 1507 B.C., *Rome* the year 751 B.C., and *Venice* A.D. 456.

Fig. 216. View of Genoa, from the *Supplementum Chronicarum*, Venice 1486.

The edition of Benalius is notable for its inclusion on the first three leaves of three subject cuts, the *Creation of Eve: a Roundel* (based on the cut in the Cologne Bible), the *Fall and Expulsion from Paradise* and the *Story of Cain and Abel*. The *Fall and Expulsion* is certainly by the same designer and cutter (Hieronymus de Sanctis) as the frontispiece in Sacro Busto's *Sphaera Mundi* of 1488, a subject to which I shall recur later.[1]

Rizus' editions contain the same blocks, and an additional *Building of the Tower of Babel* (fig. 217) which offers an attractive illustration of building operations taken from contemporary Italian life.

The edition printed by Rizus, 15th February 1492/93 (H. 2809, E. 345), is further embellished by a border twice used, first as a frontispiece including the cuts of the *Six Days of Creation* (from the Malermi Bible of 1490), and then round the first page of text. The border itself (with eight children at the vintage in the lower part) appeared a few months earlier in Jacobus de Voragine, *Legenda Aurea*, issued by Bonellis, 10th December 1492 (E. 678), and in St. Jerome, *Vitas Patrum*, printed by CAPCASA in February 1493/94 (cf. E. 569, of February 1492).

[1] See p. 463.

The use of the same borders by various printers, working contemporaneously, is a sidelight on the general conditions governing the supply of
woodcuts in Venice.[1]

We have mentioned Ratdolt's editions of the *Fasciculus Temporum*, which
were issued when he was carrying on his printing establishment alone (between 1480 and 1486). The earliest borders in Venetian books intended to

Fig. 217. Building of the Tower of Babel, from the *Supplementum Chronicarum*, Venice 1490.

stand on their own merits, untouched by the illuminator, were those issued
earlier by Ratdolt when in partnership with Bernhard (Maler), and Peter
Löslein (1476–78).[2] Bernhard, who, like Ratdolt, was a native of Augsburg,
appears to have been the predominant partner, and as he is designated a
painter he was probably the designer of the borders and initials. Ratdolt
was no doubt from the first the expert printer, and Löslein acted as editor
and proof-reader of the firm (*corrector et socius*).

[1] See pp. 399, 468, 502-504.
[2] See G. R. Redgrave, *Ratdolt and his Work at Venice*, London (Bibliographical Society)
1894; L. Baer, *Bernhard, Maler von Augsburg, und die Bücherornamentik der italienischen
Frührenaissance*, Monatshefte für Kunstwissenschaft, 1909, p. 46.

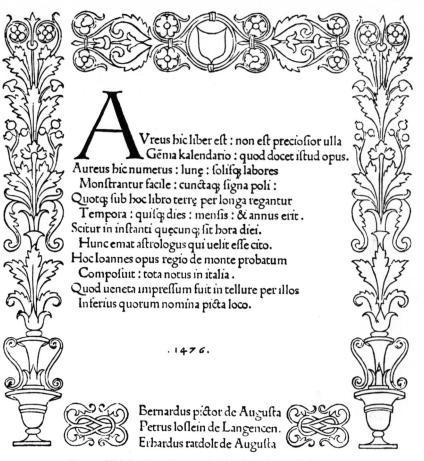

AVreus hic liber eſt : non eſt precioſior ulla
Gēma kalendario : quod docet iſtud opus.
Aureus hic numerus : lunę : ſoliſcʒ labores
Monſtrantur facile : cunctacʒ ſigna poli :
Quotcʒ ſub hoc libro terrę per longa regantur
Tempora : quiſcʒ dies : menſis : & annus erit.
Scitur in inſtanti quęcuncʒ ſit hora diei.
Hunc emat aſtrologus qui uelit eſſe cito.
Hoc Ioannes opus regio de monte probatum
Compoſuit : tota notus in italia.
Quod ueneta impreſſum fuit in tellure per illos
Inferius quorum nomina picta loco.

. 1476 .

Bernardus pictor de Auguſta
Petrus loſlein de Langencen.
Erhardus ratdolt de Auguſta

Fig. 218. Title-border to Johannes Müller, *Calendarium*, Venice 1476.

Four border designs were used by the firm between 1476 and 1478, one
of them in three variants. The first, composed of five pieces in outline with
conventional plants growing out of vases at the sides, was made for Johann
Müller (Regiomontanus), *Calendarium*, 1476, quarto (H. 13776, E. 247;
Ital. ed., H. 13789, E. 248; fig. 218). All the others were designed in
white on a black (or coloured) ground. The first version of the second
design, a complete four-sided border with branch work and foliage, wreath
and shield in lower panel, was used, sometimes printed in red, at the head

of Part I. of Appianus, *Historia Romana* (*De Bellis Civilibus*), 1477, folio (H.1307, E.221). A three-sided border of similar design but closer pattern and smaller branch-work, and with empty wreath of scale-like pattern in the lower panel, was prefixed to Part II. of the same work. The third version of the second design was a fairly close repetition in smaller size of the first version, and used in Dionysius Periegetes, *Cosmographia*, 1477, quarto (H.6226, E.255).

The third design, also a complete four-sided border, and the most delicate of all, formed of branch-work and foliage, crossed shields in circle in the lower panel, appeared with a beautiful capital Q of the same design on the first page of Coriolanus Cepio, *Gesta Petri Mocenici*, 1477, quarto (H.4849, E.254).

The fourth design, somewhat bolder than the preceding, consisting of branch-work with oak-leaves and acorns, and an empty wreath in the lower panel, appeared in Celsus Maffeus, *Monumentum Compendiosum pro Confessionibus Cardinalium*, 1478 (E.275; fig.219). Altogether these borders form an incomparable series, those on black ground unsurpassed in later Venetian work, as in the whole field of book-decoration.

Matching the borders in style were various series of initials, of which examples are here reproduced from the outline set used with the first border (fig.220); black ground branch-work capitals corresponding to the Appianus border (fig.221), and black ground branch-work with oak-leaves and acorns corresponding to the fourth design (fig.222). The partnership which produced these beautiful works was too soon dissolved, the cause no doubt being a severe epidemic of plague in Venice in 1478, visitations which so constantly accounted for the rapid changes of fortune noted throughout the century in the history of the different printers. Ratdolt only retained part of the stock (some of the type and initials passing into the hands of Renner), and though he used many of the initials, he only reprinted one of the borders, the three-sided version of the second design (in some copies of his 1482 *Euclid*, British Museum, IB.20513, variant of H.6693, E.282). And he only added one further border to his stock in these later years (chain-work on black ground, with a seven-pointed shield at the foot), used for example in Johann Müller, *Calendarium*, 1482 (H.13777, E.250). Ratdolt carried some of his stock of initials back to Augsburg, an example such as the Q reproduced in fig. 222 being also used in his *Augsburg Obsequiale* of 1487.[1]

In his later years at Venice, Ratdolt was chiefly interested in the publication of astronomical and mathematical books, and decoration in itself was

---

[1] See p. 300.

Suo Reuerendiſſimo patri & Domino.D.B.Ze
no diuina miſeratione preſbytero Cardinali ſan
ctę Marię i porticu.Celſus Mapheus ueronenſis
canonicus regularis congregationis Lateranenſis
Salutem ęternam & cōmendationem peroptat.

I reuerendiſſime pater & domine
dixerimus quia peccatum non ha
bemus iuxta Iohannis apoſtoli ſen
tentiam noſmetipſos ſeducimus &
ueritas in nobis non eſt.Ideo pie ac
recte a ſancta matre eccleſia inſtitutū arbitror: ut
omnis utriuſcʒ ſexus ſemel ſaltem i anno propria
cōfiteat̄ peccata:quo per huiuſmodi confeſſionis
humilitatē auctori noſtro reconciliari mereamur
cum quo peccando inimicitiam contraxeramus.
A quo quidē ſalutari pręcepto nec uos qui eccle
ſiaſtica pręeminentia inſigniti eſtisı exemit. Cū
magis deceat eos qui excellentiori fulgent digni
tateıetiā puriori conſcientia nitere:Cęterıſcʒ qui
bus pręſunt fidelibus non ſolū beneuiuendi pre
cepta tradere: ſed etiā exempla monſttare. Tuo
itacʒ precipuo hortatu & iuſſu ac nō nulloʒ alioʒ
patrum in hoc breui ſcrutat̄ riolo aliqua congeſſi

a

Fig. 219. Title-border to Celsus Maffeus, *Monumentum* Venice 1478.

Fig. 220. Initial L, from Müller, *Calendarium*, Venice 1476.

no longer an important aim. His use of woodcuts was largely technical, and in this respect his work is notable in showing the earliest attempts at printing in colour from more than one block,[1] a practice which he also introduced and carried much further in Germany. The most interesting of his Venetian colour-woodcuts appeared in his Hyginus, *Poetica Astronomica*, first issued in 1482 (H. 9062, E. 285), with its pictorial representation of the Constellations, Signs of the Zodiac and Planets. Verses at the end of the book seem to indicate that the invention of the figures was due to JOHANNES SANTRITTER, but how far this implies their actual drawing is vague. From its numerous editions the book must have been extremely popular. It was reprinted by Ratdolt in 1485 (H. 9063, E. 286), and a later edition with more crudely cut copies was issued by THOMAS DE BLAVIS in 1488 (H. 9065, E. 287), these copies being used again in R. F. Avienus, *Opera* (in the section *Fragmentum Arati Phaenomenon*), printed by ANTONIUS DE STRATA, in the same year, 1488 (H. 2224, E. 431). In addition to the constellation cuts of crude German character, the *Avienus* contains a few charming little outline designs, notably those illustrating the constellations of *Bootes* (with the waggon), at sig. h. vii, verso, and of the *Pleiades*, at sig. k. iv (fig. 223). They are cut with admirable precision, and fall in character between the popular and the classic styles, to which we shall soon devote our attention. These delicate little outline figures are matched by a charming little cut of *Three Girls and an old Woman* in L. B. Alberti, *Hecatomphyla, sive De Amore*, printed by BERNARDINUS DE CHORIS, 1491 (H. 421, E. 562), and by others in the more classic style (less finished in execution) in the horoscopes of Joannes Angelus, *Astrolabium Planum*,

Fig. 221. Initial R, from Appianus, *Historia Romana*, Venice 1477.

Fig. 222. Initial Q, from *Euclid*, Venice 1482.

printed by J. Emericus de Spira, 1494 (H. 1101, E. 433), which were based on the German cuts in Ratdolt's Augsburg edition of 1488 (H. 1100, E. 432).[2]

---

[1] E.g. in J. Müller, *Calendarium*, 1482 (H. 13777, E. 250).

[2] The frontispiece of an *Astronomer, with an Astrolabe, seated in a Landscape*, signed N, is

Another astronomical book of Ratdolt's printing, Johannes de Sacro Busto (John Hollywood), *Sphaera Mundi*, 1482 (H. 14101, E. 258), has little but technical diagrams, and the same diagrams, recut, were used in the 1488 edition printed by Hieronymus de Sanctis and J. L. Santritter (H. 14112, E. 260), where their invention was definitely attributed to Santritter. The colophon verses in this 1488 edition are again somewhat vague as to their explicit connotation. As

Fig. 223. The Pleiades, from Avienus, *Opera*, Venice 1488.

Santritter was a man of learning in astronomy and astrology, I should infer as certain that he designed the technical diagrams, but should regard it as highly improbable that he drew the allegorical frontispiece (fig. 224). Nor is it probable, from the custom of the time, that De Sanctis was more than the cutter, so that the designer of this frontispiece and of other illustrations in a similar style must at present remain, like most of his contemporary designers, in anonymity. Other woodcuts in a similar style which Kristeller[1] has grouped about the *Sphaera Mundi* frontispiece of De Sanctis include:

(1) J. P. Foresti (Bergomensis), *Supplementum Chronicarum*, Venice (B. Benalius) 1486 (H. 2807, E. 342): the four Old Testament subjects, the nearest in details of style to the *Sphaera Mundi* being the *Fall and Expulsion from Paradise*.

(2) *Fior di Virtù*, Venice (H. de Sanctis) 1487 (E. 387, Oxford): with an attractive cut of a monk gathering blossom.

(3) *Libro di S. Justo*, Venice (n.pr.) 1487 (E. 356, Manchester): with a small cut illustrating 'the appearance of the Fortune of the World to S. Just'.

(4) St. Thomas Aquinas, *Opusculum*, Venice (H. de Sanctis and J. L. Santritter) 1488 (H. 1502, E. 447).

more ambitious. In style of design it is midway between several of the cuts noted among Kristeller's attributions to H. de Sanctis, and the more purely classical style of the cuts in the *Ovid* of 1497. Another more important cut representing *Two Astronomers seated by a large Astrolabe* appeared in J. Müller (Regiomontanus), *Epitome in Almagestum Ptolemaei*, printed by J. Hamman, 1496 (H. 13806, E. 895).

[1] Graphische Gesellschaft, Berlin, ix., 1909.

(5) John Estwood (Eschuid), *Summa Astrologiae Judicialis*, Venice (J. L. Santritter for F. Bolanus) 1489 (H. 6685, E. 450): with a map of the world with wind faces.[1]

(6) Cherubino da Spoleto, *Spiritualis Vitae Compendiosa Regula*, Venice, n.d., n.pr. (B. Benalius) (E. 1268): cut of the saint holding books and flowers.

(7) *Fior di Virtù*, Brescia (B. Farfengo) 1491, and Brescia (B. Misinta) 1495: with cut of student at his desk. Cf. p. 507.

The frontispiece of the *Sphaera Mundi* and the *Fall and Expulsion* from the *Supplementum Chronicarum* are in a classic style, influenced by Mantegna, foreshadowing the *Ovid* of 1497 and the *Hypnerotomachia Poliphili* of 1499. Certain details of design which occur in both *Sphaera Mundi* and the *Fall*, i.e. the ground with flowers and rabbits, will be met again in the *Petrarch*, printed by Bernardinus Rizus in 1488, though the cutting of the latter is distinctly more angular in character.[2]

I have already alluded to the *popular* and *classic* styles in Venetian woodcut. The distinction is vital to the understanding of book-illustration in Venice, and seems to indicate the existence of two master designers, who are probably to be found among the miniaturists and painters, and not among the craftsmen who cut the blocks. I will speak of these designers respectively as the '*popular*' *designer* or the *Illustrator of the Malermi Bible of 1490* and the '*classic*' *designer* or the *Illustrator of the Malermi Bible of 1493*. Nicolò Malermi (*b.* 1422) was the author of the Italian translation, and the issue in 1490 of this *Biblia Vulgar Istoriata*, printed by GIOVANNI RAGAZZO for Lucantonio Giunta (H. 3156, E. 133), was the earliest illustrated edition.[3] The edition of 1493 (E. 135) was printed by GULIELMUS ANIMA MIA (Tridinensis, de Monferrato).[4]

---

[1] A still earlier woodcut map of the world appeared in Pomponius Mela, *Cosmographia*, Venice (Ratdolt) 1482 (H. 11019, E. 274).

[2] See p. 484.

[3] The earliest edition of Malermi's Bible was printed by Vindelinus de Spira, 1st August 1471 (H. 3150), and the new version was also adopted half-way through the printing of the Bible issued by Adam de Ambergau, 1st October 1471 (H. 3148, E. 131).

[4] For notes on both editions see F. Weitenkampf, *The Malermi Bible in the Spencer Collection*. Bulletin of the New York Public Library, November 1929. Later editions of the 1490 Bible, with variations and additions in the cuts, were printed by Ragazzo for Giunta in 1492 (H. 3157, E. 134), and Jo. Rubeus for Giunta, 1494 (H. 3158, E. 136). Certain differences between the cuts and their arrangement in the Bible of 1493 (E. 135) from either the 1490 or 1492 editions inclined Mr. A. W. Pollard to assume the possibility of a lost Ragazzo-Giunta edition of about 1491. The 1493 Bible was not reprinted, so that it was evidently less popular. A

It may be assumed that Lucantonio Giunta, who was the most enterprising publisher in Venice between 1490 and 1510, was chiefly responsible for the form of the 1490 edition. It is a medium-sized folio printed in two columns, illustrated by numerous little cuts of column width (the average dimension of the blocks being $1\frac{3}{4} \times 2\frac{7}{8}$ inches). Its form became a pattern for a great number of Venetian illustrated books of the succeeding two decades. Such small illustrations have often been described as sign-posts to help the reader find his place without page headings or index; and they are certainly valuable as memorisers of the main episodes of a long text. But for all that they are very true illustrations, vividly drawn, though seldom of original invention. As illustrations they do not

Fig. 224. Frontispiece to Johannes de Sacro Busto, *Sphaera Mundi*, Venice 1488.

always claim to be more than typical of incident; so that one block will frequently serve for more than one story. The general elements of the compositions were to a large extent borrowed from the woodcuts of the

small selection of its cuts appeared in *Fioretti della Bibbia*, printed by Antonio e Rinaldo di Trino, 1493 (E. 159). A limited number of the cuts from the 1490 Bible also appeared in the *Latin Bible* printed by Bevilaqua, 1498 (H. 3124, E. 138).

Cologne Bible of about 1478–79,[1] which had become a model for the majority of Bible-illustrators of the period. But the designer adopted his originals with great independence, using contemporary costume, and imparting thereby a sense of surprising reality to his little illustrations. They are almost entirely in outline: they tend to a certain angularity of drawing, in which bearded faces resemble the designer's characteristic stubbled ground, made up of short parallel and nearly perpendicular strokes.

The *Malermi Bible* of 1493 was based closely on the edition of 1490, both in its form as a book and in the design of its woodcuts. But the style of the illustrations was entirely transformed from the vernacular into a classic rendering inspired by the influence of Andrea Mantegna. Contemporary costume yielded to a more typical classic; the angular gave way to a more rhythmic and curving treatment of fold and figure; the figure itself was not hidden by its clothes, but often rendered with considerable science beneath a more clinging drapery. This description may sound as if I magnify the *classic* designer to the detriment of his *popular* rival, but this is far from my intention. As an illustrator the popular designer possesses by far the more vivid touch; he is not shy of indecencies, which the classical designer discreetly covers (e.g. in Potiphar's wife); moreover, the cuts of the classic designer are often blunted renderings, wanting in life, for all their greater science in drawing.

And it is seldom that the designer of the Bible of 1493 shows real independence from his predecessor in invention (one of the few examples being the illustration to the *Building of the Tower of Babel*, where both designers drew directly from contemporary building operations). But where he does exert independence, he generally achieves the better and certainly more dignified result, e.g. in the *Death of Abel*, and in such revisions of the poorer designs of the 1490 Bible as *Christ preaching from the Boat* (Matthew xiii.).

Even the greater science displayed by the classic designer is not always seconded by the cutters, who are certainly several, and of very varying quality. In general there is more regularity and excellence in the cutting of the blocks in the 1490 Bible than in the 1493 edition, though the best cutter of the latter edition is equal to the best of 1490.

In the 1493 Bible the style of drawing is more consistent than the quality of cutting, so that it may perhaps be inferred that all the illustrations are due to one draughtsman. On the other hand, in the 1490

[1] See p. 358.

Bible the woodcuts certainly disclose two designers, and my designation the 'Illustrator of the Malermi Bible of 1490' must be referred to the chief designer. Most of the Old Testament subjects are the work of this master, the chief exceptions being contained in 'Solomon's Song', the 'Wisdom of Solomon' and 'Ecclesiasticus'. This poorer designer was also responsible for a great part of the New Testament. The difference, moreover, consists in style, and not merely in quality of cutting (though each designer may be affected by the latter contingency).

Many of the cuts of the 1490 Bible are signed *b* or ·*b*·, and as this is found on examples by both designers, it can definitely be assigned to cutter and not designer.[1] One of the cuts (Deuteronomy xxv.) has the two signatures *b* and ·*b*·, the second signature ·*b*· being perhaps added, as the former might have been confused with the ground; in any case this example seems to show that *b* is identical with ·*b*·. The one other signature is ·Mb·, found once only on Apocalypse xvii. The majority of the cuts are without signatures, and these include many of the finest quality, equal to the best of those signed *b*, and probably cut by the same hand. It is difficult to explain the irregularity of signature. It is possible that a considerable number of subjects might have been cut on a larger block, and divided before printing, and in this case the cutter might have economised in his signatures.

The only signature on the cuts in the 1493 Bible is *N*, and this not nearly so frequently as the *b* in the 1490 Bible. Apart from those signed *N*, there are certainly various hands among the cutters; a good craftsman (including *N*); an inferior cutter, and a third craftsman of very poor talent (responsible for such crude cuts as Deuteronomy xviii. and xxi.).

The natural inference is that there were two distinct woodcutters' workshops, those of the master *b*, and the master *N*, each with various craftsmen.

Cuts signed *b* in Venetian books of the period are all, as far as I can find, in the 'popular' style, except the examples in the *Hypnerotomachia Poliphili*. Those signed *N* on the other hand are consistently of the 'classic' style. This might incline one to think that the workshops included a designer; but it seems to me more in keeping with the general history of the art to think that the designers were painters or

---

[1] There is a slight possibility that these letters have some workshop signification distinct from the individual cutters. My further references to the Master *b*, etc., must be read with this potential qualification.

illuminators outside the cutters' shops, and that the designers, who would probably be appointed by the publisher or printer for the illustrations, would tend to employ particular workshops for the cutting of their blocks.

A careful tabulation of cuts in the two styles used by the various printers and publishers reveals little in the way of exclusive relations between certain printers and one or the other workshop. I do not know that Anima Mia, Luere or Aldus used any but the 'classic' style; while Ragazzo, B. Benalius, Capcasa, Plasiis and Pensis chiefly favoured the 'popular' manner. The publisher Giunta used illustrations of both kinds, and the same may be said of other printers, such as Gregoriis, Jo. Rubeus, Bonellis, Locatellus, and J. Hamman.

It would seem, therefore, that the cutters' shops were independent of the printers, and worked for any printer or designer who commissioned them, and that the designers were more attached to particular cutters than were the printers. The same independence was certainly exemplified in the cutters of the outline borders used as a basis for illumination between the years 1469 and 1472, for the same atelier of illuminators and cutters supplied these borders, as we have seen, to several publishers indiscriminately.[1]

Moreover, an examination of the borders of the last decade of the century seems to show that the woodcutters' workshops must have kept some of their miscellaneous stock, hiring it out as occasion required to any publisher according to his requirement.[2]

These considerations have differentiated our treatment of Venetian woodcut illustration from that of most German towns, where we had more often been able to arrange our description of book-illustrations under the various printers.

Other signatures which appear on cuts of the 'popular' style are:

 i (e.g. *Malermi Bible*, printed by Ragazzo for Giunta, 1492, E. 134; S. Jerome, *Vitas Patrum*, Ragazzo for Giunta, 1491, E. 568, and later editions; Jacobus de Voragine, *Legenda Aurea*, Bonellis, 1492, E. 678).

 F (e.g. *Malermi Bible*, Ragazzo for Giunta, 1492, E. 134; *Legenda Aurea*, E. 678, and Livy, *Decades*, Jo. Rubeus for Giunta, 1493, E. 33; *Trabisonda Istoriata*, Pensis, 1492, E. 661; Petrus de Crescentiis, *De Agricultura*, Capcasa, 1495, E. 842).

---

[1] See p. 399.   [2] See pp. 502-504.

£ (Jerome, *Vitas Patrum*, Ragazzo for Giunta, 1491, E. 568, and later editions).

Mɓ (*Malermi Bible*, 1490 and 1492, E. 133 and 134).

The only other signature apart from *N* found at all frequently on the cuts in classic style is 1 a (e.g. Ovid, *Metamorphoses*, printed by Jo. Rubeus for Giunta, 1497, E. 223; *Officium B.V.M. Virginis*, printed by J. Hamman, 1497, E. 462; and *Breviarium Romanum*, B. Stagninus, 1498, E. 919, in which the shaded style is used). The letters of this signature are not divided by stops, so that it more probably indicates some Jacobus (Giacomo), and the possibility that it might be Jacob of Strassburg has been already mentioned.[1]

My remarks have shown that I regard the designers of Venetian book-illustration as distinct from the cutters, and of greater artistic importance in our history. It would be of far greater interest to identify any of these designers than find an explanation for any of the monograms of cutters which we have cited.

The style of the 'classic' designer or designers is strongly influenced by Andrea Mantegna, possibly through the medium of such painters as Cima and Benedetto Montagna. Cima studied under Benedetto's father, Bartolommeo Montagna, in Vicenza, and was later under the influence of Giovanni Bellini. He painted various little mythological pictures somewhat after the manner of Bellini's five *Allegories* in the Academy, Venice, but nearer in style to the more angular manner of his Vicentine master, and of the line-engravings of his master's son Benedetto. The woodcuts which are nearest in style to Benedetto Montagna's line-engravings, containing certain correspondences in design, occur in the edition of Ovid's *Metamorphoses*, printed by Jo. Rubeus for Giunta, 1497 (H. 12166, E. 223), e.g. the *Apollo and Marsyas* at f. 49, verso (fig. 225), and the *Apollo and Pan* at f. 93, comparable respectively with B. Montagna, B. 31 and 22. Only a few paintings by Benedetto Montagna are known, and it seems more than probable that as an engraver of small subjects he may also have been supplying Venetian printers with designs for woodcuts. There are a few woodcuts signed *b. M*[2] (a *Sibyl beneath an Arch* in Valerius Probus, *De Interpretandis Romanorum Litteris*, Venice, printed by J. Tacuinus, 1499, H. 13378, E. 1179, the *St. John the Baptist with the Lamb*, one of Tacuinus's printer's marks,

---

[1] See p. 433.

[2] The signature on the *Sibyl* is certainly *b. M*. In the *St. John the Baptist* an *o* above the *M* makes *b. Mo*, or it may only be part of the ground. It is reproduced in Lippmann, *Wood-Engraving in Italy*, 1888, p. 127.

Kristeller 328, not used until the early years of the XVI century,[1] and the large and powerful cut of *St. Michael* in the *Camaldolensian Missal* printed by Antonius de Zanchis, 1503 (E., *Missals*, 235), which are not unlike the Vicentine's style), but this is more likely to represent a cutter than a designer, and it is improbable that the painter and line-engraver Benedetto Montagna would have practised woodcutting as well. On the other hand,

Fig. 225. Apollo and Marsyas, from Ovid, *Metamorphoses*, Venice 1497.

if any of the Venetian illustrations are Benedetto Montagna's design, nothing is more likely to be his than the Ovid.

The style of the 'popular' designer does not seem so nearly related to any of the well-known painters as that of the 'classic'. Though the best work of the kind is certainly that of a very talented hand, yet he might well belong to the company of illuminators, of whom so few are identified, rather than the panel painters. Benedetto Bordone[2] is one of the known illuminators of the period who has been compared with some of the 'popular' illustrations (e.g. Essling has compared his work with the New Testament cuts in the Malermi Bible of 1490, and with the two illustrations in Marco

[1] It appears in Cicero, *De Officiis*, Venice 1506.

[2] See notice of his work in Thieme-Becker, *Künstler-Lexicon*. He worked in Venice from about 1480 to 1539. There is a Missal illuminated by his hand, about 1525, in the British Museum (Add. MS. 15813).

dal Monte S. Maria in Gallo, *Libro de la Divina Lege*, printed by Nicolaus de Balaguer de Castilia, 1486, E. 355), but I see no real case for identification, and the *b* that recurs on the cuts is again more likely to denote cutter than designer.

If any of the greater painters might be mentioned as showing something of the spirit of the 'popular' designer it would perhaps be Carpaccio, but I find no real relation in style of draughtsmanship, in which he is in fact nearer to the 'classic' side.

The clearest indication of the two styles is given in the

Fig. 226. Jacob's Blessing, from the *Malermi Bible*, Venice 1490.

illustration of *Jacob's Blessing* taken from the Malermi Bibles of 1490 and 1493 (figs. 226, 227), and the general origin for the composition of both may be seen in the *Cologne Bible* (fig. 168). In the 1493 edition the

Fig. 227. Jacob's Blessing, from the *Malermi Bible*, Venice 1493.

figures show greater stability, drawing of a more structural character and costume of a more classic, or fanciful classic, tendency; but they lack the vivid qualities of the earlier designer. The cuts in the 1493 edition are slightly smaller than those of 1490, but are made up to column breadth by decorative border-pieces at the sides, and generally provided with upper and lower borders as well.

The column itself is about a quarter of an inch wider in the 1493 edition, and the general appearance of the page, with less careful printing and a somewhat untidy effect from the combinations of little cuts and borders, by no means so satisfying as the 1490 Bible.

I have already spoken of the greater variety in the quality of the cuts in the 1490 Bible. Of the examples here reproduced, the cuts of *Jacob's Blessing* (fig. 226), of *Nicolò Malermi in his Study* (fig. 228), of *Solomon's Messengers before King Hiram*, of the *Monks and Choristers singing*, signed *b* (fig. 229),

Fig. 228. Nicolò Malermi in his Study, from the *Malermi Bible*, Venice 1490.

are by the better designer, while *Christ in the House of Martha and Mary*, signed ·*b*· (fig. 230), is by the weaker master.

From the 1493 Bible the illustration of *Heliodorus driven from the Temple* (fig. 231) shows a powerful design with skilfully foreshortened figures but somewhat careless cutting; while the cut of *Solomon in his Court* within the same border as was used in the frontispiece and first page (fig. 232) is a most masterly piece of design, almost worthy of Mantegna himself. The border itself is one of the most beautiful of all the outline borders of the time, and the panel at the foot with Tritons and Nymphs is again thoroughly Mantegnesque in vein.

Two *Latin Bibles* (*cum postillis N. de Lyra*),[1] printed by B. LOCATELLUS for O. Scotus in 1489 (H. 3168, E. 132), and by PAGANINIS in 1495 (H. 3174, E. 137), contain a few woodcuts, but mostly mere diagrams (of the ark, the temple and its treasures, etc.), and little of artistic

Fig. 229. Monks and Choristers singing, from the *Malermi Bible*, Venice 1490.

interest except the *Creation of Eve* in the 1489 edition. In style of figure and design this illustration is more classic than the woodcuts of the 1490 Malermi Bible, and nearer to the cut of the *Fall and Expulsion from Paradise* in the *Supplementum Chronicarum* of 1486,[2] rather than to the classic designs of the 1493 Bible. But in manner of cutting, with its delicate line, it is certainly related to the 1490 Bible.

Another book with cuts comparable with the Malermi Bible of 1490 is

[1] Cf. p. 370.   [2] See p. 457.

Bonaventura's *Devote Meditazioni sopra la Passione* printed by CAPCASA, 27th February 1489/90 (E. 405). The majority of the cuts are in the same manner as the poorer illustrations in the Malermi Bible, exemplified by many in the New Testament, and are probably by the same designer. But three stand out from the rest, the *Christ before Pilate*, the *Flagellation* and the *Mocking of Christ* (fig. 233), and are probably by the Master Illustrator of the 1490 Malermi Bible. The *Mocking of Christ* is excellent in its study of character, while the *Flagellation* has a

Fig. 230. Christ in the House of Martha and Mary, from the *Malermi Bible*, Venice 1490.

dignity in both figure and setting which places it among the best illustrations of the time.

The 1490 Malermi Bible was twice reprinted for the original publisher, L. A. Giunta, with a few additional cuts (some signed *F* and *i*), by Ragazzo

Fig. 231. Heliodorus driven from the Temple, from the *Malermi Bible*, Venice 1493.

in 1492 (E. 134), and by Jo. Rubeus in 1494 (E. 136), which proves its greater popularity than the edition of 1493. Many of the cuts from both Malermi Bibles are also found reprinted in various other books of the period, e.g. numerous illustrations from the 1490 Bible in the *Epistole et Evangeli* issued by Anima Mia about 1492 and in 1494 (E. 185 and 187), by Capcasa in 1493 (E. 186) and by Manfredus de Bonellis in 1495 (E. 188), and in the *Vita della preziosa Vergine Maria* printed by Jo. Rubeus for Giunta in 1492 (E. 630); and cuts from the 1493 Bible issued by their original printer, Anima Mia, in his *Epistole et Evangelii* of 1494 (H. 6642, E. 187). The fact that Anima Mia, the printer of the 1493 Bible, was also using some

Fig. 232. A page from the *Malermi Bible*, Venice 1493, with Solomon in his Court.

of the cuts of Ragazzo's 1490 Bible while Ragazzo was still active in printing, shows clearly how promiscuously the woodcutters must have supplied their blocks to the printers.

I will mention the more important books with illustrations by the 'popular' designer, nearly all column cuts of the same size and form as those of the 1490 Bible.

St. Jerome, *Vitas Patrum*, printed in 1491 by Ragazzo for Giunta (H. 8624, E. 568), contains nearly four hundred illustrations and on the front page an attractive larger cut of *Episodes in the Life of the Hermit St. Paul* within the border from the 1490 Bible (fig. 234). Another lively example, of a *Story of the Abbot Daniel of Egypt*, where the child points to its father, most delicate in line and subtly expressive,

Fig. 233. The Mocking of Christ, from Bonaventura, *Devote Meditazioni*, Venice 1489/90.

is in the best style of the 'popular' designer. Capcasa's edition of February 1493/94 (E. 569), which has the border from the *Supplementum Chronicarum* printed by Rizus, 1492 (E. 345), reprints the same small cuts. Jacobus de Voragine, *Legenda Aurea*, in Malermi's Italian translation (*Legendi di Sancti vulgare storiado*), first printed by Manfredus Bonellis, 1492 (E. 678, Modena), and in 1494 by Capcasa (E. 679), include numerous cuts of the same character.

Capcasa's edition, which contains well over two hundred illustrations, is largely independent of the earlier issue. Two excellent initials, P with Jacobus de Voragine (fig. 235) and a smaller E with Nicolò Malermi, appear on the first leaf. The *Transportation of the Body of St. Lucy* at f. 14 (repeated at f. 164, *de Sancto Lamberto*) is an unusual example in this kind of illustration of a composition with many small figures (fig. 236). It looks as if it were based on some picture by Gentile Bellini, comparable with his *Discovery of the Relics of the Cross* in the Academy at Venice,[1]

---

[1] Reproduced Venturi, *Storia dell' arte italiana*, vii. (4), fig. 134.

Fig. 234. Episodes in the Life of the Hermit St. Paul, within the border from the *Malermi Bible* of 1490, a page from St. Jerome, *Vitas Patrum*, Venice 1491.

Fig. 235. Initial P from *Legenda Aurea*, Venice 1494.

or by one of his immediate followers (e.g. G. Mansueti, or Lazzaro Bastiani).

A good example, with figures in the usual scale, is the *Group of Monks standing in a Portico* (*S. Sabba Abbate*), on f. 222, verso. Another interesting illustration of a *Group of Monks* (in this case seated, and with the injunction SILENTIUM) may be referred to in comparison, in St. Bernardus, *Sermones de Tempore*, printed by J. Emericus, 1495 (H. 2849, E. 806).

A third group of rather similar composition, *St. Thomas Aquinas lecturing*, in Thomas Aquinas, *Commentaria in libros Aristotelis*, printed by Otinus de Luna for A. Calcedonius, 1496 (H. 1495, E. 897; reprinted in Petrus Bergomensis, *Tabula Operum Thomae Aquinatis*, 1497, Jo. Rubeus, H. 2820, E. 914), may be noted here, though its design is in the 'classic' manner.

A book entirely suited to the vein of the 'popular' designer, with his naïve and occasionally naughty wit, was Boccaccio's *Decameron*, which he illustrated with his usual small cuts in the editions printed by Joannes and Gregorius de Gregoriis, June 1492 (H. 3277, E. 640, dated; E. 641, undated). They were reprinted by Manfredus de Bonellis, 1498 (H. 3278, E. 642). One of the two larger cuts which occur at the heads of the 'Giornate', with two charming groups, is here

Fig. 236. Transportation of the Body of St. Lucy, from *Legenda Aurea*, Venice 1494.

reproduced (fig. 237).[1] Equally attractive is the illustration of the whole company seated in a garden, framed within the border that surrounds the first page.

---

[1] The example reproduced occurs throughout E. 641, and at the fourth, seventh and tenth days in E. 640. The other example appears at the head of the other days in E. 640.

The same border and a certain number of the small cuts from the *Decameron* recur in the same printers' edition of Masuccio's *Novellino*, July 1492 (H. 10888, E. 668), with many new illustrations of a similar character (fig. 238). The little cuts of the *Cobbler* (f. 1, verso; fig. 239) and the *Preacher*, *Frate Hieronimo da Spoleto*, with its excellent rendering of a crowd, are among many vivid renderings of contemporary life.

Another work by the 'popular' designer, as lavishly illustrated as the *Vitas Patrum*, is the Livy (*Deche di Livio vulgare historiate*) printed by Jo. Rubeus

Fig. 237. From Boccaccio, *Decameron*, Venice 1492.

for L. A. Giunta, 1493 (H. 10149, E. 33; reprinted in Latin by Philippus Pincius, 1495, H. 10141, E. 34). One of its best illustrations, inscribed BOOZ, used for more than one subject (e.g. Decas III. lib. viii. c. 50, lib. ix. c. 22, and Decas IV. lib. iii. c. 32), was originally intended to represent *Boaz seated with his Kinsmen and Elders at the City Gate* (fig. 240), and appeared at the head of Chapter IV. of *Ruth* in the Malermi Bible of 1492 (H. 3157, E. 134), though it did not figure in the original edition of 1490. The faces are most expressive and the figures equally significant in gesture and pose. The cuts made for the *Livy* are about 2⅛ inches high (see fig. 241), while others which belonged originally to the 1490 Bible are within 2 inches.

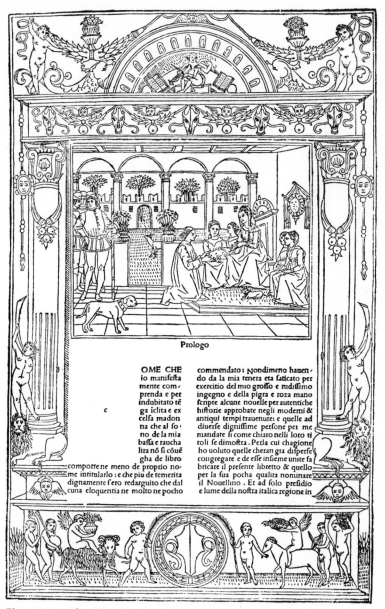

Prologo

OME CHE io manifesta mente com‚ prenda e per indubitato te‚ ga iclita e ex celsa madon na che al fo‚ no de la mia baffa e raucha lita no fi coue gha de libro comporre ne meno de proptio no‚ me intitularlo : e che piu de temerita dignamente fero redarguito che dal cuna eloquentia ne molto ne pocho commendato : Nondimeno hauen‚ do da la mia tenera eta faticato per exercitio del mio groffo e rudiffimo ingegno e della pigra e roza mano fcripte alcune nouelle per autentiche hiftorie approbate negli moderni & antiqui tempi trauenute: e quelle ad diuerfe digniffime perfone per me mandate fi come chiaro nelli loro ti‚ toli fe dimoftra . Per la cui chagione ho uoluto quelle che tan gia difperfe congregare e de effe infieme unite fa bricare il prefente libretto & quello per la fua pocha qualita nominare il Nouellino . Et ad folo prefidio e lume della noftra italica regione in

Fig. 238. A page from Masuccio, *Novellino*, Venice 1492, with the author presenting his book.

Cuts of a similar character, including many battle scenes, had appeared in *Trabisonda Istoriata*, printed by Pensis, 1492 (H. 15585, E. 661). Several were used again in the *Livy*. The average quality is high, an illustration of a

Fig. 239. The Cobbler, from Masuccio, *Novellino*, Venice 1492.

Banquet on sig. pp. v being one of the most interesting.

Among other cuts by the popular designer is that of a *Monk gathering flowers in a walled garden* which appears in various editions of the *Fior di Virtù* (Capcasa, 3rd April 1490, E. 389; Ragazzo, 30th December 1490, E. 390; Capcasa, 14th July 1492 and 3rd June 1493, E. 391 and 393). The reproduction given shows it in its second state, in which the clouds and star, which somewhat disturb the composition as it appears in the 1490 edition, have been cut away (fig. 242). The book also contains small column cuts of fables, and a larger cut of *Four figures at a farm* on the end page.

Several of the cuts from the *Fior di Virtù* and the *Livy* reappear in Petrus de Crescentiis, *De Agricultura*, printed by Capcasa, 1495 (H. 5839, E. 842). The larger cut of a *Farmstead*, under the title, is specially interesting from its subject, as are numerous illustrations of country occupations, e.g. that of *Threshing* on sig. L. vi. verso (fig. 243).

Plutarch's *Lives*, printed by Ragazzo for Giunta, 1491 (H. 13129, E. 594; re-

Fig. 240. Boaz and his Kinsmen at the City Gate, from the *Malermi Bible*, Venice 1492.

printed by B. Zanis, 1496, H. 13130, E. 595), contains another of the best designs in the same style, that of *Theseus and the Minotaur*.

The *Vita de la preciosa Vergine Maria* (Jo. Rubeus for Giunta, 1492, E. 630) has an attractive cut of *Joachim's Offering* on the first page, a little upright *Annunciation*, and among numerous little oblong cuts several from the 1490 Malermi Bible.

An unusually large wood-cut in the style of the 'popular' designer (but with parallel shading rarely found in his work) is the *Seated Figure of a Man* from whose head and hands sprouts a tree of consanguinity in Joannes Crispus de Montibus, *Repetitio Tituli de Heredibus*, printed by J. Hamman 19th October 1490 (H. 11607, E. 527; fig. 244). The figure is generally printed in brown, the text in red, and the leaves coloured (either by printing or stencil) in green.

Fig. 241. The Roman Navy, from *Livy*, Venice 1493.

Similar again in style and in its shading is the larger woodcut in St. Augustinus, *De Civitate Dei*, printed by B. Locatellus for Octavianus Scotus, 1489 (H. 2065, E. 73).

Of other works in the manner of the 'popular' designer I would mention illustrations in:

> Joannes Climacus, *Scala Paradisi*, printed by [B. Benalius and] Capcasa, 1491 (H. 5468, E. 565; the same and other cuts in ed. Pensis, 1492, H. 5467, E. 566).
>
> *Miracoli della Madonna*, printed by B. Benalius and Capcasa, 1491 (E. 605).
>
> St. Augustine, *Sermones ad heremitas*, printed by V. Benalius, 1492/93 (H. 2004, E. 695) (with an interesting cut of a Baptism).
>
> *Processionarium*, printed by Emericus, 1494 (H. 13381, E. 751).
>
> Pulci, *Morgante Maggiore*, printed by M. de Bonellis, 1494 (H. 13588, E. 759).
>
> S. Caterina, *Dialogo della Divina Providenza*, printed by Capcasa, 1494 (H. 4692, E. 738).
>
> Robertus Caracciolus, *Specchio della Fede*, printed by Jo. Rubeus, 1495 (H. 4494, E. 833) (with an attractive cut of Fra Roberto preaching).

An illustration of a school class in Nicolaus Perottus, *Regulae Sypontinae*, printed by PENSIS, 1492/93 (H. 12682, E. 622; 1493/94, H. 12683, E. 623; 1495, H. 12688, E. 624), is particularly entertaining (fig. 245),

Fig. 242. A monk gathering flowers, from *Fior de Virtù*, Venice 1493.

and one of the printer's marks used by Tacuinus, with centaurs and nymphs, is another excellent example of the work of the 'popular' designer (fig. 246). Another interesting illustration of a *School Class* is contained in the border of Guarinus Veronensis, *Grammaticales Regulae*, printed by NICOLAUS DE BALAGUER, 1488 (E. 315). This is probably by the 'popular' designer, while a corresponding copy in the border of Augustinus Datus, *Elegantiolae*, printed by J. B. SESSA, 1491, is probably by the designer of the New Testament and poorer illustrations of the 1490 Malermi Bible. Still another example of a border containing an illustration of a school is J. E. B. Pylades, *Grammatica*, printed without date by BERNARDINUS VENETUS DE VITALIBUS (E. 861).

The best books are often the least happy in their illustration, and there is no exception in the three chief editions of Dante's *Divine Comedy*, printed with woodcuts in the xv century, those of Brescia, 1487 (printed by Boninus de Boninis, H. 5948), and of Venice (printed by B. Benalius and Capcasa, March 1491, H. 5949, E. 531; and by Petrus de Plasiis, November 1491, H. 5950, E. 532).

All go back either directly or indirectly to Botticelli's designs, of which only the first nineteen, for Cantos i.-xix. of the *Inferno*, were engraved on copper for Landino's *Dante*, printed at Florence, 1481 (H. 5946).[1] The Venice designers may have known the Florentine edition, but probably used the Brescia edition as their immediate source. The illustrations of the Brescia edition, which precede each canto up to *Paradiso* i., where they cease, are all full-page within

Fig. 243. Threshing, from Petrus de Crescentiis, *De Agricultura*, Venice 1495.

black-ground borders of two patterns (see fig. 247),[2] somewhat in the style of the Venice *Petrarch* of 1488. The cuts are for the most part done with parallel shading, a practice which only became common in North Italian book-illustration in the last years of the century, and some are much more crudely cut than others (e.g. *Inferno* xxi., and many of the *Purgatorio*). The best designs are in the earlier part of the *Inferno*, where the Florentine engravings would be available as models. Great deterioration is noticeable in the later illustrations, so that the designer could hardly have known any of Botticelli's unpublished drawings. Benalius and Capcasa's edition contains full-page cuts within outline borders at the head of each book, and only small cuts (about $2\frac{1}{2}$ inches square) for each canto (see fig. 248); Plasiis' edition has only the small cuts (about $3\frac{1}{4}$ inches square; see fig. 249). The cuts in both are very much of the same character and quality, and, considering the close relationship of their designs and the small interval of six months between the two editions, it seems almost more

---

[1] See A. M. Hind, *Catalogue of Early Italian Engravings in the British Museum*, p. 83. For Botticelli's drawings at Berlin and in the Vatican, see F. Lippmann, Berlin 1887, and J. Strzygowski, Berlin 1887.

[2] Pattern (*a*)—Cherub's head (below), candelabra (sides), grotesque head (above) (fig. 247); pattern (*b*)—dolphins (below), candelabra (sides), scroll (above).

likely that the cuts to both were provided by the same firm of cutters, rather than that the designer or cutter of the later edition copied the earlier. The illustrations of both are nearly related in style to the work of the 'popular' designer, though for the most part very inferior in quality, especially, as in the Brescia edition, in the later parts of the work.

Petrarch is somewhat better served in the three chief Venetian editions of his *Trionfi*, printed respectively by Rizus, 1488 (H. 12787, E. 76; see

Fig. 244. Seated Man, from Crispus de Montibus, *Repetitio Tituli de Heredibus*, Venice 1490.

fig. 250), Plasiis, 1490 (H. 12771, E. 77; reprinted 1492, H. 12773, E. 78), and Capcasa, 1492/93 (H. 12774, E. 79; see fig. 251).[1] The six designs to the 'Triumphs' in each of these editions are full-page cuts within decorative borders, those of Rizus and Plasiis being on black ground, and Capcasa's the same outline border which had been used in the *Dante* of March 1491. The illustrations of the 1488 edition have already been compared in certain details (the ground with rabbits and flowers) with the *Fall and Expulsion* in the *Supplementum Chronicarum* of 1486 and frontispiece of the *Sphaera*

[1] For Petrarch illustration in general see Essling and Müntz, *Pétrarque*, Paris 1902.

Mundi of 1488, and their general style is allied to the Venetian designers of the 'classic' school, though somewhat more angular in cutting. The cuts of the 1490 edition are different designs, freely copied from the Florentine line-engravings, and preserving the same method of shading in open parallels.[1] This imitation of line-engravings in the 'Broad Manner' no doubt had some influence in developing the 'shaded' manner of Venetian woodcut. The adaptation might have been made by the 'popular' designer, or one of his school.

Fig. 245. A School Class, from Perottus, *Regulae Sypontinae*, Venice 1492/93.

The Florentine designs are again followed in Capcasa's issue of 1492/93, probably through the medium of the 1490 edition. In style they are nearly related to the 'classic' designer of the Malermi Bible of 1493, but if by the same hand they are not his best performance. They were reprinted by Zanis in 1497 (H. 12776).

Fig. 246. Printer's mark of Tacuinus, Venice.

I have already described and illustrated the Venetian edition of *Aesop* in connection with the Verona *editio princeps* of 1479.[2] The better of the two Venetian series of cuts is that first issued by Manfredus de Bonellis in 1491 (E. 360, GW. 432), and their author is possibly identical with the 'classic' designer of the 1493 Malermi Bible. An interesting cut of similar

---

[1] See A. M. Hind, *Catalogue of Early Italian Engravings in the British Museum*, 1910, p. 115.

[2] See p. 413.

Fig. 247. Inferno, Canto II., from *Dante*, Brescia 1487.

character is that of *St. Aloisius at his forge* prefixed to Giordano Ruffo, *Arte di cognoscere la Natura dei Cavalli*, printed by PETRUS DE QUARENGIIS, about 1493 (H. 14034, E. 692). And not unlike the Bonellis *Aesop* designs is the woodcut of *Master and Pupil* in *Lucidario* (*Libro del Maestro e del Discipulo*), printed by Bonellis, 1st March 1495 (E. 812), which is copied in a much cruder manner in the edition issued with the same printer's name, but probably at Milan, on the 12th July 1495 (E. 813).[1]

The same classic style is shown

Fig. 248. Inferno, Canto III., from *Dante*, Venice (Benalius and Capcasa) 1491.

in the woodcuts to the *Terence* printed in 1497 by SIMON DE LUERE for L. SOARDIS (H. 15429, E. 864), and reprinted by SOARDIS alone in 1499 (H. 15430, E. 866). The small illustrations (measuring about 2 × $3\frac{1}{4}$ inches), which are in many cases based on those of the edition printed by Trechsel at Lyon in 1493, are well designed, chiefly in outline, but somewhat carelessly cut. Their effect is somewhat spoilt by the printing or stamping of the names of the characters (or abbreviations for the same) in ordinary

Fig. 249. Inferno, Canto I., from *Dante*, Venice (Plasiis) 1491.

[1] See p. 522.

Fig. 250. Triumph of Chastity, from Petrarch, *Trionfi*, Venice 1488.

type on the woodcut impression, which introduces a heavier tone than the woodcut line. More important are the two fine full-page frontispieces, representing *Terence and his Commentators in a Classic Hall* and the

Performance in a Theatre (fig. 252).

Somewhat more Vicentine in style are the numerous and excellent cuts of the *Metamorphoses* of Ovid, printed by Jo. Rubeus for Giunta, 1497 (H. 12166, E. 223), and reprinted by F. MAZALIS at Parma, 1505. The style of design is consistent throughout, but the quality of the cuts varies considerably, several hands taking part, as is evidenced by the two signatures 1 a and N. Those by 1 a, whose signature occurs here for the first time, are among the best and most firmly cut. The possibility of Benedetto Montagna being the designer of the Ovid has already

Fig. 251. Triumph of Love, from Petrarch, *Trionfi*, Venice 1492/93.

been discussed.[1] I would here note how in general character they lead on to that masterpiece of the classic style in Venetian illustration, the *Hypnerotomachia Poliphili*, by Francesco Colonna, printed by Aldus in 1499.[2]

[1] See pp. 469, 470.
[2] Albert Ilg, *Ueber den kunsthistorischen Werth der H. P.*, Vienna 1872; C. Popelin, *Le*

Fig. 252. Performance in a Theatre, from *Terence*, Venice 1497.

The theme of the author's love for Polia is set in a most elaborate embroidery of classical lore, filled out with the lengthiest descriptions of real or imagined works of art. The Elizabethan translation of 1592, 'The Strife

Fig. 253. Poliphilus in a wood, from *Hypnerotomachia Poliphili*, Venice 1499.

of Love in a Dreame', covered less than half the work, and omitted much of the elaborate embroidery, but even so it was regarded by its contemporaries in an age of literary conceits as precious to excess. Little wonder that the book lives now only for its beautiful illustrations and printing.[1]

Songe de P. littéralement traduit . . . avec une introduction, Paris 1883; C. Ephrussi, *Étude sur le songe de P.*, Paris 1888 (Bulletin du Bibliophile); *Facsimile of 168 Woodcuts in H.P., with notice by W. J. Appell*, London (Science and Art Department) 1888; Facsimile of 1499 edition, London (Methuen) 1904; J. Poppelreuter, *Der anonyme Meister des P.*, Strassburg 1904; O. Pollak, *Der heutige Stand der P.-Frage*, Kunstchronik, N.F., xxiii., 1912, 433; *Hypnerotomachia, The Strife of Love in a Dreame* [translation of a part, by R. D(allington?)], London 1592; Philip Hofer, *Variant copies of the 1499 Poliphilus*, New York (Public Library) 1932.

[1] See the note in the British Museum Catalogue of the Huth Bequest, London 1912, No. 39

Whoever the designer, he is not far removed from the author of the *Ovid* woodcuts, and his work is in direct descent from cuts such as the *Fall and Expulsion from Paradise* in the *Supplementum Chronicarum* of

1486,[1] a relation particularly noticeable in the style of drawing faces and mouths. In general the influence of Giovanni Bellini is evident, but its specific expression, with a tendency to sharp folds and straight lines at the foot of long drapery, is Vicentine rather than purely Venetian. One thinks again of Benedetto Montagna, or Cima, and on occasion of Carpaccio (e.g. sig. E. 1, verso), but no definite clue has been found to fix the identity of a designer who is manifestly an artist of charming

Fig. 254. Ruined Temple, from *Hypnerotomachia Poliphili*,
Venice 1499.

invention and sensitive genius. Certain of the illustrations seem to disclose a knowledge of the work of Botticelli, possibly of the drawings to Dante,[2] e.g. the cut of *Poliphilus in a wood* (sig. a iii, verso; fig. 253), and *Poliphilus and Polia walking by an arched trellis.* He has a good understanding of classic decoration, a remarkable faculty for beauty of architectural design (e.g. in the *Ruined Temple*, sig. p iii; fig. 254), and a fine sense of rhythm in figure drawing (e.g. *Poliphilus and the Dragon*, sig. d iii, verso). And the book is ennobled by the pure beauty of type and printing that char-

[1] See p. 456.   [2] See p. 483.

acterises most of Aldus's work. A decorative design of a *Siren* (sig. n iv) and one of the outline initials, which occur in the book, are also reproduced (figs. 255 and 256).

The *Hypnerotomachia* is the only book Aldus issued with numerous illustrations.[1] Apart from woodcut capitals, head- and tail-pieces (generally in delicate tendril and leaf pattern), there is seldom more than a single cut, and that only in occasional books. His main interest was centred in the printing of classical, especially Greek texts, and this richly illustrated book must

Fig. 255. A Siren, from *Hypnerotomachia Poliphili,* Venice 1499.

have been entirely due to Leonardus Crassus of Verona, who in his address of the Duke of Urbino states that he financed the undertaking.

Fig. 256. Initial letter P, from *Hypnerotomachia Poliphili,* Venice 1499.

The greater connoisseurs of the period cared for books for their literary contents and printing, and not for the illustrations, which they despised as vulgar substitutes for their more precious illuminations.

It is noteworthy that the presentation copy of Landino's *Dante* (Florence 1481) to the Signoria, which is preserved in the National Library, Florence, is without any of the engraved illustrations; and the contempt for engraved or woodcut illustration was sometimes accompanied by a complete contempt for all printed books, for it is known that none was admitted to the library of Federigo, Duke of Urbino.[2]

Other woodcuts in the style of the illustrations of the *Hypnerotomachia Poliphili* occur in:

Constitutiones Fratrum Ordinis B.V.M. de Monte Carmelo, printed by Johannes Emericus for Giunta, 1499 (H. 5652, 13242, E. 1182).

---

[1] See A. A. Renouard, *Annales de l'imprimerie des Aldes,* Paris 1834.

[2] See the *Lives* of the bookseller Vespasiano da Bisticci, translated by William George and Emily Waters, London 1926, p. 104: "In this library all the books are superlatively good, and written with the pen, and had there been one printed volume, it would have been ashamed in such company".

Regulae SS. Benedicti Basilii Augustini Francisci, printed by Johannes Emericus, 1500 (H. 13827, E. 1216), with cut of *Monk and Nun standing*.

Catarina da Siena, *Epistole*, 1500 (H. 4688, E. 1230), with a cut of *St. Catherine*.

A rare edition of Bonaventura, *Meditazioni*, issued without printer's name in 1500 (E. 415, Verona and Essling), shows an attractive form of page, the woodcut subject above and the printed text below enclosed within a black-ground woodcut border. One of its cuts, *Christ's Entry into Jerusalem*, is nearly related to the *Hypnerotomachia* both in style of design and cutting, and the figure of Christ corresponds closely with that of an old man on an ass in the *Triumphus Quartus* of the *Hypnerotomachia* (sig. l iv, verso). The other cuts are much poorer in quality and differ in having parallel shading; three are signed by the woodcutter *N*, and one, the *Entombment*, is based on a line-engraving of the school of Mantegna (Bartsch 2).

Retracing our steps some years, our attention is demanded by the greatest piece of illustration in the classic style in xv-century Venetian books, i.e. the *Fascicolo di Medicina*, printed by Joannes and Gregorius de Gregoriis on the 5th February 1493/94, the work of a German physician resident in Venice, Johannes de Ketham (E. 586).[1] The Latin edition of 1491, *Fasciculus Medicinae* (H. 9774, E. 585), contained six blocks, the first a mere diagram, the remaining five being human figures with anatomical and medical notes. One of these blocks (a nude man with marginal lists of various diseases) was reprinted as plate iv. in the Italian edition; the remaining five subjects were cut on new blocks. But the value of this second edition lies in the four new subjects, illustrating the physician's and surgeon's activities. Even if the author of the technical figures were the designer of the new subjects, a purely artistic treatment, seconded by more careful cutting, puts them on an entirely different level. The designs themselves contain larger figures than any of the Venetian illustrations hitherto described,[2] and their style has a dignity worthy of Mantegna. They are almost near enough in character to justify an attribution of the design to the master himself, only there is lacking, perhaps, something of the rhythm which adds such distinction to the 'Triumph of Caesar' on which he was working at this period. This lack of rhythm, combined with a stability and classic sense inspired by Mantegna, suggests Mantegna's brother-in-law, Gentile Bellini, with whose style Lippmann rightly compared them. Whoever the designer, it can hardly

---

[1] See A. Blum, *Le Fasciculus Medicinae de J. Ketham*, Byblis v. (1926).   [2] Except fig. 244.

Fig. 257. The doctor's visit to a plague patient, from Ketham, *Fascicolo di Medicina*, Venice 1493/94.

be doubted that these woodcuts are the invention of a painter of genius.

The first of the new illustrations, the frontispiece, shows the professor, *Petrus de Montagnana in his pulpit*; the second, *Petrus, his students and an attendant with a flask of urine*; the third, a *Doctor's visit to a plague patient* (fig. 257); the last, a *Lesson in Dissection*. The last subject is sometimes found printed in colours in the same manner as simpler examples, already quoted, by the printer Ratdolt,[1] and there is a fine impression in the British Museum copy, printed from three colour-blocks in red, green and yellow, in addition to the outline in black. It has sometimes been suggested that the colour might have been achieved by stencils, but the mottled yet regular quality of the pigment proves that it was printed, and probably by hand pressure.

Fig. 258. S. Lorenzo Giustiniani, from his *Doctrina della Vita Monastica*, Venice 1494.

There were three later editions during the succeeding few years, all in Latin, printed respectively on the 15th October 1495 (H. 9775, E. 587), 28th March 1500 (H. 9776, E. 588) and 17th February 1500/01 (H. 9777, E. 589). The third subject, the *Doctor's*

---

[1] See p. 462. Other copies, beside that in the British Museum, with the *Lesson in Dissection* printed in colour, are in the Pierpont Morgan and Dyson Perrins Collections. See B. Berenson, *Three Essays in Method*, Oxford 1927, p. 32, for reference to the change of fashion indicated by the plain coloured hose in the 1493/94 edition, and striped hose of the 1500 edition (cf. E. P. Goldschmidt & Co., London, Catalogue III., No. 14). Colour-printing is only found in certain copies of the 1493/94 edition; colour, if it occurs in the later edition, is added by hand.

Visit, occurs in a second state in the edition of March 1500, the block being cut about ¾ inch along the foot, and the cat being removed. The fourth subject, the *Lesson in Dissection*, is re-cut on a new block for the edition of 1495, and an elderly Petrus de Montagnana replaces the younger man of the Italian edition in the pulpit. Moreover, the left-hand window, which was only slightly open on the first block, is now completely open, showing a view of buildings on the waterside. This new block is cut down along the foot for the edition of March 1500, similarly to the third illustration, and the basket beneath the table disappears.

Another book printed in the same year as the *Fascicolo di Medicina*, the *Doctrina della Vita Monastica*, by S. Lorenzo Giustiniani (B. Benalius, 20th October 1494; H. 9477, E. 757), contains a woodcut definitely known to be based on Gentile Bellini (fig. 258). It is the portrait of Lorenzo Giustiniani, who was Patriarch of Venice, 1451–56, and canonised in 1690, walking, preceded by an acolyte bearing a cross, which renders in reverse [1] and in modified form Gentile's picture of 1465 now in the Academy, Venice. The modifications, especially in the background and figure of the acolyte, are considerable, and it is possible that Gentile may have provided the new design for the woodcutter. Comparable with the Ketham and Giustiniani cuts are certain large woodcuts of single figures of Mantegnesque design, i.e. a *Christ with the Instruments of the Passion* signed by the cutter *N* in Bonaventura, *Devote Meditazioni*, n.d., n.pr., about 1493 (E. 411), the figures of the famous warriors, in the books of *Guer(r)ino chiamato Meschino*, printed by Pensis, 1493 (E. 715; reprinted by J. Alvisius, 1498/99, H. 8145, E. 716), and of *Altobello*, printed by J. Alvisius, 1499 (H. 884, E. 1187). The figure of *Altobello* is perhaps the best of these, and his book is interesting as well for its smaller cuts, some, in the popular style, taken from *Trabisonda Istoriata* (Pensis, 1492),[2] others newly designed in the classic style, and showing a draughtsman of considerable power (fig. 259).

The *Guerino* subject was reprinted by Pensis in 1494 in the *Libro della Regina Ancroia* (H. 965, E. 740), in which a woman's head was pieced into the old block.

An example of movable pieces in a block is seen in a large woodcut of *St. Gregory*, which is certainly a Venetian work, though it appears in certain copies of St. Gregory's *Moralia in Job*, originally issued by Nicolaus Laurentii (Alamannus) at Florence in 1486 (H. 7935, E. 321, Kristeller 211). This work was the last book printed by Laurentii, and as the woodcut

---

[1] The reproduction in Lippmann, *Wood-Engraving in Italy*, 1888, p. 105, appears to be erroneously reversed.   [2] See p. 480.

can hardly date much earlier than 1500, and is accompanied by a title printed in red in a type such as was used by Emericus at Venice, it was undoubtedly an insertion, procured from Venice, made by some distributor of Laurentii's stock after the original issue. Both St. Gregory's head and the church held in his hand show in the impressions as separate pieces, a fact which proves that the cutter was evidently prepared to supply other saints at request with economy to himself, though I have not found examples of the figure differently used.

Fig. 259. From *Altobello*, Venice 1499.

Other examples in which the printer exercised economy by the use of composite blocks (like Grüninger, at Strassburg) are the woodcuts of classical authors and their commentators, in which names and parts of the blocks are changed to suit the occasion, e.g. in Juvenal, *Satires,* printed by Tacuinus, 1494/95 (H. 9710, E. 784), Persius, *Satires*, Tacuinus, 1494–95 (H. 12738, E. 794), Ovid, *Fasti*, Tacuinus, 1497 (H. 12247, E. 1124), and Horace, *Opera*, printed by J. Alvisius, 1498 (H. 8896, E. 1164).

One other work in the classical style may be mentioned, i.e. the frontispiece to Johann Müller (Regiomontanus), *Epitoma in Almagestum Ptolemaei*, printed by Johannes Hamman, 1496 (H. 13806, E. 895). Ptolemy and Müller are seated in a landscape beneath a large planisphere, the subject being enclosed within a black-ground border of leaf and strap-work design. Müller must have been a well-known figure at Venice (though information is lacking about the dates of his visits to Italy), and he may well have been represented in an actual portrait.

We have already referred to certain missals printed by Octavianus Scotus in 1481–82 for their outline woodcuts.[1] In the last decade of the century a large number of liturgical and devotional books were produced in Venice, printed chiefly by the German settlers, Johannes Hamman, and Johannes Emericus of Speier.

[1] See p. 416.

The form of the *Officium Beatae Virginis Mariae,* or the 'Hours of the Blessed Virgin' (*Horae*), would seem to have originated in France, where it was the most popular book of devotions throughout the xv century.[1] The earliest printed examples issued in Paris with woodcut illustrations appeared about 1485–1486, and Venice followed soon after with an edition of 23rd July 1489 printed by ANDREAS TORRESANUS (E. 451, Venice), and another of 1490 printed by Johannes Hamman (E. 452, Parma).

The borders and illustrations to these two editions of Torresanus and Hamman are entirely French in character, and might both have been produced by craftsmen from the school of Jean Dupré, whose other relations with Venice will be noted below.[2] Especially near to Dupré's *Horae* of about 1488 in the British Museum (IA. 39817),[3] not only in style, but in details of design, is the Hamman edition, E. 452.

Two subsequent *Horae*

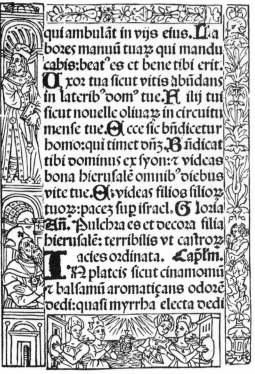

Fig. 260. From *Officium B.V. Mariae,* Venice 1493.

issued by Hamman (3rd December 1491, E. 453, Paris; E. 454, 4th February 1492, Paris), and others printed by Emericus of Speier 6th May 1493 and later issues (E. 455, Paris; E. 458, 459, Paris; E. 460, Modena), are without the complete borders, and the little cuts, largely in outline, are Italian in character, and comparable with the illustrations in the Naples editions of 1486 and 1487, which seem to be the earliest of the Italian *Horae.*[4]

---

[1] See p. 676. [2] See pp. 500 and 628. [3] See p. 683.
[4] See p. 410.

Then Hamman produced a few very beautiful *Horae* with borders, and with some suggestions from French designs, but largely Italian in style, e.g. that of 1493 (E. 456, B.M., IA. 23362; fig. 260), and 1st October 1497,

for Scotus (E. 462, Parma). Some of the cuts in the latter are signed 1 a. A Sarum *Horae*, not described by Essling, still smaller in form, was printed by Hamman for London booksellers, G. Barrevelt and F. Egmont, in 1494 (Duff, 181, S.T.C. 15874, only known in fragments, e.g. B.M., IA. 23403; fig. 261). The *Annunciation* shown in the reproduction also occurs in E. 456, so that other cuts as well were probably used in both editions.

Purely Venetian in design is the *Officium* printed by Hieronymus de Sanctis in 1494 (E. 457, Paris; see fig. 262), its woodcut borders and subjects being among the most delicate achievements of Italian illustration. The de-

Fig. 261. From *Sarum Horae*, Venice 1494.

signer of this edition was also in part at least responsible for the designs to Hamman's issue of 1st October 1497 (E. 462, Parma).

In the early xvi century the French style again appears, and several of the Venetian prayer-books show borders with black ground after the model of the majority of Paris *Horae* about 1500, the first noted by Essling being published by the Giunta in 1501 (E. 465). And the black-line style of Dupré recurs in editions by Zuan Ragazzo for B. Stagnino, 24th October 1504 (E. 467, Vienna), and by Gregorius de Gregoriis (E. 472, Berlin), and a comparison, which I have been unable to make between these two editions and the Dupré-Caillaut group,[1] might show that not only designs, but actual blocks from Dupré's workshop were used.

To the Missals, which are for the most part larger folios, the late Prince d'Essling devoted a special volume of his work on Venetian illustration.[2]

[1] See p. 683.   [2] *Les Missals imprimés à Venise de 1481 à 1600*, Paris 1896.

They are generally limited in illustration to a large cut of the *Christ on the Cross* at the *Canon of the Mass* (usually called on that account the *Canon* cut), but occasionally have fine borders, and more frequently attractive initials.

Among the pictorial initials those in the Roman Missal printed by Emericus for Giunta, 10th November 1497, are among the best (fig. 263). Similar initials had been used earlier in the *Processionarium* printed by Emericus in 1494 (E. 751). Other subjects most usually found in Italian Missals are the *Annunciation* and a little roundel of the *Agnus Dei*, but a variety of Old and New Testament subjects also occur. Though Germany may claim priority by a year, and France by some three months, in Missals illustrated with woodcuts,[1] Venice was perhaps the most important centre in their production during the xv century, and continued to print liturgical books for many foreign dioceses well into the xvi century. Nevertheless, Paris and Lyon vied with Venice in the number of their illustrated Missals during the xv century, and began their publication in the same year, 1481. Later in the xvi century Antwerp, and the Plantin press in particular, gradually absorbed the trade.

Fig. 262. From *Officium B.V. Mariae*, Venice 1494.

The large folio Choir Book (*Graduale*) printed by Emericus for Giunta in 1499 and 1500 (H. 7844, E. 1208) is one of the most interesting of the larger Venetian service books of the xv century for its series of historiated initials (fig. 264). They were used again in Giunta's smaller folio *Graduale* of 1513–15 (E. 1209), in which two full-page cuts also appeared, a *Christ on the Cross with the Virgin, St. John, and the Magdalene* (copied from ·I·B·⁂·),[2]

<hr />

[1] See pp. 283 and 628.   [2] See p. 442.

Fig. 263. Initial used as E, in *Missale Romanum*, Venice 1497.

and a *Death of the Virgin*, the latter signed ı a. The initials are in the same style as the larger cuts, and it is possible that the cutter ı a may be responsible for them all. The larger cuts may have been done for the edition of 1499–1500, but they do not occur in the only two copies known (British Museum and Venice). They are all in the shaded style, comparable to the work of Jacob of Strassburg, a style which was becoming general in Venetian woodcuts by the beginning of the xvi century.

The turn of the century also saw a certain reflection of the Florentine style, in an increased use of white line on black ground. A few of the illustrations in the *Hypnerotomachia Poliphili* show this manner in the treatment of the ground

Fig. 264. Initial letter S, from *Graduale*, Venice 1499.

(e.g. *Europa and the Bull*, at sig. k iv), and an edition of Ovid, *Epistolae Heroides*, printed by TACUINUS, 1501 (E. 1136), offers similar and more frequent examples. Comparison of two editions of A. Cornazano, *Vita de la Madonna*, those of Bonellis, 1495 (E. 821), and of Sessa, 1502 (E. 823), illustrates the same change in style.

I have said little about the *borders used in Venetian books* during the last decade of the xv century, reserving them for separate treatment, chiefly because the same blocks were used by various printers in different books. I have already referred to this practice as an argument in favour of the independence of the woodcutters from the printers in Venice.[1] I add here, in two groups,

[1] See p. 468.

a list of the more important borders, and the principal books in which they occur:

A. BLACK-LINE BORDERS

(1) *Two Cupids on horses* (below); *pilasters with medallion heads* (sides); *two eagles flanking lunette* (above). Folio. Fig. 234.

   (*a*) *Malermi Bible*, Ragazzo for Giunta, 1490 (H. 3156, E. 133). With dove in lunette.

   (*b*) St. Jerome, *Vitas Patrum*, Ragazzo for Giunta, 1491 (H. 8624, E. 568). With God the Father in lunette (as reproduced in fig. 234).

   (*c*) Plutarch, *Vitae*, Ragazzo for Giunta, 1491 (H. 13129, E. 594).

   (*d*) Livy, *Decades*, Jo. Rubeus, 1493 (H. 10149, E. 33). With scholar standing at desk in lunette.

(2) *Two Cupids supporting shield* (below); *columns with sphinxes and naked youths* (sides); *lions flanking lunette* (above). Folio. Fig. 251.

   (*a*) *Dante*, Benalius and Capcasa, March 1491 (H. 5949, E. 531). With God the Father in lunette.

   (*b*) Petrarch, *Trionfi*, Capcasa, 1492–93 (H. 12774, E. 79).

   (*c*) Voragine, *Legenda Aurea*, Capcasa, 1494 (E. 679).

   (*d*) Marsilio Ficino, *Epistole*, Capcasa, 1495 (H. 7059). In *c* and *d* with four additional outside border-pieces.

(3) *Cupids on rams* (below); *columns with putti and lions* (sides); *putti and dolphins flanking lunette, and putto playing viol in lunette* (above). Folio. Fig. 238.

   (*a*) Boccaccio, *Decamerone*, Gregoriis, June 1492 (H. 3277, E. 640).

   (*b*) Masuccio, *Novellino*, Gregoriis, July 1492 (H. 10888, E. 668).

   (*c*) Boccaccio, *Decamerone*, Bonellis, 1498 (H. 3278, E. 642).

(4) *Eight children at Vintage* (below); *columns* (sides); *sphinxes flanking lunette* (above). Folio.

   (*a*) Voragine, *Legenda Aurea*, Bonellis, 1492 (E. 678).

   (*b*) Foresti, *Supplementum Chronicarum*, Rizus, 1492/93 (H. 2809, E. 345). With the dove in lunette.

   (*c*) St. Jerome, *Vitas Patrum*, Capcasa, 1493/94. With God the Father in lunette.

(5) *Tritons and Nymphs* (below); *ornament panels* (sides); *cupid and vases* (above). Folio. Fig. 232.

   (*a*) *Malermi Bible*, Anima Mia, 1493 (E. 135).

(6) *Putti on griffins* (below); *naked youths with torches* (sides); *sirens* (above). Quarto.

    (*a*) *Vita de la Preciosa Vergine Maria*, Jo. Rubeus for Giunta, 1492 (E. 630).

    With Man of Sorrows above.

    (*b*) Niger, *De Modo Epistolandi*, Capcasa, 1492 (H.C. 11867, E. 671).

    (*c*) *Trabisonda Istoriata*, Pensis, 1492 (H. 15585, E. 661).

    In *b* and *c* with scholar writing at desk above.

    (*d*) *Lucidario* (*Libro del Maestro e Discipulo*), Bonellis, 1495 (E. 812).

    With vacant space above.

(7) *A second block of same design as No. 6, but less well cut.* Quarto.

    With Man of Sorrows above.

    (*a*) *Vita de la Madonna Storiada*, Tacuinus, 1493 (E. 631).

    (*b*) *Epistole ed Evangeli*, Anima Mia, 1494 (H. 6642).

B. BLACK-GROUND BORDERS

(1) *Nymphs on centaurs supporting medallion head* (below); *candelabra* (sides); *dolphins and head* (above). Fig. 250.

    Petrarch, *Trionfi*, Rizus, 1488 (H. 12787, E. 76).

    The style of borders (1) and (2) similar in style to the two borders used in the Brescia *Dante* of 1487 (H. 5948; see fig. 247 and p. 483).

(2) *Two cupids playing viol and pipe* (below); *candelabra* (sides); *sphinxes* (above).

    Petrarch, *Trionfi*, Plasiis, 1490 and 1492 (H. 12771, 12773; E. 77 and 78).

    Plutarch, *Vitae*, B. de Zanis, 1496 (H. 13130, E. 595).

(3) *Panel with the Choice of Hercules* (below); *candelabra* (sides); *panel with satyr and ram* (above). Fig. 265.

    Herodotus, *Historiae*, Gregoriis, 1494 (H. 8472, E. 735).

    St. Jerome, *Opera*, Gregoriis, 1498 (H. 8581, E. 1170).

(4) *Eagle, cornucopiae and winged animals* (below); *candelabra* (sides); *grotesque head* (above); similar in style of design to No. 3.

    Lucianus, *Vera Historia*, Bevilaqua, 1494 (H. 10261, E. 747).

(5) *Two lions seated back to back* (below); *candelabra* (sides); *scroll-work* (above).

    Lucan, *Pharsalia*, Bonellis, 1495 (H. 10248, E. 851).

    Mandeville, *De le più maravigliose cose del Mondo*, Bonellis, 1496 (H. 10656, E. 907).

Fig. 265. First Page with border, in *Herodotus*, Venice 1494.

(6) *Strap work in a regular series of knots.*

Pacioli, *Summa de Arithmetica*, Paganinis, 1494 (H. 4105, E. 779).

Fig. 266. Initial L from Pacioli, *Summa de Arithmetica*, Venice 1494.

The first page of the Luca Pacioli also contains a black-ground initial L interesting for its portrait of the author (fig. 266), and an excellent black-line initial N is reproduced from St. Jerome, *Opera*, printed by Gregoriis, 1498 (fig. 267).

The decorative head-pieces used in Greek books printed by ZACHARIAS CALLIERGES are individual, though not very attractive, in character. They are generally printed in red, but occasionally in gold (e.g. in the British Museum copy of Ammonius, ὑπόμνημα, 1500, H. 927).

An earlier example of the printing of type in gold is that of the dedication in Ratdolt's *Euclid* of 1482 (H. 6693, E. 250, British Museum).

Attractive pieces of decoration are occasionally offered by the printer's marks, and several examples are here reproduced (figs. 268-70).

VICENZA—VERONA—BRESCIA

Fig. 267. Initial N from St. Jerome, *Opera*, Venice 1498.

Passing from Venice to the neighbouring towns, there is nothing of importance to record at Treviso or Padua, and little more at Vicenza. Apart from the *Herbal* printed by Leonardus Achates and Gulielmus of Pavia at Vicenza in 1491 (H. 8451),[1] the only Vicentine cut to which I would refer is a good three-side border (outline scroll-work with cupids and animals), and initials in the same printers' *Euclid* of 1491 (H. 6694). The importance of Verona lies in the beginnings of Italian book-illustration and has already been dealt with,[2] but in passing one might note an attractive little cut of *Viol and Bow* in Aurelius Augurellus, *Carmina*, printed anonymously at Verona in 1494.

[1] See pp. 352, 403.   [2] See p. 410.

Brescia offers somewhat more interest, midway between the influence of Venice and Milan, but reflecting in its woodcuts the more powerful though more distant Venice. We have already referred to its editions of *Aesop* and *Dante*, both printed by Boninus de Boninis in 1487,[1] and to an illustration in the *Fior di Virtù*, printed by Battista Farfengo, 1491 (and by Bernardinus Misinta, 1495), which Kristeller has compared with the style of woodcuts attributed to the Venetian printer Hieronymus de Sanctis. The *Fior di Virtù* cut (representing a student at his desk)[2] certainly has Venetian character, but I would hesitate to place it without qualification in the Sanctis group. Another Brescian cut in similar style, though with some parallel shading, is the *Virgin and Angels under a Canopy*, which occurs in the *Miracoli della Gloriosa Maria*, printed by Farfengo, 1490 (Reichling 630, Naples; fig. 271). The same subject occurs with some

Fig. 268. Printer's mark of Simon Bevilaqua, Venice.

Fig. 269. Printer's mark of Balaguer, Venice.

modification in a somewhat larger woodcut with title *Sta Maria di Loreto*, now in the collection of Baron Edmond de Rothschild.[3] I incline to regard the 1490 version as the earlier.

Apart from two excellent versions of Misinta's printer's mark (Husung 24 and 25), the only other interesting Brescian cut to which I would refer is that of the *Author in his Study* in *Aesopus Moralisatus*, printed by Misinta for Angelus Britannicus, 1497 (GW. 419). It is not unlike Farfengo's two cuts, but somewhat thinner in its line, and with more classic ornament.

FERRARA

Returning somewhat on our tracks, but keeping within the centre of Venetian influence, Ferrara next demands our attention.[4]

[1] See pp. 413 and 483.

[2] Reproduced in Mitteil. der Gesellschaft für vervielfält. Kunst,Vienna 1908, p. 13. Cf. p. 464.

[3] Described and reproduced by L. Arrigoni, Milan 1884. It should also be compared with a line-engraving, Passavant, v. 15, 9 (Liechtenstein Collection).

[4] See Gustave Gruyer, *Les Livres à gravures sur bois publiés à Ferrare*, Gazette des Beaux-Arts, 2ᵉ pér., xxxviii., 1888, 89, 339, 416; 3ᵉ pér., i., 1889, 137, 241, 339.

Fig. 270. Printer's mark of Hieronymus Blondus Florentinus, Venice.

Here the earliest woodcut illustrations reflect the style of Cosimo Tura, the most characteristic, and in some respects the most mannered, of the xv-century Ferrarese painters. The earliest of these, representing a *Pope seated between two Cardinals* (fig. 272), appeared in Bonifacius VIII., *Sextus Liber Decretalium*, printed by AUGUSTINUS CARNERIUS, 1478,[1] and in the *Constitutiones* of Clement V., issued by the same printer, in 1479. The next in order known to me is the woodcut of *St. Maurelius standing beneath an Arch* prefixed to the *Leggendario e vita e miracoli di S. Maurelio*, printed by LAUREN-TIUS DE RUBEIS (ROSSO), 1489 (H. 10918). It is a dignified subject, somewhat carelessly cut (fig. 273).

Gruyer cites a variant edition in the Ferrara library with the title *Leggenda de sancto Maurelio*, which contains a second cut on the verso of the last leaf of the volume representing *St. George and the Dragon*. It appears to be by a different hand from the other, and more nearly related to the Venetian cuts in the 'popular' style. The

Fig. 271. The Virgin and Angels, from *Miracoli della Gloriosa Maria*, Brescia 1490.

[1] My reference is taken from Katalog No. 1 of Dr. Ignaz Schwarz, Habsburgergasse 3,

design might have been suggested by Tura's panel of *St. George*, of 1469, in the Cathedral at Ferrara (once an organ wing), but it is not near enough in detail to render the relation at all certain.[1]

Another woodcut entirely under the same influence of Tura, with the characteristic bulging folds of drapery, is that of *Alfraganus and his editor* ('Heremita') in Alfraganus, *Rudimenta Astronomica*, printed by ANDREAS BELLFORTIS, 1493 (H. 822).

Contrasting with the cuts in the style of Tura is another group more nearly related to the work of the 'popular' designer at Venice. Among these

Fig. 272. Pope between two Cardinals, from Bonifacius VIII., *Sextus Liber Decretalium*, Ferrara 1478.

may be mentioned a *Virgin and Child standing beneath a Canopy, within a border of classic design*, the frontispiece to Petrus Pallagari Tranensis, *De Ingenuis Adolescentium Moribus*, printed by L. de Rubeis, 1496 (H. 15597). Similar in style are also the little outline cuts in the *Officium* printed by L. de Rubeis, 1497 (H. 11972), and in the *Corona Beatae Virginis*, n.d., by the same printer, which is appended to the *Officium* in the British Museum copy. There are some delicate figured capitals in the *Officium* (e.g. a *D* with David playing the Harp).

The most attractive of all the Ferrarese illustrations are contained in the

Vienna 1919, No. 11, where the cut is described as appearing on f. 5 of the Bonifacius book. My illustration was kindly supplied me by Dr. G. Agnelli (Director of the Biblioteca Publica, Ferrara), who confirms Gruyer's description of the *Constitutiones* as of 1479.

[1] Tura's painting is reproduced in Venturi, *Storia dell' arte italiana*, vii. (3), fig. 398. Dr. G. Agnelli, Director of the Ferrara library, informs me that the second edition with the cut of St. George was actually printed by Franciscus de Rubeis (son of Laurentius) in 1544. See p. 74 and fig. 33, for a book-cover design with a similar subject.

Epistles of St. Jerome, printed by Laurentius de Rubeis, 12th October 1497 (H. 8566). Their author is evidently inspired by the 'popular' designer at Venice, in particular by the cuts in his *Vitas Patrum* of 1491 and *Legenda Aurea* of 1494.[1] They are small column cuts of similar form and dimensions, and in the same outline style. They have a certain roundness in linear character which distinguishes them from the Venetian designer, and a characteristic emphasis of the black pupil of the eye, which adds to their vivacity of expression. The artist is a most conscious humorist in the wonderful variety of facial expression he gives to St. Jerome's lion, offering its naïve comment on the various episodes of the saint's life (fig. 274). As illustrations of con-temporary custom,

Fig. 273. St. Maurelius, from *Legendario di S. Maurelio*, Ferrara 1489.

the woodcuts in the last section of the book, dealing with the rules of monastic life, are peculiarly interesting (fig. 275).

Less humanly attractive, but more individual in their technical manner, are the woodcuts in Jacobus Philippus Foresti (Bergomensis), *De Claris Mulieribus*, issued a few months earlier by the same printer, 29th April 1497 (H. 2813). They are a series of illustrations of the famous women

[1] See p. 475.

of history and fable, in which a few contemporary examples are undoubtedly portraits. Most of the cuts have backgrounds in white line, probably suggested by the Florentine practice. Several of the blocks serve to represent more than one character, e.g. the *Proba Poetrix* (f. 115, verso; as *Angela Nugarola*, f. 149, and as *Isota Nugarola*, f. 151), which is one of the few examples chiefly in black line, and the *Marcella Romana* (f. 116, verso, who also appears as *Paula Gonzaga*, f. 142, verso, *Genebria Cambare*, f. 150, and *Hippolyta, wife of King Alphonso of Naples*, f. 159, verso). Among the contemporary person-

Fig. 274. St. Jerome and pupils, from his *Epistole*, Ferrara 1497.

ages which appear to be based on portraits from the life are *Bianca Maria Sforza* (f. 153, verso), *Catherina Countess of Forlì and Imola* (f. 160), *Leonora of Aragon, wife of Ercole d' Este* (f. 161, verso),

Fig. 275. Visit to a Convent, from St. Jerome, *Epistole*, Ferrara 1497.

and *Damisella Trivulzia* (f. 167; see fig. 276). The *Damisella Trivulzia* is certainly based on a Milanese painting or drawing.

The *Medusa* (f. 24) is one of the most excellent of the illustrations as decorative design (fig. 277). The black-ground (white-line) woodcuts make a good balance to the heavy Gothic type of the text.

Two attractive outline borders in the Venetian style, by the same designer as the St. Jerome illustrations, appear in both the *St. Jerome* and the *De Claris Mulieribus*. One of them (with four children below, little cavaliers at the sides, and six children making music, flanking a lunette, above) bears a date 1493, but I have not found it in any book before the two in question. The second contains sirens and two children with trumpets (below), children on griffins (sides), and children playing viol and pipe, flanking a lunette (above). Each shows certain differences of state, according as *God the Father* (in the final border), the *Resurrection*

Fig. 276. Damisella Trivulzia, from Foresti, *De Claris Mulieribus*, Ferrara 1497.

(in the second border), or merely lettering, appears in the respective lunettes.

In the *De Claris Mulieribus* the first border is used on the back of the title to contain a cut of the author presenting his book to Beatrice of Aragon, Queen of Hungary and Bohemia, and also to surround a second frontispiece with *Scenes from the Life of the Virgin*.

Though a few years beyond the limits of my study, I would refer to the large outline cut of *St. Christopher*

$(6 \times 4$ inches)[1] in the *Carthusian Missal* issued by the Carthusian Monastery at Ferrara in 1503; it is closely related to Venetian style, and probably by the designer of the St. Jerome illustrations. On the other hand, the *Canon* cut of the *Christ on the Cross* in the same missal is in the white-line manner, somewhat crude in execution. There are some good figured initials, e.g. an M with a Priest celebrating Mass.

MILAN—SALUZZO—MONDOVÌ
—PAVIA—MANTUA

Milanese woodcut achieved no individual position during

Fig. 277. Medusa, from Foresti, *De Claris Mulieribus*, Ferrara 1497.

[1] Reproduced in the Dyson Perrins Catalogue, No. 166.

the xv century comparable with the schools of Venice or Florence. There were probably fewer workshops devoted in any special way to either line-engraving or woodcut, and what was done, as Kristeller rightly observed, shows the variable quality that would denote occasional work by craftsmen engaged in other fields.

The same remark applies to Lombardy and Piedmont in general, and the book-illustration of all this region is most naturally treated as a single group.[1]

As in painting, the most distinguished Milanese achievement in woodcut was in portraiture. The earliest book-illustration to which I can refer (apart from woodcut initials) is the *Profile Portrait of Paolo Attavanti* (fig. 278), which appears in his *Breviarium totius juris canonici*, printed by PACHEL and SCINZENZELER, 28th August 1479 (H. 7159, P.K. 38), and later in the same year in the same author's and printer's *Quadragesimale de reditu peccatoris ad Deum* (H. 7166, P.K. 39), and *Comento volgare e latino del psalmo lxxxx*,

Fig. 278. Paolo Attavanti, from his *Breviarium totius juris canonici*, Milan 1497.

and in his undated *Modo utile di Confessione* (Reichling IV. 1309, P.K. 40). The letters at the foot, M.P.F.O.S.S., can be interpreted as *Magister Paulus Florentinus Ordinis Sancti Spiritus*. The block shorn of its pediment appeared soon after in the *Penitential Psalms* (Latin and Italian), printed without date or printer's name, but almost certainly by Ratdolt at Venice, about 1480 (H. 7165, British Museum).[2]

A most attractive little composition is the *Portrait of Bernardo Bellinzone*

---

[1] See Paul Kristeller, *Die lombardische Graphik der Renaissance*, Berlin 1913 (including catalogue of books printed at Milan, Como, Pavia, Turin, Asti, Savona, Saluzzo and Mondovì); Paul Kristeller, *Books with Woodcuts printed at Pavia*, Bibliographica, vol. i., 1895, 347.

[2] Copies appeared in editions of the *Breviarium Decretorum* printed by Matthias Hus and Jean Battenschue of Lyon, 1484, and by Albrecht Kunne, at Memmingen, 1486.

which appears in his *Rime*, printed by PHILIPPUS DE MANTEGATIIS, 1493 (H. 2754, P.K. 52; fig. 279). There is a line-engraving of the same subject, known in only one impression, now in the collection of Baron Edmond

de Rothschild,[1] from which the woodcut may be copied, unless both are based on the same original. The figure is evidently drawn from nature with its rendering of an easy and unconventional attitude, and Kristeller's suggestion that Leonardo da Vinci might have been responsible for the drawing is by no means unreason-

Fig. 279. Bernardo Bellinzone, from his *Rime*, Milan 1493.

able.[2] Bellinzone, who died in 1491, was, like Leonardo, a Florentine engaged at the court of Lodovico Sforza, and they must have frequently met.

Two other notable Milanese woodcut portraits fall just outside the limits of our date, i.e. in the early years of the XVI century, but they demand some reference, i.e. the large *Portrait of Bernardino Corio seated writing*, which appeared in his *Patria Historia*, issued by Alexander Minutianus, Milan 1503 (P.K. 116; measuring over 11 × 6¼ wide),[3] and the striking *Profile Portrait of the Marquis of Saluzzo* (fig. 280), in J. L. Vivaldus, *Opus Regale*, printed by JACOBUS DE CIRCHIS and SIXTUS DE SOMASCHIS, Saluzzo 1507 (P.K. 365).

Another book of J. L. Vivaldus, *De Veritate Contricionis*, printed by the brothers GUILLERMI LE SIGNERRE at Saluzzo 1503, contains a *St.*

---

[1] Reproduced Kristeller, *Lombardische Graphik*, pl. ix.

[2] See André Blum, *Léonard de Vinci graveur*, Gazette des Beaux-Arts, August 1932.

[3] A folio book which also contains a fine classical design of a figure of Virtue.

Dies mei velociores fuerũt cursore. fugerũt
et non viderũt bonum: pertransierunt quasi
naues poma portantes. ficut aquila volás ad
escam. Job.viiij.cap.

Fig. 280. The Marquis of Saluzzo. from Vivaldus, *Opus Regale*, Saluzzo 1507.

Jerome kneeling before a Crucifix, within a fine classical and heraldic border, which is one of the most decorative of Lombard woodcuts.

Returning on our tracks, one of the earliest Milanese cuts appears to be

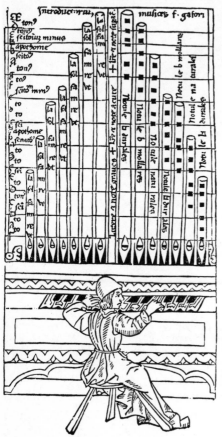

that of the *Organist* (fig. 281) in Franchinus Gafurius, *Theorica Musicae*, printed by Philippus de Mantegatiis, 1492 (H. 7406, P.K. 161). The block was issued earlier in an edition printed by Francesco di Dino at Naples in 1480 (H. 7404, Fava-Bresciano, 170),[1] but the style was unlike anything else in Neapolitan book-illustration, and the Lombard musician Gafurius, who only stayed about two years at Naples (1478–80), no doubt had the block cut in his own province. The style shows kinship to Brescian work, like most of the earlier Milanese illustration. The other illustration in the Naples edition of 1480, *Figures at an Anvil (Tubal Cain)*, was re-cut in the Milan edition.[2]

In their somewhat loose style of drawing and shading the Gafurius cuts are not unlike the allegorical title-cut in Baptista Fulgosius, *Anteros*, printed by Leonardus Pachel, 1496 (H. 7393, P.K. 160).

Another work by Gafurius, the *Practica Musicae*, printed by Le Signerre, 1496 (H. 7407, P.K. 162), has one of the most attract-

Fig. 281. The Organist, from Gafurius, *Theorica Musicae*, Milan 1492.

ive borders. From 1484 Gafurius, who was priest as well as musician, directed the music in the Cathedral at Milan, and he is shown in the

---

[1] See p. 405.

[2] For another block first used at Naples and printed later in Lombardy (at Soncino), the border to Tuppo's *Aesop* of 1485, see p. 405.

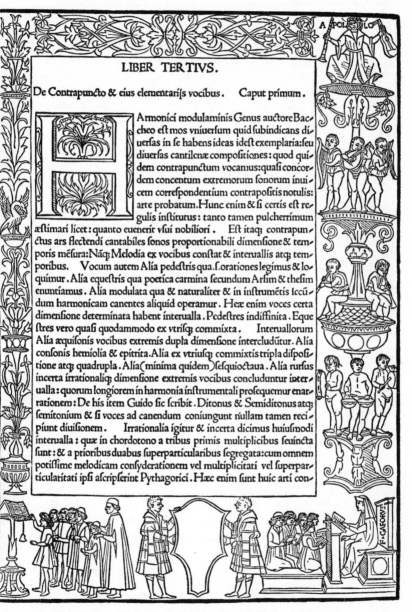

LIBER TERTIVS.

De Contrapuncto & eius elementariis vocibus.   Caput primum.

Armonici modulaminis Genus auctore Baccheo est mos vniuersum quid subindicans diuersas in se habens ideas idest exemplaria:seu diuersas cantilenæ compositiones: quod quidem contrapunctum vocamus:quasi concordem concentum extremorum sonorum inuicem correspondentium contrapositis notulis: arte probatum.Hunc enim & si certis est regulis institutus: tanto tamen pulcherrimum æstimari licet:quanto euenerit vsui nobiliori .   Est itaq; contrapunctus ars flectendi cantabiles sonos proportionabili dimensione & temporis mesura:Náq; Melodia ex vocibus constat & interuallis atq; temporibus.   Vocum autem Alia pedestris qua.s.orationes legimus & loquimur.Alia equestris qua poetica carmina secundum Arsim & thesim enuntiamus. Alia modulata qua & naturaliter & in instruméris lecúdum harmonicam canentes aliquid operamur. Hex enim voces certa dimensione determinata habent interualla.Pedestres indiffinita.Eque stres vero quasi quodammodo ex vtrisq; commixta.   Interuallorum Alia æquisonis vocibus extremis dupla dimensione intercludútur.Alia consonis hemiolia & epitrita.Alia ex vtriusq; commixtis tripla dispositione atq; quadrupla.Alia(minima quidem)sesquioctaua.Alia rursus incerta irrationaliq; dimensione extremis vocibus concluduntur interualla:quorum longiorem in harmonia instrumentali prosequemur enarrationem:De his item Guido sic scribit.Ditonus & Semiditonus atq; semitonium & si voces ad canendum coniungunt nullam tamen recipiunt diuisionem.   Irrationalia igitur & incerta dicimus huiusmodi interualla : quæ in chordotono a tribus primis multiplicibus seuincta sunt:& a prioribus duabus superparticularibus segregata:cum omnem potissime melodicam considerationem vel multiplicitati vel superparticularitati ipsi ascripserint Pythagorici.Hæc enim sunt huic arti con

Fig. 282. Page with Border, in Gafurius, *Practica Musicae*, Milan 1496.

border training his choir (fig. 282). The border occurs before the first and third books, while a second border with Amphion, Orpheus and Arion, and cupids supporting a shield, is prefixed to books two and four.

The interesting frontispiece to the *Antiquarie prospetiche Romane composte per prospectivo Melanese depictore*, n.d., n.pr. (P.K. 21, Munich, Rome, Casanatense; fig. 283),[1] is related to Brescian work in the resemblance of its border to that of the frontispiece of the Brescia *Aesop* of 1497 (GW. 419, see p. 507), but in its subject, the nude figure amid Roman architecture, is very near in style to Bramantino. Whether the author of these curious verses on the 'Mirabilia Romae', who calls himself *Prospectivo Melanese depictore* and signs the frontispiece with the initials P M, is Bramantino or some similar stylist is still unsolved. The verses dedicated to Leonardo da

Fig. 283. Frontispiece to *Antiquarie prospetiche Romane*, Milan, about 1499–1500.

Vinci contain references which support a date of about 1499–1500.

Another attractive cut, of *Two Lovers*, is described and reproduced by Kristeller from Fossa Cremonese, *Inamoramento di Galvano*, printed without date by Petrus de Mantegatiis (P.K. 152), but another version, which may be the earlier block, appeared in Aeneas Sylvius Piccolomini (Pius II.), *Historia di due Amanti*, printed by ALEXANDER DE PELIZONIS, 1500.[2]

---

[1] The book described and frontispiece reproduced by G. Govi, *Intorno a un opusculo rarissimo della fine del secolo xv*, Rome 1876 (Reale Academia dei Lincei, 16th January 1876). For a recent attribution of the book to the printer J. Besicken at Rome, see my additions, Vol. I. p. 265.

[2] First described and reproduced by E. P. Goldschmidt & Co., Catalogue VIII., No. 11.

Two editions of Bernardino de Busti, *Mariale*, contain attractive little cuts of the *Virgin and Child*, no larger than initial letters, and printed at the beginning of sections like initial letters. Two designs occur in the *Mariale*, printed by Uldericus Scinzenzeler, 1492 (H. 4159, P.K. 81a), each several times repeated. They are simple outline cuts, of excellent classical design, and give the impression of being based on larger works of painting (see fig. 284).

Fig. 284. The Virgin and Child, from *Mariale*, Milan 1492.

In the edition of the *Mariale* printed by Leonardus Pachel, 1493 (H. 4160, P.K. 81b), the *Virgin and Child* is a white-line metal-cut. The same edition also contains a little outline *Annunciation*, repeated many times like the *Virgin and Child*. The *Annunciation* lacks clear linear quality, and I am inclined to think that it might be printed from metal casts of a wood-block, as an economy in printing where so much repetition was required, as with initials.[1]

Another Lombard book with metal-cut illustrations is the Aesop, *Vita et Fabulae*, printed at Mondovì (Piedmont) by DOMINICUS DE VIVALDIS, 1481 (Paris, H. 295, P.K. 3a). They are rough metal-cuts somewhat in the manner of Neumeister's edition of Turrecremata, *Meditationes*, 1479.

It has been suggested by Kristeller (*Lombardische Graphik*, p. 48) that the *Portrait of Attavanti*, mentioned above, might be cut in metal. It seems to me unlikely that metal would be used for direct cutting in outline work of this delicate line, but metal casts, on the other hand, might have been made from the original block for purposes of repeated printings.

Among other small cuts of delicate outline style in Milanese books may be mentioned a *Pietà* in Busti, *Defensorium Montis Pietatis*, printed by Scinzenzeler, about 1497 (H. 4167, P.K. 86), and a little *Annunciation* in St. Bernardus, *Sermones de Tempore*, printed by Leonardus Pachel, 1495 (H. 2850, P.K. 59), and later in the *Miracoli della Madonna*, printed by P. de Mantegatiis, 1496 (P.K. 224). The *Sermones* also contains a full-page cut in a broader style representing *St. Bernard in his Study*, which also appears in his *Epistole*, Pachel, 1495 (H. 2873, P.K. 60). In its strong outline and parallel shading it is not unlike the style of the *St. Jerome before a Crucifix* in St. Jerome, *Vita et Transita*, printed by P. de Mantegatiis, 1495 (H. 8650, P.K. 178).

---

[1] See Index of Subjects (under *Casts*).

Fig. 285. The Triumph of Fame, from Petrarch, *Trionfi*, Milan 1494.

Interesting in relation to the use of wood and metal at Milan is the edition of Petrarch, *Trionfi*, printed by ANTONIUS ZAROTUS, 1494 (H. 12762, P.K. 279 b; fig. 285). The six Triumphs are derived from the Florentine broad-manner line-engravings, in part directly and in part through the medium of the woodcuts in the Venetian edition, printed by Plasiis, 1490 (H. 12771, E. 77). The Triumphs of Love and Chastity are woodcuts; the others are white-line metal-cuts. They are all enclosed in black-ground borders of two types: (*a*) with cupids playing musical instruments, below, (*b*) with tritons and nymphs, below. The first three have border (*a*), which is certainly cut on wood; the last three have border (*b*), which appears to be on metal.

Another series of the 'Triumphs of Petrarch', copied from the Venice edition of Plasiis, was issued by Scinzenzeler, 1494 (H. 12775, P. 279 a). These are all on wood, and one of them, the *Triumph of Divinity*, also appeared in Bernardus, *Sermoni sopra la Cantica*, 1494 (H. 2861, P.K. 58).

The *Missale Ambrosianum*, printed by Leonardus Pachel, 1499 (P.K. 247 c), also contains a metal-cut copy from a Florentine broad-manner engraving, i.e. the *Annunciation* (after P. v. 51, 1, Hind, B.I. 1). Among other cuts, it contains a *Christ on the Cross* which appeared earlier in the *Missale Ambrosianum* printed by Zarotus, 1488 (H. 11256, P.K. 247 a), and a *St. Ambrosius with SS. Protasius and Gervasius*, nearer in style to Pavia woodcuts of the early XVI century.

Though woodcut is manifestly more suited to book-illustration than line-engraving, as intaglio plates would require printing in a separate press, it is noteworthy that the earliest book-illustrations, both at Milan and Florence, were from intaglio plates, i.e. at Milan in Fra Pacifico de Novara, *Summula de pacifica Conscientia*, printed by FILIPPUS DE LAVAGNIA, 24th March 1479 (H. 12259), and at Florence in Bettini, *Monte Santo di Dio*, printed by NICOLAUS LAURENTII, Alamannus, 1477 (H. 1276). Though the practice was not continued at Milan, and only repeated, then only partially, in the *Dante* of 1481, at Florence, it probably offers some evidence that engraving on metal was in more general vogue than woodcut in both these places before 1480.

A considerable proportion of Milanese woodcut of the last decade of the XV century is characterised by heavy outlines, regular parallel shading, and crude and somewhat angular design. It is German in manner, though often based on Venetian originals.

Several books originally printed by Bonellis at Venice appear in Milanese type, e.g. that of Scinzenzeler, and with Milanese woodcut decoration, though in some cases the name of Bonellis still appears (in what exact signification is obscure): e.g. there is an issue of Lucan, *Pharsalia*, which still bears the name of the Venetian printer Bonellis, and the date 1495 (like H. 10248, E. 851),[1] but is in Scinzenzeler's type, and has the same border and other decorative pieces as in Scinzenzeler's editions of Mandeville, *De le più maravigliose cose del Mondo*, 21st October 1497 and 6th December 149[7?] (British Museum, H. 10658?), and was certainly printed at Milan about 1497 (British Museum, IA. 26759). The same border also occurs in a reprint of *Lucidario* (*Libro del Maestro e Discipulo*) originally printed by Bonellis, 12th March 1495 (E. 812), which is signed and dated Bonellis, 12th July 1495, and contains a characteristic Milanese copy of the original cut (E. 813, formerly Fairfax Murray).[2] A fourth appearance of the same border is in the Italian *Aesop*, printed by Scinzenzeler, 1497 (H. 352, P.K. 3 b, GW. 439), in which the subject-cuts are copied from the Venetian edition printed by Bonellis, 1491 (GW. 432, E. 360). In another Italian edition of *Aesop*, printed by Le Signerre in 1498 (H. 284, P.K. 3 c, GW. 440), the cuts are copied in reverse from Scinzenzeler's issue. Similar in style to the *Aesop* are the two 'miracle' subjects within four-piece borders in the *Miracoli della Madonna* printed by Mantegatiis, 1496 (P.K. 224).

By far the most important series of cuts in this strong and angular style appeared in the *Specchio dell' Anima*, edited by Giovanni Pietro Ferraro, and printed by the brothers Le Signerre, 1498 (P.K. 143). Apart from the border round the dedication, the book contains seventy-eight prints from seventy-six blocks—the Creation, and the Fall leading up to the Life of the Virgin and of Christ. Behind the crude cutting is revealed a designer of considerable power; the *Christ taking leave of his Mother* (sig. c 2)[3] shows a noble simplicity, and the *Flight into Egypt* (sig. b 1) is a fine decorative composition (fig. 286).

Fifty-eight of the cuts from the *Specchio* were reprinted (with the original narrow borders cut away so as to fit the subjects into broader *passe-partout* borders) in the *Tesauro Spirituale* by the same editor and printers in 1499 (P.K. 144, Oxford, Berlin).[4] Five new subjects were added (sig. d 2, *Preaching of Christ*, reproduced, Lippmann, Italian woodcut, after p. 144; a 3, the *Visitation*; e 2, *Christ taking leave of his Mother*; i 6, *Christ bearing the Cross* (leading in the Oxford copy); m 2, the *Apostles with the Holy Women*, reproduced, Kristeller, Lombardische Graphik, p. 49), the last four noted being in a somewhat more detailed and pictorial manner, in some respects weaker in character and possibly under Netherlandish influence.

---

[1] See p. 504.   [2] See p. 487.

[3] Reproduced, Kristeller, *Lombardische Graphik*, p. 47, from the *Tesauro Spirituale*, 1499.

[4] For a later edition of the cuts in 1563, and further notes, see Vol. I. p. 265.

The development towards a more pictorial manner, and a more pliable scheme of cutting, is more marked in the early XVI century in a group of cuts which seem inspired, if not designed, by Cesare da Sesto (e.g. Assaracus,

Trivultias, 1516, P.K. 36, Berlin), and are comparable with the group of line-engravings of the 'Master of the Beheading of John the Baptist'.[1] But this is already beyond the limits of my work.

At Pavia the earliest book with any cuts of interest is Stephanus Costa, Tractatus de Consanguinitate et Affinitate, printed by MARTINUS DE LAVALLE 1489 (H. 5788). It is a thin folio containing two large

Fig. 286. The Flight into Egypt, from Specchio dell Anima, Milan 1498.

cuts, the first showing a king supporting a table of consanguinity, the second, another table embellished with attractive outline figures.

Apart from this there are a few cuts in service-books, e.g. the crude outline Crucifixion in the Missale Romanum, printed by JOANNES ANTONIUS BIRRETA and FRANCISCUS GIRARDENGUS, 1491 (H. 11396, P.K. 249), the Priest presenting his Book to the Pope in the Breviarium Romanum, printed by Girardengus, 1494 (H. 3917; P.K. 73), and the St. Ambrose and St. Augustine in Albericus de Rosate, Lexicon Juris, printed by MICHAEL and BERNARDINUS DE GARALDIS, 1498 (H. 14000, P.K. 307).

One of the most pleasing designs is the Mercury adopted as printer's mark in and after 1506 by Bernardinus de Garaldis at Pavia, though it was used earlier by the Venetian printer Joannes Tacuinus in the Decreta Marchionalia Montisferrati, 1505 (E. 1498, Vienna). The latter book was

[1] See A. M. Hind, Catalogue of Early Italian Engravings in the British Museum, 1910, p. 520.

printed for a bookseller, Nicolaus de Panibus, at Casale Monferrato (between Vercelli and Alessandria), so that the block was probably a Lombard or Piedmontese work. It has also been noted in a book probably printed at

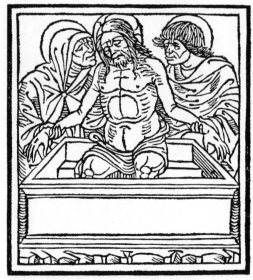

Rome,[1] and in another printed at Paris,[2] but none of the references explain the letters I.G.S.

Of other Lombard towns, Mantua may be mentioned for a woodcut *Pietà* (Christ in the Tomb supported by the Virgin and John), which occurs on the last page of *Quaedam Auctoritates ad misericordiam inducentes*, issued without printer's name in 1485 (B.M.L., IA. 30674; fig. 287). It is cut in strong outline, and a somewhat exaggerated Mantegnesque style of design, comparable in certain respects with wood-

Fig. 287. Pietà, from *Quaedam Auctoritates*, Mantua 1485.

cuts, which will be noted below, in books printed at Modena by Dominicus Rocociolus.

PARMA—FORLÌ—MODENA—BOLOGNA

Before coming to Florence, which was the only other centre of comparable artistic importance with Venice in xv-century book-illustration, we will pass in rapid review the unimportant production of a few towns of the Emilia. Venice was not infrequently called on for the loan of blocks, e.g. in the Ovid, *Metamorphoses*, printed by FRANCISCUS MAZALIS at Parma, 1505 (reprinted from the Venice edition of Jo. Rubeus, 1497),[3] and in

---

[1] *Soleñis repetitio . . . per . . . Franciscum de Pepis Florentinum . . . edita Romae . . . per Fabianum de Giocchis* (Munich).

[2] *Lectura aurea . . . Petri de Bellapertica . . . super librum Institutorum . . . Parisiis sub signo duorum cygnorum . . . impensis Nicolai Vaiautierii et Charoli Dudecii* (Olschki, Catalogues LIII, No. 405, and LXII, Florence 1906).

[3] See pp. 469, 470, 489. Mazalis describes himself as *calcographus* in the colophon, which must not be confused with its other technical use as line-engraver. It implies no more than

Nicolaus Ferrettus, *De Structura Compositionis*, printed by HIERONYMUS MEDESANUS at Forlì in 1495 (H. 6974), with two borrowed blocks, the *School*

Class, from the *Regulae Sypontinae* printed by Pensis, 1492/93,[1] and *Theseus and the Centaur* from the edition of Plutarch, printed by Ragazzo, 1491.[2]

At Modena a few woodcuts appeared in books printed by DOMINICUS ROCOCIOLUS, by far the most attractive being the *Adoration of the Magi* in the *Legenda sanctorum trium Regum*, 1490 (H. 9399; fig. 288). Kristeller has attributed its design to the author of the frontispiece to Alfraganus, *Rudimenta Astronomica*, issued at Ferrara in 1493. There is certainly a relationship in manner, but it seems to me less immediately

Fig. 288. Adoration of the Magi, from *Legenda Sanctorum Trium Regum*, Modena 1490.

inspired by Cosimo Tura than by some such master of the Lombard school as Vincenzo Foppa. It is a design of real strength and dignity.

A *Madonna and Child seated beneath an Arch*, which appeared in Antonio Cornazano, *Vita di Nostra Donna*, 1490 (H. 5726), with hard outline

printer (a 'writer in metal-type'), and other instances of its use may be noted with Bartholomaeus Cremonensis in his colophon verses in Hain 13035 (Venice 1472), and with Benedictus Hectoris in Hain 14868 (Bologna 1498).

[1] See p. 482 and fig. 245. [2] See p. 480.

and some parallel shading, is far poorer in quality than the *Adoration of the Magi*, and the illustrations in the same printer's two undated editions of Johann Lichtenberger's *Prognosticatio* (H. 10081 and Proctor 7208) are

merely adaptations of the woodcuts in the anonymous and undated German editions (S. 4499, H. 10080).[1]

Bologna, standing midway between Florence and Venice, shows the influence of both schools of illustration.[2] As at Florence, its earliest illustrated work, the *Cosmographia* of Ptolemaeus, printed by DOMINICUS DE LAPIS, 23rd June 1477, was embellished with line-engravings on copper, the first published series of engraved maps in Italy.[3]

The earliest woodcut, and perhaps the most individual of Bolognese xv-century illustrations, is the *Visitation* (fig. 289), which appeared in two editions of the *Formulario di Epistole*, printed by UGO RUGERIUS, the first, of 20th April 1485, issued under the name of Bartolommeo Miniatore (H. 11167), the

Fig. 289. The Visitation, from Landinus, *Formulario di Epistole*, Bologna 1485.

second, 23rd June 1485, under that of Christophorus Landinus (H. 9857). The *Epistole* of S. Caterina da Siena, printed by Joannes Jacobus de Fontanesis, 18th April 1492 (H. 4687), contains a crudely cut *St. Catherine with figures kneeling under her protection* (Sorbelli, pl. xxi.). A *Storia di S. Giorgio*, printed without date or printer's name, and assigned to Florence by Proctor (6348 a) and Kristeller (194 a), is now attributed in the British Museum Catalogue to the Bolognese printer FRANCISCUS PLATO DE BENE-

[1] See p. 345.
[2] See Albano Sorbelli, *Storia della stampa in Bologna*, Bologna 1929.
[3] See L. Sighinolfi, *I mappamondi di Taddeo Crivelli*, Bibliofilia, x., 1908, 241.

DICTIS. It contains a cut of *St. George and the Dragon*, showing in reverse the same design as the cut in an undated Florentine *Rappresentazione di S. Giorgio* (P.K. 195a and his fig. 67), from which it is almost certainly copied.

The black-ground border (with Christ and two angels below, candelabra at sides, and Veronica napkin above) which surrounds the first page of *Lucidario*, printed by CALIGULA DE BAZALERIIS, 20th March 1492 (Reichling 559, Sorbelli, pl. xviii.), and again in 1496, is also certainly based on a Florentine cut. A border of similar design is known in the *Fior di Virtù* issued by the Societas Colubris at Florence in 1498 (British Museum, IA. 28049), and as there are other reasons for assuming a lost Florentine edition of the same book before July 1494 (when one of the *Fior di Virtù* cuts, P.K. fig. 8, appeared on the title of Miscomini's *Lucidario*, P.K. 244 c), the original edition and border probably went back before 20th March 1492. An attractive initial H also appears on the same page of the Bologna *Lucidario*.

Another book of the same printer, *Buova d' Antona*, 1497, has a crude cut of *Sir Bevis fighting a monster*, within a haphazard collection of border pieces, partly Florentine in style.

Examples of Bolognese borrowings from Venice may be noted in the *Aesop* (Zucco's Italian version) printed by ERCOLE NANI, 1494 (GW. 435, Sorbelli, pl. xxii.), in which the cuts are based on the edition of Bonellis, 1491. The same title-cut and border also appears in Domenico Cavalca, *Pungi Lingua*, issued by the same Bolognese printer, in 1493 (H. 4775).

Another Bolognese copy of a Venetian original is the woodcut of a *Monk gathering Blossom* in Stefanus de Flandria, *Quaestio de subiecto*, printed by GENTILIS DE ROVEIS (Ravaglis), 1497 (H. 7128; Sorbelli, pl. xx.), which is based on the illustration in the *Fior di Virtù*, printed by de Sanctis, 1487 (E. 387).

FLORENCE

We have already noted that the earliest book-illustrations at Milan and Florence[1] were done in line-engraving.[2] In Florence the goldsmiths formed an important section of the artistic community, and to judge from the rarity of single woodcuts of the period, prints from intaglio plates were probably regarded with greater favour. It is therefore not surprising that Botticelli, who was working for some time under the influence, if not in the service, of Antonio Pollaiuolo, should have turned to the line-engravers

---

[1] Paul Kristeller, *Early Florentine Woodcuts, with an annotated list of Florentine Illustrated Books*, London 1897.　　　　[2] See p. 521.

for the reproduction of his designs to *Dante*, printed by Nicholaus Laurentii in Landino's edition of 1481 (H. 5946).[1] Line-engravings in the same style had been successfully used in Antonio Bettini's *Monte Sancto di Dio* issued by the same printer in 1477.[2] But in that volume there were only three illustrations, and the trouble of separate printing for the copper plates was in consequence small. The same condition in relation to the numerous plates proposed for the Divine Comedy (one for each Canto) was no doubt partly the cause of the breakdown of the project, and after the nineteenth plate no further progress was made, and the blank spaces remained in the printed copies, as a record of thwarted intention. Only a very few copies contain all the illustrations done, the majority having no more than the first two plates; and as token of the small regard paid to the illustrations, the copy on vellum presented to the Signoria, and now in the National Library at Florence, was entirely without plates.

A more successful venture in illustration with copper plates was Berlinghieri's *Geographia*, with its numerous engraved maps, printed by Laurentii about 1480–82. The same medium was used in the two other contemporary series of maps (Ptolemy, *Cosmographia*, of Bologna 1477, and Rome 1478), but separate printing would be essential with large folding maps, whether from wood or copper, so that the same objection did not exist. After these publications no illustrated books appeared in Florence for some eight or nine years, and the woodcut illustration with which we have to deal falls entirely within the last decade of the century.

There were comparatively few fully illustrated books: the exceptions being three works printed for Piero Pacini, the *Epistole e Evangelii* of 1495, the *Aesop* of 1496, and Pulci's *Morgante Maggiore* of 1500/01, and if we trespass slightly into the succeeding century, Frezzi's *Quadriregio* of 1508 (also done for Pacini).

Most of the books are small quartos, within $8\frac{1}{2} \times 6$ inches; the *Epistole e Evangelii* and Frezzi's *Quadriregio* are exceptionally large examples with a page of about 11×8 inches.[3] Few had more than two woodcuts, at beginning and end, and a large proportion only a frontispiece, or small cut

---

[1] See A. M. Hind, *Catalogue of Early Italian Engravings in the British Museum*, 1910, p. 83.

[2] *Ibid.*, 1910, p. 81. These illustrations were copied with considerable freedom in woodcut in the edition printed by Lorenzo Morgiani and Johannes Petri, 1491 (P.K. 60), the *Christ in a Glory* reappearing in D. Cavalca's *Frutti della Lingua*, issued by the same printers in 1497 (P.K. 96).

[3] Another of the larger-size Florentine books with woodcuts is the edition of the *Monte Sancto di Dio*, mentioned in the preceding note.

beneath the title. The cuts themselves are very uniform in size and shape, by far the greater number being small oblongs about 3 × 4 inches in size, nearly adapted to the width of the type surface, whether a single column of prose, or two narrow columns of verse.

There is far less fine printing and careful book-making at Florence than at Venice, but in spite of a certain amateur character in book production, there is no lack of artistic sense in the balance of the page of type and the woodcut illustration.

The books themselves are largely of popular character, poetry, romance and religious tracts. Technical books were seldom provided with illus-

Fig. 290. Piero Pacini's marks, from Frezzi, *Quadriregio*, Florence 1508.

trations as at Venice, a point on which the Florentines may have been guided by their artistic sensibility.

It is the very cheap and popular character of the books (often no more than pamphlets in extent) that has rendered them so scarce. They were disregarded by connoisseurs of the period, and few reached the libraries of great collectors, and the well-worn pages may have largely ended in the waste-paper basket within a few decades of their production.

PIERO PACINI DÀ PESCIA published (through various printers) a large proportion of the best of the Florentine illustrated books, and he evidently aimed at producing attractive books, but in general there is evidence that those who desired production of greater efficiency, at least as regards the text, went to Venice. Marsilio Ficino was amongst them, as is clear from his *Epistole* printed by Capcasa at Venice in 1495 (H. 7059), with its references on ff. 146b and 177a to Alopa's Florentine edition of his translation of Plato (1484–85, H. 13062), and the Venetian edition printed by De Choris in 1491 (H. 13063).

Moreover, the most notable publisher in Venice at this period, Lucantonio Giunta, was a Florentine, who probably chose his residence for its provision of better printing.

Fig. 291. From *Lucidario*, Florence 1494.

A considerable number of the Florentine woodcuts appear in the books of more than one printer, so that it is no more feasible here than at Venice to order one's descriptions according to printers. Another difficulty is presented by the frequent lack of dates in the books, and the absence of the printer's name adds a further obscurity in description. The study of types, chiefly promoted by Robert Proctor, has resulted in assigning a great part of the anonymously printed books to BARTOLOMMEO DI LIBRI (for only eight of his books from a total of about one hundred and twenty contain his name).

There are indications that certain editions have been lost, e.g. a *Fior di Virtù* of about 1492, and a xv-century *Ninfale Fiesolano*.

The earliest edition of the *Fior di Virtù* which is preserved is that printed by the SOCIETAS COLUBRIS (COMPAGNIA DEL DRAGO) in 1498,[1] but a cut which was manifestly made for this work appeared in the *Lucidario* printed by Miscomini in 1494 (fig. 291), and reasons have been given above[2] for thinking that the original edition of the *Fior di Virtù* was issued before 20th March 1492.

Boccaccio's *Ninfale Fiesolano* is only known with the Florentine cuts in the edition of 1568 (P.K. 66, Paris; Met. Museum, New York; fig. 292),

[1] B.M.L., IA. 28049. Kristeller, 150 a, confuses with that of Bonaccorsi and Francisci, 1488 (H. 7108).

[2] See p. 527.

but their style is that of the xv century (or at least not later than Frezzi's *Quadriregio* of 1509) and the inspiration that of Botticelli, no doubt through the medium of some less notable designer.

The descriptions of Florentine editions in Hain and Kristeller are so frequently ambiguous that wherever possible I will add references from the British Museum Catalogue of Books printed in the xv Century.

Fig. 292. From Boccaccio, *Ninfale Fiesolano*, Florence 1568.

No doubt the printers, or the publishers, dealt with various independent ateliers; but there is no evidence as to whether they commissioned the painter-designers, or dealt with the wood-cutters direct. They probably took either course according to opportunity.

The chief printers who issued books with cuts were ANTONIO DI BARTO-LOMMEO MISCOMINI; BARTOLOMMEO DI LIBRI, who printed the largest number of Savonarola tracts, and plays sacred and profane;[1] FRANCESCO BONACCORSI, and LORENZO MORGIANI, in part with JOHANNES PETRI (Giovanni di Piero da Maganza), who also printed many of Savonarola's works. A few illustrated books only were issued at the beginning of the last decade of the century by FRANCESCO DI DINO, and at the end by the SOCIETAS COLUBRIS (COMPAGNIA DEL DRAGO), and by three partners, ANTONIO TUBINI, LORENZO (DE ALOPA) VENEZIANO, and ANDREA GHIRLANDI, of whom the first and last had belonged to the Societas Colubris.

Florentine woodcut illustrations have a special character in being nearly always enclosed within a narrow border on the block itself, while broader *passe-partout* borders are used when occasion demands to adapt the usual small type of woodcut to fill a whole page. The artist evidently aimed

---

[1] There is a useful understanding between certain American University libraries with regard to their collection of early books. Thus the Widener Library, Harvard, makes a special point of collecting *Savonarola* tracts and *Sacre Rappresentazioni*, and reproductions of the same. Princeton, on the other hand, specialises in *Virgil*, and Cornell in *Petrarch* and *Dante*.

at presenting something of the illusion of a framed picture in his little woodcuts.

In the earlier illustrations the borders are for the most part a simple design of three-lobed leaf either in outline or on a black ground: the black ground sometimes sufficing for the limitation of the border, and later more often defined with separate outer and inner border-lines. The corner-pieces contain some simple pattern, such as five dots or a star.

In the *Epistole e Evangelii* printed by Morgiani and Petri for Pacini in 1495 [1] there are as many as fourteen different border designs.

Of the broader *passe-partout* borders the following are the most important designs:

(1) Flower, scroll, and shield (below); candelabra (sides); wreaths (above). Black ground. $4\frac{1}{4} \times 3\frac{1}{8}$ inches.

Augustinus, *Sermones* (Dino), 1493. H. 2009; P.K. 11; B.M., IA. 27707.

(2) Man of Sorrows and two angels (below); candelabra (sides); Veronica napkin (above). Black ground. $6\frac{3}{4} \times 4\frac{7}{8}$.

Fior di Virtù (Societas Colubris), 1498. B.M., IA. 28049. (Probably appeared in an earlier edition before 20th March 1492.)

(3) Four cupids holding wreaths about escutcheon (below); candelabra (sides); I.H.S. and two grotesque heads (above). $6\frac{3}{8} \times 4\frac{1}{4}$.

Sogni di Daniel Profeta (Morgiani), n.d. B.M., IA. 27920.

Pietro Bernardo, *Compendio di Contemplatione* (Tubini), n.d. B.M., IA. 28075.

(4) Veronica napkin (below), scroll (sides), God, Father and Dove (above). $5 \times 3\frac{3}{8}$.

Savonarola, *Trattato dell' Umiltà* (Miscomini), n.d. H. 14372; B.M., IA. 27250.

Savonarola, *Trattato dell' Umiltà* (Libri), n.d. H. 14373; B.M., IA. 27506.

(5) Eagles (below), scroll (sides), tritons (above). Black ground. $6\frac{3}{4} \times 4\frac{3}{8}$. P.K., fig. 17.

Passavanti, *Specchio di Vera Penitenza* (Libri), 1495/96. H. 12435; B.M., IA. 27317.

Savonarola, *Predica dell' Arte del bene morire* (Libri), n.d., after 2nd November 1496. B.M., IA. 27321.

Angelo da Vallombrosa, *Lettera ai Signori e popolo Fiorentino* (Libri), n.d., after 1st January 1496/97.

[1] See p. 538.

GW. 1911; B.M., IA 27324.

Savonarola, *Trattato contra gli Astrologi* (Libri), n.d., H. 14378; B.M., IA. 27512.

(6) Children tilting on pigs (below); candelabra (sides); hare and hounds (above). Black ground. $6\frac{7}{8} \times 4\frac{3}{4}$. P.K., fig. 13.

This border cannot be later than 1493, when it was copied in Anianus, *Compotus*, printed by Andreas Freytag, at Rome.

Canzone per andare in maschera per carnesciale, fatte da più persone (by Lorenzo de' Medici and others) (Morgiani and Petri), n.d. (about 1493–97). P.K. 284; B.M., IA. 27887.

Ippolito Buondelmonti e Dianora de' Bardi (Morgiani and Petri), n.d. (about 1493–97). GW. 575; P.K. 72 a; B.M., IA. 27935. *Uberto e Filomena*, n.d., n.pr. P.K. 421 a (Erlangen).

(7) Cupids on deer (below); candelabra (sides); cupids supporting medallion with profiles of man and girl (above). Black ground. $6\frac{7}{8} \times 4\frac{1}{2}$. P.K., fig. 15.

Storia di Bradiamonte, n.d., n.pr. P.K. 70 (Erlangen).

Apart from the borders and *passe-partouts* the purely decorative features of Florentine book-illustration are scanty. Woodcut initials are not so common as at Venice, nor so varied or interesting. A good representative example is the capital F from St. Augustine, *Sermones*, printed by Francesco di Dino, 1493 (H. 2009, P.K. 11 b, B.M., IA. 27707).

The woodcut designs show a remarkably high level in invention and composition. In subjects which admit of dramatic rendering there is no lack of expressive representation, made all the more vivid by the limitation of the means at the draughtsmen's disposal. In stories of sentiment, the reader is touched by motives of gentle reserve and unaffected charm; while religious themes are accorded their pictures of grave, yet harmonious dignity.

The designers were undoubtedly painters, and in many illustrations one finds reflection of the style of the greater artists of the time, and of Botticelli and Ghirlandaio in particular. But there are no woodcuts whose character claims by indubitable signs such exalted paternity. The probabilities are all in favour of lesser artists under their influence devoting their energies to woodcut design, and perhaps only a small number, as the variety of style shown in the cuts of this decade is not very large.

Thus Mr. Berenson [1] has ventured to attribute the larger proportion

[1] See Burlington Magazine, i., 1903, 6. The *Master with Seven Pupils* reproduced in our fig. 294 is among the many so attributed.

of the cuts of about 1490–1500, reproduced by Kristeller, to his Alunno di Domenico, now identified as BARTOLOMMEO DI GIOVANNI, a painter who is known to have done the *predelle* to Ghirlandaio's *Adoration of the Kings* in 1488. It is the same painter to whom the late Mr. Herbert Horne attributed the design of the line-engraving, the *Triumph of Bacchus and Ariadne*, only known in the British Museum.[1] There is unfortunately no evidence beyond that of style, and the inevitable difficulty of comparing the painter's style with the modified reflection in work of another convention adds another obstacle.

Mr. A. W. Pollard certainly voiced more scientific opinion in his scepticism of undocumented attributions, but such attributions do not thereby lose their value, for they at least place the illustrations near their probable artistic milieu, and may at any time help to find the link required.

Another possible clue might be found in research of the unidentified work of FRANCESCO ROSSELLI, the little known brother of Cosimo Rosselli. A *Map of the World* engraved by him on copper after Giovanni Matteo Contarini in 1506 (the first-known printed map showing the Discoveries of Columbus) was recently acquired by the British Museum.[2] Apart from this line-engraving nothing is known of his work beyond conjectures based on the inventory of his son ALESSANDRO DI FRANCESCO ROSSELLI, 1528, which contains a large number of engravings and woodcuts of the most various character.[3] Several of the known line-engravings of the xv century figure in the list, and it is extremely probable that Francesco Rosselli, who is described as an illuminator of prints (*miniatore e stampatore*) was the engraver of some of these in addition to the Contarini Map. It is equally probable that he was woodcutter as well, and responsible for many of the woodcuts described. Whether any of these are book-illustrations is uncertain, though entries such as *7 Lisime di fogli stampati in sonetti e in chomedie* imply the possibility that he was among the makers of woodcut illustrations. But I can do no more than suggest a possible direction for research.

Another link might be offered by drawings such as a sheet of studies by an anonymous Florentine artist in the Uffizi,[4] which contains a variety of studies for narrow borders, and is probably on that account by a designer

---

[1] A. M. Hind, *Catalogue of Early Italian Engravings in the British Museum*, 1910, p. 44, A. II. 11.

[2] Published with description and facsimile by the British Museum, 1924.

[3] See I. del Badia, *Miscellanea fiorentina*, vol. ii. No. 14, p. 24 (Florence 1894); A. M. Hind, *Catalogue of Early Italian Engravings in the British Museum*, 1910, p. xxix.

[4] The reverse of Schönbrunner and Meder, 277. Both sides reproduced by O. Fischel, *Die Zeichnungen der Umbrer*, Berlin 1917, p. 40, figs. 40, 41.

who worked for woodcut illustration (fig. 293).[1] One of the figures is nearly related to Donatello's *St. George*; others appear to be based on subjects of the heroes of antiquity done by Ghirlandaio, probably with the collaboration of Perugino, in the Palazzo della Signoria at Florence about 1482. But of the dozen designs for borders on this sheet, I have only connected two with published work. The topmost pattern occurs (*a*) in the cut of the *Master with Seven Pupils* in C. Landinus, *Formulario*, printed by Miscomini, 1492 (P.K. 230 b, H. 9862, B.M., IA. 27203), which also appears in *Flores Poetarum*, printed without date or printer's name (P.K. 153), and in Nicolaus Valla, *Ars Metrica*, n.d., printed by Bonaccorsi (B.M., IA. 27651, fig. 294);

Fig. 293. Sheet of Studies. Pen drawing in the Uffizi, Florence.

and (*b*) in borders in the *Aesop* printed by Bonaccorsi for Pacini, 1496 (P.K. 137 a, H. 1350 a, and later editions). The second example, four rows from the foot of the drawing, i.e. the series of triangles, corresponds with borders of certain cuts in Frezzi's *Quadriregio* of 1508, and there are unmistakable Umbrian characteristics in these illustrations as

---

[1] But it must be remembered that armourers used similar border designs, and panels of trophies such as appears as one of the drawings (cf. armour illustrated in the Bulletin of the Metropolitan Museum of Art, New York 1930, p. 93).

well as in the drawing. Nevertheless this correspondence in character is not enough to support any conclusions.

The last clue to authorship is the signature LV which occurs in the first illustration of Frezzi's *Quadriregio* (fig. 295), which is repeated on sig. B. 2.

Fig. 294. Master with Seven Pupils, from Valla, *Ars Metrica*, Florence.

It has been connected with Luca Signorelli (*Luca Venturi*), but though certain subjects, such as the *Battle of Naked Men* (f. 68, verso), are reminiscent of his style, there is little foundation for the conjecture. Inference from other examples of signed cuts and the general practice of the period[1] renders it far more probable that the LV denoted the cutter rather than the designer, and it is not beyond reason that it might be the cutter Lucantonio degli Uberti, only his usual initials were LA, and it seems probable that in the few years preceding 1508 he was out of Florence.[2]

Our indications have thrown little illumination on the possible authorship of Florentine woodcuts, but in spite of paucity of results they are set down in the hope that they may lead other researchers to some solution.

I will conclude this section with a short survey of the more important Florentine books, beginning with the few more fully illustrated examples.

[1] See Index of Subjects (under *Designer and Cutter*).   [2] See p. 452.

One of the most attractive of these in the earlier style of pure outline, is Filippo Calandri, *Arithmetica*, printed by Morgiani and Petri, 1491/92 (P.K. 77 a, H. 3156, B.M., IA. 27782). There are borders to the tables throughout, of charming scroll and figure design, and even the pages of problems have their appropriate illustrations, and nothing could be imagined more alluring to the young student of arithmetic (fig. 296).

Jacobus de Cessolis, *Libro di Giuoco di Scacchi*, printed by Miscomini, 1493/94 (P.K. 101, H. 4900, B.M., IA. 27205), contains, under the guise

Fig. 295. Frontispiece to Frezzi, *Quadriregio*, Florence 1508.

of the game of chess, a picture of the various occupations of men, in a frontispiece and thirteen other illustrations. The frontispiece of the *Game of Chess* (fig. 297) is one of the finest of Florentine illustrations, and, added to its sensitive draughtsmanship, has a certain largeness of style which is remarkable even amid the high average attained by Florentine work of the period. It is nearly related to Botticelli, and undoubtedly the design of a painter, and of a really gifted artist. The remaining illustrations are good, but lack the rhythmic quality of the frontispiece, and can hardly be by the same designer.

The most considerable achievement of xv-century Florentine book-illustration is contained in the *Epistole e Evangelii,* printed by Morgiani and Petri, for Pacini, 27th July 1495 (P.K. 135 b).[1]

Only two copies of the original edition of 1495 are known, one in the Corsini Library at Rome (see fig. 298), the other belonging to Mr. C. W. Dyson Perrins. The latter, which came from the collection of Richard Fisher, was reproduced in facsimile by the owner for presentation to the Roxburghe Club, with descriptive text by Mr. A. W. Pollard, in 1910. Unfortunately it had suffered by fire; the full-page frontispiece being considerably damaged and made up, and a few of the other small cuts also having suffered. In addition to the frontispiece,[2] it contains 144 illustrations of the standard Florentine size (i.e. about 3 × 4 inches, a small number being uprights), with some fourteen varieties of border design, as well as twenty-five small half-lengths of prophets, evangelists, and epistle-writers, and a little St. Sebastian. The colophon emphasises the numerous

Fig. 296. Page with border, from Calandri, *Arithmetica,* Florence 1491/92.

leaves and woodcuts, no doubt to compare the achievement favourably with the less ambitious Venetian edition of the same work.[3]

---

[1] The complete title is *Epistole e Evangelii e Lectioni vulgari in lingua toschana,* i.e. the Epistles, Gospels and Lessons as read in the Mass.

[2] The inset cuts of the Evangelists, from small blocks which also occur in the text, differ in the later editions. For other woodcuts comparable in style with this frontispiece, see p. 74.

[3] See p. 473. It is noteworthy that another Florentine edition which appeared a few months after Morgiani's issue, printed by Bartolommeo di Libri on the 24th October 1495

Some of the cuts are in outline, such as the *Last Supper*, f. 47 b (with its inevitable reflection of the versions in fresco by Castagno and Ghirlandaio), the *Flagellation*, f. 60, and the *Mocking of Christ*, f. 49, verso (with something of the style of Pollaiuolo), and the *Last Judgment*, f. 22 a (fig. 299), the

Fig. 297. Frontispiece to Cessolis, *Libro di Giuoco di Scacchi*, Florence 1493/94.

last being a design of great dignity; but the majority are in the usual Florentine manner, with white-line ground. A few of the cuts had appeared in Bonaventura, *Meditazioni sopra la Passione*, printed by Miscomini about 1494 (P.K. 69 a; B.M., IA. 27248), and it is from this edition that I reproduce the *Christ entering Jerusalem* (fig. 300).

There were later editions of the *Epistole e Evangelii* in 1515 (P.K. 135 c, Victoria and Albert Museum, Biblioteca Riccardiana), and in 1551 (Dyson

(P.K. 135 a, Essling 189, Florence), was illustrated entirely with Venetian blocks, e.g. from Jacobus de Voragine, *Legendario di Sancti*, 10th December 1492 (Essling 678, Modena).

Fig. 298. Frontispiece to *Epistole e Evangelii*, Florence 1495.

Perrins, W. M. Ivins, Jr.) and 1559/60 (British Museum). Some of the cuts also appeared subsequent to 1495 in other works, e.g. the *Feast of the Prodigal Son* in the *Rappresentazione del Vitello Faggiato*, n.pr., n.d. (P.K. 434, Oxford, etc.), the *Agony in the Garden* and *Christ bearing the Cross* in Savonarola, *Sermone dell' Orazione*, Morgiani and Petri, n.d. (P.K. 382 c, B.M., IA. 27956), and the *Agony* alone in Savonarola, *Esposizione del Pater Noster*, Morgiani and Petri, n.d. (P.K. 384 a, B.M., IA. 27953), and eleven cuts in Bernardo Pulci, *La Passione del Nostro Signore*, n.pr., n.d. but before 1559 (P.K. 340, British Museum).

Only two copies of any xv-century Florentine edition of Aesop's *Fables* are cited by Kristeller, those of Prince Trivulzio and the Biblioteca Riccardiana, Florence (printed

Fig. 299. Last Judgment, from *Epistole e Evangelii*, Florence 1495.

by Bonaccorsi for Pacini, P.K. 137 a). But some of the sixty-five cuts of this edition reappear in editions of 1514 and 1520 (P.K. 137 b and c). A variant of the last edition from the Fairfax Murray Collection is now in the library of Mr. Wilfred Merton,[1] and it is from this copy that I reproduce the *Sick Vulture and his Mother* (fig. 301), a design of fine decorative quality. The subjects show a general dependence on the editions of Verona (1479) and Naples (1485), but other sources may well have been used in designs of such traditional character.

Pulci's *Morgante Maggiore*, published by Piero Pacini 1500/01 (P.K. 347,

---

[1] The cuts of Mr. Merton's copy are reproduced in *Aesop's Fables: Samuel Croxall's Translation with a bibliographical note by Victor Scholderer*. Arranged by Bruce Rogers for the Limited Editions Club, 1933.

Vienna; Berlin, incomplete), contains some 149 cuts, of which 14 also appear in other books (mystery plays and romances). Mr. Scholderer has identified the printers with the *Societas Colubris* or *Compagnia del Drago* (Antonio Tubini and Antonio Ghirlandi).[1] The cuts show a variety of styles, some near to that of the earlier Florentine illustration, others in the more angular and piquant manner of the *Epistole e Evangelii* and of many books of about 1495, and the largest group in an apparently later style in which the

Fig. 300. Christ entering Jerusalem, from Bonaventura, *Meditazioni sopra la Passione*, Florence, about 1494.

figures are in general shorter and drawn with more rounded contours and delicate lines (see fig. 302). Kristeller has compared the style of this last group with Piero di Cosimo.

Frezzi's *Quadriregio del Decorso della Vita Umana* of 1508 (P.K. 164), which has already been mentioned in the discussion of possible authorship of Florentine woodcuts in general,[2] is the last of the books with more copious illustration which demands our attention (see figs. 295 and 303). It was printed for Piero Pacini, in part at least by Filippo Giunta, but

<hr />

[1] By comparison with an edition of Perottus, *Rudimenta Grammatica*, 1500, which contained the imprint of the Societas Colubris, and the device of the Dragon with initials A A for Antonio Tubini and Antonio Ghirlandi (the only known copy submitted to Mr. Scholderer by Mr. E. P. Goldschmidt in 1930).   [2] See p. 536.

a change in type half-way through the book complicates the typographical problem. It is one of the larger-size Florentine books, the verses being

Fig. 301. The Sick Vulture and his Mother, from *Aesop*, Florence.

printed in double column on a page of about 11 × 8 inches. Its illustrations (title-border and 116 subjects) are remarkable for their general high

Fig. 302. From Pulci, *Morgante Maggiore*, Florence 1500/01.

level of quality; many are very beautiful in design, and full of life and motion, while the black and white lines are perfectly combined in the cutting. Here is certainly the culmination in the development of Florentine woodcut illustration both in design and technical quality; some of the charm of the earlier woodcuts may have been lost in a more uniform achievement, but I cannot agree with Kristeller's conclusion that 'in their conventional correctness, in the lifelessness of the scratchy lines, in their tedious repetitions of the same forms and movements and of the background, these and other similar cuts are very far removed from the simple illustrations of the xv century, which were full of spirit, character, and artistic life.' [1]

Fig. 303. The Pursuit of Cupid, from Frezzi, *Quadriregio,* Florence 1508.

The earliest type of Florentine illustration seems to be seen in the *Christ on the Cross with the Virgin and St. John* (P.K. cut 2) and the *Man of Sorrows with two Angels* (P.K. cut 3; fig. 304) which appeared in various books about 1490–92, both occasionally within the same border of interlaced pattern. They are good designs, roughly cut in outline and parallel shading, in a style that probably had its source in the Broad Manner line-engravings. In the impressions known the blocks already seem worn, so that they were possibly done earlier, either as separate cuts or for books which were not issued or of which no copies remain.

Both subjects in their earlier state have a border of interlaced pattern,

[1] *Early Florentine Woodcuts*, p. xxxix.

the border of the Crucifixion subject having a rosette in each corner, that of the Man of Sorrows a leaf. In the books in which they occur the blocks, inclusive of the border, are too large for the page, and they are found cut or masked in the impression, another fact which favours the probability that they were done for some earlier works. The *Christ on the Cross* appears with its border in D. Cavalca, *Specchio di Croce*, printed by Dino, Florence 1490 (P.K. 95 b, Florence), and in Savonarola, *Trattato del Sacramento*, printed by Miscomini, Florence, n.d. (P.K. 391 a), and with its border cut away in Savonarola, *Trattato dell' Amore di Jesu*, Miscomini, Florence 1492 (P.K. 374 f).

Fig. 304. The Man of Sorrows, from Savonarola, *Dell' Umiltà*, Florence 1492.

The *Man of Sorrows* is only known in Savonarola, *Trattato dell' Umiltà*, printed by Miscomini, Florence 1492, where it appears with its border (P.K. 394 d).

Then between 1490 and 1495 a considerable number of cuts appeared in a much more sensitive style of draughtsmanship, largely in outline. One of the finest examples occurs in Jacopone da Todi, *Laude*, printed by Bonaccorsi, 1490 (P.K. 220), the *Virgin adored by the Author* (fig. 305), a cut similar in quality to the *Last Judgment* in the *Epistole e Evangelii* of 1495 (fig. 299). Others of the same group (though probably by a variety of designers) are:

Christ standing with Cross and Chalice in a Niche, in Thomas à Kempis,

Imitatio Christi (Miscomini), 1493 (P.K. 227 b), and Passavanti,
   Specchio di Vera Penitenza (Libri), 1495/96 (P.K. 323);
Christ standing with Cross and Chalice in a Landscape, in Thomas à
   Kempis, *Imitatio Christi* (Libri), n.d. (P.K. 227 a);

Fig. 305. The Virgin adored by the Author, from Jacopone da Todi, *Laude*, Florence 1490.

The title-cut of Granollachs, *Lunare* (Morgiani), 1491 and 1496
   (P.K. 210 a and b) (P.K. cut 11);
St. Francis receiving the Stigmata (P.K. cut 27), in S. Francesco,
   Fioretti, n.d. (P.K. 155 a, Vatican), and the *Rappresentazione di
   S. Francesco* by Antonia Pulci (Libri), n.d. (P.K. 158 a),
The Agony in the Garden, in Savonarola, *Sermone dell' Orazione*, n.d.

(P.K. 382 a), and *Dell' Orazione Mentale* (Libri), n.d. (P.K. 383 a), comparable with another representation of the subject in the *Epistole e Evangelii* of 1495;

St. *Augustine in his Study, turned to the left* (fig. 306) in St. Augustine, *Soliloquii* (Morgiani), 1491 (P.K. 10 a), and as *St. Antoninus* in Antoninus, *Confessionale* (Morgiani), 1493 (P.K. 25);

Fig. 306. St. Augustine in his Study, from his *Soliloquii*, Florence 1491.

St. *Augustine in his Study, turned to the right* in St. Augustine, *Sermoni volgari* (Miscomini), 1493 (P.K. 11 c);

Master with Seven Pupils (fig. 294, $5\frac{7}{8} \times 4$ inches), in C. Landinus, *Formulario di Lettere* (Miscomini), 1492 (P.K. 230 b); *Flores Poetarum*, n.d. (P.K. 153); Nicolaus Valla, *Ars Metrica* (Bonaccorsi), n.d. (B.M.);

Smaller subject of a *Master with Seven Pupils* ($4 \times 3\frac{1}{4}$ inches) in C. Landinus, *Formulario di Lettere* (Libri), n.d. (P.K. 230 a), and N. Perottus, *Regulae Sypontinae* (Libri), n.d. (B.M.);

Master and Pupil in *Lucidario* (Libri), n.d. (P.K. 244 a), and F.
Berlinghieri, *Protesto alla Signoria* (Libri), n.d. (H. 2826);

Young Man at a Desk (P.K. cut 22) in Luca Pulci, *Epistole* (Libri),
n.d. (P.K. 342);

Turbaned Sage at a Desk in *Il Savio Romano* (Morgiani), n.d. (B.M.);

Fig. 307. Confessions in a Church, for Capranica, *Arte del ben Morire*, Venice (?) 1490.

Astrologer in his Study in Pietrobono Advogario, *Pronostico dell' Anno
1496* (Morgiani) [1495–96] (P.K. 332), *Pronostico dell' Anno 1497*
(Morgiani) [1496–97] (P.K. 333), Granollachs, *Lunare* (Morgiani),
1496 (P.K. 210 b), and Giuliano Dati, *Prete Janni* (Prester John)
(Morgiani), n.d. (P.K. 122 a);

Prester John in Giuliano Dati, *Prete Janni* (Morgiani), n.d. (P.K. 122 a);

The Mount of Piety (freely adapted from the large Florentine line-engraving in the Broad Manner, B. xiii. 88, 7), in Marco del Monte Santa Maria, *Tavola della Salute* (Miscomini), 1494 (P.K. 257), and the same author's *Libro dei Commandamenti di Dio*, 1494 (P.K. 258);

Confessions in a Church (with two Confessors), which, though printed probably at Venice, in Capranica, *Arte del ben morire* (Clein and Himel) 1490 (Essling 271; H. 4402), is likely to be Florentine work (fig. 307), and the original of which there is a modified copy in Antoninus, *Confessionale: Summa omnis mortalium cura* (Libri), n.d. (B.M.) (P.K. cut 108).

Confession in a Church (with one Confessor) in Antoninus, *Confessionale: Curam illius habe* (Morgiani and Petri) 1493 (P.K. 25), and Antoninus, *Tractato volgare intitolato Defecerunt* (Morgiani and Petri), 1496 (P.K. 26).

One of the most important groups of Florentine illustrated books is that of the Savonarola tracts.[1] Illustrations from several of these have already been mentioned (see pp. 532, 541, 545, 546, 547), and I would now add a list of the other sermons and tracts which contain the chief woodcuts, mostly examples in which a greater use of white line is seen:

Predica dell' Arte del ben morire (Libri), n.d. (about 1496)[2] (P.K. 375 c and d): Title cut within a border, and three other cuts.

Compendio di Rivelazione (Morgiani and Petri), 1st September 1495 (H. 14335): four cuts (one repeated), with a most vivid representation of *Savonarola preaching* (fig. 309).

De Simplicitate Christianae Vitae (Morgiani): two editions, 1496 (P.K. 392 a and b), and *Epistola a tutti gli eletti* (P.K. 379; Corsini), containing a cut representing *Savonarola writing in his Cell* (fig. 308).

---

[1] See Gustave Gruyer, *Les Illustrations des écrits de Savonarole publiés en Italie au XVᵉ et au XVIᵉ siècle*, Paris 1879. The Widener Library, Harvard University, has added to its original Savonarola tracts a large collection of facsimiles. Cf. p. 531, footnote 1.

[2] Facsimile, Wiegendruck Gesellschaft, Berlin 1926 (Einleitung von Erich von Rath). The facsimile is made from P.K. 375 c (Berlin). The same cuts appear in two slightly varying editions in the B.M. (IA. 27321 and 27320) which Kristeller includes under his 375 d. Kristeller 375 a, printed, according to von Rath, by Morgiani and Petri (Stuttgart, Paris; not in the B.M.), contains three cuts, variants on the last three cuts in 375 c and d, with the first repeated on the title. It is only the later issue of this variant, P.K. 375 b (printed by Tubini and Ghirlandi, after 1500; B.M., 3905 dd. 118), which contains the *Triumph of Death* cut from Petrarch, *Trionfi* of 1499 (P.K. 328) on the title. The three blocks in these editions seem to me inferior to Libri's, but it is difficult to say whether they are modified copies of Libri's blocks, or based on the same original drawings.

Sopra i dieci Commandamenti (Morgiani), n.d. (P.K. 377 a), containing cuts (*a*) *Savonarola presenting his book to kneeling nuns in a chapel*; (*b*) another oblong subject of *Monk and Nuns*, at the end.

Predica e Rivelazioni (Libri), 5th September 1495 (H. 14380),
Sopra i dieci Commandamenti (Libri), 24th October 1495 (P.K. 377 b),
Epistola a un amico (Libri), n.d. (P.K. 380 a), with the upright

Fig. 308. Savonarola in his Cell, from his *De Simplicitate Christianae Vitae*, Florence 1496.

subject of *Two Monks receiving Nuns* (P.K. cut 32) which occurs in various other tracts printed by Libri.

Tractato del Sacramento (Libri), two undated editions: H. 14352 and 14353 (B.M., IA. 27498 and 27552), with two woodcut versions of the *Elevation of the Host* (one being reproduced by Kristeller, cut 109).

Dell' Orazione Mentale (Libri), n.d. (P.K. 383), and *Regola del bene vivere* (Libri), 1498 (P.K. 389), with a subject of a *Monk kneeling before the Altar* (P.K. cut 42).

Trattato contra gli Astrologi (Libri), n.d. (P.K. 376), with a cut of *Monk and Astrologer*.

Another group of great interest is offered by the *Sacre Rappresentazioni*, or Mystery Plays, published in such numbers by the Florentine printers.[1]

xv-century editions are rare, but the popularity of such plays is evidenced in the numerous reprints of the xvi century. Many of the later editions contain cuts printed from the original blocks, and in the absence of early issues may be of considerable interest. Several collected editions containing numerous plays (which had no doubt in most cases been printed separately) are known, with a special lettering or signature affixed to each play and

Fig. 309. Savonarola preaching, from his *Compendio di Rivelazione*, Florence 1495.

index to the series added. Two of these *collectanea*, issued by the Giunta, are preserved in the Museo Poldo-Pezzoli, Milan, *Il Primo Libro di Rappresentationi et Feste, di diversi Santi e Sante*, 1555, and *Il Secondo Libro di Feste et Rappresentationi*, 1560, and titles occur in the same collection for *Il Terzo Libro di Feste, Rappresentationi, et Comedie Spirituali*, 1578, and for another series of 1591.

Most large collections such as that of the British Museum show various late issues in which the signatures occurring on the title-pages show that they had belonged to one or another of such collected editions.

The title nearly always contains a cut of the *Angel of the Annunciation*, generally placed above another woodcut illustrating the play. The text of the play occasionally contains further illustrations.

The earliest type of this *Angel of the Annunciation* is in outline within a border of trefoil on black ground, with the lower border removed, probably for convenience of space. A good example is seen in the *Rappresentazione di San Panunzio*, by Feo Belcari, printed by Libri, n.d. (P.K. 321; fig. 310). The same design of angel is found in xvi-century editions without the border, and a third design, in which the figure is shaded in parallel lines, is also commonly found.

A very beautiful *Annunciation* (fig. 311) appears on the first page of the

Fig. 310. Title-cuts to Feo Belcari, *Rappresentazione di San Panunzio*, Florence.

Rappresentazione della Festa della Annunziazione (Libri), n.d. (P.K. 365 a), and another excellent cut probably by the same hand is the *Last Judgment* on the title-page of the *Rappresentazione del Dì del Giudicio* by Antonio Araldi (?) (Libri), n.d. (P.K. 206a).

From the numerous *Sacre Rappresentazioni* issued in Florence in the xv and xvi centuries, I would also note the following as among the more important examples of which there are editions of the xv century, or

Fig. 311. The Annunciation, from the *Rappresentazione della Festa della Annunziazione*, Florence.

the early years of the xvi century (collections are only cited when early editions are not in the British Museum):

La Rappresentazione

di Santa Agata, n.d. (P.K. 7 a, Oxford);
di Santa Cristina (Libri), n.d. (P.K. 115 a);
della Natività di Cristo (Libri), n.d.;
della Regina Esther, n.pr., n.d. (P.K. 138 a);
di Santa Felicita Hebrea, n.d. (P.K. 144 a);
del Figliuol Prodigo, n.d. (P.K. 148 a);
di San Francesco, by Antonia Pulci (Libri), n.d. (P.K. 158 a);
di San Giorgio (Libri), n.d. (P.K. 195 a, Oxford);

di San Giovanni Battista, by F. Belcari (Libri), n.d. (P.K. 199 a);
di San Giovani e Paolo, by Lorenzo de' Medici (Libri), n.d. (P.K. 285 a);
di San Giovanni Gualberto, n.d. (P.K. 203 a);
d' un Miracolo del Corpo di Cristo (Libri), n.d. (P.K. 180 a);

Fig. 312. The Death of Lucretia, from the *Storia e Morte di Lucrezia*, Florence.

d' un Miracolo di Nostra Donna (Libri), n.d. (P.K. 270 a);
di Santa Orsola, n.d., P.K. 309 d. (good early cut of a Martyrdom of Six Saints, in ed. 1554, B.M.);
di San Valentino e Santa Giuliana, n.d. (P.K. 422 a, Florence).

Sometimes the title, as with novels, will be *Storia* or *Historia*, and *Festa* is often added, e.g.:

La Hystoria e Festa di Susanna, n.d. (P.K. 408, *bis*);
La Hystoria di Sancta Maria Magdalena e Lazaro e Martha, n.d. (P.K. 250 c, Corsini).

Many of the editions described in Kristeller without name of printer may have been issued by Libri, who printed more of these plays than any other Florentine printer in the xv century. A certain number of such plays were also printed at Siena, more particularly those about Saint Catherine of Siena.

Novels and romances, in prose and verse, form another large group of the Florentine illustrated books, and two of the most attractive examples appeared in the *Storia di Ippolito Buondelmonti e Dianora Bardi* (Morgiani), n.d. (P.K. 72 a), and in the *Storia e Morte di Lucrezia* (Morgiani), n.d. (P.K. 245 a, fig. 312), the latter being very typical of Florentine work in its vivid and expressive quality.

Fig. 313. Market Scene, from *Contrasto di Carnesciale e la Quaresima*, Florence.

The following *novelle* might also be noted (Erlangen being one of the richest collections of the rare early editions):

> *Novella di due preti et un cherico innamorati duna donna*, n.pr., n.d. (P.K. 300, Kupferstichkabinett, Berlin; Erlangen).
> *Storia di Maria per Ravenna*, n.pr., n.d. (P.K. 272, Erlangen).
> *Novella della figliuola del Mercante*, n.pr., n.d. (P.K. 299, Erlangen).
> *Storia di Bradiamonte*, n.pr., n.d. (P.K. 70, Erlangen) (woodcut within the *passe-partout* border, described as No. 7 on p. 533).
> *La Nencia de Barberino*, n.pr., n.d. (P.K. 282 a, Erlangen).
> *Storia di Uberto e Filomena*, n.pr., n.d. (P.K. 421 a, Erlangen) (woodcut within the *passe-partout* border, described as No. 6 on p. 533).
> *Novella di Gualtieri e Griselda*, n.pr., n.d. (P.K. 215 a, Erlangen).

I will conclude this section on Florence with reference to various other illustrations of interest:

> *Monte dell' Oratione* (Bonaccorsi), 1496 (P.K. 288 a, Florence) (the first cut reproduced, Delaborde, *Gravure en Italie*, p. 219).

Chapel scene, in *Laude facte da piu persone* (Libri), n.d. (P.K. 232 a and b, and cut 73).

Scene at a Banker's, in Chiarini, *Libro di Mercatanzie* (Libri), n.d. (P.K. 104); reprinted in the *Rappresentazione di Agnolo Hebreo*, 1554.

Domestic and Market Scenes, in *Contrasto di Carnesciale e la Quaresima* (Morgiani), n.d. (P.K. 85 a; fig. 313).

Monk arguing with two other monks and five laymen, in Domenico Benivieni, *Tractato in defensione della Doctrina di Savonarola* (Bonaccorsi), 1496 (P.K. 52).

A Ring of Dancing Girls before the cornice of a building with the Medici arms (fig. 314), in Lorenzo de' Medici, Politiano and others, *Ballatette* (Libri), n.d. (about 1496) (Gamba, No. 262, Florence; the B.M. copy lacks the woodcut); the cut is reprinted in the later edition of 1568 with title *Canzone a ballo* (e.g. Metropolitan Museum, New York).[1]

The larger cut in the 1533 edition of the *Canzone a ballo* (P.K. 283 a),[2] in which the scene takes place before an archway on a squared pavement, and the young man in the foreground is on the right, instead of left ($6\frac{7}{8} \times 4\frac{3}{4}$ inches), and which contains the device of the printer Francesco di Jacopo della Spera, is based on the woodcut reproduced in fig. 314. Kristeller also describes a third and smaller version ($4\frac{1}{2} \times 3\frac{1}{8}$ inches) in an edition of 1557 (Corsini).

Carnival Scene (P.K. 284, within the *passe-partout* border described as No. 6, on p. 533; see frontispiece), in *Canzone per andare in Maschera per Carnesciale fatte da piu persone* (Lorenzo de' Medici and others) (Morgiani and Petri), n.d. (about 1493–97).

Group of Seven Men with a Dog, in Lorenzo de' Medici, *La Compagnia del Mantellacio*, n.pr., n.d. (P.K. 280 and P.K. fig. 18, Ferrara, private collection): same style as the preceding *Carnival Scene* and the *Dancing Girls* in the *Ballatette*.

The Murder of Duke Galeazzo Sforza, in *Lamento del Duca Galeazo Sforza* (B. Zucchetta), 1505 (P.K. 400 a and P.K. cut 63, Trivulzio).

---

[1] This edition was reproduced in facsimile (including facsimile of the woodcut) by Gamba, in 100 copies, at Milan 1812. The British Museum only possesses the reprint.

[2] Reproduced in Kristeller, *Italienische Buchdrucker- und Verlegerzeichen*, Strassburg 1893, pp. 18 and 19, No. 61.

Captive Youth, and a girl shooting at Cupid, in Luca Pulci, *Driadeo d'Amore*, n.pr., n.d. (P.K. 341, Oxford), and Tebaldeo da Ferrara and others, *Canzoni*, n.pr., n.d. (P.K. 411, and P.K. cut 171).

Fig. 314. Ring of Dancing Girls, from *Ballatette* by Lorenzo de' Medici,
Politiano and others, Florence.

and to illustrations in the following books:

Angelo Politiano, *La Giostra di Giuliano di Medici* (Tubini), n.d.
(P.K. 336 a, cuts from Pulci, *Morgante Maggiore*, 1500, and from
the *Epistoli e Evangelii*, as well as others done for the book).
Petrarca, *Trionfi*, printed for Pacini, 1499 (P.K. 328, Rome, Vitt.
Emman.). Facsimile, Rome 1891. The *Triumph of Death* appears

in one edition of Savonarola, *Predica dell' Arte del ben morire* (see
p. 550, footnote 1), and the *Triumph of Love* on the title of Frezzi,
Quadriregio, 1508.
Guerra e Conquesta di Granata (Morgiani), n.d.
La Schiatta de' Reali di Francia, n.pr., n.d. (P.K. 160).
La Caccia di Belfiore, n.pr., n.d. (P.K. 76 and P.K. cut 72), noted
by Kristeller for careless cutting, the mouth of the horseman on the
left being forgotten).
S. Bernardo, *Sermoni* (Morgiani), 1495 (P.K. 56).
Bernardino di Firenze, *Le Bellezze di Firenze* (Morgiani), n.d. (about
1496), (P.K. 53, and cut 1, a *View of Florence*).
Giuliano Dati, *Lettera delle Isole che ha trovato il Re di Spagna* (Mor-
giani), n.d. (about 1493–94) (P.K. 125).
Simone Sardini, *Cerbero* (Morgiani), n.d. (P.K. 372 a, a cut which
Kristeller describes as Sienese in style).

Bibliography

DELABORDE, H. La Gravure en Italie avant Marcantoine. Paris 1883.

LIPPMANN, Friedrich. Der italienische Holzschnitt im xv Jahrhundert. Berlin 1885.

VARNHAGEN, Hermann. Über eine Sammlung alter italienischer Drucke der Erlanger Uni-
versitätsbibliothek. Erlangen 1892.

KRISTELLER, Paul. Italienische Buchdrucker- und Verlegerzeichen. Strassburg 1893.

POLLARD, A. W. Italian Book Illustration, chiefly of the xv century. London 1894.

FUMAGALLI, G. Lexicon Typographicum Italiae. Dictionnaire géographique d'Italie pour servir
à l'histoire de l'imprimerie dans ce pays. Florence 1905.

OLSCHKI, Leo S. Le Livre en Italie à travers les siècles, démontré par une collection exposée à
Leipzig. Florence 1914.

PERRINS, C. W. Dyson. Catalogue of the Early Italian Printed Books in the Library of C. W. D. P.,
by A. W. Pollard. London 1914.

MARINIS, Tammaro de. Catalogue d'une collection d'anciens livres à figures italiens appartenant
à T. de M. Préface de Seymour de Ricci. Milan [1925].

ORCUTT, William Dana. The Book in Italy during the xv and xvi centuries, shown in facsimile
reproductions of the most famous printed volumes, collected under the auspices of the Italian
Ministry of Instruction. Introduction by Guido Biagi. Explanatory Text and Comment by
W. D. O. [on basis of Paris Exhibition of 1900]. London (printed Norwood, Mass.) 1928.

BERTIERI, Raffaello. Editori e stampatori Italiani del Quattrocento. Milan 1929.

HUSUNG, M. J. Die Drucker- und Verlegerzeichen Italiens im xvi Jahrhundert. Munich 1929.

CHAPTER VII

BOOK-ILLUSTRATION AND CONTEMPORARY SINGLE CUTS IN THE NETHERLANDS

Louvain—Utrecht—Culenborg

THE earliest known cut in books printed from movable type in the Netherlands is a small oval portrait of the printer JOHANN OF PADERBORN (JOHANN OF WESTPHALIA), used as his printer's mark, which first appeared in his edition of Justinian, *Institutiones*, Louvain, 21st November 1475 (CA. 1052, CN. v. 1, The Hague, fig. 315). It is an attractively cut profile head on dark ground, rather in the manner of a cameo. It appeared in several versions (Juchhoff 47-49) in various books issued by the same printer between 1475 and 1484, printed either in black or red. Another little profile portrait, that of CONRAD OF PADERBORN (CONRAD OF WESTPHALIA), even more delicate in workmanship, occurs as his printer's mark in his edition of Maneken (Carolus Virulus) *Epistolares Formulae*, Louvain 1st December 1476 (CA. 1202, CN. v. 6, Juchhoff 50, The Hague).

Fig. 315. Printer's mark and Portrait of Johann of Westphalia, 1475-84.

But these woodcuts are isolated in character and can hardly be compared with anything else of the period except certain decorative pieces such as the first mark of the printer Jan Veldener, which first appeared in the Role-

Fig. 316. Printer's mark of Jan Veldener, Louvain 1475.

winck, *Fasciculus Temporum*, issued at Louvain, 29th December 1475 (Juchhoff 46; fig. 316). There is a variant form in which the right-hand shield is blank, the name being sometimes omitted (e.g. in his *Epistelen en Evangelien*, Utrecht 1481, CA. 690; see Juchhoff 41 and 54). This, in its turn, is comparable in design with Gerard Leeuw's first mark, of two shields hanging from a branch (Juchhoff 30). The woodcut marks of the Netherlandish printers are above the average in interest, and several others will demand our attention in their place.

A few months later than Johann of Westphalia's printer's mark, appeared the first series of woodcut illustrations in a Netherlandish book, those in the *Fasciculus Temporum*, printed by Jan Veldener at Louvain, 29th December 1475 (CA. 1478, CN. v. 3).

In subjects these illustrations follow the pattern set by the Cologne edition of Arnold Ther Hoernen of 1474,[1] the *Christ blessing* (fig. 317) being drawn by a distinctly better hand than its original. This block is found in various other books of Veldener's press, such as the *Epistelen en Evangelien*, 1479 and 1481 (CA. 688 and 690), in the edition of 1479 above the printer's mark. Veldener's

Fig. 317. Christ Blessing, from Rolewinck, *Fasciculus Temporum*, Utrecht 1481.

second edition of the *Fasciculus Temporum*, printed at Utrecht 19th April 1481 (CA. 1479), contains additional cuts, such as the *Building of Rome* and the *Storming of a Town*, for the most part based on illustrations in that other compendium of universal history, the *Rudimentum Noviciorum* (Lübeck, Lucas Brandis, 1475, H. 4996). Of its independent cuts the most attractive is that of *St. Peter at the Gate of Heaven* (f. 76 b, reprod. Schretlen, pl. 40, B), a four-piece scroll border and large initial G (fig. 318).[2] The border and initial G also occur in his *Passionael*

Fig. 318. The Initial G, from Rolewinck, *Fasciculus Temporum*, Utrecht 1481.

of 12th September 1480 (CA. 1757, Oxford, Cambridge, The Hague).

Veldener's second printer's mark (Juchhoff 55), with blank shield sup-

---

[1] See p. 357.   [2] For another initial of the same style see p. 583, and cf. also p. 725.

ported by two lions, has a border in similar scroll-work (reprod. Holtrop, pl. 39 [29], 3). The style of decoration originated in Ulm, but has its nearest counterpart in a border used by Knoblochtzer, Strassburg, e.g. in his *Aesop* (S. 3021, H. 325). The *Passionael* (CA. 1757) also contains an interesting full-page cut illustrating the *Martyrdom of Various Saints* (CN. vi. 8).

A series of thirty-nine crudely cut Bible subjects, for the most part small uprights about $3\frac{1}{8} \times 2\frac{1}{4}$ inches, appeared in Jan Veldener's edition of the *Epistelen en Evangelien*, Utrecht, 19th April 1481 (CA. 690, CN. vi. 9). This edition also contains, on its last two leaves, fragments from the block-book *Speculum Humanae Salvationis*. Mention has already been made of the appearance of such fragments in printed books,[1] and I would here supplement my earlier reference by a list of the fragments and of the books in which they were printed:

I. SPECULUM HUMANAE SALVATIONIS. Its twofold blocks, divided into their two subjects, appear in:—

Epistelen en Evangelien, Utrecht (Veldener) 1481. CA. 690, CN. iii. E (two subjects only).

Speghel onser Behoudenisse, Culenborg (Veldener) 1483. CA. 1573, CN. iii. F (all the blocks, with twelve added subjects in the same style, i.e. 128 subjects in all).

Kruidboeck, Culenborg (Veldener) 1484. CA. 918, CN. iii. G (two subjects only).

II. BIBLIA PAUPERUM (Schreiber, ed. I). Forty-four pieces cut from the blocks appear in:—

Epistelen en Evangelien, Zwolle (Pieter van Os) 1487. CA. 697, CN. i. B (The Hague).

(*Note.*—Conway states that the fragments are from his ed. B = Sotheby II = Schreiber V. I have not examined The Hague copy of the *Epistelen*, but the blocks in later books printed by Pieter van Os in the British Museum are from Schreiber I, and so presumably would be those in the *Epistelen*, 1487.)

Among the numerous books printed by Pieter van Os at Zwolle between 1487 and 1500, in which the fragments occur, may be mentioned *Die Passie ende dat Liden ons Heren*, 1489, CA. 1163.

---

[1] See p. 213.

III. CANTICUM CANTICORUM (ed. I). The upper half of the first subject appears in:—

Rosetum Exercitiorum Spiritualium, Zwolle (Pieter van Os) 1494. CA. 1224, CN. ii. B.

Other fragments of a similar character, which probably represent a lost block-book of the Legend of the Holy Cross (Historia Sanctae Crucis), appeared in the Boec van den Houte, printed by J. Veldener at Culenborg, 6th March 1483 (CA. 940, CN. iv. B).[1]

From the presence of the fragments of the Speculum blocks at Utrecht, Bradshaw inferred that the Speculum block-book was originally printed at the same place. But considering the way in which printers moved from place to place, and borrowed blocks from other printers, such an inference is by no means certain, either in the case of the Speculum and Utrecht, or of the Biblia Pauperum and Canticum in relation to Zwolle. Even the addition of blocks in a similar style need not imply the same workshop, for a careful designer might easily imitate the earlier series.

The last illustrations issued by Veldener which I would mention are 150 cuts of plants in the Kruidboeck in Dietsche, printed at Culenborg, 1484 (CA. 918, CN. vi. 12 A), copied in reverse from the editio princeps, the Herbarius Latinus printed by Schoeffer at Mainz (S. 4203, H. 8444).[2] As the issues come within the same year, it looks as if some arrangement had been made by which Veldener was lent proofs to copy. Veldener also printed a Latin edition about a year later (CA. 916, CN. vi. 12 B).

Another of the earliest illustrated books issued at Utrecht, 30th March 1480, was Otto van Passau, Boeck des Gulden Throens, with a printer's mark of a palm-tree with two blank shields and Ǧ (the initial G with a cross)[3] (CA. 1342, CN. vi. 4, Holtrop, pls. 42-44 [40-42]). They are probably by the same designer or cutter who did the additional cuts in Veldener's second edition of the Fasciculus Temporum (1481) and his Epistelen en Evangelien of 1481, and are of little artistic interest. They are curious, however, for the economy by which various figures are fitted into different Gothic architectural borders. The illustrations are conversations between an Elder and a female figure, representing the Soul.

There are six varieties of Elder, five varieties of the Soul, and four

---

[1] For reproduction and notes see John Ashton and S. Baring Gould, The Legendary History of the Cross, London 1887.

[2] See pp. 348-352.

[3] Read by Campbell and Proctor 8861, incorrectly, as G.L. It is the same monogram as Juchhoff 56 and 57.

varieties of the border, in addition to the first illustration, on a single block, of *Elder and the Soul with Christ enthroned.* The whole series, in which nineteen combinations are made out of the single figures and borders, are reproduced by Holtrop.

GOUDA

Much more attractive is the series of 121 small woodcuts in the *Dyalogus Creaturarum* printed by GERARD LEEUW at Gouda, 3rd June 1480 (CA. 560,

Fig. 319. Initial S and border-pieces, from *Dyalogus Creaturarum*, Gouda 1480.

CN. viii. 2), and in various later editions in Latin and Dutch (*Twispraec der Creaturen*) printed by Leeuw at Gouda and Antwerp, and by Snellaert at Delft (1481–91).

The popularity of this book of fables is evidenced by the fact that as many as nine editions were printed in the Netherlands in these years, and a French edition, with copies of the original cuts, at Lyon in 1483.

The first page of the text (sig. a. 2) has a four-piece scroll border of the same character as Veldener's *Fasciculus Temporum* of 1481, and a handsome initial S on black ground (fig. 319), in addition to the cuts of the Sun, Moon and Clouds. It is an attractively printed book in Gothic type, in which the cuts of the fables are small oblongs about 2 × 4⅜ inches (nearly the width of the text). They are simply cut, for the most part in outline, with an occasional use of white on black (e.g. for the crow, sigg. f. 6, verso, f. 8, verso, and g. 3), and by no means lacking in verve and humour (fig. 320).

The relationship of this designer, or cutter, to the block-book tradition is seen even more clearly in his full-page cuts to the *Gesten van Romen* (*Gesta Romanorum*) first printed by Leeuw at Gouda, 30th April 1481 (CA. 826, CN. viii. 6 A, Paris). Only six of the series appeared in this first edition, nine were issued in the edition (*Gesten der Romeynen*) printed by Pieter van Os at Zwolle, 1484 (CA. 828, CN. viii. 6 B), and a tenth cut (with three of the others) in *Sielentrost*, Zwolle, P. van Os, 1485 (CA. 1547, CN. viii. 6 c). In their simplicity of design and cutting they are more reminiscent of the *Apocalypse* than the *Biblia Pauperum* and *Speculum*

Fig. 320. The Fowler, from *Dyalogus Creaturarum*, Gouda 1480.

block-books. The *Story of the Emperor Conrad*, which only appears in the two editions of the *Gesten van Romen*, is reproduced from the edition of 1484 (fig. 321).

Near in style again to the *Dyalogus* and *Gesta Romanorum* woodcuts are the four illustrations[1] to the *Vier Uterste*, Gouda (G. Leeuw) 1482 (CA. 1316, CN. viii. 4, Brussels, The Hague), which were also printed (probably earlier, 1481–82) by AREND DE KEYSERE at Audenarde (*Quatre Dernières Choses*, CA. 586, Brussels, Ghent); and another set of four in the *Historia Septem Sapientum Romae* (*Die Seven wise mannen van Romen*) printed at Gouda, first (undated) by the same printer who later issued the first edition of the *Chevalier Délibéré*, possibly Gotfridus de Os (CA. 952, CN. viii. 5 A, Haarlem),[2] and about 1482 by G. Leeuw (CA. 947, CN. viii. 5 B, Cambridge, Oxford). But both these sets are inferior in interest to the Gouda books before mentioned.

---

[1] *St. Peter at the Gate of Heaven* is reproduced by Holtrop, pl. 95 (98) b, and Delen, pl. xxx.
[2] See pp. 585, 588.

Conway arranged the Netherlandish woodcuts in sections under various woodcutters whom he called the 'First Gouda Woodcutter' (i.e. the author of the *Dyalogus*, etc.), 'Second Gouda Woodcutter' (the author of the *Devote Ghetiden*,[1] etc.) and by other similar local titles. I am not following these distinctions, except for occasional reference, as I feel that the foundations of one's knowledge are too insecure. In the first place, I would prefer to make distinctions by *designer* rather than by *cutter*, but the two factors are in such constant interplay—the same designer being interpreted by various cutters, and the identity of a designer being sometimes, perhaps, obscured by bad cutting—that I would, for the most part, avoid dogmatic distinctions.

Fig. 321. Story of the Emperor Conrad, from the *Gesten van Romen*, Gouda 1481.

Schretlen in his study of Dutch and Flemish woodcuts unites in single personalities two or more of Conway's 'sectional' woodcutters. Thus he regards the series of small cuts for a *Devote Ghetiden van den Leven ende Passie Ihesu Christi* (a book of devotions for various times and seasons, comparable to the French *Horae*),

---

[1] *Ghetiden* is the Dutch equivalent for *Horae* in the sense of Canonical Hours, and is used in relation to Hours of the Virgin, of the Holy Cross, of the Life and Passion of Christ, etc. Cf. pp. 566, 568, 581, 583 and 584.

which we are about to describe, as by the same artist as the *Dyalogus Creaturarum*, in the same way that he attempts to identify Conway's 'Third Gouda Woodcutter', the author of *Godevaerts van Boloen* and of the *Chevalier Délibéré*, with JACOB CORNELISZ.

Fig. 322. The Flight into Egypt, from the *Devote Ghetiden*, Antwerp, about 1484.

A series of sixty-eight small upright cuts, illustrating the Life of Christ, measuring about $4\frac{1}{4} \times 3\frac{1}{4}$ inches, first appeared complete in the *Devote Ghetiden van den Leven ende Passie Iesu Christi*, printed by Leeuw at Antwerp about 1484 (CA. 1115, CN. ix. 2 E, Leyden, Soc. de litt. néerl.; see fig. 322). Portions of the same series had appeared earlier in (*a*) *Liden ons Heren*, Gouda (Leeuw), 29th July 1482 (CA. 1156, CN. ix. 2 A, The Hague, Brussels); (*b*) *Lyden ons Heeren*, Haarlem (Bellaert), 10th December 1483 (CA. 1157, CN. ix. 2 C, Enschedè Sale, 374); and (*c*) *Epistelen en Evangelien*, Gouda (G. de Os), 23rd June 1484 (CA. 693, CN. ix. 2 D, Cambridge). And probably between (*a*) and (*b*) were issued the sheets with thirty-six of the cuts with Dutch verses (in Leeuw's type), preserved at Erlangen (CA. 746, CN. ix. 2 B).[1] Thereafter portions of the series appeared in a variety of books issued by Leeuw at Antwerp and certain other Netherlandish printers until the beginning of the XVI century.

The *Devote Ghetiden* (*getyden*) *van den Leven ende Passie Iesu Christi* is a rare form of devotional 'Hours', the regular *Ghetidenboeck* being the Hours of the Blessed Virgin. Its illustration is practically the same as would be

---

[1] Reproduced and described by M. Zucker, *Einzelformschnitte in der Kupferstichsammlung der kgl. Universitäts-Bibliothek Erlangen* (Einblattdrucke, herausgegeben von Paul Heitz), Strassburg 1913. See Schreiber, vol. i. 12, etc.

Fig. 323. Christ preaching from the Ship, and the Parable of the Sower, from Ludolphus, *Leven ons Heeren*, Antwerp 1487.

Fig. 324. The Disciples plucking the Ears of Corn, from Ludolphus, *Leven ons Heeren*, Antwerp 1487.

required for a Life of Christ, such as that of Ludolphus de Saxonia, and some fifty of the series appeared in Leeuw's edition of *Ludolphus*, issued in 1487, generally with two architectural side-pieces, or some other subject block added to make up the width of page. The series may have been originally done for a lost or unachieved *Devote Ghetiden* or even for a *Ludolphus*. That there is only one copy known of the 1484 *Devote Ghetiden* renders it quite possible that an earlier edition was completely lost. Or it may be that before the project for the *Devote Ghetiden* was complete, part of the series of blocks was used for works in which fewer blocks were required.

The subjects are related to Israhel van Meckenem's line-engravings, his *Smallest Passion Series*.[1] The designs must have been very popular at the period, as numerous examples appear in a variety of forms, in line-engraving

[1] See M. Geisberg, *Verzeichnis der Kupferstiche I. v. Meckenem*, Strassburg 1905, p. 3, and M. Lehrs, *Geschichte und kritischer Katalog*, ix. 62-120. Geisberg dates the Meckenem series about 1475-78. Described by Willshire, *Early German and Flemish Prints in the British*

Fig. 325. The Disciples plucking the Ears of Corn, from Ludolphus, *Leven ons Heeren*, Delft 1488.

and woodcut, in Germany and the Netherlands, from the *Biblia Pauperum* block-book downwards.[1]

In other Netherlandish woodcuts the same designs appear in a series by the Haarlem woodcutter who worked for Bellaert, in his *Epistelen en Evangelien*, 1486 (CA. 695, CN. xi. 9 A, The Hague), reprinted in Ludolphus, *Leven ons Heeren*, Zwolle (P. van Os) 1499 (CA. 1185, CN. xi. 9 B, The Hague, Cambridge), and in the Ludolphus, *Leven ons Heeren*, Delft (Snellaert) 1488 (CA. 1182, CN. xxi. 7).

In German books with woodcuts some of the same designs appear in the *Rudimentum Noviciorum*, Lübeck (Brandis) 1475 (S. 5159, H. 4996), and *Die Nye Ee und det Passional van Ihesus und Marien*, Lübeck (Brandis) 1478 (S. 3349, H. 4061).

Museum, vol. ii. p. 339, 16, under IA. of Zwolle, and Conway's discussion (*Woodcutters of the Netherlands*, p. 44) is based on this description. Lehrs refers Meckenem's designs back to the so-called 'Master of the Martyrdom of the 10,000 Christians' (L. iii. p. 358, 8-53), and these again largely to the Master E.S.

[1] See Geisberg, *Israhel van Meckenem, Anhang*, p. 279; Lehrs, *Geschichte und kritischer Katalog des deutschen . . . Kupferstichs im xv Jahrhundert*, iii. p. 358, No. 8, etc.

The whole subject is very complex, and there is no present solution in regard to the original designs for the series.

The style of cutting is very distinct from the illustration of the *Dyalogus Creaturarum* and its group. The outlines are clearly cut and angular; and there is a very regular scheme of shading in short parallel strokes, against the outlines as well as for inner shading. The cutter makes considerable use of white on black.

Characteristic work by the same designer and cutter is contained in the seven cuts in *Van den Seven Sacramenten*, Gouda (Leeuw) 1484 (CA. 1492, CN. ix. 4). A block of *Master and Pupil* is printed at the side of each subject, making it up to the breadth of the page.

ANTWERP

I would now consider the other woodcut illustrations in the Ludolphus, *Leven ons Heeren*, printed by Leeuw at Antwerp, 1487 (CA. 1181, CN. x. 6 A, 7 A, 8, xii. 3 A).

There are, in the first place, a considerable number of full-page and half-page cuts which Conway has described as by his 'First Antwerp Cutter' (CN. x. 6), many of them based on the subjects in the Cologne Bible. I incline to think that their designer and cutter is the same as the author of the *Devote Ghetiden*. Some of the full-page cuts are near in style to the line-engravings of Allart du Hameel, who worked at Bois-le-Duc, Louvain and Antwerp from 1478 till the early XVI century, particularly in his engravings of the *Brazen Serpent* (B. 1, Lehrs 1) and *Constantine the Great and the Vision of the Holy Cross* (P. 11, Lehrs 5). Among the nearest in this respect are *Christ preaching from the Ship (with the Parable of the Sower)* (fig. 323) and the *Feeding of the Five Thousand*.

Others, such as that of the *Disciples plucking the Ears of Corn* (fig. 324), are related in style of drawing to the cuts in the *Ludolphus*, printed by Snellaert at Delft in 1488 (CA. 1182, CN. xxi. 2; fig. 325).

Finally, there is another series of full-page and half-page cuts in the style of the designer and cutter who worked for Bellaert at Haarlem (CN. xii. 3), e.g. *Christ appearing to Three Holy Women* (fig. 326).

On the title-page is a small subject of the *Redeemer* ($5\frac{1}{8} \times 3\frac{1}{4}$ inches), which is replaced by a larger and better cut of different design in Leeuw's edition of 1488 (CA. 1182). The latter is reprinted in the Zwolle (Pieter van Os) edition of 1495 (CA. 1184) ($7\frac{1}{8} \times 5$ inches, Schretlen, pl. 45, B).

Delft

The Delft issue of Ludolphus, *Leven ons Heeren* (CA. 1182, CN. xxi.
12, The Hague, Oxford, Cambridge), was published by Snellaert in 1488,
i.e. the year after Leeuw's Antwerp edition. The subjects largely correspond, and it is natural on that account to assume, with Conway, that
Snellaert's cuts are copied from these of Leeuw, but Schretlen estimates the
quality of the Delft cuts more highly, and thinks they are the originals,
though not published till after the Antwerp edition. The woodcuts in the

Fig. 326. Christ appearing to Three Holy Women, from Ludolphus, *Leven ons Heeren*,
Antwerp 1487.

Delft edition are fairly uniform in style throughout, with very angular
cutting, the hair being represented in curious strands. In general, I would
say of the Antwerp edition that the drawing was more correct and the
cutting more precise, though the Delft cuts are sometimes even more
spirited. It may, I think, be accepted that the Delft subjects corresponding
with the *Devote Ghetiden* are copied from that series; it is more difficult
to be certain in the case of other subjects, where the Antwerp edition has
something of the Delft cutter's style (e.g. in the *Disciples plucking the Ears*

of Corn; fig. 324). Here I am more inclined to regard the Delft designer as the inspirer (fig. 325). But the whole subject of these Ludolphus editions is full of difficulty, as well as interest, and I cannot pretend to have

mastered its problems.

The designer of the Delft *Ludolphus* and of numerous other woodcuts printed at Delft from about 1483 by JACOB VAN DER MEER, CHRISTIAN SNELLAERT and HENRIK ECKERT of Homburg (who worked after 1500 at Antwerp), Conway's 'Second Delft Cutter', is a very distinct mannerist, and has been conjecturally identified

Fig. 327. Printer's mark of Christian Snellaert, Delft.

by Dr. Max Friedländer with the painter called the 'Master of the Virgo inter Virgines'.[1]

The earliest book in which his work is recognised is the *Historie van die Seven Weise Mannen*, Delft (Meer), 13th January 1483 (CA. 953, CN. xxi. 2, Utrecht), with cuts based on Leeuw's Gouda edition of 1482 (CA. 947, CN. viii. 5 B, Oxford, Cambridge).

More interesting are the thirteen small cuts (about $3 \times 2\frac{1}{4}$ inches, within double border-lines), with single figures illustrating the game of chess, in Jac. de Cessolis, *Scaecspul*, printed by J. van der Meer, 14th February 1483 (CA. 421, CN. xxi. 3; fig. 328). They are cut with greater regularity and precision than are most of the illustrations in the Delft *Ludolphus*, as is also the *King and Ten Counsellors* on the first page of Jean Boutillier, *Somme Rurael*, printed by Van der Meer, 19th August 1483 (CA. 361, CN. xxi. 4), on which also appears an elaborate woodcut initial S on black ground.

---

[1] See Max J. Friedländer, *Altniederländische Malerei*, v., Berlin 1927, p. 65.

On 25th March 1486 appeared for the first time the fifty-eight small upright Bible illustrations (about 4 × 3¼ inches), based in part on the Gouda and Antwerp *Devote Ghetiden* series, in the *Vier Uterste* (Delft, Meer, CA. 1319, CN. xxi. 7 A, The Hague). They were reprinted in the same year, 29th November, in Van der Meer's *Epistelen en Evangelien* (CA. 696, CN. xxi. 7 B, The Hague), in the *Ludolphus* of 1488, already described, and in several other editions of the Epistles and Gospels, *Passionael, Ludolphus,* etc., by Van der Meer and Snellaert at Delft, and by Eckert at Delft and Antwerp. Further cuts of a similar character appeared in the *Passionael,* printed by Van der Meer, 1st March 1487 (CA. 1763, CN. xxi. 9, The Hague, Cambridge), and these also occur in the 1488 *Ludolphus,* and in several later *Passionael* and other books printed by Snellaert and Eckert at Delft and Antwerp, while other blocks of the same type were cut for the first time for Snellaert's *Passionael* of 1489 (CA. 1765, CN. xxi. 15).

Fig. 328. The Notary, from Cessolis, *Scaecspul,* Delft 1483.

A series of copies from the *Ars Moriendi* block-book were printed by Snellaert in 1488 (*Sterfboeck;* CA. 1619, CN. xxi. 14), and occasional illustrations by the same Delft designer, or directly inspired by him, appeared in various Delft books till nearly the end of the century, e.g. a *Confession* in *Devotus Libellus de Modo Confitendi,* Snellaert, 14th February 1494 (not in CA.), a *Monk (St. Bernard) giving instruction* (CN. xxi. 29), e.g. in *Expositio Hymnorum,* 1496 (CA. 722), and a large *Christ on the Cross with the Virgin and St. John* in the *Missale Trajectense,* Snellaert, about 1495 (CA. 1262, CN. xxi. 30, The Hague).

The illustrations in Eckert's edition of the *Fables of Aesop* (1498, CA. 29, CN. xxi. 31) are carelessly cut copies from the series first issued at Ulm by Johann Zainer about 1476–77,[1] with eight separate side-pieces (figures and trees) used to fit the subjects to the width of the page. If the same designer as before is responsible for this series, his work has considerably suffered by the poor cutting of the blocks.

[1] See p. 306.

The only cuts in Delft of any interest which preceded the work of the presumed 'Virgo inter Virgines' Master are three illustrations in Johannes Gerson, *Boec van den gheboden Gods*, printed by Van der Meer, 1482 (CA. 802, CN. xx. 2, The Hague, Cambridge), representing *Instruction*, *Confession* and *Absolution* (reproduced, Schretlen, pl. 54 a and b). They are, in strong outline with little shading, nearer in style to the *Dialogus* designer.

HAARLEM

Haarlem was another centre of interest in the development of Dutch book-illustration, and the designer who worked for the printer Jacob Bellaert certainly manifested a style nearer than other book-illustrators in the Netherlands to the tradition of the *Biblia Pauperum*, *Canticum Canticorum* and *Speculum* block-books.

We have already spoken of the tradition surrounding the name of Laurens Janszoon Coster of Haarlem in the chapter on the Block-books,[1] and discussed the later claim made for him in regard to the discovery of printing. The relation in style of early Haarlem book-illustration to the three block-books mentioned, at least gives some support to the theory that Coster's part in that development was in the making of some of these block-books, and that craftsmen of his school carried on his traditions in ordinary book-illustration. Of Coster the printer, himself, nothing is known in documents, unless he be the Laurens Jansz Coster recorded to have left Haarlem in 1483.

We have already noted an edition of the *Devote Ghetiden* cuts in a *Lijden ons Heeren* printed by JACOB BELLAERT at Haarlem in 1483,[2] but here the printer is using blocks which were lent him from another source. The first of his books which contained cuts by the Haarlem designer who follows so closely in the tradition of the *Speculum* and allied block-books is Jacobus de Theramo, *Der Sonderen Troest* (*Belial*), issued on 15th February 1484 (C.A. 1656, CN. xi. 2). The book includes a full-page cut illustrating the *Fall of the Angels and Man*, *Noah's Ark*, *The Destruction of Pharaoh's Host and The Baptism of Christ* (fig. 329), six half-page oblong cuts, eight quarter-page upright cuts, and various narrow side-pieces to make up the uprights to the breadth of the page.

Schretlen very rightly compares the designer's style with the miniatures in the MS. Dutch Bible of 1474 in the British Museum,[3] noting a close

---

[1] See pp. 208, 209.   [2] See p. 566.

[3] Add. MS. 16951 (the Books of Genesis, Exodus, Leviticus, Numbers, Deuteronomy,

relation in detail between the full-page woodcut and the *Destruction of Pharaoh's Host* in the Bible (see Schretlen, Appendix, pl. E). A considerable number of the composite subjects show Christ or Solomon as Judge, in the centre, and side-pieces of the oppos-ing pleaders, Belial and others. Bel-laert's printer's mark, with its four-piece border, which occurs in this and other books, is prob-ably by the same designer and cutter (Juchhoff 37; fig. 330, without the border which oc-curs in fig. 332). A few of the blocks also appear in *Die Vier Uterste* (Bellaert, November 1484, CA. 1318), and in certain other borders issued by Bellaert and other printers in the Netherlands.

Fig. 329. The Early History of Man and the Baptism of Christ, from Jacobus di Theramo, *Der Sonderen Troest*, Haarlem 1484.

Cuts of very similar character, as well as some attract-ive illustrations of natural history sub-jects and a plate of roundels of the months, occur in Bartholomaeus Anglicus, *Boeck van den Proprieteyten der*

Joshua, Judges and Ruth), written by Hugo Gerritsz at Noordwÿk, 1473–74. A. W. Byvanck and G. J. Hoogewerf, *Noord-Nederlandsche Miniaturen*, 1921, pl. 98; Schretlen, Appendix, pls. E-I.

Dingen, 24th December 1485 (CA. 258, CN. xi. 8; fig. 331), and four slight cuts in Bellaert's edition of Otto van Passau, *Boeck des Gulden Throens*, 1484 (CA. 1343, CN. xi. 4). But more individual and varied in

character are the illustrations in the two medieval romances,[1] the *Historie van Jason* of about 1485 (CA. 1092, CN. xi. 6) and the *Historie van Troyen*, 1485 (CA. 1095, CN. xi. 7), of which the only impressions to which I can refer are in the Bibliothèque Nationale, Paris. A full-page frontispiece of the *Author presenting his book to Philip the Good*, within the same border with which Bellaert surrounded his printer's mark (fig. 332),[2] and twenty half-page oblong cuts appeared in both books, and the condition of the blocks shows that the undated *Jason* is the earlier work. Then twenty-five new half-page cuts in the same form first appeared in the *Historie van Troyen*. The designs are very spirited, and here and there show a good decorative sense, as in the occasional use of white on black for the grass ground.

Fig. 330. Printer's mark of Jacob Bellaert, Haarlem.

The last two books with woodcuts by the same hand, issued by Bellaert at Haarlem, are Pierre Michault, *Doctrinael des Tyts* (CA. 1254, CN. xi. 11, The Hague), and the *Boeck vanden Pelgherijm* (CA. 1376, CN. xi. 12), Brussels, Berlin Print Room), both printed in 1486. Earlier in the same year Bellaert had issued the series of scriptural cuts in his *Epistelen en Evangelien*, to which we have already referred.[3]

The best work of the Haarlem designer, who has a natural tendency to

[1] First issued in the French of Raoul Le Fèvre, the English translation of William Caxton by Colard Mansion and Caxton at Bruges, about 1474–76.

[2] The frontispiece of the *Author presenting his book* appeared without the border-pieces in Pierre Michault, *Doctrinael des Tyts*, printed by Bellaert, 1486 (CA. 1254), and in *Sydrac*, printed by Hugo Janszoen of Woerden, at Leyden, 1495.

[3] See p. 569.

Fig. 331. The Birds, from Bartholomaeus Anglicus, *Boeck van den Proprieteyten der Dingen*,
Haarlem 1485.

anecdote, is full of life and spirit, and the interest in landscape and architecture is characteristic of the Dutch art of the period. The cutting is not very precise, but it is in harmony with the naturalistic vein of the Dutchman's design.

Fig. 332. The Author presenting his book to Philip the Good, from the *Historie van Jason*, Haarlem, about 1485.

No books were issued by Bellaert after 1486, and his designer (whether identical with the cutter or not) probably migrated to Antwerp, for a considerable number of the illustrations in books printed by Gerard Leeuw, up to his death in 1493, and by other Antwerp printers for a few years later, are in the same style, though of varying quality.

The blocks done for Bellaert were scattered, and used by Leeuw at Antwerp, and by a variety of other Netherlandish printers. Even his printer's mark, with its original borders, reappeared without revision in the *Sydrac* (*Schoone Historie gheheeten Sydrac*), printed at Leyden in 1495, and attributed by Proctor to the printer HUGO JANSZOEN of Woerden (CA. 981). The *Author presenting his book*, and the *Creation and Fall of the Angels* in *Sydrac*, are likewise Bellaert's blocks, the former from the *Historie van Jason* of about 1486, the latter from Glanville, *Proprieteyten der Dingen* of 1485.

ANTWERP (*continued*)

The illustrations in the *Histoire de Paris et de Vienne* issued by G. Leeuw, 15th May 1487 (CA. 941, CN. xii. 1), and four days later in Dutch, *Historie van Parijs ende Vienna* (CA. 942), of which the only copies known to me are in the Bibliothèque Nationale, Paris, are in just the same style and form as the *Jason* and *Troy* cuts (see fig. 333). They were probably done at Haarlem, and might have been originally issued there, but there is no trace of an edition earlier than 1487.

We have already alluded to a section of the cuts in the Leeuw's *Ludolphus* of 3rd November 1487 as in the same style (CA. 1181, CN. xii. 3; fig. 326),[1] and the twelve illustrations in the same printer's *Hoofkyn der Devotien*, of 28th November 1487 (CA. 985, CN. xii. 4, The Hague, Cambridge), are also by the same designer.

Fig. 333. Frontispiece to the *Historie van Paris ende Vienne*, Antwerp 1487.

The same hand again appears in the *Historie van die seven wise mannen van Romen*, issued by Claes Leeuw in 1488 (CA. 954, CN. xii. 9), and by Gerard Leeuw in a Latin edition under the title *Historia Calumniae Novercalis*, 6th November 1490 (CA. 950). In the interval the blocks had been lent to Johann Koelhoff at Cologne, who printed an edition earlier in 1490.[2] The cutting is rather heavier than most of the cuts printed by Bellaert at Haarlem, so that I incline to think that Bellaert's designer continued to work for both Claes and Gerard Leeuw, but not the same cutter.

[1] See p. 570.   [2] See p. 362.

There are numerous little cuts of a similar character issued by Gerard Leeuw in various books of devotion, the most attractive being perhaps the *Van die gheestelike kintscheyt Ihesu*, 1488 (CA. 1074, CN. xii. 6 A), and

the *Corona Mystica Beatae Virginis Mariae*, 1492 (CA. 997, CN. xii. 19).

The same designer was probably also responsible for the woodcut of the *Arms of England supported by Angels* on the title-page of the *Cronycles of the Londe of Englond*, printed by Gerard Leeuw, 1493 (CA. 511, CN. xii. 20), framed within three parts of Bellaert's four-piece border (seen in fig. 332).

The woodcuts in Leeuw's edition of Aesop's *Fables*, 1486 (CA. 26, CN. xv.), are copies from the cuts in the Ulm edition of Johann Zainer,[1] and not, as described by Conway, the original German blocks. The series which appear in the Aesop printed by Eckert at Delft in 1498 were probably based on those in Leeuw's edition.

Gerard Leeuw used three printer's marks, all showing the Castle of Antwerp (Juchhoff 3-5), and the best of these is here reproduced (fig. 334; Juchhoff 3).[2] Other attractive devices used by Antwerp printers are those of GOVAERT BAC (Juchhoff 6-12, all but one showing a bird-cage), ROELANT VAN DEN DORPE (Juchhoff 13, Knight Roland), and MATHIAS GOES (*Wild man with Shield of Brabant*, Juchhoff 1, and a *Three-masted Ship*, Juchhoff 2; fig. 335). The three-masted ship is of a similar type to the ship engraved on copper by the anonymous Master W✣ (Lehrs, 1895, No. 30, and *Kritischer Katalog*, No. 41).

---

[1] See p. 306.

[2] The same block was used by later printers at Antwerp, Mathias Goes and Thierry Martens.

Mathias Goes also used an attractive series of woodcut initials (see Holtrop, pl. 100 [47] and fig. 336).

Among other Antwerp cuts I would mention the *Master and Five Pupils* (e.g. in *Cato Moralisatus*, 1485, CA. 406, CN. x. 3, and in Petrus Hispanus, *Logicalia*, 1486, CA. 1394, CN. x. 3, both printed by Gerard Leeuw), and a lengthy series illustrating the *Historie van Meluzine*, printed by Gerard Leeuw, 1491 (CA. 975, CN. x. 11, Brussels), all somewhat similar in style to the *Devote Ghetiden* series.

Another lengthy and interesting series of cuts was issued by Rolant van den Dorpe in the *Cronyke van Brabant* of 1497 (CA. 508, CN. xxxvii. 1, Oxford, Cambridge, The Hague), and effective designs are often made of the battle scenes with their spears and standards.

A certain number of cuts in the French style (if not actually French blocks) appeared in various small books of devotion, chiefly issued by Gerard Leeuw and ADRIAEN

Fig. 335. Printer's mark of Mathias Goes, Antwerp.

VAN LIESVELT at Antwerp. The *Duytsche Ghetiden*[1] printed by Leeuw, 16th August 1491 (B.M. IA. 49836, cf. CN. xvi. 1 A), is the earliest example to which I can refer, the whole text being printed like the French *Horae*, within four-piece borders, with occasional subjects cut in the text (fig. 337). Very similar is the *Horarium Trajectense* (Utrecht Hours of the

---

[1] This is the complete title on the first page, but the colophon expands its connotation: *Hier in desen boeck sal men vinden die getijden van onser vrouwen ende van den heylighe cruce, Een oracie van den heylighen gheest. Die vii psalmen. Die Vigilie met ix lessen. Die xv pater nr. metten ghebeden van der passie ons heeren* [etc.].

Fig. 336. Initial S, from St. Augustine, *De Virtute Psalmorum*, Antwerp, n.d.

Virgin) printed by Liesvelt, 1495 (CA. 990, CN. xvi. 11), which contains some of the cuts, but the borders are from a different set of blocks. The borders of both books are comparable in their alternate spaces of black and white ground with a set of cuts in the *Horae* manner in the Lyon edition of the *Mer der Hystoires*, 1491.[1]

Before leaving Antwerp I would mention a series of fifty woodcuts illustrating the *Life and Passion of Christ* which were printed at Antwerp by Hendrik Eckert of Homburg, in editions of 1500, 1503 and 1510.[2] Twenty cuts of the series have been described, on account of their two owners, as the Delbecq-Schreiber Passion (see fig. 338). These twenty impressions had been coloured and mounted in a manuscript book of devotion, and Schreiber conjecturally dates them about 1480 (S. 148, etc., now in the Bibliothèque Royale, Brussels). There are also copies of the same series at Linz and Vienna.[3] The subjects derive chiefly from the cuts of the block-book *Speculum Humanae Salvationis*, but in certain subjects they are nearer in detail to the *Devote Ghetiden* series described above.[4] Unless one could depend on more definite proof in regard to the date of the MS. to which the Delbecq-Schreiber impressions belonged, I should be more inclined to date the blocks nearer 1490 than 1480.

ZWOLLE

I have already referred to the printer PIETER VAN OS of Zwolle for his reprints from fragments of block-books, and from blocks issued earlier by Bellaert and Leeuw. He also issued copies of the *Ars Moriendi* block-book in his *Sterfboeck* printed in 1488 and 1491 (CA. 1620, 1621, CN. xvii. 7). Among work for which he was originally responsible, the *Vision of St. Bernard*, which appeared in S. Bernardus, *Sermones*, Zwolle, edd. 1484–85 and 1495 (CA. 275, 276, CN. xvii. 2; fig. 339), is the most interesting

---

[1] See p. 613.

[2] The British Museum has them in *De Leven ons heeren*, 1510.

[3] See W. Molsdorf, *Die niederländische Holzschnitt-Passion Delbecq-Schreiber*, Einbl., Strassburg 1908; G. Gugenbauer, ditto, II. Teil, Einbl., Strassburg 1913; W. L. Schreiber, Sale Catalogue, Vienna 1909, No. 65; W. L. Schreiber, *Manuel*, No. 14 a, etc., No. 148, etc.

[4] See p. 566.

and one of the best Dutch woodcuts of the period.[1] The printer's mark of an *Angel kneeling in a niche holding the shield of Zwolle* (Juchhoff 60 and 61), which occurs in the edition of 1484–85, is certainly by the same hand. Another full-page cut which occurs in the issue of 1495, the *Annunciation*, is by another hand and of harder and more angular design. It appeared earlier in the *Vaderboeck* of 1490 (CA. 938, CN. xviii. 3, The Hague, Brussels, Cambridge, Darmstadt).

A head-piece representing *Beehives and Bees* in Thomas Cantipratanus, *Der Bien boeck*, printed by Pieter van Os, 1488 (CA. 1658, CN. xvii. 6; fig. 340), is an attractive design, in which the white and black line is well combined by the cutter. Mention should also be

Fig. 337. The Annunciation, from the *Duytsche Ghetiden*, Antwerp 1491.

made of a large woodcut capital H (102 × 105 mm.) which appeared in his *Passionael* of 1490 (CA. 1766, Holtrop, pl. 92 [83]) in the style of the G used by Veldener in his *Fasciculus Temporum*, 1481, though slightly larger.[2]

DEVENTER

Little work of importance was produced at Deventer. Most of the books printed by RICHARDUS PAFRAET and JACOBUS OF BREDA were small, and few contained cuts.

Of woodcuts in Pafraet's book I would mention a *Master with five pupils*

---

[1] Variants of the subject are found in two dotted prints of the period, S. 2565 (Nuremberg) and 2565 a (Breslau). Cf. Dodgson, *Catalogue of Early German and Flemish Woodcuts in the British Museum*, i. p. 234.   [2] See p. 560.

(CN. xxviii. 13),[1] which occurs in many of his books (e.g. in *Gemmula Vocabulorum*, 1487, CA. 792), a *Master and Youth standing* (CN. xxviii. 16), e.g. in Albertus de Eybe, *Boeck van den Echten Staete*, about 1493 (CA. 724), and his two devices representing *St. Lebuin* (Juchhoff 27 and 28).

Fig. 338. Christ before Pilate, from the so-called Delbecq-Schreiber Passion, Antwerp 1500.

A cut on a black ground, with the *Sacred Monogram and the Signs of the Evangelists in roundels*, is found in certain of his books, e.g. Baptista (Spagnuolo) Mantuanus, *Carmen in praeconium Rob. Severinatis*, 1495 (CA. 239), and was also issued by Jacobus of Breda, e.g. in Alanus, *Doctrinale*, 1494 (CA. 56, Juchhoff 29). Juchhoff describes it as Jacobus of Breda's device, but it may be no more than a frontispiece cut. There are two other blocks of the same design, one, with the scroll of the S cutting the lower margin, and more crudely cut than Pafraet's block, used by Pieter van Os at Zwolle, e.g. in Prudentius, *Psychomachia*, n.d. (CA. 1458), and the other used by GOVAERT BAC at Antwerp, in which the eagle is on the right (in the two others it is on the left), and placed by Juchhoff among his printer's marks (10).

LEYDEN

HUGO JANSZOEN of Woerden, printer at Leyden, was one of the printers who became possessed of some of Bellaert's old blocks, and he even used Bellaert's printer's mark in its original form.[2]

Apart from this he chiefly deserves mention for his small books of devotion, though they are of less interest than those printed by Gerard Leeuw and Liesvelt at Antwerp, the blocks being for the most part cut in a hard manner. Examples of such books are the *Ghetyden van onser lieuer vrouwen*, 1495 (CA. 838, CN. xxix. 1), Bernardus, *Onser lieuer vrouwen Souter*, n.d. (C.A. 279, CN. xxx. 1 E), *Dat Leven ons liefs heren*, 1498

---

[1] Similar in general design (master on throne and the pupils grouped in lower foreground) to the cut issued by G. Leeuw (see p. 581), but the master is reading from a book, while in the latter he holds a birch. [2] See pp. 575, 576.

(CA. 1111, CN. xxx. 1 A), and *Dat Leven onser lieuer vrouwen*, 1500 (CA. 1122, CN. xxx. 1 G). A cut of the *Annunciation* which appears in the first three of these books is in the Haarlem style, even if it did not come from Bellaert (CN. xiv. 2).

Gouda (*continued*)

We have already considered the earliest woodcuts printed at Gouda.[1] We now return to the study of books printed at the same place under the

Fig. 339. The Vision of St. Bernard, from S. Bernardus, *Sermones*, Zwolle 1484–85.

names and initials, GOTFRIDUS DE OS, GOVAERT VAN GHEMEN and G.D., who, according to Holtrop, are possibly one and the same person. Govaert van Ghemen also printed at Leyden about 1490,[2] and from 1493 until 1510 at Copenhagen, spelling his name Gotfridus af Ghemen.

[1] See p. 563.

[2] See CA. 1256, Juchhoff 44. The printer's mark copied by the *Collacie Broeders*, Gouda 1496 (CA. 36).

Fig. 340. Head-piece, from Cantipratanus, *Der Bien boeck*, Zwolle 1488.

Fig. 341. Initial A, Gotfridus de Os, Gouda.

The only book known to me issued with the name of the printer Gotfridus de Os is the *Quintupertitum Opus Grammaticale*, 1486 (CA. 1331, CN. xxv. 3, Cambridge). It contains a cut of *Master and three Pupils*, and a good series of initials on black ground, several with grotesque faces (Holtrop, pl. 72 [111] and fig. 341). They were used later by Wynkyn de Worde in England.[1] They resemble but are slightly larger than a series used by Gerard Leeuw at Antwerp about the same period (e.g. in his *Ludolphus* of 1487, see Holtrop, pl. 104 [59]). The *Master and Pupils* cut is certainly by the same hand as the series in the *Historie hertoghe Godevaerts van Boloen*, about 1485–86 (CA. 968, CN. xxv. 1), issued with the printer's mark of an Elephant and Castle, the letters G.D., and the arms of the Archduke Maximilian and the town of Gouda (Juchhoff 35, Holtrop, pl. 77 [125], CN. xxv. 2).

Most interesting is the first cut, showing *Pope Urban II. preaching the First Crusade at Clermont*. The printer's mark is also by the same hand, and one of the most attractive Dutch blocks (fig. 342). Both are thoroughly naturalistic works and must have been originally based on the life. Holtrop refers to a record in the *Cronycke van Hollandt* printed by J. Seversoen, 1517, under the year 1484, of 'a living elephant conducted round Holland from town to town, to the great profit of its master, and drowned near Muiden when embarking for Utrecht'. Holtrop thinks this event offers a *terminus a quo* for the dating of both the *Godevaert van Boloen* and the *Chevalier Délibéré*.

Another block of the same mark and probably by the same cutter, in which the elephant walks to the left, appears in the first edition

[1] See p. 725.

of the *Chevalier Délibéré* (Juchhoff 34, Holtrop, pl. 75 [118], CN. xxv. 7).

The *Chevalier Délibéré*, by Olivier de la Marche, is one of the most important illustrated books of the period. It is an alle-
gorical romance in verse, in which the author, or actor (*l'acteur*), recounts the adventures of the autumn of his life, how *Thought* tells him he must meet the Knights *Accident* and *Weakness* in the Forest of Fate; his encounter with *Hutin*, one of their retainers; his retreat to the abode of the Hermit *Un-
derstanding*; his en-
counter with *Age*, his temptation near the *Palace of Love*; his welcome at the *Manor of Good Hap* by the Lady *Fresh Memory*; his attend-
ance with her at the lists where Duke Philip and Duke Charles of Burgundy

Fig. 342. Mark of the Printer G.D. (Gotfridus de Os?), Gouda.

are overcome by *Accident*; his return to the Hermit *Understanding*, and his preparation for death.

Olivier de la Marche (1425–1502) was a faithful servant of the House of Burgundy; witnessed the death of Charles the Bold, and was himself taken prisoner at the Battle of Nancy, 1477; and later served both Mary of Burgundy and her consort Maximilian as *premier maître d'hôtel.*

The first edition of the *Chevalier Délibéré*, issued in Holland, was printed at Gouda between 1486 and 1490 with the printer's mark of the *Elephant and Castle* and letters G.D. (Juchhoff 34), and it is therein stated that the treatise was completed in April 1483 (CA. 1083, CN. xxv. 6, Baron Edmond de Rothschild, from the Ganay and Davillier Collections).[1] The poem and its sixteen full-page cuts were reprinted at Schiedam, about 1498–1500 (CA. 1084),[2] certainly after the *Vita Lijdwine* of 1498, where the same printer's mark is in earlier impression. The series of cuts also appeared in *Den Camp van der Doot*, issued at Schiedam in 1503. Two of the blocks were reprinted in the *Vaderboeck*, by Seversoen, Leyden 1511, and finally cut up into sections in Seversoen's *Cronycke van Hollandt*, 1517.

One of the MSS. of the poem (Bibliothèque Nationale, MS. français, 1606) gives the author's directions for its illustration, including both design and colour. These directions are closely followed in the only known copy of the first Gouda edition, in the library of Baron Edmond de Rothschild, Paris, in which the cuts are coloured. I cannot find that any of the contemporary illuminated MSS. (of which a list is given by Picot and Stein),[3] contain designs corresponding to the woodcut series in either the Dutch or French editions.

The designs of the Gouda woodcuts are the work of an artist (probably a painter) of real merit. Dr. Friedländer thinks that they belong to the local school, probably by some painter in the following of Geertgen of Haarlem, and compares the style of a picture of the *Disciples of St. John the Baptist and*

---

[1] The earliest editions printed in France are 8th August 1488 and 1493 (Cl. ii. 221), so that the Gouda issue might be the *editio princeps*. The cuts in the first two Paris editions are entirely different designs from the Gouda edition. For the work and its various editions see E. Picot and H. Stein, *Recueil des pièces historiques imprimées sous le règne de Louis XI.*, Paris (Société des Bibliophiles François) 1923, p. 305. The work must have been very popular in the XVI century, for in addition to the various French editions there were two Spanish versions printed at Antwerp in 1555, and another at Salamanca in 1560 (*El Cavallero determinado*). The Spanish version of Hernando de Acuna was translated into English by Lewis Lewkenor and issued under the title *The Resolved Gentleman*, London 1594.

[2] An edition known in imperfect copies at the Bibliothèque Nationale and the Bibliothèque de l'Arsenal, Paris, and in the Musée Plantin, Antwerp. See the reprint and facsimile of woodcuts for this edition (based on the Paris copies) with preface by F. Lippmann, issued by the Bibliographical Society, London 1898. Above the printer's mark on the last page is an excellent *Memento Mori* cut, the *Three Skulls* (CN. xxxii. 7).

[3] E.g. in the Musée Condé, Chantilly, and Fitzwilliam Museum, Cambridge.

Fig. 343. Combat between the Actor and Age, from Olivier de la Marche, *Chevalier Délibéré*, Gouda, about 1486–90.

of Christ in the J. G. Johnson Collection, Philadelphia.[1] It seems almost certain that the edition was done under the direction of the author himself, and, apart from such comparison, we might have expected that he would have

turned to some artist of the Southern Netherlands, and in some respects I feel a nearer relation in these designs to French art than in any other Dutch woodcuts. On the other hand, the cutter is more likely to have been a local craftsman, and was probably the same who worked on other books printed by Gotfridus de Os (and his doubles).

Fig. 344. St. Lydwina's Fall on the Ice, from Brugman, *Vita Lijdwine*, Schiedam 1498.

Schretlen believes that these designs are the early work of Jacob Cornelisz, but the evidence seems to me insufficient to support the conjecture.

One of the nearest relations in style to the *Chevalier Délibéré* may be seen in the woodcuts of *Les Neuf Preux* at Hamburg, of which only two of the three blocks are preserved (S. 1948, and vol. vi., 1893, pl. xvi a). Apart from the same large qualities of design, there is resemblance in details of technical method, such as the perpendicular shading of the legs.

SCHIEDAM

Allusion has already been made to the *Vita Lijdwine*, by Johannes Brugman, printed at Schiedam, 1498 (CA. 383, CN. xxxii. 5), as it bears the same printer's mark as the second edition of the *Chevalier Délibéré* (Juchhoff 53). In the *Vita Lijdwine* the mark bears the imprint *Schiedam in Hollandia* in type; in the *Chevalier Délibéré* there are further breaks in the woodcut border-lines and the imprint reads *Schiedam in Hollant*. Most of the cuts are half-page oblongs, about 3 × 3⅝ inches, and the subject of

---

[1] Max J. Friedländer, *Altniederländische Malerei*, v., Berlin 1927, p. 61, No. 37, pl. xxv.

S. Lydwina's Fall on the Ice (fig. 344) shows a Dutch designer with the gift for simple representation from daily life so characteristic of later Dutch art. Both designer and cutter might be the same as the author of the cuts in the *Historie her-toghe Godevaerts van Boloen*.[1]

SCHOONHOVEN

Near to the *Vita Lijdwine* in type of work are certain cuts in devotional books printed by the Augustinian Canons of St. Michael, near Schoonhoven, of which copies are very rare outside Holland (there are a few in the University Library, Cambridge). The *Virgin and Child in Glory* in the *Gheti-denboec* of 1498 (CA. 842, CN. xxxii. 1, Cambridge) and the

Fig. 345. Pyramus and Thisbe, from Ovid, *Metamorphoses*, Bruges 1484.

St. Augustine in the *Breviarium Windesemense* of 1499 (CA. 368, 369, CN. xxxii. 2, The Hague) may be noted.

A *Liber Horarum* of 10th March 1500 (CA. 988), one of the few Schoonhoven books in the British Museum, contains an attractive little cut of the *Annunciation* (84 × 59 mm.) of rather different character.

BRUGES

Outside Antwerp there was considerably less woodcut book-illustration in the xv century in the Southern Netherlands than in Holland. The earliest and most interesting was the *Metamorphoses* of Ovid (*Métamorphose moralisé*

[1] See p. 586.

par Maistre Thomas Waleys) issued by COLARD MANSION at Bruges in May 1484 (CA. 1348, CN. vii.).[1] It is a folio printed in two columns of large Gothic type, containing seventeen large cuts illustrating the stories (about two-thirds of the page in size, $7\frac{1}{4} \times 6\frac{1}{2}$ inches) and the same number of upright column cuts of gods and goddesses (about $4\frac{1}{2} \times 3$ inches). They are drawn in a broad and open manner, awkward and angular in cutting, but not without a certain gauche charm (see fig. 345). Very similar in character and possibly by the same designer are the cuts which appeared in *L'Abusé en Court* printed anonymously at Lyon about 1480, and in one or two other books by the same printer, e.g. in Pierre Michault, *Doctrinal du Temps passé* and the *Quatre Filz Aymon*.[2] They formed a very definite source of inspiration to the chief woodcut designer in Vérard's workshop after 1490.[3]

Mr. Henkel has demonstrated the close relationship of the designs to Flemish miniatures in MSS. at Paris (Bibliothèque Nationale, MS. français 137) and Copenhagen (Royal Library, MS. Otto Thott 399). There are probably many other cases unidentified where the early woodcut designer has based his work on miniatures.

Colard Mansion's only other illustrated book, if we are right in regarding it as such, is his Boccaccio, *De Casibus virorum et foeminarum illustrium* of 1476, but there he used line-engravings, and only two copies are known with the series pasted in.[4]

BRUSSELS

Somewhat similar in their broad and angular style of cutting are the two cuts in the *Legenda Henrici Imp. et Kunegundis* printed at Brussels by the Fratres Communis Vitae[5] in 1484, representing the *Emperor Henry II. and Kunigunda seated* and the *Arms of Anthony of Rotenhan, Bishop of Bamberg* (CA. 1100, CN. xxii. 1, Holtrop, pl. 62 [74] and 63 [75]).

[1] See M. D. Henkel, *De Houtsneden van Mansion's 'Ovide Moralisé'*, Bruges 1484. Amsterdam (Koninklijk Oudheidkundig Genootschap) 1922. Bradshaw first noted two editions both with imprint of Colard Mansion and date May 1484, but the second probably printed by Jean Gossin who took over Mansion's rooms after his disappearance in 1484. The British Museum copy is of this second issue. Cf. Henkel, *Nederlansche Ovidius-Illustratien van de 14ᵉ tot de 18ᵉ Eeuw*. Oud-Holland 1921, p. 149, and *Engravings and Woodcuts after Flemish Miniatures*, Burlington Magazine, li. 209 (Nov. 1927).

[2] See p. 600.   [3] See p. 666.

[4] See my *History of Engraving and Etching*, 3rd ed., 1923, pp. 32-3. The Newbattle copy is now in the Boston Museum of Fine Arts. The other copy with the engravings is at Göttingen. There is a line-engraving at Boston of *Jason subduing the Oxen*, in the style of the Boccaccio illustrations, which shows that Mansion had originally thought of using engravings for his *Ovid* as well.   [5] Cf. p. 213.

Louvain (*continued*)

By the same hand as the Kunigunda woodcuts are the illustrations in Boccaccio, *De claris mulieribus*, printed by AEGIDIUS VAN DER HEERSTRATEN, Louvain, 1487 (CA. 294, CN. xxii. 3). They are freely adapted from the woodcuts which appeared in the Ulm edition of 1473 printed by Johann Zainer,[1] and some are as good and as spirited as the originals.

Two other Louvain books may be mentioned, both printed by LUDOVICUS RAVESCOT, the *Visio Lamentabilis* of about 1487 (CA. 1745, CN. xxiii. 1), with four vivid but crude cuts representing a hermit's dream, and the adventures of the soul after death, and Petrus de Rivo, *Opus Responsivum de Anno die et feria dominicae Passionis*, 1488 (CA. 1405, CN. xxiii. 4, 5).

The most interesting of the four cuts in the latter book is the *Virgin and Child in a Church, adored by the author*, which appears on the first page, and is reproduced by Juchhoff as though it were a device of the printer (Juchhoff 52; fig. 346). It gives the impression of having been based on a painting of a similar design to

Fig. 346. The Virgin and Child adored by the author, from Petrus de Rivo, *Opus Responsivum*, Louvain 1488.

the Berlin Van Eyck. Ravescot's actual printer's mark occurs in the colophon of the same book (Juchhoff 51).

[1] See p. 305.

Miscellaneous Single Cuts

In the latter part of the xv century book-illustration everywhere plays by far the most important rôle in the history of woodcut, and in the Netherlands there are few single cuts of any importance. A series of *Les Neuf Preux* (S. 1948) has already been mentioned,[1] and the only other cut of equal interest is the *Good Shepherd*, a large cut preserved in the Stadtbibliothek at Breslau (S. 838; fig. 347). The design is similar to an engraving by the Master of the Amsterdam Cabinet (Master of the Hausbuch, Lehrs 1894, No. 18), which is possibly the original on which the cut is based, though both might derive from a common source.[2] It has inscriptions in both Dutch and French, and probably belongs on that account to the Southern Netherlands, and from the dialect, according to the late M. Henri Hymans, to the region of Liége. It was preserved with a woodcut from the Lübeck *Rudimentum Noviciorum* of 1475, in the binding of an undated Missal of about 1470–80, and this is about the period to which one would assign the block.

A large and crudely cut *Christ Child in a Heart* (S. 796, Berlin) deserves mention if only for its signature, *peter de wale*, which is probably that of a craftsman of the Netherlands, or Lower Germany, in the last quarter of the xv century.

Then there is a little woodcut of *Christ on the Cross* (S. 444, Paris, Lemoisne, pl. xcvii.) inscribed *Actum Gandavi*, i.e. done at Ghent, and there are several small cuts in the British Museum and in various Dutch collections related in style to the Netherlandish illustration of the last decade of the xv century, and possibly themselves unidentified book-illustrations,[3] but they do not merit more than a passing reference.

Bibliography

HOLTROP, J. W. Monuments typographiques des Pays-Bas au xvme siècle. Collection de fac-simile. The Hague 1868.
CAMPBELL, M. F. A. G. Annales de la typographie néerlandaise au xvme siècle. The Hague 1874.
CONWAY, William Martin (Lord Conway of Allington). Woodcutters of the Netherlands. Cambridge 1884.

[1] See p. 157.
[2] A somewhat different treatment of the same theme is seen in S. 839 and its variants (see p. 322).
[3] See M. D. Henkel, *Holzschnitte in holländischen Sammlungen*, Einbl. 49, Strassburg 1918.

Fig. 347. The Good Shepherd. S. 838.

BRADSHAW, Henry. List of the Founts of Type and Woodcut Devices used by Printers of Holland in the xv century. Collected Papers, 1889, p. 258.

SCHRETLEN, M. J. Dutch Woodcuts, 1480–1500. *Print Collector's Quarterly*, viii., 1921, 329.

SCHRETLEN, M. J. Dutch and Flemish Woodcuts of the xv Century (with a foreword by Max J. Friedländer). London 1925.

SCHRETLEN, M. J. Het Vroege Werk van Jacob Cornelisz. Oudheidkundig Jaarboek. Utrecht v. 143·(November 1925).

DELEN, A. J. J. Antwerpsche Drukkersmerken. *Gulden Passer.* 1923.

DELEN, A. J. J. Histoire de la gravure dans les anciens Pays-Bas, Première Partie. Des origines à 1500. Paris and Brussels 1924.

JUCHHOFF, Rudolf. Drucker- und Verlegerzeichen des xv Jahrhunderts in den Niederlanden, England, Spanien, Böhmen, Mähren und Polen. Munich 1927.

NŸHOFF, Wouter. Nederlandsche Houtsneden, 1500–1550. Reprodukties van oude Nord-en Zuid-Nederlandsche houtsneden op losse bladen. The Hague 1931–35.

CHAPTER VIII

BOOK-ILLUSTRATION AND CONTEMPORARY SINGLE CUTS
IN FRANCE AND FRENCH SWITZERLAND

THE story of book-illustration in France in the xv century offers peculiarly difficult problems. The various editions of numerous early works are often most confusing, a confusion which is rendered more obscure by the extreme rarity of so many. Without a first-hand survey of provincial libraries in France many problems must be left unsolved. Moreover, among French publishers and printers the practice of lending blocks was even commoner than elsewhere, and in the *Horae*, which form so important and characteristic a part of French illustrated books, the slight variations between different issues introduce many ambiguities.

Happily, the study has been very considerably clarified by the researches of the late M. Claudin contained in his monumental history of early French books, and on this basis I can at least hope to be a little more definite in my references than would otherwise have been possible.

The beginnings of book-printing and book-illustration were everywhere nearly related to the crafts of the scribe and miniaturist, but perhaps nowhere is this relation so clearly seen as in France. Several of the early printed books, such as *Les Croniques de France*, printed by Pasquier Bonhomme, 1476 (Cl. i. 172, Paris, Bibl. de l'Arsenal), and the *Valerius Maximus* in French, of about 1476 (Cl. i. 199),[1] have spaces left blank for the miniature painting, and many of the vellum copies of the finest books with woodcuts have the woodcuts almost completely covered by the opaque colours of the illuminator.[2] In certain cases we know that publishers and printers had

---

[1] *Le Livre de Valerius Maximus translaté de latin en françois par Simon de Hesdin*, n.p., n.d., n.pr. (Paris, certainly not later than 1477). There are two copies in the Bibliothèque Nationale and one in the Bibliothèque St. Geneviève (from the Moreau Collection), with miniatures; another was described in the Fairfax Murray Catalogue, H. W. Davies, 1910, No. 557. There is no copy in the British Museum.

[2] A good example in the British Museum is the *Croniques de France*, printed by J. Maurand for Vérard, 1493 (C. 22. f. 1-3). No doubt several of the illuminated vellum copies of Vérard's books in the British Museum were copies purchased by Henry VII., though the only one about which I find definite evidence is the *Grant Boèce de Consolation*, 1494 (Macf. 37), where the name of Henry VII. has been substituted for Charles VIII. in the second line of the Prologue. An uncoloured paper copy of the *Ortus Sanitatis* (Macf. 140) appears to be the copy mentioned in the Privy

been, and possibly continued to be, illuminators, e.g. the printer Pierre Le Rouge, and the publisher Antoine Vérard, and the illuminators may also have turned their hands, with the change of the times, to the designing of woodcuts.

It is natural therefore that the woodcut subjects as well as the decorative portions of various early printed books should show a close relation to miniatures, or even a direct dependence on known illuminations. This is especially true of such books as the *Cité de Dieu* of St. Augustine, printed by Pierre Gérard and Jean Dupré (Abbeville 1486), and the *Mer des Hystoires* printed by Pierre Le Rouge (Paris 1488–89). Moreover, the 'bastard' type (a cross between pure Gothic and Roman, a Gothic with its flamboyance reduced) contributed in its freer form to give the appearance of manuscript. The borders of the early *Horae* of Jean Dupré and Antoine Vérard also show fairly direct translations into wood of the illuminator's style.

Up to about 1495 this border decoration of Books of Hours was in the indigenous French tradition, but thereafter appears a gradual infiltration of classical elements in design which culminated in *Horae* printed by Geoffroy Tory. These Books of Hours form the most characteristic feature, and the finest flower of French woodcut illustration, and we shall treat them separately at the end of this chapter.

Antoine Vérard of Paris was by far the most important publisher of illustrated books in France in the xv century, though he was rivalled by Simon Vostre in the issue of liturgical books. Occasionally a colophon claims Vérard as printer (*impressum per*), but this is less likely to have been the literal truth than a publisher's licence of language in cases where he did not choose to cite the name of the printer he commissioned. Vérard undoubtedly possessed a large supply of blocks, for he was primarily interested in illustration, while in other cases it was no doubt the printers themselves who possessed their own material, type and block, and were their own publishers.

Printers from Paris occasionally helped out provincial publications with their craftsmen and material, e.g. Jean Dupré at Abbeville and

Purse expenses of Henry VII., 1502, 'to Anthony Vérard for two bokes called the gardyn of helth, £6'.

There are various examples of Vérard's illuminated vellum copies, done for royal presentation, in the Bibliothèque Nationale, Paris (see Cl. ii. 466). Paul Durrieu, in his *Jacques de Besançon* (Paris 1892), argued against the probability of Vérard illuminating his own printed books, and attributed most of this work in Vérard's books between 1492 and 1498 to Jacques de Besançon. But M. Durrieu's attribution of this and other works of illumination to Jacques de Besançon (including many works now ascribed to Maître François, 'Egregius Pictor Franciscus') is quite uncertain, and for the most part abandoned by the author himself since the publication of his book.

Rouen,[1] and were frequently called on to print provincial Missals.[2] An example of the loan and return of blocks from Paris has been noted by Claudin in the illustrations to the *Légende Dorée* first printed by Jean Dupré in Paris, May 1496, later by Jean de Vingle at Lyon, 1497, thereafter returning to Paris and used by N. de la Barre, 1499, but I have been unable to check his statements.[3] One instance has also been noted of a French block used at Cologne, the *Author in a Chamber*, which first appeared in Couteau and Menard's edition of the *Danse Macabre des Hommes*, Paris 1492 (Cl. ii. 176). It occurs, cut about $\frac{1}{8}$-inch along the foot, as a representation of the commentator Albertus Magnus in Aristotle, *De Anima cum comentario Alberti Magni*, printed by Quentell, at Cologne, 1499 (S. 3349, H. 1711, Schramm 493, e.g. at Berlin).[4]

It is natural that the most refined and characteristic examples of French woodcut illustration should have been produced in Paris, which was already the centre of French culture.

LYON

Lyon was equally important as a commercial centre and as a house of call on the main roads of communication between France, Switzerland and Italy, on the one hand, and Germany, France and Spain, on the other, and it is not surprising on that account that woodcut illustration should have been introduced at Lyon earlier than at Paris, and that German craftsmen should have taken a considerable part in its development.

We shall therefore begin our survey of French illustrated books at Lyon,[5] reserving the purer French style shown in Paris books for the latter part of the chapter. For the most part Lyon illustration is cruder in design and cutting than contemporary Paris work, but we shall find occasional exceptions, e.g. in the precise woodcut of the monogrammist ID, in the work of the gifted designer of Trechsel's *Terence*, and in certain Italianate cuts such as appeared in some of Sacon's books, and in Dupré's *Éternelle Consolacion* (Cl. iii. 488, Paris).

---

[1] See pp. 622-625.　　　　　　　　　　　　　　[2] See p. 631.

[3] See Cl. ii. 290-92, iv. 230. The edition referred to as printed by Jean Dupré may be that published by Vérard, 20th May 1496 (Paris). I cannot refer to the locality of the other editions. Cf. Index of Subjects (under *blocks, transfer of*).

[4] Cf. pp. 361, 362, also for comment on supposed kinship between the style of woodcut work in France and Cologne.

[5] Natalis Rondot, *Les Graveurs sur bois et les imprimeurs à Lyon au XV siècle*. Lyon, Paris 1896; Rondot, *La Gravure sur bois à Lyon au XV siècle*. Bibliographica iii. (1897) 46; Rondot, *Graveurs sur bois à Lyon au XVI siècle*. Paris 1897.

The first of the Lyon books, the *Mirouer de la Redemption* printed by MARTIN HUSS, 26th August 1478 (Cl. iii. 158), contains illustrations re-printed from the original German blocks of Richel's Basle edition of 1476.[1] The book must have been very popular, for it was re-issued by Martin Huss

Fig. 348. From *L'Abusé en Court*, Lyon, about 1480.

in 1479 and 1482, and several times later by Matthias Huss.

Some of the earliest Lyon illustrations were issued about 1480 by the anonymous printer gener-ally known by the title of one of his books, *L'Abusé en Court* (Cl. iv. 365, B.M., C. 6. b. 9), a satirical allegory on Court life, which contains eleven woodcuts (see fig. 348).[2] Another of his books is Pierre Michault, *Doctrinal du temps passé* (Cl. iv. 375, Paris), a satire on contemporary moral instruction, in which Virtue conducts the author round various lecture-halls, illustrated in the cuts. The work was written by Pierre Michault in 1466, and dedicated to Philip the Good, Duke of Burgundy. Of curious interest in relation to the antiquity of woodcut in the region of Burgundy, is the description of the prints hanging on the walls as *aucunes histoires entaillés et gravées*.

In style these cuts show close kinship to the illustrations in the Bruges *Ovide Moralisé*, printed by Colard Mansion, 1484,[3] and it is possible they are by the same designer.

From the same press, about the same date, and with woodcuts possibly by the same hand is the *Quatre Filz Aymon*, one of the numerous romances printed at Lyon (Cl. iv. 392-93, B.M., IB. 42244; see fig. 349).[4] The

<hr/>

[1] *Spiegel menschlicher Behältnis*, see p. 325. The Lyon issue contained some 256 illustrations, about twenty-one less than the Basle edition.

[2] Facsimile reproduction of the cuts and types of *L'Abusé en Court* and the *Doctrinal*, edited by Cl. Dalbanne and E. Droz, Lyon (Association Guillaume Le Roy) 1926. Another early edition of *L'Abusé en Court* was printed by Peter Schenck at Lyon, 1485 (C. iii. 383, and iv. 360, Pellechet 24, Paris).   [3] See pp. 591, 592.

[4] Other illustrated editions of this romance were printed by Le Roy about 1484–88 (Cl. iii. 88,

most attractive part of the woodcut decoration consists of the numerous initial letters in outline, with branch and scroll patterns embellished with animals or grotesque heads (see fig. 350).

Perhaps even earlier than either of the books just mentioned is the woodcut of the *Virgin standing with the Child before a curtain* (fig. 351), which appeared as frontispiece to *L'Histoire du Chevalier Oben* (Owain), printed without date by GUILLAUME LE ROY (Cl. iii. 46). Even if the book is no earlier than about 1480, the block probably goes back somewhat earlier, as it appears already in a somewhat worn condition. Here we have a thoroughly French design, cut with a considerably thinner line than the Lyon blocks of German type, and it is one of the most attractive of the Lyon illustrations.

Fig. 349. From *Le Quatre Filz Aymon*, Lyon, about 1480.

Guillaume Le Roy was the earliest of the Lyon printers, and for the first decade of his work after 1473 his books were financed by a rich merchant, Barthélemy Buyer, whose name appeared in company with Le Roy's. Virgil's *Énéide*, 1483 (the year of Buyer's death), was the first in which Le Roy's name stood alone. It contains crude and angular cuts with some parallel shading, rather in the manner of Ulm and Augsburg illustrations.

Similarly Teutonic, and probably by the same designer and cutter as the *Quatre Filz Aymon*, are the woodcuts (two full-page and numerous half-page oblongs) in the romance of *Fierabras*, printed by Le Roy about 1485 (Cl. iii. 72; fig. 352).

The cuts in *L'istoyre du chevalier Pierre de Provence et de la belle Maguelone*, printed by Le Roy about 1485 (Cl. iii. 84), are less interesting than the frontispiece to *Fierabras* which we reproduce, but somewhat more

probably by the same designer as the *Pierre de Provence*, Cl. iii. 84, see above), and by Jean de Vingle, 1493 (Pierpont Morgan 611). The cuts in the latter are probably by the designer of Trechsel's *Terence* of 1493 (see p. 609).

Fig. 350. Initial O, from *Le Quatre Filz Aymon*, Lyon, about 1480.

advanced in drawing or more closely shaded. *Le Livre des faisz de Bertrand du Guesclin*, Le Roy, about 1487 (B.M., IB. 41544), has an attractive frontispiece representing the knight, and numerous half-page oblong cuts, some in the crude style of the *Aymon* and *Fierabras*, and others more finely drawn and cut. Probably between the latter two romances was printed Pierre Michault, *Danse des Aveugles*, which is attributed to Le Roy, about 1485 (Cl. iii. 100, Paris). The cuts were reprinted by Michel Topié and Jacobus of Herrnberg, about 1492. They probably derive from the earlier cuts illustrating the same work printed by Louis Cruse at Geneva, about 1480. The *Danse des Aveugles* printed by Le Petit Laurens, Paris, about 1495 (Fairfax Murray, Davies 277), is illustrated with cuts taken for the most part from Syber's edition of the *Roman de la Rose*, Lyon, about 1485 (Bourdillon, Ed. B).[1]

Prestre Jehan, printed by Le Roy, about 1490 (Cl. iii. 106, Paris), is of interest for the figured initial P of its title.

The printers, NICOLAUS PHILIPPI (Müller) from Bensheim and MARCUS REINHARD from Strassburg, used for the most part blocks of German character, so that they no doubt brought German craftsmen in their employ. The illustrations in their Aesop (*Fables d'Ésope*) of 26th August 1480 (Cl. iii. 120, Tours)[2] were based on the original Ulm cuts, or on one of the numerous German editions (e.g. Knoblochtzer, Strassburg, about 1480), if indeed they are not actually one of the versions printed in Germany, not yet identified. They were used later in an edition printed by Matthias Huss and J. Schabeler, 1484 (Paris). The cuts of another Lyon *Aesop*, printed by Topié and Herrnberg, about 1490, are also derived from the same source, but are much poorer in quality.

Another book of Philippi and Reinhard, Rodericus Zamorensis, *Mirouer de la Vie Humaine*, 1482 (Cl. iii. 132: Pierpont Morgan 598), contains cuts printed from the original Augsburg blocks of Günther Zainer's *Spiegel menschlichen Lebens* (about 1475–76), interspersed with certain copies from the same source, and the same series was used later still by Pablo Hurus[3] at Saragossa (1491).

---

[1] See below, p. 606.

[2] For reproduction and notes on this and other Lyon editions of *Aesop* see Cl. Dalbanne, E. Droz and J. Bastin, Lyon (Association Guillaume Le Roy) 1926.

[3] See p. 741. Claudin surmised that Pablo and Juan Hurus (Huss) of Constance, who printed at Saragossa, may have been of the same family as the Huss at Lyon.

Philippi and Reinhard appear to have issued the earliest Lyon edition of the Golden Legend (*Legenda Aurea*, about 1480, Cl. iii. 124-30, Fairfax Murray, Davies 589)[1] with crude cuts of German character. Other Lyon editions were printed by Matthias Huss and Petrus of Hungary, 1483 (*Légende Dorée en François*, Cl. iii. 255, 331, Lyon), with small upright column cuts, about $3\frac{1}{4} \times 2\frac{3}{8}$ inches, and by Matthias Huss alone, 1486 (*Legenda Aurea*, Cl. iii. 275, Paris, Fairfax Murray, Davies 588), with similar blocks but largely different from those in the French edition of 1483, about $3\frac{1}{8} \times 2\frac{5}{8}$ inches.

About 1482 Marcus Reinhard disappeared from Lyon, and prob-

Fig. 351. The Virgin and Child, from *L'Histoire du Chevalier Oben*, Lyon, about 1480.

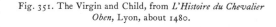

ably returned to Strassburg to work with his kinsman, Johann Grüninger (Reinhard), and was printing independently at Kirchheim, 1490–91.[2]

---

[1] For notes on these Lyon editions of the Golden Legend see Cl. Dalbanne, *Remarques sur l'illustration de quelques légendes dorées imprimées à Lyon au XVe siècle* (Documents Palaeographiques, Monographiques, Typographiques, Lyon, Bibl. de la Ville, 1923, etc., viie fascicule, 1928); Cl. Dalbanne, *La Légende Dorée. Mathieu Husz et Pierre Hongre*, 1483. Lyon (Association Guillaume Le Roy) [1924].

[2] See p. 340, and Robert Proctor's article on Reinhard and Grüninger.

After Reinhard's departure Philippi printed an edition of Guillermus, *Postilla super Epistolas et Evangelia*, with numerous small cuts, about 1483–84 (Cl. iii. 141; locality of copy unknown to me).

Ficrabras.

Fig. 352. From *Fierabras*, Lyon, about 1485.

Martin Huss, whom we have already mentioned as the printer of the first book-illustration at Lyon, issued an edition of Jacobus Palladinus de Theramo, *Le Procès de Belial à l'encontre de Jhesus*, 1482 (Cl. iii. 173), with numerous small oblong cuts and a larger frontispiece, in a crude German style. After this year his press was carried on by MATTHIAS HUSS, from Bottwar in Würtemberg, who worked well into the xvi century. His was the first French illustrated edition of Bartholomaeus Anglicus, *Le Propriétaire des Choses*, 1482 (Cl. iii. 245), and it is one of his most interesting books, with its full-page cuts at the head of each section (see fig. 353), with its thin lines, angular design, and open parallel shading, characteristic of so much Lyon woodcut. It was reprinted by Huss in 1485, and most of the same blocks, with some replacements and new decorative work and border and initials, appeared in his edition of 15th March 1491/92 (Cl. iii. 291). The large initial *L with St. George and the Dragon* which appeared in the title was first used at Lyon by Dupré in his edition of the *Mer des Hystoires*, 1491,[1] and again by Matthias Huss in his *Grant Danse Macabre*, 1499/1500. The designs first used by Matthias Huss,

[1] See p. 612 and fig. 364.

adapted by a more powerful cutter, appeared in Jean Syber's edition of the *Propriétaire des Choses*, about 1485–86 (Cl. iii. 200; fig. 354). According to Claudin the new blocks were made for an edition printed by Le Roy, 26th January 1485/86,[1] and lent to Syber after that date (Cl. iii. 63, 202, Lyon).

Fig. 353. The Ages of Man, from Bartholomaeus Anglicus,
Propriétaire des Choses, Lyon 1482.

A few cuts occur in the Boccaccio, *Livre de la Ruyne des Nobles Hommes et Femmes*, printed by MATTHIAS HUSS and JEAN SCHABELER, 1483 (Cl. iii. 256), and one to each of the books of *Le Livre de Valerius Maximus translaté en François*, Huss, 1485 (Cl. iii. 269), but of much greater interest is Huss's edition of *La Grant Danse Macabre*, 18th February 1499/1500 (Cl. iii. 318). The subject of the *Danse Macabre* will be treated at more length in the description of the Paris edition of Guy Marchant.[2] The present edition is partly based on Marchant's cuts and partly on those of Couteau and Menard's edition (1492). Its chief original interest lies in the representation of *Death and the Printers*, which is not known in the other edition (fig. 355).

Most of the subjects of the *Danse des Hommes*, and the two cuts representing *Les Trois Morts et les Trois Vifs*, are copied fairly closely from Couteau and Menard (who apparently continued no further in the work),[3] while the *Danse des Femmes*, *Death on a Horse*, the *Trumpeter of Death*, and the *Débat du corps et de l'âme*, are based on Marchant. Other illustrations,

---

[1] I cannot refer to locality of this edition.   [2] See p. 644.
[3] See p. 647.

i.e. *La Complainte de l'âme damnée*, *L'Exhortation de bien vivre et de bien mourir*, and *La Vie du mauvais antechrist*, are independent designs.

At the head of the section of 'Les Quinze signes' appears a late state of the woodcut by ID representing *Robertus de Licio preaching before Pope and Cardinals* with the artist's initials removed.[1]

The earliest illustrated edition of the *Roman de la Rose*[2] appears to be

Fig. 354. The Birds, from Bartholomaeus Anglicus, *Propriétaire des Choses*, Lyon, about 1485–86.

that printed by GASPARD ORTUIN and PETER SCHENCK, at Lyon, about 1480 (Bourdillon A). It contains some eighty-six cuts, the first a double subject the width of the page (fig. 356), another half-page block, the *Building of the Tower*, the rest small column cuts. Another Lyon edition with cuts derived from this edition, somewhat larger, and more expressive in drawing, was printed by JEAN SYBER about 1485 (Pierpont Morgan 601), and its blocks were reprinted by Guillaume Le Roy, Lyon, about

[1] See p. 615.

[2] See F. W. Bourdillon, *The Early Editions of the 'Roman de la Rose'*, Bibliographical Society's Monographs, xiv., London 1906.

1487 (Pierpont Morgan 606), and in Paris by Jean Dupré, about 1494 (Cl. i. 280), by Le Petit Laurens for Jean Petit and Vérard, about 1497, and by N. Des Prez for Jean Petit, and other publishers, between about 1498 and 1505, a few blocks being lost in the progress (Bourdillon B, C, D, F, G).

Another Paris edition of the *Roman de la Rose*, published by Vérard,

Fig. 355. Death and the Printers, from *La Grant Danse Macabre*, Lyon 1499/1500.

probably between 1494 and 1498 (Bourdillon E, Cl. ii. 250; printed by Etienne Jehannot?), contains an incomplete series of copies near the style of Vérard's chief designer, carelessly cut except for the subjects on the first page. It also includes numerous cuts from Petrus de Crescentiis, *Prouffitz Champestres*, and the *Cent Nouvelles Nouvelles*,[1] 1486, and from other earlier books published by Vérard.

A later edition issued by Vérard, in smaller size, about 1505 (Bourdillon H), contains another series of woodcuts, smaller than the rest, more uniform in character than his earlier edition, and better cut. The cuts for

[1] See p. 655.

this edition were also issued in Jean Molinet's prose version, *le Roman de la Rose moralisé*, also issued by Vérard (Bourdillon X). Bourdillon dates this about 1500, and regards it as the model followed by Balsarin, Macfarlane (186) and others date it about 1511.[1] In this edition the cuts were

Fig. 356. From the *Roman de la Rose*, Lyon, about 1480.

framed in a border of gothic arcading, which Vérard used in several of his later books.

Molinet's prose version was also issued at Lyon by Balsarin in 1503, with still another series of woodcuts, very wooden in character (Bourdillon Y).

Le Roman du Roy Ponthus et de la belle Sidoyne (Cl. iii. 391-94, Oxford, Proctor 8535) is another undated romance printed by Gaspard Ortuin, with blocks of more advanced design and cutting than his *Roman de la Rose*, and probably issued about 1484. There is also an edition with the same cuts, probably earlier, printed by Guillaume Le Roy in a type similar to that of his *Énéide* of 1483 (Cl. iii. 394-95, Chantilly).[2]

JOHANN NEUMEISTER, who has already been mentioned for his work at Mainz,[3] was printing at Albi about 1480–83, and from 1483 to 1498 at Lyon. His most distinguished work at Lyon is contained in two missals, the *Lyon Missal* of 1487 (Cl. iii. 360, Paris, Lyon), and the *Uzès Missal*,

---

[1] See p. 654.

[2] See reproduction of the 41 cuts used in the editions of G. Le Roy and Gaspard Ortuin, edited by Cl. Dalbanne and E. Droz, Lyon (Association Guillaume Le Roy) 1926.

[3] See p. 194.

Fig. 357. Initial T from the *Lyon Missal,*
Lyon 1500/1501.

which he printed in collaboration
with Michel Topié in 1495 (Cl. iii.
369). Apart from the *Canon* cuts,
the latter contains a fine series of
pictorial initials on black ground.

The same initials were used later
by Petrus of Hungary in his *Lyon
Missal* of 16th April 1500/1501 (Cl.
iii. 343-51, Lyon), in addition to a
larger and still more interesting *Initial
T with Abraham's sacrifice* (fig. 357).

The high-water mark of book-
illustration at Lyon in the xv century
is reached in the Terence *Comoediae,*
printed by JOHANN TRECHSEL, 1493.
Trechsel, who came to Lyon from
Mainz about 1487, has already been mentioned for some colophon verses
touching on early printing.[1] He had married the widow of Nicolaus
Philippi, who died in 1488, and so came into possession of that printer's
stock.

It is more than probable that the designer of the *Terence* is German or
Netherlandish in origin, working in a style that recalls Erhard Reuwich's
illustrations to the original Mainz *Breydenbach* of 1486.

Kristeller and Friedländer have both compared the *Terence* cuts with
the Lübeck *Dodes Dantz* (1489) and *Bible* of 1494,[2] and Friedländer has
suggested identity of authorship. I admit the kinship, but there is a peculiar
manner of curved lines in the *Lübeck Bible* which is quite distinct. Whatever his origin, the designer's hand may perhaps be traced in various stages
of progress in other Lyon books in the last decade of the century, but the
series of woodcuts to Trechsel's *Terence* is his masterpiece. The book
opens with a fine full-page frontispiece representing the *Theatre* (fig. 358),
and the plays are illustrated with a variety of smaller oblong cuts, in which
the actors are shown on the stage, disposed with a fine sense of design, and
drawn with a vivid and humorous touch (see fig. 359).

Among Lyon woodcuts allied in style to Trechsel's *Terence* I would
mention in the first place the illustrations to Raoul Le Fèvre, *Recueil des
Hystoires de Troye,* printed by MICHEL TOPIÉ and JACOBUS OF HERRNBERG,
1490 (Cl. iv. 11-23, Paris), reprinted by JACQUES MAILLET in 1494. The

[1] See p. 209.   [2] See pp. 362-367.

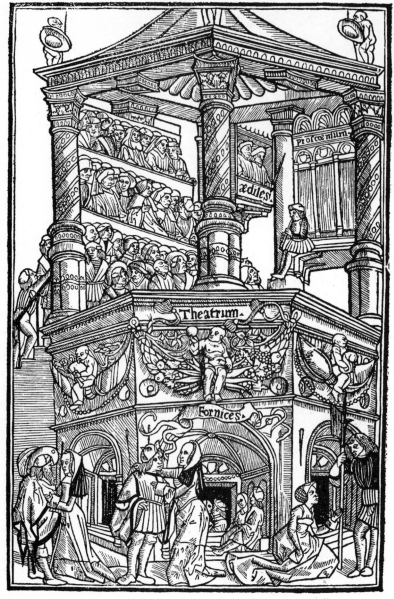

Fig. 358. The Theatre, from Terence, *Comoediae*, Lyon 1493.

illustrations vary considerably in quality, possibly owing to the varying skill of the cutters, but in the best examples the peculiar virtue of the Terence designer is evident. The title contains a delightful initial *L with monkeys* (fig. 360).[1]

Topié and Herrnberg were the printers of the first French edition of Breydenbach[2] in Nicole Le Huen's version *Des Sainctes Peregrinations de*

Fig. 359. From Terence, *Comoediae*, Lyon 1493.

Jherusalem, 1488 (Cl. iv. 1), which contained copies of the Mainz blocks, nine woodcuts after the smaller subjects, the folding views being engraved on copper plates. It is conceivable that the Terence designer assimilated something of the Mainz master's character through this work, in which he might have taken part. The second French edition of Breydenbach, in the more faithful translation of Jean de Hersin, *Le saint voyage et pélerinage de Hierusalem*, was issued in February 1489/90 without name of printer (Cl. iii. 397, Proctor 8618), and has been attributed variously to Ortuin (Claudin), Maillet (Proctor) and Le Roy (Pellechet). The illustrations in this edition were printed from the original Mainz blocks.

Two further books in which the style of the Terence designer is clearly seen are Martial d'Auvergne, *Les Vigilles de la Mort du Roy Charles VII.*, n.d.

---

[1] Reprinted in Maillet's edition of Jean Boutillier, *La Somme rural(e)*, 1494 (Cl. iv. 109).

[2] See pp. 352-356.

Fig. 360. Initial L, from *Recueil des Hystoires de Troye*, Lyon 1490.

(Cl. iv. 155, École des Beaux-Arts, Paris, from J. Masson), and the Cicero, *Offices*, 1493 (H. 5236, Paris) and 1496 (Paris, Mazarin), printed by CLAUDE DAYNE (Cl. iv. 150). The earlier edition of the Cicero is without printer's name, but it has the same initials and woodcut as the later (*Cicero presenting his book to his son Marcus*), so that it is probably by the same printer.

Another book printed by Dayne, *Le Livre de Matheolus qui monstre les biens qui vieignent pour soy marier*, 1492,[1] contains on its title a characteristic *Initial L with fool and girl kissing* (fig. 361) which might also be by the Terence designer. It recurs on the title of Guy de Roye, *Doctrinal de Sapience*, printed by Dayne in 1497/98 and 1498/99 (Cl. iv. 162, Paris).

Similar again in style is the large *Initial C with a sick woman in bed* on the first page of Boethius, *De Consolatione Philosophiae* (*Commentum Duplex in Boethium*), printed by JEAN DE VINGLE, 1498 (HC. 3417). Vingle's excellent printer's mark also occurs in the same book (Meyer 69; fig. 362). And the same printer's editions of *Les Quatre Filz Aymon*, 1493, 1495, 1497 and 1499 (Cl. iv. 222; for first edition see Pierpont Morgan 611), also contains a series of woodcuts probably by the Terence designer.

Different in style from the *Terence* designs, but equally vivid in characterisation is the illustration of a *Boys' School* (fig. 363) in the *Cathon en François* printed without date by PIERRE BOUTEILLER, Lyon (Cl. iii. 433, Toulouse).

For richness of decoration one of the most notable of Lyon books is the *Mer des Hystoires* printed in 1491 by JEAN DUPRÉ,[2] who must not be confused with the Paris printer of the same name. Most of the subject cuts are copied from the Paris edition printed by Pierre Le Rouge, 1488–89, and are

---

[1] The wording of the colophon in the B.M. copy confirms this date. Claudin (iv. 164) places it about 1498.

[2] E.g. Paris (B.N.). This edition is wanting in the British Museum.

Fig. 361. Initial L, from *Le Livre de Matheolus,* Lyon 1492.

considerably inferior to the originals; the borders and other decorative pieces are derived in style from the same source, but show more independence and offer much of beauty and interest. Thoroughly independent are the borders to the little series in the manner of a *Book of Hours* in volume ii.; in alternate spaces of light and dark ground they are akin in character to certain Flemish Books of Devotion, printed by Gerard Leeuw and Adriaen van Liesvelt at Antwerp, 1491 and 1495.[1] I have not found them used outside the folio *Mer des Hystoires*. The large *Initial L with St. George and the Dragon* of the title-page (a variant of Le Rouge's L) appeared here for the first time (fig. 364), being used later by Matthias Huss in the *Propriétaire des Choses*, 1491/92, and *La Grant Danse Macabre*, 1499/1500.[2] Most of Dupré's blocks for the *Mer des Hystoires* were reprinted at Lyon by CLAUDE DAVOST in an edition of 1506, and many appeared later in various books issued in Paris by Enguilbert de Marnef and F. Regnault.[3] Davost's edition contains some curious initial letters, with flower and figure on black ground, which had appeared earlier in his issue of *Le Propriétaire des Choses*, 1500 (Cl. iv. 339, Paris, Bibl. du Musée d'Histoire Naturelle).

I would also mention the initial letters used by the printer JEAN CLEIN, righly designed leaf and floral design on black ground (Cl. iv. 281).

A woodcut of the *Virgin and Child in Glory*, and the *Stigmatisation of St. Francis*, which appeared on the verso of the title-page of *L'Éternelle Consolacion* (*De Imitatione Christi*) printed without date by Dupré (Cl. iii. 488, Paris), stands apart from most Lyon book-illustration and is much more nearly related to Venetian work. Another example in a similar

---

[1] See pp. 581, 582. [2] See p. 605.

[3] The edition of the *Mer des Hystoires* published by E. de Marnef and F. Regnault about 1517 (B.M., 582. l. 7) contains cuts from the editions of both Le Rouge and Dupré.

Fig. 362. Printer's mark of Jean de Vingle, Lyon.

style, possibly by a designer from North Italy, is the small *Crucifixion* in the *Missale Romanum*, printed at Lyon by JACQUES SACON, 26th April 1500 (Cl. iv. 303, École des Beaux-Arts, Paris, from J. Masson Collection). Moreover, one of the designs used by Sacon as his printer's mark, an allegorical figure of Virtue (Silvestre 548), is copied from a woodcut in Bernardino Corio, *Patria Historia*, Milan 1503.[1]

Sacon also printed an edition of Sebastian Brant's *Stultifera Navis*[2] under the title *Salutifera Navis*, and dated 1488 (evidently in error for 1498), a translation into Latin verse by Jacques Locher from the original German *Narrenschiff*. Except for the title-cut, the blocks had appeared at Paris in 1497 in an edition printed by J. Lambert (?) for J. Philippe (Manstener) and G. de Marnef, a translation of Brant into French verse by Pierre Rivière, entitled *La Nef des Folz du monde*. Another Lyon edition of the same work, a French version by Jean Drouyn, *La Grant Nef des Folz*, was printed by BALSARIN at Lyon in 1498 and 1499. Cuts in these French editions are all derived directly or indirectly from the original Basle editions.

From other books printed by Sacon, the most interesting woodcut is perhaps that of *Five Commentators of Virgil* on the title-page of Virgil, *Opera*, 1499 (Cl. iv. 301).

Woodcuts by the Master ID
in Books printed at Lyon, Toulouse and in Spain

The designer who uses the initials ID holds an unimportant but unique position in book-illustration at Lyon. His work appears in the following books printed at Lyon:

---

[1] See p. 514.   [2] See p. 331.

Robertus de Licio (Caracciolus), *Quadragesimale Aureum de Peccatis*, printed by Trechsel, 9th February 1488/89: a small cut of *Robertus de Licio preaching before Pope and Cardinals* (Cl. iii. 83).[1]

Les Mistères de la Sainte Messe, printed by G. Le Roy, n.d. (about 1490) (Cl. iii. 82; Claudin-Ricci, No. 202, Paris): a small *Annunciation*, copied from Schongauer, B. 3, Lehrs 1 f.

Ars Moriendi, Latin text, n.d., n.pr. (about 1490) (Cl. iii. 83, iv. 436):[2] twelve cuts, including the complete series of eleven subjects copied

Fig. 363. A Boys' School, from *Cathon en François*, Lyon, n.d.

from the block-book, and a woodcut title in large Gothic letters on black ground on the last page of the volume.

---

[1] It appeared in later state, with the monogram ID removed, at the beginning of the section on 'Les Quinze Signes' in *La Grant Danse Macabre*, printed at Lyon by Matthias Huss, 1499/1500 (see p. 606).

[2] There is another Lyon series of octavo copies after the *Ars Moriendi* block-book which occurs in several editions:

    (1) [*L'Art et Disposition de bien mourir*]. Pierre Bouteiller, n.d. [about 1485], Cl. iii. 443 (in Claudin's possession, from Rosenthal, Munich, who had placed it as a Grenoble book). The eleven block-book subjects. The title was lacking in the only copy known, and is inferred from (2).

    (2) *L'Art et Disposition de bien mourir*. Jean Syber (?). After 1485. Cl. iii. 445. Chantilly.

    (3) *Ars Moriendi*. Latin text. Jean Syber (?). About 1490? Cl. iii. 209. H. 1832. R. Proctor,

Apart from books printed at Lyon, another of ID's woodcuts, the *Stoning of St. Stephen*, appeared in the *Toulouse Missal* printed by Étienne Cléblat, at Toulouse, 1490 (Cl. iii. 83, Toulouse).[1] This cut is perhaps the most interesting of all his designs, showing the saint in the centre stoned by three men, a bishop kneeling on the right, and a tiny St. Paul (*Saulus*), like a child in size and character, seated to the left on cloak and sword, watching the performance (fig. 365).

Finally a large *Christ on the Cross between the Virgin and St. John* appeared in a Spanish book of 1517, but the block probably belonged like the rest to the end of the xv century.[2]

The woodcuts of ID are Netherlandish in style, clear in design, hard in cutting, with strong outline and great regularity of shading, parallel series of short lines being often used in the background. Kristeller thought that ID was the designer of the cuts in the Naples *Aesop* of 1485, and of various blocks in Spanish books, besides the signed *Christ on the Cross*, and he regarded ID as a Northern artist (possibly from the region of Alsace) who worked successively at Naples, in France and in Spain.[3] The border to *Tirant Lo Blanch*, Valencia 1490, is certainly comparable with that in the Naples *Aesop* of 1485, and the woodcut representing the *King in Council* in the *Usatges de Barcelona e Constitucións de Cataluña* (Barcelona 1495) is equally near to the Naples *Aesop* and to the cuts signed ID, but I do not feel prepared to unite their respective authors in a single personality without more definite evidence.

Returning from this digression, I propose to continue the survey of provincial towns, all the more cursory because woodcut published in the

The Library, 2nd Ser. III., October 1902, p. 339. B.M., Paris, Auxerre, Munich. Attributed by Claudin to Jean Syber, by Pellechet to J. Dupré of Lyon, in the British Museum to Engelhard Schultis, about 1492.

The B.M. copy contains 12 illustrations from 10 blocks, i.e. copies after the whole original series except the last subject, *Triumph in face of Death*. This is replaced by a repetition of the *Inspiration of the Angel against Avarice* (*quid faciam?*), and the same cut is also repeated as frontispiece.

(4) *Tractatus succinctus de arte et scientia perfecte vivendi beneque moriendi*. Pierre Mareschal, n.d. (about 1515).

[1] Tibulle Desbarreaux-Bernard, *Catalogue de incunables de la Bibliothèque de Toulouse*, Toulouse 1878, No. 167, and reproduction, *Figures*, fol. 22. Cf. I. van Meckenem, Lehrs 383.
[2] See pp. 752 and 754 for this, and other cuts of similar style issued in Spain.
[3] Identification with Jean de Dale, maker of playing-cards at Lyon, has also been suggested (see p. 87, and N. Rondot, *Les Graveurs sur bois à Lyon au xve siècle*, p. 133), but his signed playing-cards give no support to the suggestion.

Fig. 364. Initial L, from the *Mer des Hystoires*, Lyon 1491.

more important of these, apart from Lyon, derived directly from the fountain-head of Paris.

GENEVA

Apart from varying political relations, Geneva[1] is naturally grouped in the present study with France, as Basle had been with Germany. The output of Genevese printers is small, but a few books of some interest may be noted.

In the first place five small woodcuts, attractive in design, but primitive in their outline style, illustrating Pierre Michault, *La Danse des Aveugles*, printed by LOUIS CRUSE about 1480 (Proctor 7809). Then a striking figure of *Fierabras*, as frontispiece to the romance of that name, issued in 1483 (Proctor 7811; fig. 366), a work which also contains numerous small oblong cuts, chiefly in outline, analogous in style to the work of the Lyon *Abusé en Court*,[2] and a full-page subject of the *Emperor and his Court*, used here as Louis Cruse's printer's mark. More strictly his printer's mark is the full-page *Heraldic cut with two negresses and his name Loys M. Cruse* (Meyer 17) which appears in Rolewinck, *Fasciculus Temporum*, issued in 1495 (Proctor 7817). The *Fierabras* also contains cuts of the various subjects usual in this work.

Another edition of the *Fasciculus Temporum*, issued without printer's name

[1] See Paul Heitz, *Genfer Buchdrucker- und Verlegerzeichen*, Strassburg 1908.

[2] See p. 600.

at Geneva, in 1495 (Proctor 7820), has an interesting full-page frontispiece of the *Author at a Desk*, as well as some good initials on black ground.

A few less important cuts appeared in books printed by JEAN BELLOT, e.g.

Fig. 365. The Master ID. The Stoning of St. Stephen, from the *Toulouse Missal*, Toulouse 1490.

in the small *Missale Lausannense* of 1500, where the little cut of the *Virgin of Lausanne* is of cruder quality than the rest, and points to earlier editions.

CHAMBÉRY

At Chambéry, ANTOINE NEYRET issued a few books of interest, the first being Maurice de Sully, *Exposition des Évangiles*, 1484, with two full-page woodcuts of effective design in open linear style, *Christ on the Cross, with the Signs of the Evangelists*, and the *Resurrection*, in addition to numerous small illustrations. Then a curiously calligraphic woodcut representing *Baldwin Count of Flanders*,[1] in which the rich trappings of the horse bear the printer's

---

[1] Reproduced in A. Blum, *Les Origines du livre à gravures en France*, 1928, pl. lxxvii. It is probably based on the frontispiece of the *Fierabras*, printed by Louis Cruse at Geneva, 1483 (see p. 617).

name, occurs in *Le Livre de Baudoin Comte de Flandres*, 1485. The book contains various other smaller oblong cuts, roughly executed.

A characteristic woodcut of *Master and Pupils* appeared in Jean Dupin, *Livre de la Bonne Vie appelé Mandevie*, 1485 (H. 6460), a morality in the form of a romance, shared by *l'Acteur 'Mandevie'* (representing the Life of Man) and the virtues, vices and other characters.

And finally, there is a series of crude but interesting cuts illustrating hunting, as well as a full-page allegory, in *Le Livre du Roi Modus et de la Reine Racio*, 1486 (H. 11447), a sort of 'Chasse Moralisée' after the pattern of the more famous morality on Chess by Jacobus de Cessolis.

Fig. 366. Frontispiece to *Fierabras*, Geneva 1483.

ALBI—TOULOUSE

Of towns in the South of France, Albi has already been mentioned for the second impression of the series of metal-cuts illustrating Turrecremata, *Meditationes*, 1481, which JOHANN NEUMEISTER, settled here between 1480 and 1483, had brought with him from Mainz, where he had published the first edition in 1479.[1]

Toulouse has also been noted in relation to the work of the monogrammist ID.[2] Apart from the woodcut there described, I would merely refer to a rough cut of *Christ carrying the Cross, with a kneeling Monk* in the *Imitation de Jesus Christ*, printed by HEINRICH MAYER, 28th March 1488,

[1] See p. 194; and for his work at Lyon, p. 608.
[2] See p. 616.

Fig. 367. Doctor and Patient, from *El Libro de proprietatibus rerum en romance*, Toulouse 1494.

as it is the first French edition of that famous book (H. 9120, Claudin-Ricci 633, Paris).

Mayer also printed a certain number of books in Spanish for export into Spain, one of the most notable being Bartholomaeus Anglicus, *El Libro de proprietatibus rerum en romance*, 1494. The woodcuts are naïvely crude in design and cutting, but of some interest for the style which seems to indicate a Spanish craftsman. The woodcut of *Doctor and Patient*, at the head of Book VII., *De las enfermedades*, is the most entertaining (fig. 367).

Poitiers—Bréhan-Loudéac—Dijon

Proceeding North to Poitiers, JEAN BOUYER and GUILLAUME BOUCHET may be noted for a delicately cut printer's mark of heraldic design (Meyer 169), and the same hand was certainly responsible for the attractive little woodcut of a *Preacher* in Guillaume Alexis, *Les Faintises du Monde*, issued by the same printers about 1494 (Claudin-Ricci 448-450, G.W. 1241, Vienna).

At Dijon, I would only mention two full-page cuts of the *Vierge de*

Miséricorde and of the *Members of the Cistercian Order* which occur in Joannes de Cirejo, *Privilegia ordinis Cisterciensis*, printed by PETRUS METLINGER, 1491.

Turning North-West, I would touch at Bréhan-Loudéac (a small place near Rohan, a little south of Loudéac, in Brittany), referring to an edition of Pierre Michault, *La Danse des Aveugles*, printed by ROBIN FOUCQUET and JEAN CRÈS, about 1485, which is only known in the Pierpont Morgan Library, New York (Pierpont Morgan 621, Claudin-Ricci 1926, No. 82). The cuts are crudely executed

Fig. 368. Annunciation, from Nicolaus de Lyra, *Les Postilles*, Troyes 1492.

in outline, and based on the Geneva edition of Louis Cruse (of about 1480), or the Lyon edition of about 1485.[1]

CHABLIS—TROYES

At Chablis and Troyes, Guillaume Le Rouge published a few books with woodcuts, between 1489 and 1493, before finally settling in Paris, where we shall meet another famous member of the family, Pierre Le Rouge.[2] Interesting cuts appeared in Maurice de Sully, *Les Expositions des Évangiles*, Chablis 1489 (Monceaux ii. 47, G. Le Rouge No. 2, Claudin-Ricci 92-99, Paris), and later, with additions, in Nicolaus de Lyra, *Les Postilles et Expositions des Épitres et Évangiles* (French version by Pierre Desrey), Troyes, 30th March 1492 (Monceaux ii. 57, G. Le Rouge No. 3, Claudin-Ricci 677-679).

A remarkable full-page cut of the *Crucifixion with the Three Crosses* (reprod. Claudin-Ricci 92), and numerous column cuts, appeared in both, and a few attractive woodcuts were added in *Les Postilles*. These included

---

[1] See pp. 617, and 602.
[2] See Henri Monceaux, *Les Le Rouge de Chablis*, Paris 1896.

on f. 1 an *Annunciation* (fig. 368) within a four-piece border (one piece bearing G. Le Rouge's name), and a *Resurrection* (about 4⅝ × 3¾ inches, reprod., Monceaux ii. 12, and Claudin-Ricci 679), a subject of which Dupré had a larger version (7¼ × 6 inches).[1] But most directly relevant to the later book were the illustrations on f. 2 of *Author and Scribe*, probably representing the translator Pierre Desrey with Jean des Barres (reprod., Monceaux ii. front., and Claudin-Ricci 678),[2] and, on the last leaf, *St. Jerome seated writing before a saintly assembly.*[3]

At Troyes, Guillaume Le Rouge printed, in 1491, *La Danse Macabre hystoriée* (Monceaux ii. 50, G. Le Rouge No. 2; Claudin-Ricci 672-77, Bourges), largely based on Marchant's Paris series, and much poorer in quality. Then about 1496, or a few years later, *La Grande Danse Macabre des hommes et des femmes* was printed at Troyes by Nicolas Le Rouge (Monceaux ii. 219, N. Le Rouge 2; Claudin-Ricci 682-84, Oxford, Le Mans, Dresden), in which the cuts of the dance proper were printed from Marchant's original blocks. At the end of this edition is the subject of the *Printer adoring the Virgin and Child*, which first appeared in Dupré's *Horae* of 4th February 1488/89.[4] The original shield is altered to contain Nicolas Le Rouge's initials.

ABBEVILLE—ROUEN

The last two provincial towns that claim our attention, Abbeville and Rouen, were provided directly from Paris with their best woodcuts, by the famous printer Jean Dupré. And it is known that Dupré assisted both PIERRE GÉRARD of Abbeville and JEAN LE BOURGEOIS of Rouen in the foundation of their presses, providing type as well as blocks, and lending one of his most experienced craftsmen, Pierre Violette.[5]

Raoul de Presles' French version of St. Augustine, *La Cité de Dieu*, issued at Abbeville in two volumes, of the 24th November 1486 and 12th April 1486/87, bears imprint of Jean Dupré and Pierre Gérard in collaboration. The book opens with a woodcut representing *Raoul de*

---

[1] E.g. in the *Sarum Missal*, printed by Dupré and his successors, Paris 1500 and 1504 (see p. 629). A close copy appeared in Pynson's *Sarum Missal* of 1512 (see p. 722).

[2] Reprinted by G. Tavernier, *La Règle des Marchands*, Provins 1496 (Claudin-Ricci 608, 609, Provins).

[3] The same block was used in Dupré's edition of St. Jerome, *Vie des Saints Pères Hermites*, Paris 1486. G. Le Rouge may have intended it to represent Nicolaus de Lyra.

[4] See p. 687.

[5] See Cl. i. 272.

Presles and Charles V., and thereafter each of the twenty books is headed by a woodcut (see fig. 369). The subjects are closely related to illuminations in certain manuscripts of the *Cité de Dieu*, being especially near to a MS. at Turin, done in 1466 for the Grand Bastard Antoine of Burgundy.[1]

In 1486, Gérard also printed an edition of Boutillier, *La Somme rurale* (Paris), containing the interesting full-page cut of *Charles VIII. enthroned*,[2] which also occurred in Nicolaus de Lyra, *Postilles sur le Livre des Psaumes*, printed by Pierre Le Rouge, Paris, about 1490 (Cl. i. 477), and in Martial d'Auvergnac, *Les Vigilles de la Mort du feu roy Charles VII.*, printed

Fig. 369. The Expulsion, from St. Augustine, *La Cité de Dieu*, Abbeville 1486–87.

at Paris by Dupré, 1493 (Cl. i. 275). It is impossible to say whether the block emanated originally from the workshop of Dupré or Pierre Le Rouge; but the double transfer led Claudin to suggest that Le Rouge might have been responsible for its making. In any case it shows the close relations that existed between Paris printers.

Le Triomphe des Neuf Preux, 30th May 1487, only bears Gérard's name in the colophon, but here again it is probable that Jean Dupré provided the

[1] For a detailed study of the MSS. see Alexandre de Laborde, *Les Manuscrits à peintures de la Cité de Dieu de Saint Augustin*, Paris 1909 (Société des Bibliophiles Français). Count de Laborde suggests that Pierre Le Rouge might have been the draughtsman and cutter who translated the miniatures for the printed work.

[2] Reproduced, Blum, *Les Origines du livre à gravures en France*, 1928, pl. iv.

blocks. Most attractive is the full-page frontispiece, with the *Author presenting his Book* (fig. 370), designed and cut in a freer manner than the rest in consonance with the contemporary scene. The heroes themselves are

Fig. 370. The Author presenting his book, from *Le Triomphe des Neuf Preux*, Abbeville 1487.

designed in a more decorative convention, powerful, if somewhat grotesque, in form, and cut in firm lines. The only exception to their flamboyant design is the subject of *Bertrand du Guesclin* himself, a bullet head which is proved to have been based on an authentic portrait tradition (fig. 371).

The most important illustrated book printed at Rouen is the first volume of Walter Map, *Le Livre des vertueux faix de plusieurs nobles chevaliers specialement du chevalier Lancelot du Lac*, issued by Jean Le Bourgeois, 24th November 1488. It was printed in Dupré's type, and Dupré himself printed the second volume at Paris, and his date of 16th September 1488 was no doubt an indication of the greater experience and dispatch of his own establishment (Cl. i. 272). There are half-page cuts at the head of the First and Second Parts of the Rouen volume (the second, representing a *Combat with Long Swords*, having also appeared at Abbeville in *La Cité de Dieu*, 1486–87).[1]

[1] It appeared later in Vérard's *Lancelot du Lac*, 1494.

But by far the most important illustration is the large woodcut of *King Arthur and his Knights at the Round Table*, within a four-piece border, with which the book opens (fig. 372). The outline borders are entirely in the manner of Dupré's atelier, and the fact that one of the other cuts had been used in a book in which Dupré collaborated with Gérard at Abbeville, apart from the con-nection with Dupré in the prints of the second volume of the work, renders it certain that Jean Le Bourgeois obtained his blocks from the same source.

Fig. 371. Bertrand du Guesclin, from *Le Triomphe des Neuf Preux*, Abbeville 1487.

Another splendid production of Rouen printing (no doubt seconded by Dupré) is the *Sarum Missal*, printed by MARTIN MORIN, 12th October 1492.[1] In addition to the full-page subjects regu-larly found in French Missals at the Canon of the Mass, *Christ on the Cross with the Virgin and St. John*, and *God the Father enthroned, with signs of the Evangelists*,[2] there is a beautiful four-piece border, with branch, bird, beast and flower motives, in the style of the Paris atelier of Jean Dupré. It occurs thrice, and at its first occurrence, at sig. a. 1, encloses a woodcut of the *Mass of St. Gregory* (about $5\frac{7}{8}$ inches square) which is near the work of Vérard's chief designer, and is freely modelled on the same subject in Dupré's *Verdun Missal* of 1481.[3] The original shows white stars on a black ground behind God the Father, while the

---

[1] See Ed. Frère, *De l'imprimerie et de la librairie à Rouen dans les XVe et XVIe siècles, et de Martin Morin*, Rouen 1843.

[2] This second subject is not found in German or Italian missals.   [3] See p. 628.

Morin version is in black line throughout. The border is not repeated in the British Museum copy of another edition of Morin's *Sarum Missal*, of about 1497 (IC. 43967), in which the full-page Canon cuts are also different (and within architectural framework), but it occurs in certain later editions printed at Rouen (e.g. one of 1513).[1] The edition of about 1497 bears on its title-page an interesting woodcut initial M with dragon, grotesque head, and Morin's name, and below a woodcut of *St. George and the Dragon* (about $6\frac{1}{2} \times 6$ inches),[2] with king and queen looking on from the city walls on the right, and at f. 126 a *Crucifixion of St. Andrew* ($5\frac{5}{8}$ inches square). Morin's edition of 1510 (Law Society's Library) has a smaller copy of the *St. George and the Dragon* ($4\frac{7}{8} \times 3\frac{1}{8}$ inches) below the title, and Canon cuts which appear to correspond with those in the 1492 edition, but other cuts as in the edition of about 1497.

Morin's printer's mark (Meyer 178) appears framed in four attractive border-pieces in the edition of about 1497.

PARIS

In my survey of Paris books I will first deal with the independent work of certain early printers (falling largely between 1481 and 1492), then with books published by Antoine Vérard from 1485 to the beginning of the xvi century (many being by the same printers after they came into his employ, chiefly after 1492), and thirdly with other printers in their independent work during the last decade of the fifteenth century.

The independent printers of the earlier group with whom I shall be concerned are Jean Dupré, Pierre Le Rouge, Jean Bonhomme, Antoine Caillaut and Louis Martineau, Pierre Levet, Guy Marchant, Gilles Couteau and Jean Menard.

I have already spoken of JEAN DUPRÉ for his collaboration with printers at Abbeville and Rouen. Apart from the fine quality of the woodcut work which proceeded from his workshops, he is notable as the printer of the first illustrated book published at Paris. His borders and decorative pieces, largely in outline, with designs of bird, beast, branch and flower, in the best tradition of medieval French illumination, are among the most beautiful

---

[1] Reproduced, J. Lieure, *La Gravure en France au XVIe siècle: La Gravure dans le livre et l'ornement*, Paris 1927, pl. ii.

[2] This occurs later on the reverse of the title of the *Art of good lyvynge and good deyng*, published by Vérard, Paris 1503 (see p. 662).

Fig. 372. King Arthur and his Knights at the Round Table, from Walter Map, *Le Livre des vertueux faix de plusieurs nobles chevaliers*, Rouen 1488.

productions of the time. This side of his work is seen at its best in the *Book of Hours*, which will be treated separately later in this chapter.

His earliest illustrated book is the *Paris Missal* of 22nd September 1481, which he printed in collaboration with DESIDERIUS HUYM (Cl. i. 209, H.C. 11339, Pr. 7920), containing the usual *Canon* cuts in French Missals, *God the Father enthroned, with the signs of the Evangelists*, and the *Christ on the Cross with the Virgin and St. John*, each full-page, designed with a certain stiff dignity and powerfully cut, slightly arched above, and with a cross outside the border-line below.[1]

In his *Verdun Missal* of 28th November 1481 (Cl. i. 218, Paris), added to his *Canon* cuts, is a large woodcut of the *Mass of St. Gregory* within four-piece borders.[2] And the same Missal also contains a variety of smaller upright subjects, averaging about $4\frac{1}{4} \times 3$ inches (the *Adoration of the Shepherds*, *Presentation in the Temple*, *La Cour Céleste*, *Les Trois Morts* being reproduced by Claudin). Throughout his career (1481–1504) Dupré was printing Missals, Breviaries and Synodical Statutes for many dioceses outside Paris, among the earliest being the *Chartres Missal* of 1482 (Cl. i. 217, Paris) and the *Limoges Missal* of 1483/84 (Cl. i. 220, Limoges). In the dedication of the latter he makes the interesting statement that the work had been achieved by the help of Venetian craftsmen whom he had brought to Paris (*per Venetos arte impressoria magnificos et valde expertos completum*), adding in the colophon that it was printed in the Venetian manner (*Venetica forma*).[3] Venice was at this period the chief centre for the printing of liturgical books, and Claudin refers to a *Nantes Missal* of 1482 having been printed at Venice,[4] and several later French Missals printed at Venice are described by Essling (e.g. 149, *Paris Missal*, 1487, by J. Hamman de Landoia and J. Emericus de Spira, and 144, *Clermont-Ferrand Missal*, 1492, by Joannes Antonius Birreta).

Angers, Arras, Besançon, Meaux, Reims, Troyes, are among the dioceses for which Dupré provided liturgical books. His *Sarum Missal* of 30th

---

[1] Claudin, *Documents sur la typographie et la gravure en France*, ed. S. de Ricci, 1926, No. 242. Four copies are known, Paris (Bibl. Nat., Bibl. St. Geneviève, and Seymour de Ricci) and Oxford.

[2] Leo S. Olschki, *Le Livre illustré au XVᵉ siècle* (Florence 1926, No. 117, and fig. 181), reproduces the *Mass of St. Gregory* within the same borders as from the *Paris Missal* of 22nd September 1481, but M. Seymour de Ricci informs me that its type is not Dupré 1 and 2 (as in the 1481 ed.), and that it is probably an issue of about 1491.

[3] For other business transactions between Dupré and Venetian printers see p. 630, note 5.

[4] Described as printed by Bartholomaeus de Alexandria (de Blavis), Andrea d' Asola (Torresanus) and Maphaeus de Salodio (Paterbonis) (Cl. i. 220). It is not described by Essling.

Fig. 373. Initial T, from the *Sarum Missal*, Paris 1500 and 1504.

September 1500 (Cl. i. 263, Duff 331, STC. 16175) shows how far-reaching was his fame. There are copies in the Law Society's Library, at Christ's College, Cambridge, and in the Cathedral Library at Ely, but the last named is the only one complete with *Canon* cut. Of the *Sarum Missal* the British Museum has a later edition printed by Dupré's heirs in 1504 (STC. 16178), with a printed note on the title-page that it was sold by booksellers in St. Paul's Churchyard (*Venales apud bibliopolas in cimyterio sancti Pauli Londoñ. invenientur*).

Besides the *Canon* cut, and a small initial T[1] on dotted ground, with a *Christ on the Cross between the Virgin and St. John* (fig. 373), it contains the *Mass of St. Gregory*, to which we have already alluded, as in Dupré's *Verdun Missal* of 1481, a *Resurrection* (about 7¼ × 6 inches), of the same design as a smaller cut in *Les Postilles* of Nicolaus de Lyra, printed by Guillaume Le Rouge at Troyes, 1492,[2] and a smaller column cut of the *Descent of the Spirit*. The illustrations noted are from the same blocks as those in the edition of 1500.

Missals and Breviaries being made for use in churches are inevitably rare in private collections. Even those compiled according to the rite of different dioceses or monastic orders, which all gave way to the uniform Roman ritual after the Council of Trent (1563), mostly remained in their respective dioceses or convents, and are as rare outside as the liturgies which remained in use. Of liturgical books it is chiefly the small Books of Hours, made for private devotion, that have been available to collectors.

Dupré's edition of Laurent du Premier-Fait's translation of Boccaccio, *Les Cas et Ruynes des nobles hommes et femmes*, 26th February 1483/84 (Cl. i. 222), appears to have been the earliest illustrated book in French printed at Paris (see fig. 374). Its nine woodcuts, beginning with the *Author writing, and the Expulsion from Paradise*, which are somewhat sketchily designed and cut, were borrowed by Richard Pynson for John Lydgate's English version, the *Fall of Princes*, which he printed at London in 1494.[3]

Not unlike in character is the frontispiece, the only woodcut in Vérard's edition of Boccaccio, *Les Cent Nouvelles*, 22nd November 1485, a French version of the *Decameron* by the same translator (Cl. i. 226, Paris), and typographical reasons also favour the inference that Dupré was commissioned by Vérard to print this edition. In its loose style of handling

---

[1] Originally in Pierre Le Rouge's *Toul Missal*, 1492.   [2] See p. 621.   [3] See p. 732.

(contrasting with the decided line of most of Vérard's later woodcuts) it is comparable with such woodcuts as the *Translator presenting his book to the King*, which appeared in the edition of Caesar, *Commentaires* (French version by R. Gaguin), 1485, attributed by Claudin (vol. i. p. 417, Paris, Bibl. Mazarine, and St. Geneviève) to Pierre Levet, and in Sydrach, *La Fontaine de toutes Sciences*, Vérard, 1486/87 (Macf. 5),[1] and with the similar subject in the *Triomphe des Neuf Preux*, printed by Gérard, Abbeville 1487.[2]

Fig. 374. The Death of Saul, from Boccaccio, *Les Cas et Ruynes des nobles hommes et femmes*, Paris 1483/84.

To 1486 belongs Dupré's edition of St. Jerome, *Vie des Saints Pères Hermites* (Cl. i. 228), with a full-page frontispiece of *St. Jerome seated writing before a saintly assembly*,[3] numerous column cuts, well designed and clearly cut, somewhat Netherlandish in character (see fig. 375), and interesting initials with figures and grotesque heads.

The earliest French illustrated editions of the *Lives of the Saints* appear to be those published at Lyon,[4] but Dupré followed soon after with his *Légende Dorée* of 7th October 1489 (Cl. i. 264, École des Beaux-Arts, Paris, from J. Masson), with the usual small column cuts.[5] He also printed, in col-

[1] Reproduced, A. Blum, *Les Origines du livre à gravures en France*, 1928, pl. xxviii., and J. Macfarlane, *Antoine Vérard*, London (Bibliographical Society) 1900, pl. v.

[2] See p. 623.

[3] Used later by Guillaume Le Rouge at Troyes (see p. 622).   [4] See p. 603.

[5] These blocks, as well as others from his *Vie des Saints Pères Hermites* of 1486, were printed in Venetian issues of the Golden Legend in 1504 and 1514 (see Essling, *Livres à figures vénitiens*, Nos. 682 and 686), and E. P. Goldschmidt & Co., *Medieval Literature and Science*, List 5, London [1932], No. 157 A. The fact that Dupré had a second series cut for his edition of 1493/94

laboration with André Bocard, a larger folio of the same work, 10th March 1493/94 (Cl. i. 269), with a different series of cuts, and an edition of May 1496, whose blocks, according to Claudin, were printed later by Jean de Vingle at Lyon, 1497 (Cl. iv. 230), and again in Paris by Nicolas de la Barre, 1499 (Cl. ii. 290-92). I might add here that Vérard also published editions of the *Légende Dorée*, 10th February 1490/91 (Macf. 14, Vienna), 2nd June 1493 (M. 28, Paris, Pierpont Morgan 505), and 20th May 1496 (Macf. 45, Paris), and an edition of St. Jerome, *Vie des Pères*, on 15th October 1495 (Macf. 43).[1]

Fig. 375. St. Ammon, from St. Jerome, *Vie des Saints Pères*, Paris 1486.

I will here interpolate some account of the printer PIERRE LE ROUGE, returning later to other works printed by Dupré, in which he used blocks from Le Rouge's most famous book, *La Mer des Hystoires*. He belonged to a large family of scribes and illuminators, turned printers.[2] Jacques Le Rouge (Jacobus Rubeus), the earliest of the printers, friend and compatriot of Nicolaus Jenson, was working at Venice from 1470 to 1478, and in other parts of Italy till 1481 or later, afterwards returning to France, and printing a local Breviary at Embrun (Dauphiné) in 1489–90. He describes himself in this Breviary as a Frenchman of the diocese of Langres, so that Chablis, where others of his name worked, was probably the cradle of the family. Of the four other printers of the name, Jean, Pierre, Guillaume and Nicolas, only Guillaume, Nicolas and Pierre come within our survey. We have already spoken of books printed by Guillaume at Chablis and Troyes, 1489–92; and by Nicolas at Troyes (about 1496).[3] Of Guillaume's later activity in Paris, 1493–1517,

renders it probable that the original blocks had been disposed of before that date, though no Italian edition containing them has been identified before that of 1504. It should also be noted that many of the subjects (and possibly some of the blocks) from Dupré's *Books of Hours* were used in Venetian *Horae* of the early XVI century (Essling, Nos. 467 and 472).

[1] See p. 671.

[2] See Henri Monceaux, *Les Le Rouge de Chablis: Étude sur les débuts de l'illustration du livre au XVᵉ siècle*, 2 vols., Paris 1896. The book is full of interesting material about French book-illustration in general. Its fault is the wholesale attribution of woodcut work to one or other of the Le Rouge, on purely conjectural grounds. References may frequently be given to his catalogue even though the attributions are incorrect, as it contains the fullest descriptions available of many books. [3] See pp. 621, 622.

no books of any certain attribution belong to our period, for Monceaux's list is largely conjectural. Pierre Le Rouge (who from 1487 describes himself as 'imprimeur du Roi') remains incomparably the most important member of the family, and chiefly on account of the *Mer des Hystoires*, which he printed for Vincent Commin in two volumes, July 1488 and February 1488/89 (B.M., Paris, Pierpont Morgan Library, New York). The two large folios, with 257 numbered leaves in vol. i., and 271, in addition to 28 unnumbered leaves, in vol. ii., printed in double columns, contain an immense amount of material in historical and legendary lore, with a very large number of woodcut illustrations. The number of blocks used is far less than the number of illustrations, for the prints are often stock subjects, repeated in many different positions throughout the work.

The book itself is translated from that epitome of legend and history, the *Rudimentum Noviciorum*, first printed by Brandis at Lübeck, 1475,[1] the chronicle being continued to 1483 (the Coronation of Charles VIII.), by the anonymous translator. The illustrations are also derived to a considerable extent from the same source, but they render the originals very freely, and they include a great variety of new subjects and a wealth of new decorative material. The borders are particularly beautiful, following in outline the best traditions of the French illuminators, a charming medley of branch, leaf, bird, beast and man (see fig. 376). There are three immense decorative initials, P with the author writing, T with the Redeemer, and S in the form of a dragon, in addition to the gothic L with St. George and the Dragon of the title-page. The most important full-page cut, again very near to the illumination of the period, is the twofold subject, the *Baptism of Clovis and the Battle of Tolbiac*, at f. 214 of the second volume (fig. 377). The other full-page or double folio plates are maps of the world and the Holy Land, and many genealogies designed as in the *Rudimentum Noviciorum* in the form of chains, interspersed with little scriptural and historical scenes. Then

Fig. 376. Border-piece from the *Mer des Hystoires*, Paris 1488–89.

[1] See p. 363

Fig. 377. Baptism of Clovis and the Battle of Tolbiac, from the *Mer des Hystoires*, Paris 1488–89.

there are numerous column cuts of various sizes, largely little upright subjects, the scriptural and historical subjects being generally more elaborate and less interesting than the freshly designed scenes from

contemporary life. They are all repeated time after time as stock illustrations of similar scenes and personages, for innumerable are the opportunities for using the death of a king in battle (the best and most expressive of the historical series), a battle scene, the storming of a city, a meeting of kings, king in council and the like. Among the subjects treated more completely in the vein of contemporary genre, and applied to saints, philosophers and men of learning are — a monk seated writing,[1] a monk standing reading and a woman visiting a doctor (fig. 378), a nagging philosopher, the astronomer, the lecturer, the preacher, the congregation. They are probably by

Fig. 378. Woman visiting a Doctor, from the *Mer des Hystoires*, Paris 1488–89.

the same designer as the woodcuts to *Maistre Pierre Pathelin* printed by Levet and Germain Bineaut.[2] Then two good large oblong subjects, one of the *Destruction of Pharaoh's Host* and the other a two-fold illustration of *Soldiers by a River outside a City, and Procession of Priests in a Church.* Finally, between ff. 70 and 107 in volume ii., a series of ten little cuts (measuring about $2\frac{7}{8} \times 1\frac{7}{8}$ inches) within borders, illustrating the life of the Virgin and the life of Christ (fig. 379).[3] These cuts and borders, with a woodcut surface covering about $4\frac{1}{2} \times 3$ inches, correspond in style to the Dupré-Caillaut group described below,[4] while seven of the subject-blocks are actually printed in Meslier's *Horae* of 14th February 1489/90.[5]

In a second edition of the *Mer des Hystoires* published by Vérard about 1503 (B.M., C. 7. d. 4, 5), the book is largely the same in text and illustration, with the addition of some thirty-eight folios of text in the second

---

[1] E.g. at f. 44, verso, within single border-line, measuring 74×60 mm. Another cut of a *Monk seated writing*, slightly larger and within triple border-lines (95×77 mm.), done in a more detailed setting, occurs at f. 42, and elsewhere (fig. 380), and was repeated in Vérard's *Art de bien Mourir* of 1492, and in various other books.   [2] See pp. 642, 643.

[3] Eight of these are reproduced by Claudin, i. 466-67.

[4] See p. 683.   [5] See p. 685.

volume, bringing the history down to the Italian expedition of Louis XII., in 1499–1500. A considerable number of small initial letters (Gothic calligraphy with grotesque heads) have been added where spaces were left in the first issue for the rubricator, and a very large folding cut (about $14\frac{1}{4} \times 30$ inches) illustrating the *Battle of Fornovo* (1495) is added after f. 292 in the second volume. Reference has already been made to the edition printed by Jean Dupré at Lyon in 1491.[1] Successive editions both at Paris and Lyon, e.g. those of Davost, Lyon 1506, and of Enguilbert de Marnef and François Regnault, Paris, about 1517, bring down the history to about the time of printing. It is noteworthy that the illustrations of the edition of Marnef and Regnault are printed promiscuously from the blocks of both Le Rouge and Dupré.

Fig. 379. The Annunciation, from the *Mer des Hystoires*, Paris 1488–89.

The excellence of the *Mer des Hystoires* probably induced Antoine Vérard to enlist Pierre Le Rouge among the various printers who worked on his publications. We have already mentioned one other independent work of Pierre Le Rouge (Nicolaus de Lyra, *Les Postilles sur le Livre des Psaulmes*, Paris, about 1490), for the woodcut of Charles VIII. enthroned (fig. 381), which had appeared earlier at Abbeville, and was used in 1493 by Dupré.[2]

Further examples of the relations between Dupré and Pierre Le Rouge may be cited in the use of various blocks from the *Mer des Hystoires* in Martial d'Auvergne, *Les Vigilles de la Mort du Roy Charles VII.*, Paris, 8th May 1493 (Cl. i. 275), and Honorat Bonnor, *L'Arbre des Batailles*, Paris, 22nd June 1493 (Cl. i. 275), both printed by Dupré. In one case two

[1] See p. 612.   [2] See p. 623.

subjects are made by dividing the oblong block of *Soldiers by a River outside a City and Procession of Priests in a Church*, noted among the illustrations of the *Mer des Hystoires*. Claudin refers to the fact that no books bear

Fig. 380. Monk seated writing, from the *Mer des Hystoires*, Paris 1488–89.

Pierre Le Rouge's name from 1483 (at Chablis) until 1488 (at Paris), and in view of the various relations we have noted between Le Rouge and Dupré at Paris and Abbeville, he conjectures that Le Rouge might have been working on blocks for Dupré during this period of 1483–87.

The conjecture is reasonable, and Pierre Le Rouge may be responsible for designing (or even cutting) such blocks as those of the Abbeville *Cité de Dieu*,[1] but it must be remembered that it is pure conjecture. Far more hypothetical are the attributions to Pierre and Guillaume Le Rouge made by Monceaux of the printing of so many of the books published by Vérard.[2] They are based chiefly on the fact that many of the cuts from the *Mer des Hystoires* are used in Vérard's books, but as they also appear in books printed independently by Dupré the argument is invalidated.[3] Monceaux's attributions equally lack support from more recent typographical research. There is, in fact, no more specific evidence of the activity of any of the Le Rouge family as designers or woodcutters than there is of Vérard himself, who from his education as scribe and illustrator might equally have designed many of the illustrations of his own books. But busy printers and publishers are more likely to have used other craftsmen for cutting their blocks.

---

[1] See p. 622.

[2] Monceaux describes Guillaume, who carried on Pierre's establishment in Paris after 1493, as Pierre's son and heir.

[3] Nevertheless, after Pierre Le Rouge's death in 1492, Vérard certainly commanded the use of Pierre Le Rouge's stock of illustrations more than any other printer or publisher.

Apart from the blocks from the *Mer des Hystoires*, Martial d'Auvergne, *Les Vigilles de la Mort du Roy Charles VII.*, printed by Dupré, 1493, contains

Fig. 381. Charles VIII. enthroned, from Nicolaus de Lyra, *Postilles sur le Livre des Psaumes*, Paris, about 1490.

the same frontispiece of Charles VIII. enthroned used by Pierre Le Rouge in 1490, and by Gérard at Abbeville, 1486,[1] and various new illustrations

---

[1] See p. 623.

and initials. Several of the subjects are of interest as illustrating the history of Jeanne d'Arc, though the designs can only be regarded as imaginary representations. The woodcut reproduced in fig. 382, 'comment les Angloys amenèrent la pucelle à Rouen et la firent mourir', is strongly designed and cut in the style of a designer who constantly worked for Vérard's books.

¶ Comment les angloys amenerent la pucelle a rouen/⁊ la firent mourir

Fig. 382. Jeanne d'Arc taken to prison at Rouen, from Martial d'Auvergne, *Les Vigilles de la Mort du Roy Charles V.*, Paris 1493.

The initials are a very attractive series, in which the main part of the letter is shown as black (patterned with white branch), and decorated outside with scroll-work in delicate outline (fig. 383).

Dupré's *Arbre des Batailles* contains many of the same cuts from the *Mer des Hystoires* as *Les Vigilles*, and here again one of the blocks, which had previously appeared at Abbeville, recurs as frontispiece, i.e. the *Group of Officers outside a City* (from *Cité de Dieu*, Abbeville 1486, Bk. I.).[1]

[1] See p. 622.

Fig. 383. Initial S, from *Les Vigilles de la Mort du Roy Charles V.*, Paris 1493.

Vérard's edition of *L'Arbre des Batailles*, to which we shall refer later, is entirely different in its illustration.

Reference has already been made to the printer Pasquier Bonhomme, and his son JEAN BONHOMME carried on his press 'à l'Image de Saint-Christophe'.[1]

Two books printed by Jean Bonhomme contain woodcuts of particular interest, showing the work of a designer of individual character. Jacques Millet, *L'Istoire de la destruction de Troye*, issued 12th May 1484 (Cl. i. 182, Dresden), contains a series of oblong cuts, including many battle scenes, and

Fig. 384. Frontispiece to Jacques Millet, *L'Istoire de la Destruction de Troye*, Paris 1484.

a very attractive allegorical frontispiece, *The Author and a Shepherdess; the Author digging to the roots of the Tree of France* (fig. 384). Copies of the cuts appeared the year later in an edition printed at Lyon by Matthias Huss (Fairfax Murray, Davies 381).

---

[1] See p. 597, and Pierre Gusman, *L'Atelier typographique de 'l'Image de Saint-Christophe' in Paris, 1475–1490*, Byblis ii. (1923) 135.

The book was also reprinted with the original cuts by Jean Driart for Vérard, 1498 (Cl. ii. 331). Many of the military scenes also reappeared, printed from the original blocks, in Robert Gaguin's French version of Julius Caesar, *Commentaires*, 1485, attributed by Claudin to Pierre Levet (Cl. i. 417, Paris). There is also an edition of the *Commentaires* about 1488,

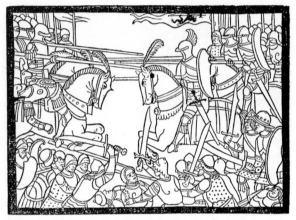

Fig. 385. Battle scene, from Caesar, *Commentaires*, Paris, about 1488.

published by Vérard, and attributed in the British Museum to the printer Pierre le Caron (Proctor 8141), which contains three of the same blocks, repeated to make eight illustrations (see fig. 385), and Vérard's Vegetius, *L'Art de la Chevalerie*, 26th June 1488 (Macf. 6), is another book which repeats some of the same series of cuts.

The second of Jean Bonhomme's books to which I alluded is Petrus de Crescentiis, *Livre des Ruraulx Prouffitz*, issued 15th October 1486 (Cl. i. 190). There are a few cuts representing country occupations and sports, but the frontispiece of the *Author presenting his book to a King* (fig. 386) is by far the most interesting, excellent in grouping and in facial expression. In style it is something of a French counterpart to the frontispiece group in Schoeffer's *Gart der Gesuntheit*, Mainz 1485 (H. 8948). Jean Bonhomme was probably also the printer of a Herbal (*Aggregator practicus de simplicibus*) issued about 1485 (Proctor 8050, Cl. i. 195), but the 150 cuts of plants are merely copies of the Mainz *Herbarius Latinus*, issued by Schoeffer in 1484 (H. 8444).[1]

Two books printed by CAILLAUT and MARTINEAU contain small cuts by

[1] See pp. 348-352.

a designer of a certain expressive quality, i.e. Jacques Le Grand, *Le Livre des bonnes Meurs*, 7th June 1487 (Cl. i. 306, locality not known to me), and the *Eruditorium penitentiale*, about 1490 (Cl. i. 320).

PIERRE LEVET is another of the printers who did independent work before Vérard secured his services. We have already mentioned the first edition

Fig. 386. The Author presenting his book to a king, from Petrus de Crescentiis, *Livre des Ruraulx Prouffitz*, Paris 1486.

of Robert Gaguin's translation of Julius Caesar, *Les Commentaires*, 1485, which is attributed by Claudin to Levet. The frontispiece, representing the *Translator presenting his book to the King*,[1] is designed and cut with a free touch, somewhat like the frontispiece to Dupré's Boccaccio, *Les Cent Nouvelles*, of 22nd November 1485, and the frontispiece of *Les Neuf Preux*, Abbeville 1487.[2] The frontispiece of the same subject in the second Paris edition of Gaguin's translation, published by Vérard about 1488,[3] is from a new block, and one that was thereafter used in many of Vérard's books (fig. 387).[4]

In 1486 Levet already appears to be working for Vérard, but three

[1] See p. 630.   [2] See pp. 623, 624, 654.   [3] See p. 640.   [4] See p. 656.

further independent works should be noted. In the first place a small
Latin Psalter, 19th February 1488/89 (Cl. i. 435), with four illustrations
of delicate design and cutting, *David and Goliath*, *David standing with his
Harp*, the *Descent of the Spirit* and the *Flight into Egypt*. The *David with his*

Fig. 387. The Translator presenting his book to Charles VIII., from
Caesar, *Commentaires*, about 1488.

Harp and the *Flight into Egypt* are also found in *Horae*, e.g. in an edition by
Dupré in the British Museum (IA. 39817), and in another *Horae* issued
by Vérard, 8th February 1489/90 and reprinted by Laurens Philippe, 1493
(B.M., IA. 40633).[1] Then the *Grand Testament de Maistre François Villon*,
1489 (Cl. i. 439, Paris, British Museum),[2] and the *Maistre Pierre Pathelin* of

[1] See pp. 683 and 689.

[2] Facsimile of the Paris copy edited by Pierre Champion, Paris 1925. The *Grand Testament
de Villon* was also printed by Jean Trepperel in 1495 and 1497 (Cl. ii. 160); facsimile of the 1497
edition, Lille 1869. The two figures of *Villon* and *Margot* are either from the original blocks or
very close copies (I have only been able to see the facsimile); *L'Évêque* and the *Three Men on the
Gallows* are considerably modified.

about the same date (Cl. i. 443, Paris). The little woodcuts in both these works are well designed and expressively cut, and three single figures in the *Testament de Villon*, representing François Villon (fig. 388), his mistress, 'la grosse Margot', and L'Évêque Thibault, were copied later in Marchant's *Danse Macabre* (in edition 4, of 1490/91) and *Compost et Kalendrier des Bergiers*.[1] The blocks of *Maistre Pierre Pathelin* were reprinted by Germain Bineaut in an edition of 20th December 1490 (Cl. ii. 304, Paris). Though Levet's edition is not dated, it is proved to be earlier by the condition of the blocks. The woodcuts of *Maistre Pierre Pathelin* seem to be by the same designer as the little cuts of contemporary genre in Le Rouge's *Mer des Hystoires* (the *Woman visiting a Doctor*, and others).

GUY MARCHANT is a printer of equal importance to Jean Dupré and Pierre Le Rouge in the history of woodcut illustration in Paris, and the two books which owe their inception to him, the *Danse Macabre* and the *Compost et Kalendrier des Bergiers*, were among the most popular works of the time and illustrated with woodcuts of great interest. In quality the first series of the *Danse Macabre*

Fig. 388. François Villon, from the *Grand Testament de Maistre François Villon*, Paris 1489.

des Hommes is perhaps the finest achievement of French woodcut in the xv century, designed with a fine expressive power and cut with beautiful precision (see fig. 389).

Marchant's woodcuts and verses seem to have been immediately based on two MSS. in the Bibliothèque Nationale from the Abbey of Saint-Victor (MS. lat. 14904 and MS. franc. 25550), but these are themselves derived from wall-paintings no longer extant, done in 1425 in the Cemetery of the Innocents at Paris.[2] Nevertheless the translation into line and into contemporary costume practically implies an independent work.

[1] The *Grand Testament* contains ten illustrations printed with repetitions from four blocks, the three figures in question and the *Three Men on the Gallows* illustrating Villon's epitaph. The episode of *Three Men on the Gallows* also appears in the woodcut of the *Entrance to Hell* which occurs in the *Danse Macabre* (ed. 2, 1486).

[2] See Valentin Dufour, *Recherches sur la Danse Macabre peinte en 1425 au Cimetière des Innocents*, Paris 1873 (and later editions of 1874 and 1875 with variant titles and reproductions of Marchant's woodcuts). The story of *Les Trois Morts et les Trois Vifs* also appeared in sculpture on the door of the cemetery church.

La Danse Macabre (*mirouer salutaire*) went through various editions,[1] and shows clearly the hand of two designers, the first (whom we shall call Designer A) responsible for the *Danse des Hommes*, the second, Designer B, responsible for most of the *Danse des Femmes* (see fig. 390). Designer B first appears in ed. 4. Designer A is by far the more distinguished, mordant in

Fig. 389. The Astrologer and the Bourgeois, from the *Danse Macabre des Hommes*, Paris (Marchant) 1491/92.

expression, and achieving his effects with subtlety of drawing and without exaggeration. He has something of the same style as Jean Bonhomme's designer referred to above.[2] Designer B is less sensitive in drawing and exaggerated in his types, with the angularity and the straight long noses characteristic of the designer who worked largely for Vérard.[3] In its expanded form, described from ed. 5 (British Museum, Huth), the work includes:[4]

> I. *La Danse Macabre des Hommes*: the frontispiece of the *Author at a desk* (1st version), the *Orchestra of Death* (1st version),

---

[1] See Claudin i. 236, etc.; Monceaux, P. Le Rouge, 1 (i.-x.), G. Le Rouge, 2, N. Le Rouge, 2.

[2] See p. 639.   [3] See p. 654.

[4] See *Catalogue of the Fifty MSS. and Printed Books bequeathed to the British Museum by Alfred Huth*, London 1912, Nos. xxv., xxvi.

20 cuts of the *Danse des Hommes,* and the *Author's Epilogue,* by Designer A; *Death on a Horse* by Designer B.

II. *La Danse Macabre des Femmes*: the *Author writing* (2nd version), the *Orchestra of Death* (2nd version), 18 cuts of the *Danse des Femmes,* the *Trumpeter of Death on a Tower,* the *Author's*

Fig. 390. The Chambermaid and the Matron, from the *Danse Macabre des Femmes,* Paris 1492.

Epilogue, and *Death on a Horse* (the last two repeated from Part I.). The first two cuts of the dance and the *Author's Epilogue* by Designer A; the remainder of the dance by Designer B; the *Trumpeter,* uncertain; the *Author writing* more powerfully cut than the dance of Designer B, and nearer to Vérard's chief designer. Poem of the *Author's Epilogue* further illustrated by three small figures of women, one copied from *La Grosse Margot* of *Le Grand Testament de Villon* (Levet, 1489), the others in the same style (possibly Designer B).

III. *Les Trois Morts et les Trois Vifs*: 2 cuts by Designer A.

IV. *Le Débat du corps et de l'âme*: 4 cuts, the soul represented in the form of a child, repeated to make 8 illustrations, by Designer A.

V. *La Complainte de l'âme damnée*: 1 cut, the *Entrance to Hell*, by Designer A.

Editions are as follows:

(1) 28*th September* 1485. Part I. only. Grenoble. 17 cuts: the *Author writing* (1st version), 15 cuts of the *Danse des Hommes*, the *Author's Epilogue.*

(2) 7*th June* 1486. Part I. ⎰H. 313. Paris.[1]
    7*th July* 1486. Part II. ⎱With title *Miroer Salutaire*, and at foot of title-page *La Danse Macabre Nouvelle.*

Part I. The *Author at a desk* (1st version), the *Orchestra of Death* (1st version), 20 cuts of the *Danse des Hommes*, the *Author's Epilogue*, 2 cuts of *Les Trois Morts* and *Les Trois Vifs.*

Part II. The *Author writing* (2nd version), the *Orchestra of Death* (1st version, repeated), 1 cut of the *Danse des Femmes* (Queen and Duchess), the *Author's Epilogue*, 4 cuts of the *Débat du corps et de l'âme* (repeated to make 8 illustrations), the *Entrance to Hell.*

(3) 15*th October* 1490. Latin edition. *Speculum salutare choree macabri.* Printed by Marchant for Geoffroi de Marnef. Paris. The cuts nearly as in ed. 2.

(4) 20*th January* 1490/91. Part I. ⎧Paris.
    10*th April* 1491. Part II. ⎪Title of Part I. *La Nouvelle Danse Macabre.*
    2*nd May* 1491. Parts III.-V. ⎨Contents nearly as in the Huth copy, B.M.

(5) 15*th April* 1491/92. Part I. ⎫
    3*rd May* 1492. Part II. ⎬British Museum (Huth).
    22*nd May* 1492. Parts III.-V. ⎭

The original blocks as well as certain copies were reprinted in various editions at Troyes, e.g. by Guillaume Le Rouge, 1491 (Bourges, and Comte de Lignerolles, Monceaux, G. Le Rouge 2),[2] and Nicolas Le Rouge, about 1496 (N. Le Rouge 2).[3] The blocks remained in the hands of the successors

---

[1] This edition reproduced in facsimile with introduction by Pierre Champion, Paris 1925.

[2] Claudin, ii. 126, refers to an edition by Le Petit Laurens, after 1494 (only known at Poitiers), which he describes as from the same blocks as G. Le Rouge, and as copies of the Marchant series.   [3] See p. 622.

of the Le Rouge press at Troyes until the XVIII century. An edition of Jean Garnier, 1728, may be cited which contains late impressions from both original blocks and copies.[1]

A most excellent series of copies of the *Danse Macabre des Hommes* was printed by COUTEAU and MENARD, Paris, 26th June 1492 (Cl. ii.

Fig. 391. The Astrologer and the Bourgeois, from the *Danse Macabre des Hommes,* Paris (Couteau and Menard) 1492.

174, Monceaux, P. Le Rouge 8, Paris). It contains the two subjects of *Les Trois Morts* and *Les Trois Vifs* but nothing else outside Part I. of the original series. In quality it is considerably inferior to the work of Marchant's Designer A; in style it is nearer to Vérard's chief designer, but it is cut with less angularity and force of line than in Vérard's most typical cuts. The use of white and black for the herbage is a decorative feature (see fig. 391).

The block of the *Author seated,* done in the style of Vérard's chief

---

[1] See E. P. Goldschmidt, London, Catalogue VIII. No. 129.

designer, was used later by Quentell at Cologne in his Aristotle, *De Anima*, 1499.[1]

As Couteau and Menard succeeded Pierre Le Rouge in printing Vérard's *Art de bien Mourir* in 1492, it is probable that their *Danse Macabre*[2] was also done at the instance of Vérard.

La Dance Macabre printed for Jean Trepperel by Nicolas de la Barre, Paris 1500, is a small book containing crude cuts in which Marchant's designs are copied very freely.

We have already described the interesting series of copies printed by Matthias Huss, at Lyon, 18th February 1499/1500.[3] The *Author seated*, the *Danse des Hommes* and *Les Trois Morts et les Trois Vifs* of this edition were copied from Couteau and Menard, but the *Danse des Femmes*, *Death on a Horse*, the *Trumpeter of Death*, and the *Débat du corps et de l'âme*, were based on Marchant, reflecting the different character of Marchant's Designers A and B in the *Danse des Femmes*. This is fairly clear proof that Couteau and Menard never completed their work, or Huss would almost certainly have used his originals throughout. The chief interest of the Lyon edition lies in its independent designs, notably the illustration of *Death and the Printers* (fig. 355).

The xv century was a time of recurrent plague throughout Europe, and moralists and preachers must have found ready listeners and readers for the vivid warnings contained in such works as *La Danse Macabre*. We have already noted other versions of the same theme in Germany,[4] and the many editions of the block-book *Ars Moriendi*, and Holbein's wonderful series of the first half of the xvi century, offer further examples of the popularity of such writings and pictures. And in the present chapter we have still to deal with Vérard's editions of *L'Art de bien Vivre et de bien Mourir*.

We should probably be wrong in thinking that these subjects suggested any exaggerated grimness in the mind of the ordinary man of the xv or xvi centuries. In Paris the Cemetery of the Innocents was a popular promenade on holidays, as cemeteries are to-day in America, and the popular enjoyment of the pomp of funerals is by no means extinct.

---

[1] See p. 362.

[2] Monceaux, P. Le Rouge 2, refers to two series of impressions of Couteau and Menard's *Danse Macabre* in the Bibl. Nationale, Paris, without title-page, printer's name or date, as done for Vérard in 1485, describing them as copies by P. Le Rouge, done almost immediately after Marchant's originals appeared. They happen to be without the *Orchestra of Death* which first appeared in Marchant's edition of 1492, but I find no certain evidence for the existence of an edition of 1485.

[3] See p. 605.   [4] See pp. 343 and 366.

Marchant's other great works, *Le Compost et Kalendrier des Bergiers* and *Le Compost et Kalendrier des Bergères*,[1] throw a happier light on contemporary life, and through the mouthpiece of the Shepherd offer a rich mine of lore relating to the whole existence of the countryman of the period. The former work as developed in its second edition included five sections:

(1) The Calendar proper.
(2) Tree of the Vices and the Pains of Hell.
(3) The Way of Health and the Tree of the Virtue.
(4) Physic and the Governance of Health.
(5) Astrology and Physiognomy.

Claudin was the first bibliographer, I believe, to describe the *editio princeps* of 2nd May 1491 (dated on the same day that he completed his *Nouvelle Danse Macabre*), of which only two copies are known, at Bourges and in the Bibliothèque Mazarine, Paris. It is a small folio of only thirty leaves, with far fewer woodcuts than appeared in the succeeding editions. It opens with the cut of the *Shepherd and the Stars* (which thereafter yielded its place of honour to the cut with *Five Shepherds*), includes in the Calendar proper the little border cuts with compartments of saints and signs of

Fig. 392. Figure symbolical of March, from the *Compost et Kalendrier des Bergiers*, Paris 1493.

the zodiac and the figures of the months (fig. 392), and in later sections the cut of the *Four Complexions*, a single block of the *Seven Planets in relation to the days of the week* (divided later into two parts), and two large upright cuts of *Shepherd with quadrant* and *Shepherd with plumb-line* (fig. 393).

In 1493 there were two editions, 18th April (Paris) and 18th July (Valenciennes, British Museum and Pierpont Morgan 508); they are both practically identical in contents, and added much new matter in text and illustration.[2]

---

[1] See Monceaux, P. Le Rouge 30, i.-vi., N. Le Rouge 3 and 13; Cl. i. 360, etc.

[2] One of two copies of the April edition in Paris is printed on vellum, illuminated and modified by Vérard, the Royal Arms covering Marchant's printer's mark and Vérard's mark superimposed on the colophon. Facsimile of 18th July 1493 (Valenciennes copy) edited by Pierre Champion, Paris 1926. The *Calendar and Compost of Shepherds*, edited by G. C. Heseltine, London 1930, is based on the cuts in the edition of 18th July 1493 (though not entirely complete), and on the English translation of R. Copland (first published by Julian Notary about 1518?) collated with the original French and revised.

The frontispiece is the *Author writing* (the second version, which appeared in *La Danse Macabre*, 1486), then the woodcut with *Five Shepherds in a Landscape* is prefixed to the prologue. Apart from the

illustrations of the first edition, the most notable woodcuts are the series of the *Sept Paines d'Enfer*, introduced by the cut of *Christ in the House of Simon bidding Lazarus speak* (copied from the woodcuts in Vérard's *Art de bien Vivre et de bien Mourir*), the *Lord's Prayer*, the *Ten Commandments*, the *Commandments of the Church* (again suggested by blocks in Vérard's book), the *Ship of Life*, *Death on a Horse* (from *La Danse Macabre*), *Man's body as dominated by the signs of the Zodiac and the Seven Planets*, the *Planets and days of the week*, a series of the *Planets and their influences*, *Death in the Tombs*, and ten small and very attractive upright subjects of single and double figures (see fig. 394), of which three were based on the cuts in *Le Grand Testament de Villon*, 1489.[1]

Several editions appeared in the succeeding years, the most attractive additions to the illustrations being *January*, one of the full-page illustrations of the occupations of the months, first issued in the *Compost et Kalendrier des Bergères*, 1499, the *Trumpeter of Death* (as in the *Compost des Bergères*), and the *Lymasson* (or *L'Escargot*), with a woman and two soldiers fighting a monstrous snail, the latter being here reproduced from the *Bergiers* of 10th September 1500, in the British Museum (fig. 395).[2]

Fig. 393. Shepherd with plumb-line, from the *Compost et Kalendrier des Bergiers*, Paris 1493.

The most important of the later French editions is that of Nicolas Le Rouge, at Troyes, 1529. The illustrations are made up partly from Marchant's original blocks and partly from copies done in Vérard's workshop. The more powerfully cut blocks, e.g. the full-page *Months* (from the *Compost et Kalendrier des Bergères*, 1499), are still in good condition.

[1] See p. 642.

[2] The last two subjects do not occur in the British Museum copy of 18th July 1493, but Monceaux notes them in his description of edition of 18th April 1493. There are variations in most copies, so that definite statements as to when a woodcut first appeared are dangerous.

As in the case of *La Danse Macabre*, the blocks remained in the hands of the successors of Le Rouge at Troyes until the XVIII century.

Of French editions outside Paris, illustrated by different cuts, Claudin notes two printed by Jean Bellot at Geneva in 1497 and 1500, and several XVI-century editions at Lyon. He also refers to German editions printed at Lübeck, 1519, and Rostock, 1523.

There were also numerous English editions up to the earlier half of the XVII century, the first, under the title of *Kalendayr of the Shyppars*, being printed by Vérard at Paris, 1503 (STC. 22407).[1] None of the blocks is from the original series but all are from Vérard's stock: the *Christ in the House of Simon*, the *Pains of Hell*, the *Lord's Prayer*, and *Twelve Apostles* from his *Art de bien Vivre et de bien Mourir*, numerous little figures from his *Terence en françois* (about 1500), *Death with a spade in a cloister* from Robert Gobin, *Les Loups Ravissans* (Vérard, Paris, about 1503),[2] the rest being copies from Marchant's series.

Fig. 394. Schoolmaster and Boy, from the *Compost et Kalendrier des Bergiers*, Paris 1493.

The first edition printed in England (*The Kalender of Shepherdes*) was issued by Richard Pynson, 1506 (STC. 22408),[3] who borrowed most of the blocks used by Vérard in 1503, in addition to that of the *Author standing, presenting his book*,[4] which came from the *Art de bien Vivre et de bien Mourir*, 1492, and various other borders printed by Vérard. Some of the

---

[1] Reproduced in facsimile and edited by Heinrich Oskar Sommer, London 1892. The facsimile was made from the complete copy in the Library of the Duke of Devonshire. There are imperfect copies in the British Museum and at Manchester. See also E. Gordon Duff, *The First Two Books printed in the Scottish Language*, Edinburgh Bibliographical Society, 1892–93. The two books discussed are Vérard's English edition of the *Kalendayr of the Shyppars*, 1503, and the *Art of good lyvyng and good deyng*, 30th May 1503 (see p. 662), which Gordon Duff shows to have been made by a Scotsman who was at Paris in 1503. The writer who revised the translation for Richard Pynson's edition of 1506 speaks of the 1503 version as in 'corrupte Englyshe', which no Englishman could understand. And Robert Copland, who made a new translation for Wynkyn de Worde in 1508, refers to it more specifically as in 'rude and Scottysshe language'.

[2] See p. 669.

[3] The text reprinted in the work of H. O. Sommer quoted above.

[4] This appeared later in Robert Fabyan's *Chronicles*, London (Pynson) 1516 (B.M., G. 6014), and in Lawrence Andrewe's edition of Vincent de Beauvais, *Myrrour of the World* (about 1527).

Terence figures were replaced by copies. It does not include the subject from *Les Loups Ravissans.*

Many of the cuts reappeared in Julian Notary's edition (Robert Copland's translation), the *Kalender of Shepardes,* of about 1518 (STC. 22410), and in various subsequent editions.

Fig. 395. Le Lymasson, from the *Compost et Kalendrier des Bergiers,* Paris 1500.

The edition printed by Wynkyn de Worde, 1508 (The *Kalender of Shepherdes,* STC. 22409, Magdalen College, Oxford), is largely composed of poor copies of the Vérard blocks, and was no doubt immediately based, at least in part, on Pynson. But it should be noted that it contains the verses on the portentous snail (*Lymasson,* or *l'Escargot*), which did not appear in Pynson's edition.

Marchant also issued, in conjunction with the publisher Jean Petit, a *Compost et Kalendrier des Bergères,* 17th August 1499, the only edition known (H. 5590). Marchant here uses his mark of *Prestre Jehan* in place of that of the *Two Cobblers* which appeared in the *Kalendrier des Bergiers.* Much of the same illustrative material was used here as in the earlier work, the chief omission being the *Christ in the House of Simon,* the *Paines d'Enfer* and the other cuts of that section up to the *Commandments.* Of the new blocks the most important are the series of full-page illustrations of the *Occupations of the Months* (of which only the *January* ever appeared in editions of the *Kalendrier des Bergiers*), in the manner of Vérard's chief designer (see fig. 396), the two cuts of the shepherdesses *Bietrix and Sebille* and the peasants *L'un et l'autre* (fig. 397), the *Trumpeter of Death amid Flowers* (which also appears in the 1500 edition of the *Kalendrier des Bergiers*) and the little frieze of *Les Trois Morts et les Trois Vifs.* The book ends with the original *Danse Macabre des Femmes* (including the first version of the *Orchestra of Death,* eighteen subjects of the dance, and the author's epilogue) and a block of *Christ carrying the Cross, with a kneeling man.*[1]

---

[1] This block, based on a cut in Toulouse edition of *L'Imitation de Jesus Christ* (1488), was first used by Jean Lambert in his edition of *L'Imitation,* Paris, 16th November 1493; then lent to

Some of the blocks of the *Compost des Bergères* had appeared in Joannes de Sacro Busto, *Sphaera Mundi*, printed by Marchant for Jean Petit, February 1498/99, e.g. the *Hand with a Sphere*, the large *Month of May* and the *Trumpeter of Death amid Flowers*.

Of other books printed by Marchant, S. Bonaventura, *Sermones de Morte*,

Fig. 396. August, from the *Compost et Kalendrier des Bergères*, Paris 1499.

February 1494/95 (Cl. i. 397), contains a small cut of *Dives and Lazarus*, of excellent design and delicate cutting, which had appeared earlier in various *Horae*, e.g. in editions by Dupré and Caillaut in the British Museum (IA. 39817, and IA. 39507).[1]

Le Bourgeois for his Rouen edition of 1498, returning to Paris for use in the *Compost et Kalen-drier des Bergères*. For note and reproduction see Claudin i. 224.

    [1] See pp. 683 and 685. A different version of the same subject, with two men serving at table, and a bed in the background, occurs in the early Dupré *Horae* of about 1488–90 at Oxford (Proctor 8044).

ANTOINE VÉRARD'S[1] activity as a publisher of illustrated books in the xv century seems to fall naturally into two periods, from 1485 to about 1492, when he used woodcuts of various styles corresponding to those used by

Fig. 397. L'Un et l'autre, from the *Compost et Kalendrier des Bergères*, Paris 1499.

Dupré, Pierre Le Rouge and other printers, and from 1492 to the end of the century.[2] He continued publishing till 1512, and died at latest in 1514. The second period, when his position as the leading publisher of books in the vernacular was assured, shows a remarkable unity in the style of his new woodcuts, which were probably designed and cut by some artist in his employ. The figures in this group of cuts are characterised by strongly emphasised types with long noses, and the drawing in general, if hard, is trenchant in characterisation and firmly cut in thick lines that would last out large editions. I have spoken of the author of the group as Vérard's chief designer. Some of the characteristics of drawing are already present in earlier illustrations of more delicate cutting, e.g. the series of contemporary genre in Le Rouge's *Mer des Hystoires*, and a dogmatism which tries to define the work of anonymous designers is balked by the inevitable variations in style caused by a variety of cutters. The two periods of Vérard's activity are divided by that most important work, *L'Art de bien Vivre et de bien Mourir*, issued by Vérard in 1492, which includes examples of both phases.

Boccaccio, *Les Cent Nouvelles*, a translation of the *Decameron* by Laurent du Premier-Fait, 22nd November 1485, the first book to bear Vérard's name, has already been discussed in relation to Jean Dupré, who was almost certainly the printer (Cl. i. 226, Macf. 1, Paris; see p. 641).

---

[1] See J. Macfarlane, *Antoine Vérard*, London (Bibliographical Society) 1900; J. Renouvier, *Des gravures en bois dans les livres d'Antoine Vérard, 1485–1512*, Paris 1859.

[2] The end of the century was a critical period for the printer, for in October 1490 his shop *Sur le Pont Notre Dame* was burnt down. After that date various addresses occur in his colophons, but Bourdillon (the *Early Editions of the Roman de la Rose*, Bibliographical Society, London 1906, Appendix A) contends that they were all actually the same house, and thereby justifies his dating of Molinet's *Roman de la Rose Moralisé* as about 1500, rather than later (see p. 608).

Then on 10th July 1486 appeared his edition of Petrus de Crescentiis, *Prouffitz Champestres et Ruraulx*, attributed to the printer Levet (Cl. i. 426, Macf. 3, École des Beaux-Arts, Paris, from Masson Collection), three months before Bonhomme's edition, to which reference has already been made.[1] It has an attractive series of cuts of country occupations, as well as an

Fig. 398. The Author presenting his book to an Ecclesiastic, from *L'Art de bien Vivre et de bien Mourir*, Paris 1492.

interesting little woodcut of a *Monk seated writing in his study*.[2] To Pierre Levet again is usually assigned the printing of Vérard's *Les Cent Nouvelles Nouvelles* of 24th December 1486 (Cl. i. 428, Macf. 4, Paris), that famous series of stories compiled at the court of Louis XI. It contains a frontispiece which appears to represent *Louis XI. and the Duke of Burgundy with courtiers* (in the manner of the frontispiece to Sydrach, 1486/87), as well as a large

[1] See p. 640.
[2] 57 × 59 mm. The monk is seated on the right in a carved Gothic chair. The cut is in the same style as the little upright of a similar subject in the *Mer des Hystoires*, 1488 (see p. 634 and fig. 380). The block was frequently reprinted.

number of small column-cuts, similar in style to those in *Les Prouffitz Champestres*.

The *Author presenting his book to the King*, used as frontispiece to Sydrach, *La Fontaine de Toutes Sciences*, 20th February 1486/87 (Macf. 5, and plate v., Paris), had already appeared in an edition of Caesar, *Commentaires*, translated by Robert Gaguin and attributed to Pierre Levet.[1] Both this and the frontispiece to the first edition of *Les Cent Nouvelles Nouvelles* are in the somewhat loose and sketchy style of the frontispiece to Dupré's *Les Cent Nouvelles* of Boccaccio,[2] and probably came from the workshop of Dupré or Le Rouge.

A second cut of an analogous subject, the *Translator presenting his Book to the King*, which appeared in Vérard's edition of Caesar, *Commentaires* (Gaguin's translation), issued about 1488 (Macf. 107, Proctor 8141, attributed to the printer Pierre Le Caron),[3] was more frequently reprinted.[4] It forms a link between the earlier style of Dupré and that of Vérard's chief designer. An early and characteristic example of this designer is the *Author standing, presenting his Book to an Ecclesiastic* (fig. 398), which first appeared in Vérard's *Art de bien Vivre et de bien Mourir*, in the part entitled 'Traicté de l'Advenement de Antechrist', dated 28th October 1492.[5]

A third cut of similar character, an *Author kneeling before a King surrounded by his court* (fig. 399), a very good example by the same designer, appeared in Paulus Orosius, *Histoires*, of 21st August 1491 (Macf. 16, Paris), and subsequent editions (e.g. Macf. 92, 1509), and in the *Gestes Romaines* of about 1508 (Macf. 164). The *Caesar* (Macf. 107) also contained several of the cuts which had first appeared in Millet, *L'Istoire de la Destruction de Troye*, printed by J. Bonhomme, 1484.[6]

Vérard's illustration of the *Chevalier Délibéré* of Olivier de la Marche, first issued 8th August 1488, and probably printed by Dupré (Cl. ii. 468; Macf. 7, Vienna), is entirely independent of the Dutch edition, and by comparison a light-weight. But its twelve blocks (made by one repetition into thirteen illustrations) are attractive, and with their lettering omitted are constantly found in later books. Thus one illustration of *Le Chevalier Délibéré and*

---

[1] See pp. 630, 641.   [2] See pp. 629, 641, 654.   [3] See p. 641 and fig. 387.

[4] E.g. in Aristotle, *Éthiques*, 8th September 1488; Aristotle, *Livre des Politiques*, Marchant for Vérard, 1489; Paulus Orosius, 1491 (including Seneca, *Des Motz Dorez*); Josephus, *Bataille Judaique*, 1492; Bonnor, *L'Arbre des Batailles*, 1493; *Les Cent Nouvelles Nouvelles*, 2nd ed., about 1495; *Terence en François*, about 1500.

[5] See pp. 660, 662. Repeated e.g. in Josephus, *Bataille Judaique*, 7th December 1492; H. Suso, *L'Orloge de Sapience*, 1493/94; *Kalender of Shepherdes*, London, R. Pynson, 1506.

[6] See p. 639.

Fig. 399. The Author kneeling before a King, from Orosius, Paris 1491.

Accident (fig. 400) is reprinted in Josephus, *La Bataille Judaique*, 1492,[1] and more appeared in Alanus (de Insulis), *Les Paraboles*, 20th March 1492/93 (Macf. 23, Blum, 1928, p. xxxv),[2] in Boccaccio, *De la louenge des nobles et*

Fig. 400. Le Chevalier and Accident, from *Le Chevalier Délibéré*, Paris 1488.

cleres dames, 28th April 1493 (Macf. 25), in Honoré Bonnor, *L'Arbre des Batailles*, 8th June 1493 (Macf. 29), alongside other cuts of weaker design; in *Le Jouvencel*, Vérard, 27th March 1493/94 (Macf. 34), and in Raoul Lefèvre, *Recueil des histoires troiennes*, about 1494 (Macf. 123), with other cuts from *L'Arbre de Batailles* and other sources. A later edition of *Le Chevalier Délibéré* with the same blocks was printed by Jean Lambert, 1493 (Cl. ii. 221). Its title-page bears an attractive capital L with three grotesque heads (fig. 401). There are altogether about six varieties of these

calligraphic capital L's with grotesque heads in frequent use on Vérard's title-pages. Commonest of all is the one with a single head on the right, which seems to have first appeared in Heinrich Suso, *Orloge de Sapience*, 10th March 1493/94 (Macf. 33),[3] and afterwards in *Lancelot du Lac*, 1494, and Froissart, about 1495, and various other works. Then a flamboyant example with two heads on the right first occurred in the *Croniques de France*, 1493 (Macf. 30),[4] and a more perpendicular design with two heads, left and

---

[1] See p. 659.

[2] In this book the cut showing *L'Acteur* and *L'Entendement* is cut in two and used in its separate parts: when used later as a single subject there are signs of this division. The book also contains cuts from Petrus de Crescentiis, *Prouffitz Champestres*, 1486, and *Les Cent Nouvelles Nouvelles*, 1486. The small lettering on the *Chevalier* cuts was type printing superimposed, which was of course omitted in the reprints. In other cases larger lettering had been cut on the blocks, and in some instances remains and in others is cut away.

[3] It was also used by Dupré and Bocard (printing also for Vérard ?) in their edition of the *Légende Dorée*, of the same day, 10th March 1493/94 (Cl. i. 269).

[4] This appears to have been first used by Pierre Le Caron in *Les Fais de Maistre Alain Chartier*, 1489 (Cl. ii. 75). It was copied and imitated by other printers, e.g. at Troyes (*Danse Macabre*,

Fig. 401. Initial L, with three grotesque heads, from *Le Chevalier Délibéré*, Paris 1493.

right, is used in the *Lancelot du Lac*, of 1504 ('1494') (Macf. 166), and in the *Figures du Vieil Testament et du Nouvel* of about the same date (Macf. 163) (fig. 402).

A more complex design with grotesque heads and dragons appeared in Jacobus de Cessolis, *Jeu des Eschez Moralisé*, 1504 (Macf. 72), and a smaller example with grotesque head and stork in *Le Pèlerinage de l'Homme*, 1511/12 (Macf. 101).

Another interesting capital L, with design of nude woman, monkey and bird, occurs on the last leaf of *Les Ordonnances de la Prévosté des Marchands et Échevinage de la Ville de Paris*, 1500/1501, which appears to have been printed for Vérard (Cl. ii. 500, Macf. 273).

Of Vérard's other large initials with grotesque heads I would mention a remarkable P with two grotesque heads which occurred at the beginning of the Prologue of *Le Livre du Faulcon*, about 1496 (Cl. ii. 487, Paris).

In these initials with grotesque heads and other figures the designers for woodcut were following the traditions of the scribes and illuminators. A copy in the Bibliothèque Mazarine, Paris, of the first book printed by Pierre Le Rouge at Chablis, *Le Livre des Bonnes Mœurs*, 1st April 1478 (Monceaux, i. 100), shows similar calligraphic initials.

Between 1490 and 1492 Vérard commanded the services of Pierre Le Rouge, for it was he who either printed or provided part of the illustrative material to *Lucan, Suetoine et Saluste*, 22nd December 1490 (Macf. 12, Paris), *Orosius*, including the *Motz Dorez* of Seneca, 1491 (Macf. 16, Paris, and 126), and Josephus, *La Bataille Judaique*, 7th December 1492 (Macf. 21). The first two of these repeat the large initial *L with St. George and the Dragon*, and the large initials P and S from the *Mer des Hystoires*, while the Josephus includes various border-pieces from the same source. After Pierre Le Rouge's death in 1492, Vérard made constant use of his blocks, even though he may not have been the absolute proprietor.[1] I shall refer later

Guillaume Le Rouge, 1491) and at Lyon. It should also be remembered that initials and decorative cuts, which were in constant use, might have been frequently repeated in casts. [1] See p. 636.

Fig. 402. Initial L, with
two Heads, from *Figures
du Vieil Testament,*
Paris, about 1504.

to the remaining illustrations in the *Josephus*, but
would first consider the pivotal work in Vérard's
activity.

L'Art de bien Vivre et de bien Mourir is the form in
which a general title for the whole work was first
issued (in the edition of 12th February 1493/94),
but the original edition appeared in sections beginning with *Le Livre intitule lart de bien mourir*. This
first part included as its second section *Leguyllon
de crainte divine pour bien mourir*, and was printed
by Couteau and Menard, 18th July 1492. Then
followed as Part II. the *Traicte de l'Advenement de
Antechrist*, the colophon bearing Vérard's name and
dated 28th October 1492. Finally as Part III. came
Le Livre de bien Vivre, with Vérard's name and date
15th December 1492.

In the editions of 12th February 1493/94, 20th
June 1496 (Macf. 46) and 15th October 1498
(Macf. 53, Paris) the general title reads *Le Livre
intitule lart de bien vivre et de bien mourir*. They correspond roughly in text and illustration with the first edition, but the parts
run in the order Part III., Part I., Part II.

L'Art de bien mourir contains eleven full-page cuts based on the block-
book *Ars Moriendi*, within border-pieces at the sides and below, which are
in the same style of decoration as those in the books of Dupré and Pierre
Le Rouge. They show considerable independence of treatment and are
powerfully designed and cut. The little upright cut of a *Monk seated writing*
(95 × 77 mm.; sig. a. iv, verso) comes from the *Mer des Hystoires* (f. 42).
Leguyllon de crainte divine has an upright cut with a *Saint writing, and two
prophets above* (sig. d. i), but its chief cuts illustrate the *Sept Paines d'Enfer*
(fig. 403) introduced by *Christ in the House of Simon bidding Lazarus speak*.
The *Traicte de l'Advenement de Antechrist* contains large cuts, each with two
border-pieces, illustrating the *Quinze Signes de l'Advenement*, followed by a
Last Judgment and a full-page cut of the *Blessed in Heaven* illustrating *Les
Joyes de Paradis*.[1] An upright cut of a *Sainted Bishop writing with two prophets
above* (a pendant to the *Saint writing* in *Leguyllon*) comes at the beginning
of the section on *Les Quinze Signes* (sig. l. ii, verso). A small column-cut

---

[1] The original block of *Les Joyes de Paradis* came to England, and appeared in Pynson's
Sarum Missal of 1512 (see p. 722).

of the *Birth of Antichrist* is borrowed from *Les Cent Nouvelles Nouvelles*, 1486.[1]

L'Art de bien Vivre contains oblong blocks of the *Annunciation and Visitation*, *The Virgin and Child adored by a Pope and others*, the *Lord's Prayer*, the *Twelve Apostles* (in two cuts illustrating the Creed), the *Ten Command-*

Fig. 403. Men broken on the Wheel, from *L'Art de bien Vivre et de bien Mourir*, Paris 1492.

ments, and smaller upright cuts in two compartments showing a harmony of subjects from the Old and New Testaments, besides separate cuts of the *Brazen Serpent* and *The Crucifixion*.[2] Finally seven full-page upright cuts

[1] See p. 655. In the second edition of *Les Cent Nouvelles Nouvelles* (about 1495), the same cut occurs at Nouvelles 76 and 77 but with the window and the two boys cut out of the block.

[2] The last two were repeated on smaller blocks in the 1493 edition.

illustrating the *Seven Sacraments* (fig. 404). The portrait of the *Author standing, presenting his Book to an Ecclesiastic,* which has been already noted and reproduced (fig. 398), appeared at the beginnings of Parts II. and III.

The illustrations of the *Quinze Signes* are below the rest in quality, possibly a difference of cutter rather than designer. Of the other woodcuts,

Fig. 404. Baptism, from *L'Art de bien Vivre et de bien Mourir*, Paris 1492.

the copies of the *Ars Moriendi*, the *Sept Paines d'Enfer* and *Seven Sacraments* are probably all by Vérard's chief designer, though the *Sacraments* show less exaggerated characterisation. The subjects of the Old and New Testament are nearer the tradition of Le Rouge, and the other smaller cuts in Part III., such as the *Lord's Prayer* and the *Twelve Apostles*, are not unlike the work of Designer A in Marchant's *Danse Macabre*, but such comparisons do not tempt me to any dogmatic attributions. Vérard also printed an English edition in 1503, under the title *The Art of good lyvyng and good deyng,* illustrated partly with the original cuts and partly with copies (Macf. 67,

STC. 791).[1] The British Museum copy is defective, but there is a perfect copy at Emmanuel College, Cambridge, which contains the original cut of the *Author presenting his Book*.[2] Other English editions are those of Wynkyn de Worde, the *Arte or Crafte to lyve well and to dye well*, 1505 and about 1506 (STC. 792, Cambridge, and 793, B.M.), with small copies

Fig. 405. Royal Hawking Party, with the Author presenting his book, from Tardif, *L'Art de Faulconnerie*, Paris 1492/93.

from Vérard and elsewhere, probably by the hand of the cutter of Wynkyn's *Castell of Laboure*, 1506.[3]

---

[1] See E. Gordon Duff, *The First Two Books printed in the Scottish Language*, Edinburgh Bibliographical Society, 1892–93 (see p. 651).

[2] This cut appeared in England, in Pynson's *Kalender of Shepherdes*, 1506, and in later English books (see p. 651).   [3] See pp. 676 and 733.

In a series of large books published by Vérard after *L'Art de bien Mourir et de bien Vivre*, the designer who may have been responsible for work such as the greater part of Marchant's *Danse Macabre des Femmes*, 1491 and 1492, the *Author presenting his Book to an Ecclesiastic* (fig. 398), and the stronger woodcuts of *L'Art de bien Mourir*, becomes more schematic in his

Fig. 406. Funeral Procession, from the *Croniques de France,* Paris (Regnault) 1514.

angular and trenchant style. In any case it is the author of this group of cuts, constantly repeated in many of Vérard's folios after 1492, whom I designate as Vérard's chief designer.

The *Bataille Judaique* of Josephus, 7th December 1492, contains borders from the *Mer des Hystoires,* and several large cuts reminiscent of the Dupré-Le Rouge manner, e.g. the *Fight in a City* (Macf. pl. xxiii.) and the *Petitioner before a King enthroned in Court,* but there are elements in both these cuts, and the same more strongly evidenced in the frontispiece, the *Reception of Charles VIII. at a City Gate, with the translator presenting his book to the King outside a tent in the background,* which seem to indicate the Vérard designer, less powerfully cut.

Already thoroughly characteristic are the *Royal Hawking Party with the Author presenting his Book* in Guillaume Tardif, *L'Art de Faulconnerie*, 5th January 1492/93 (Cl. ii. 457, Macf. 22, Paris; fig. 405), and the many new large cuts which appeared in the *Croniques de France*, 3 vols., printed by J. Maurand, 9th July–10th September 1493 (Cl. ii. 451, Macf. 30),[1]

Fig. 407. King Arthur and his Knights at the Round Table, from *Tristan*, Paris, about 1506.

La Bible des Poètes (a French version of Ovid's *Metamorphoses*), 1st March 1493/94 (Macf. 31), the *Lancelot du Lac*, 3 vols., 1st July and 30th April 1494 (Macf. 35), and the *Tristan*, about 1494 (Macf. 130).

Cuts from the *Josephus* and each successive book were constantly repeated in different context in their successors. After the issue of the *Lancelot*, large new blocks were seldom cut. Sometimes in the illuminated

---

[1] Sometimes called the *Croniques de Saint-Denys*. Covers the history to the death of Charles VII., 1461. The remarkable cut of a *Funeral Procession* (see fig. 406) is reproduced by Olschki (*Le Livre illustré au XVe siècle*, 1926, fig. 160) as from this edition, but I do not find it before the edition of François Regnault, 1514, where it is used for the Funerals of Charles VII. and of Anne of Brittany, Queen of Louis XII.

vellum copies the heavy illumination not only covers but greatly modifies the design, either to suit the particular occasion or a particular decorative framework. Thus the *Fight in a City* of the *Josephus* is turned into an entirely peaceful scene in one instance where it appears in the British Museum copy of *Les Croniques de France* by covering up all the combatants in colour (vol. i. f. 60, verso), and the same copy shows illuminated architectural framework over cuts which contain no basis for such decorative design.[1]

The *Croniques de France* also contained a multitude of column-cuts, partly from earlier books, which were repeatedly being used in later works.

The *Bible des Poètes* shows most clearly the origin of the designer's style. Its illustrations are based on the woodcuts of the *Metamorphoses* printed by Colard Mansion at Bruges, 1484.[2] The designs are better drawn and more powerfully cut, but the elements of the French designer's open style are already present in his weaker predecessor, who may also have been concerned in illustration in France, about 1480, at Lyon.

Among later books in which Vérard's large cuts from 1492 to 1494 were repeated may be mentioned Boethius, *Le Grant Boèce de Consolation*, 19th August 1494 (Macf. 37); Boccaccio, *Des Nobles Malheureux*, 4th November 1494 (Macf. 38, Paris) (and the later edition, *Des nobles Hommes et Femmes Infortunez*, about 1506, Macf. 157); Boccaccio, *Généalogie des Dieux*, 9th February 1498/99 (Macf. 56, Paris); later editions of *Tristan* (about 1499, Macf. 131, Paris (Arsenal), and about 1506, Macf. 193; see fig. 407); and a later and somewhat smaller folio edition of *Lancelot du Lac* dated 1494, but certainly belonging to the year 1504 (Macf. 166). The last-named book contains the small calligraphic initials with grotesque heads constantly used by Vérard from about 1500 onwards (see fig. 408).[3]

---

[1] Another example where the illumination entirely alters the subject of the underlying wood-cuts is the vellum copy of *Le Jouvencel*, 10th March 1493/94 (Macf. 34), in the British Museum. A second copy on paper in the B.M. shows the same cuts uncoloured. Comparison of the two copies of Boethius, *Le Grant Boèce de Consolation* (1494), in the British Museum (Henry VII.'s vellum copy, C. 22.f. 8, and a paper copy, 169. k. 17), where the illuminated subjects of the vellum are entirely different from the woodcuts, shows the indentation of the paper for the line of the blocks, but hardly a trace (except in one piece of border) of inked blocks. This seems to show that in some vellum copies, intended for illumination, the blocks would be masked from inking and printed blind. Cf. p. 597.

[2] I have not been able to confirm my conjecture that the cut reproduced in fig. 407 came from an earlier edition. The Bibl. Nationale copy of the *Tristan* of about 1494 lacks vol. ii., which should contain this subject; and the block of the same subject in the edition of about 1499 in the Bibl. de l'Arsenal is different (showing trumpeters in upper r.).

[3] E.g. in his *Ortus Sanitatis en françois*, about 1500 (Macf. 140, H.C. 8958), in his edition

Fig. 408. Initial O, with grotesque head, from *Ortus Sanitatis en françois*, Paris, about 1500.

Of the larger historical works issued by Vérard in addition to his *Croniques de France* of 1493, the Froissart, *Croniques de France*, of about 1495 (Cl. ii. 481, Macf. 111), contains no illustrations, but many of the old blocks from works just mentioned reappeared in the *Miroir Hystorial* in five folio volumes, 1495–96 (Macf. 42), and in the *Croniques*, supplementary to Froissart, of Enguerrand de Monstrelet (Macf. 144). The *Gestes Romaines*, of about 1508, Livy's Third Decade, translated by Robert Gaguin (Macf. 164), also included several of the old cuts from the *Ovid* and *Lancelot*, as well as the *Author kneeling before a King* from the *Orosius*, and smaller blocks from J. Millet, *L'Istoire de la Destruction de Troye* (J. Bonhomme, 1484), and other earlier works.

In the woodcuts which appeared in Vérard's books about 1500, of different character from those of his chief designer, there are two noteworthy groups, one exemplified in his *Ogier le Danois* of about 1498 (Macf. 121, Pierpont Morgan),[1] and the other in Robert Gobin, *Les Loups Ravissans*, about 1503 (Macf. 169).

The first group shows work of an expressive designer working somewhat in the manner of the author of Trechsel's *Terence* (Lyon 1493). The subject of the *Cradling of Ogier*, the frontispiece of *Ogier le Danois* (lacking in the British Museum copy), is also reminiscent in its decorative character of the Theatre cut in Trechsel's *Terence*. Comparable work is also seen in the romance *Paris et Vienne* printed by Jean Trepperel, 1498 (Pierpont Morgan 534).

Related in style is a most interesting full-page cut representing the *Prévôt des Marchands et les Eschevins de la Ville de Paris* (fig. 409) which first appeared in *Les Faiz Dictes et Ballades* of Alain Chartier, printed for Vérard by Pierre le Caron, about 1499 (Macf. 109).[2] It was reprinted in *Les Ordonnances de la Prévosté des Marchands et Échevinage de la Ville de Paris*, January 1500/1501 (Cl. ii. 492, Macf. 273). The latter book also contains a variety of interesting little cuts illustrating the various trades of

of the *Mer des Hystoires*, about 1503 (see p. 634). Of his other series of small initial letters, the floral designs on a black ground are the most attractive. For the original and later editions of xv-century Herbals see above, pp. 348-352. The British Museum copy of Vérard's *Ortus* was probably Henry VII.'s (see above, p. 597). For this and other xv-century French Herbals see pp. 640, 670, 672.

[1] Containing 58 prints from 13 blocks.

[2] At least before 25th October 1499, as the colophon gives the address of the Pont Notre Dame.

Fig. 409. From *Les Ordonnances de la Prévosté des Marchands et Échevinage de la Ville de Paris*, Paris 1500/1501.

the city (see fig. 410), and an amusing capital L with nude woman, monkey and bird on the last leaf, to which allusion has already been made.[1]

Other examples of the group are found in the main series of woodcut illustrations in Vérard's *Terence en françois* of about 1500 (Cl. ii. 487, Macf. 152). These illustrations are based on the *Terence* printed by Grüninger at Strassburg, 1496, not on Trechsel's Lyon edition. Vérard also follows Grüninger in his composite subjects, making up his subjects by fitting together a limited number of block-pieces with figure, architecture or landscape. Most of these subjects form oblongs of the width of the text; in one case separate pieces are used to make up a full-page subject with three rows of figures (f. 156, before *Heautontimoroumenos*).

Fig. 410. Timber-haulers, from *Les Ordonnances de la Prévosté des Marchands*, Paris 1500/1501.

Coming to the second group, the characteristic cuts in Robert Gobin, *Les Loups Ravissans*, Paris (Vérard), about 1503 (Macf. 169), occur in the second part dealing with Death and Humanity (fig. 411).[2] They show a use of the swelling line, a more natural property of line-engraving, for the mere pressure of the burin in the copper would broaden the intaglio line.

Other examples occur in the *Terence*, just mentioned, in its full-page frontispiece representing the *Theatre*, and a frontispiece to *Andria*, f. 4, which is used later in *Phormio*, f. 290, both based, like the rest of the illustrations, on Grüninger's blocks.

Other woodcuts by the same designer (or cutter) occur in the following works:

[Valerius Maximus] *Le Livre de Valère le Grant*, Paris, Vérard, about 1500 (Fairfax Murray 558).

Livy, *Les Decades*, published by G. Eustace and F. Regnault, Paris 1515 (one cut after the *Judgment of Agamemnon* in the *Bible des*

---

[1] See p. 659.

[2] The subject reproduced in fig. 411 appeared also in the *Kalendayr of the Shyppars*, printed by Vérard, 1503. See p. 651.

Poètes, 1493/94; another corresponding to a subject in the *Valerius Maximus*).

Jean Bouchet, *Les Regnards traversant les périlleuses Voyes des folles fiances du Monde*, Vérard, about 1503 (Macf. 149),[1] with a cut of the *Author writing* (which reappeared in Bonifacius Symoneta, *Le Livre des Persecucions des Crestiens*, about 1507) (Macf. 167).

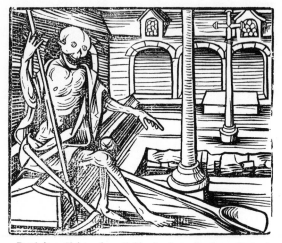

Fig. 411. Death in a Cloister, from Gobin, *Les Loups Ravissans*, Paris, about 1503.

Ortus Sanitatis en françois, Vérard, about 1500 (Macf. 140); the numerous cuts in the second part, '*Le Traictie des bestes, oyseaux poissons, pierres precieuses et orines du Jardin de Sante*', based on the *Hortus Sanitatis*, printed by Meydenbach at Mainz, 1491.[2]

Less pronounced in manner, though possibly by the same designer, are the animal subjects in *Les Loups Ravissans* and *Les Regnards*, and it must be remembered even in regard to the *Terence* that a single designer might have been interpreted in two different styles by different cutters.

---

[1] Described on the title-page as by Sebastian Brant, the name of the real author being hidden in an acrostic. Jean Bouchet prosecuted his publisher for this and other liberties taken with his work, as narrated in his *Epistres morales et familières du traverseur*, Poitiers 1545 (see Macfarlane, p. xxvii).

[2] See pp. 351, 666, and cf. 672. One of the large cuts in the second part of Vérard's *Ortus Sanitatis*, prefixed to *Le Traictie des Urines*, was copied from the cut of a pharmacy which appeared in Hieronymus Braunschweig, *Chirurgia*, printed by Grüninger at Strassburg, 1497 (see p. 342), and in other books by the same author (reprod. Muther, *Die Deutsche Bücher-illustration*, pl. 137).

Of other books published by Vérard in the xv century, there are few that call for special mention, for so much of his later illustration is from old stock. His issues of the *Roman de la Rose* have already been mentioned in relation to the earlier illustrated editions printed at Lyon.[1] His St. Jerome, *Vie des Pères*, 15th October 1495 (Macf. 43), contains numerous column-cuts, and a frontispiece of the *Joyes de Paradis* from *L'Art de bien Vivre et de bien Mourir*. The *Miroir de la Redemption Humaine* (*Speculum Humanae Salvationis*) again shows masses of column-cuts, in addition to the blocks of the *Quinze Signes* from the 1493 edition of *L'Art de bien Vivre et de bien Mourir*. *Les Figures du Vieil Testament et du Nouvel*, issued about 1504 (Macf. 163), is an imitation of the block-book *Biblia Pauperum*.

Fig. 412. Printer's mark of Felix Baligault, Paris.

Most important of the Biblical works is *La Bible Historiée* of about 1498 (Cl. ii. 481, 489, Macf. 105, Paris). Translated by Gayart Des Moulins from the Latin of Petrus Comestor, it was the most popular of the French paraphrases of Bible narrative, being reprinted by Vérard about 1507, and by his successors about 1520.[2] Even in this work, which included some two hundred illustrations, most of the blocks were old, and taken from such works as the Abbeville *Cité de Dieu* and Le Rouge's *Mer des Hystoires*. To a large extent similar in its illustration is the *Bible en françoiz*, also the work of Gayart Des Moulins, which was issued by Vérard about 1510 (Macf. 156). The most interesting cut which appeared in both the *Bible Historiée* and the *Bible en françoiz* is the *Adam and Eve* (a circular subject within a black rectangle).[3]

The above survey of Vérard's publications has embraced the work of a considerable proportion of contemporary printers. A few further names and certain works of printers already mentioned must be noted. PIERRE

---

[1] See pp. 607-608.

[2] See Seymour de Ricci, *Byblis*, ii. (1913), 15, with reproduction of the *Adam and Eve*.

[3] Reproduced by Blum, *Les Origines du livre à gravures en France*, pl. xxviii., as from the *Mistère du Viel Testament*, printed by Pierre Le Dru for Antoine Vérard (about 1495?). Claudin (ii. 66) refers to an edition of this work printed by Le Dru for G. de Marnef, about 1500.

LE CARON specialised in popular historical works; he was the gazetteer of current events, issuing such works as Pierre d'Urfé, *Ordonnance faicte par Messire Pierre d'Urfé pour l'enterrement du Roy Charles VIII.*, *L'Entrée du Roy Louis XII. à sa bonne ville de Paris*, 1498, and *Les Joustes faictes à Paris après l'entrée du Roy Louis XII.*, 1498 (Cl. ii. 85-88, Paris, St. Geneviève). We have already mentioned Le Caron as the first to use the capital L with two grotesque heads which was later in Vérard's hands,[1] and he also used two other varieties of such capitals which do not appear in Vérard's stock (see Cl. ii. 92, 93).

Fig. 413. Printer's mark of Thielmann Kerver, Paris.

Le Caron also issued a *Grant Herbier* between 1495 and 1500, largely based on the *Gart der Gesuntheit* (Mainz 1485), of which there is a complete copy in the Bibliothèque St. Geneviève, Paris (Pell. 1102, Cl. ii. 83).[2] It contains Le Caron's second mark (Meyer 112), which was not used before 1495. Before this date Le Caron used Vérard's mark with his own name inserted (Meyer 111).[3] There was an earlier French edition under the title of *Arbolayre* (n.d., n.p., n.pr.) which was probably printed by P. Metlinger, at Besançon, about 1487–88 (Pell. 1101, Cl. iv. 479, Paris).

LE PETIT LAURENS printed an edition of *L'Ordinaire des Crestiens* for Jean Petit, about 1497 (British Museum, IB. 40265).[4] The title-page has a capital L with two grotesque heads, and beneath it Jehan Petit's earliest printer's mark (Meyer 136). This mark was already cracked in Jean Petit's

---

[1] See p. 658.

[2] A perfect and uncoloured copy was recently acquired by the British Museum (see British Museum Quarterly, May 1935).

[3] For the original and later editions of the xv-century Herbals see above, pp. 348-352, and the articles by A. C. Klebs quoted in that place.

[4] This edition is described in detail, and the title-page reproduced in Catalogue VIII. No. 74 of E. P. Goldschmidt & Co., London. The B.M. copy has a mutilated title-page, but enough remains to show that its woodcuts correspond to these in the Goldschmidt copy, on which the above description is based.

edition of Joannes de Sacro Busto, *Sphera Mundi*, 1498/99 (B.M., and Fairfax Murray 492), which gives a limit for the dating of *L'Ordinaire*. Verso of the title is the cut of a *Sainted Bishop writing, with two prophets above,* which originally appeared in Vérard's *Art de bien Mourir*, 1492. A variant of this edition, without Petit's mark, and assigned to Vérard (Macf. 272, Copinger ii. 4492), is in the Bibliothèque Mazarine, Paris, so that Le Petit Laurens probably supplied both publishers. Claudin describes another edition printed by Le Petit Laurens for François Regnault, before 1499 (Cl. ii. 118), with various cuts from *L'Art de bien Vivre et de*

Fig. 414. From Gringore, *Le Chasteau de Labour,* Paris 1500/1501.

bien Mourir, the full-page cut of the *Joyes de Paradis* being a modified copy.[1]

The work was an exposition of the Catholic religion for the laity, and was probably originally written in French between 1467 and 1469. Its popularity is shown by the existence of four other editions issued by Vérard between 1490 and 1495 (Macf. 11, 20, 39, 44), but except for a single cut in the first of these (Paris) they are without illustration. It was translated into English as the *Ordinarye of Crysten Men* by Andrew Chertsey, and printed by Wynkyn de Worde, 1502 and 1506, each edition with different cuts, poor copies from Vérard's *L'Art de bien Vivre et de bien Mourir*, etc. (STC. 5198, 5199).

A good series of copies of the Basle cuts illustrating Sebastian Brant's *Narrenschiff* appears to have been first used in *La Nef des folz du Monde*, printed by J. LAMBERT for J. PHILIPPE (MANSTENER) and G. DE MARNEF, 1497 (Cl. ii. 227). Proctor (8257) attributes its printing to Baligault,

---

[1] This block is printed in Julian Notary's *Golden Legend*, London 1503/04 (see p. 734), and in Hopyl's *Passionael*, Paris (for W. Houtmart, Brussels) 1505, 1507. Claudin states that it also appears in editions of the *Légende Dorée* printed by Jean de Vingle, Lyon 1497, and by La Barre, Paris 1499, and as late as 1529 by Jodocus Badius, in *Encomium Trium Mariarum*.

who must have had close relations with Lambert, for they both used the same device, *Two monkeys beneath a tree* (Meyer 82, 83, and 108, 109). The blocks were used in 1498 by J. Sacon at Lyon,[1] and again at Paris in the French edition of Badius, *Stultifera Navis*.

Fig. 415. Mark of the Publisher Antoine Vérard, Paris.

The *Stultifera Navis* of Jodocus Badius is a shorter satirical poem suggested by Brant's work, which was issued in both Latin and French editions (the French translation by J. Drouyn) in or about 1500–1501. The Latin edition, printed by KERVER for the brothers de Marnef, is dated 20th February 1500/1501; the French edition, *La Nef des Folles*, was printed by Le Petit Laurens for Geoffroi de Marnef, without date, about the same period (Cl. ii. 127). Both editions contain six new woodcuts of lively design by the author of the cuts in Vérard's *Terence*. Kerver's edition is embellished with his own beautiful device of *Two Unicorns by a Tree* (Meyer 102; fig. 413). The French issue has in addition about a dozen cuts from the editions of *La Nef des folz* of Sebastian Brant, which have just been described.

I have already referred to JEAN TREPPEREL for his romance of *Paris et Vienne* and his edition of *Le Grand Testament de Villon*, and I would here mention another popular work, *Les Quinze Joyes de Mariage* (issued about 1499), for its illustration of a *peasant family*, a woodcut of little quality, but of entertaining character.

Most attractive of all the little popular books of the end of the century is Pierre Gringore, *Le Chasteau de Labour*, printed by PIGOUCHET for VOSTRE, 1499 (Bibl. Mazarine, Paris) and 1500/1501 (British Museum). It traces the life and thoughts of a young married couple, with their joys and sorrows, the contests between the virtues and vices, and the final triumph of virtue. The book opens with two most delicate little cuts,

[1] See p. 614.

including a *garden of love*,[1] followed by a series more broadly designed showing the lovers in bed surrounded by a variety of figures with their appropriate mottoes; then seven small cuts with dotted ground representing

Fig. 416. Les Trois Vifs et les Trois Morts; opening (two pages) from *Horae*, Paris (Dupré), about 1488.

tourneys of the virtues and vices as mounted female figures; finally another scene of the lovers in which the husband rises from bed, visits the castle of labour, with its various employments, and returns in the end to a well-earned meal and rest in his own house. The little *Tourneys of the Virtues and Vices* are in the manner of the illustrations to contemporary *Horae*,[2] and a *Tree of Jesse* in similar style which appears on the last page is found in *Horae* issued by Vostre. The others, in black line, are near in style to Vérard's Terence designer, full of life and individuality.

Several other French editions of the *Chasteau de Labour* are known or recorded, and there were also editions in English printed by Vérard in Paris,

---

[1] Which came from the calendar portion of *Horae* printed by Pigouchet for Vostre (e.g. 20th March, 17th April 1496–97, B.M., IA. 40321).

[2] I have not found these blocks in Pigouchet's *Horae*, but inferior copies appeared in Vérard's *Sarum Horae* of about 1505 (B.M., C. 35. e. 4, see p. 691).

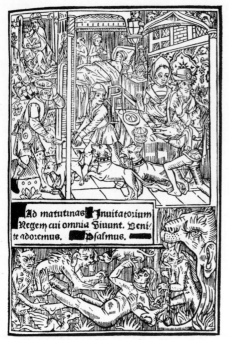

Fig. 417. Dives and Lazarus, from *Horae*, Paris
(Dupré), about 1488–90.

about 1503, and in London by Richard Pynson, about 1505 and 1506, and Wynkyn de Worde, 1506 (STC. 12379–82).[1] The woodcuts in Pynson's editions are distinctly better than Wynkyn's; in fact they are almost as well cut and as expressive as the original series. A perfect copy of Pynson's edition of about 1505 (STC. 12380) came to the British Museum from the Huth Collection. In Pynson's edition the *Tourneys of the Virtues and Vices* show some black ground without dotted work; in Wynkyn's issue these subjects are in black line only.

Pierre Gringore was also the author of *Le Casteau d'Amours*, issued by Michel Le Noir, 1500. It contains a title cut rather in the manner of the copyist of Brant's *Narrenschiff* recently mentioned, a delicate full-page of *David and Bathsheba*[2] (135 × 91 mm.) (which may have been made for a *Horae*), and Le Noir's excellent device with the two negresses (Meyer 114).

BOOKS OF HOURS[3]

Venice was the chief centre in the production of illustrated Missals, during the fifteenth century, but Paris publishers and printers first de-

[1] See *The Castell of Labour, translated from the French of Pierre Gringore by Alexander Barclay. Reprinted in facsimile from Wynkyn de Worde's edition of 1506*, with an introduction by A. W. Pollard, Edinburgh (Roxburghe Club) 1905.

[2] With cartouche in the centre for lettering DAVID, in the same form as cuts in Dupré's *Horae*, B.M., IA. 39817, but somewhat larger. At the foot of the block it shows Goliath overthrown by David.

[3] Apart from the general works on French woodcut books, see A. W. Pollard, *The Illustration in French Books of Hours, 1486–1500*, Bibliographica, iii. (1897), 430; Paul Lacombe, *Livres*

veloped, and perhaps originated, the little Books of Hours which form the most characteristic achievement of early French woodcut. In manuscript form the 'Hours of the Virgin' (*Horae Beatae Virginis Mariae*) had been favourite books of private devotion in England and France from the xi to the xiv centuries and equal in popularity to the Psalter. These manuscript *Horae* generally include: (1) Kalendar, (2) Cursus Evangelii, (3) Hours of the Virgin, (4) Hours of the Cross, (5) Hours of the Holy Ghost, (6) The Seven Penitential Psalms and the Litany, (7) Office of the Dead, (8) Memoriae, or Suffrages of various Saints;[1] and the subjects which are most regularly illustrated in the woodcuts of the printed *Horae* are the Zodiac Man, the History

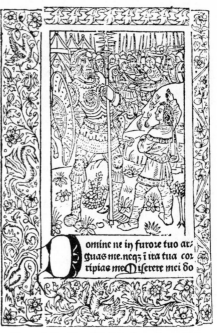

Fig. 418. David and Goliath, from *Horae*, Paris (Meslier) 1489/90.

of the Virgin and of Christ, the History of Susannah, the Parable of the Prodigal Son, the Fifteen Signs of the Judgment, the Theological and Cardinal Virtues, the Seven Capital Sins, the Twelve Sibyls, and the Dance of Death. These subjects are interspersed with contemporary *genre* in the same way as medieval church sculptors mingled saints and scripture with their own translations, simple or grotesque, from everyday life. The French illuminated *Horae* of the xv century were the immediate models for the woodcut books with their complete series of borders on every page, and occasional blocks printed in the text within the borders. This became the regular form of the illustrated *Horae* printed in France, only a few of

d'heures imprimées au xve et au xvie siècles conservées dans les bibliothèques publiques de Paris, Catalogue, Paris 1907; H. Bohatta, *Bibliographie des Livres d'Heures,* Vienna 1900 (2nd ed. 1924).

[1] See Dr. M. R. James, *Descriptive Catalogue of MSS. in Fitzwilliam Museum, Cambridge,* 1896.

the earliest examples being without the borders. Outside France (in fact outside Paris), examples of *Horae* printed and illustrated in this form are rare. There are a few in Italy, apparently inspired by the French model,[1]

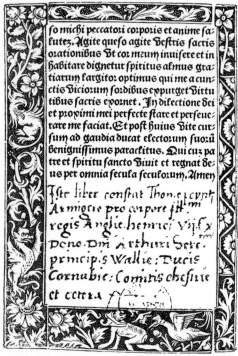

Fig. 419. Last page of the *Sarum Horae*, Paris, about 1495

rare examples in the Netherlands,[2] Germany[3] and England.[4] In Germany and the Netherlands the 'Hours' of devotion tended to centre round the Life and Passion of Christ, rather than round the Life of the Virgin. In France series of woodcuts of the Passion are in general far less common than in the North.

It is remarkable how few copies of French *Horae* in existence correspond exactly in their contents. Apart from the special forms required by the use of the various dioceses, the publishers no doubt introduced minor differences in the text, or in the arrangement of the cuts, to answer the demands of various clients. The borders in their most regular form were printed from four blocks: in other cases they were made up by the combination of a considerable number of smaller pieces, and the disposition of such pieces would lend itself to great variety of setting. In a short survey I can do little more than sketch the general development in manner of work, citing the most important of the early editions, and referring to a few others typical of the various styles.

[1] See p. 500.

[2] See pp. 581, 584. *Ghetiden* is the Dutch equivalent for Canonical Hours (*Vigilie*), and *Ghetidenboeck* is used both for Books of Hours of the Virgin and for the Breviary (i.e. the office for the canonical hours, the daily service of the Church).

[3] See pp. 328 and 340. *Zeitglöcklein* or *Horologium* (*Devotionis*) are the usual titles.

[4] See pp. 715-719. Caxton's *Fifteen O'es*, 1491, and *Horae*, printed by Wynkyn de Worde, 1494.

The early examples are largely in black line; then a plain black ground is used to throw the design into relief (e.g. in an edition issued by Caillaut about 1490, B.M., IA. 39507)[1] and punches of various patterns (plain dots,

or stars) are used to vary the design whether black on white or white on black (e.g. in edition of Dupré, 4th February 1488/89, B.M., Proctor 8045, IA. 39821); while from about 1496 a regularly dotted black ground makes an important part of the decorative character (e.g. in the edition printed by Pigouchet for Simon Vostre, 20th March and 17th April 1496, B.M., Proctor 8189, IA. 40321). The delicate line required in these little books, and particularly the manner of punching dots in a black ground, was more adapted to metal than wood, and in Dupré's edition of 4th February 1488/89 it is expressly stated that the blocks are of copper (f. 2, verso, *C'est le repertoire des histoires et figures de la bible . . . contenues dedens les vignettes de ces presentes heures imprimées en cuyure*).

Fig. 420. David and Bathsheba, from *Horae*, Paris (Dupré) 1488/89.

In the subsequent edition printed by Dupré for Vérard, 10th April 1489/90, the phrase *imprimées en cuyure* is omitted. These facts seem to imply that, both earlier and later, cuts of the sort were printed from wood blocks, but it is quite possible that here and there, even before this date, the French illustrators may have used metal for some of their delicate blocks. But they probably used metal more often for such

[1] See p. 685.

subjects as might be so frequently repeated as to justify repetition by metal casts, e.g. in initial letters and other decorative pieces. Vérard's device (Meyer 160) generally shows a bend in the upper right corner of the border-line which seems to mark it as metal rather than wood (fig. 415).[1]

Fig. 421. The Printer adoring the Virgin, from *Horae*, Paris (Dupré) 1488/89.

The best of the French *Horae* show borders spaced and laid out on the page with a perfect balance, having regard to the opening of two pages rather than the single page. The general principle of spacing which the good book-designers have followed is a gradual increase in width of margin (or border), beginning with the inner margin, and increasing with the upper, outer and lower margins respectively. This proportion is well illustrated in the opening reproduced from one of Dupré's *Horae* in the British Museum, IA. 39817 (fig. 416).[2] The borders would count as margin, so that outside the border-cut practically no margin would be left.

Most of the French Books of Hours were printed in the last decade of the xv century, and the first two or three decades of the xvi century. In view of the unity of their general character and the consistent richness of their decorative elements, these books offer most excellent material for estimating the gradual progress of Renaissance design. In the earliest examples of Dupré and others, the decoration is in the pure tradition of the medieval French illuminators; by the middle of the 'nineties there are frequent examples of Italian renaissance in candelabra and other classical inventions; by the beginning of the xvi century the Italian elements predominate, reaching their culmination in the refinement of Geoffroy Tory's books.[3]

The earliest examples, as we have noted, are mostly in black line. Then, after an intermediate stage in which dotted work predominates in

---

[1] An even more striking example of a bent border, which could only be a metal, is Richard Pynson's printer's mark (see p. 732 and fig. 466).

[2] See p. 683.

[3] See pp. 697-698.

the backgrounds, representing the most characteristic phase in the development of French woodcut *Horae*, there is a reversion to black line, and the somewhat cold severity of the Italian renaissance, as interpreted by a classicist of the pure style of Geoffroy Tory. In the middle phase borders tended to a variety of rich embellishment, decorative frills above and scroll or figured bases below (e.g. in *Horae* printed by Pigouchet for Vostre, about 1496, B.M., C. 27. e. 2, by Jehan Pychore and Remy de Laistre, 5th April 1503, B.M., Print Room, and C. 29. k. 21, and by Thielmann Kerver, 22nd June 1506, B.M., C. 29. f. 8).

Fig. 422. The Annunciation to the Shepherds, from *Horae*, Paris (Dupré), about 1490.

Most of the *Horae* are practically of pocket-book size (*Petites Heures*), the woodcut surface (which is only slightly less than the full page) varying from about $4\frac{1}{2} \times 3$ inches (e.g. Denis Meslier's edition of 14th February 1489/90) [1] to about $6\frac{1}{2} \times 4\frac{1}{4}$ inches (Vérard's edition of 8th February 1489/90). [2]

Then there is a series of somewhat larger *Horae* printed by Vérard, for the most part inscribed *imprimées par le commandement du roi*, in which the woodcut surface measures about $8 \times 5\frac{1}{4}$ inches, e.g. an edition of about 1490 (Macf. 204), [3] the work of Vérard's chief designer. These editions are generally called *Grandes Heures*, or *Heures Royales*, but not all the *Grandes Heures* are specifically printed by Royal Command, [4] while an

[1] See p. 685.   [2] See p. 689.   [3] See p. 690.
[4] E.g. that of 20th August 1490 (Macf. 202, Paris) has no reference to the Royal Command.

edition of *Petites Heures Royales* has also been cited,[1] so that the former title is the safer.

A few rare examples of *Horae* were issued in a third style, usually termed the *Agenda* form, a long narrow shape in which the woodcut surface is about $8\frac{1}{8} \times 3$ inches, e.g. the edition printed by Antoine Chappiel for Gillet Hardouin, 19th January 1504/05.[2] The majority of extant examples are printed on vellum, and many of these are illuminated.

Fig. 423. Lower half of a page, from *Horae*, Paris (Dupré), about 1490.

Then occasional attempts were made in printing in colour, but the only extant specimen to which I can refer is an edition of Jean Dupré of 1490 in the British Museum.[3] The colours used are red, blue and green. No subject is printed in more than one colour, and no single page shows more than two colours.

Many *Horae* are undated, but certain clues are offered by internal evidence. The Almanacs with Easter Tables generally cover twenty years, e.g. the earliest from 1488 to 1508, but as these are seldom advanced until well through the period, this is only a rough basis. Careful comparison with dated editions in regard to type and the condition of the blocks is the best guide.

The earliest woodcut *Horae* known was issued by VÉRARD, 6th February 1485/86, the only copy recorded, and that in fragmentary form, from the Jean Masson Collection, being now preserved in the École des Beaux-Arts, Paris (Macf. 195, described by Claudin, ii. 388-89, as printed with the type of Pierre Le Rouge). Other early editions by Vérard are 21st August 1486 and 7th July 1487, in Dupré's type (Macf. 196, 197, Cl. ii. 390-91, Paris). The fragments of the edition of 6th February 1485/86 include a few subject cuts (a *Coronation of the Virgin*, about $3\frac{1}{8} \times 2\frac{1}{2}$ inches, including upper and left border designs with a saint in a niche, and six smaller cuts about $1\frac{1}{2} \times 1$ inch, being reproduced by Claudin) as well as a

---

[1] See Cl. ii. 397; Sale of Guyot de Villeneuve, 1900, No. 44.

[2] See p. 696.   [3] See p. 688.

border-piece in Dupré's style. The edition of 21st August 1486 contains an *Annunciation* of the same size and style, and with the same two-side border design, as the *Coronation of the Virgin*, in addition to a variety of the small cuts, while the issue of 7th July 1487 has cuts only of the smaller size. They are all three of the small pocket size.

Fig. 424. Printer's mark of Jean Dupré, Paris.

Then follows a group of *Horae* with complete woodcut borders and subject cuts of uniform character, all of similar pocket-book size, where interrelation has offered considerable difficulty, and will continue to do so until they are all photographed for comparison (see Cl. i. 252-57 and 312-19). It includes the following editions:

(1) Printed by JEAN DUPRÉ (about 1488). British Museum, IA. 39817. This was dated by A. W. Pollard[1] as before 19th February 1488/89 on account of the condition of the outer border-line of the little cut of *David standing with his Harp*, which shows two further breaks in Levet's *Latin Psalter* of that date.[2] Woodcut surface about $4\frac{5}{8} \times 3\frac{1}{4}$ inches.

(2) Printed by Jean Dupré, n.d. (about 1488–90?). Bodleian Library, Oxford (Proctor 8044, Arch. D. f. 20). Has been quoted erroneously as Douce 52. Woodcut surface about $4\frac{5}{8} \times 3\frac{1}{8}$ inches (see fig. 417).

(3) Printed by ANTOINE CAILLAUT, n.d. (about 1490?). Paris, B.N. (Velins 1643). Cl. i. 312-19.

[1] The Illustration in French Books of Hours, *Bibliographica*, iii., 1897, 430.

[2] See p. 642. Such basis for dating must be used with caution as border-lines might be repaired. E.g. the *Dives and Lazarus* in the same *Horae* of Dupré has a break in its outer border near the left arm of Dives, which does not appear in the impression in the B.M. copy of Bonaventura, *Sermones*, 1494/95 (see p. 653).

(4) Anonymous printer, n.d. (about 1492?). Pierpont Morgan 567. Woodcut surface about $4\frac{1}{4} \times 2\frac{3}{4}$ inches. The blocks from Dupré's stock, partly the same as in B.M., IA. 39817 (No. 1 of this group).

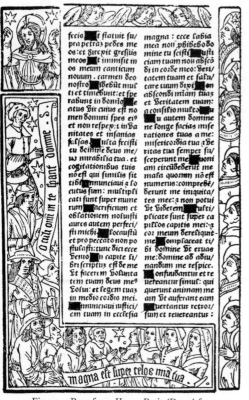

Fig. 425. Page from *Horae*, Paris (Dupré for Vérard) 1489/90.

All these four editions show four-piece black-line borders, chiefly in outline, with most attractive designs of branch, bird and beast, with an occasional figure of an angel making music and the like. They contain small subjects in about three sizes: the largest about $4\frac{1}{2} \times 3$ inches (or slightly over); the middle size about $3 \times 1\frac{7}{8}$ inches; the smallest, chiefly for single figures of saints, the size of initial letters, about $1\frac{1}{2} \times 1$ inch. The Oxford edition is entirely different in its blocks from B.M., IA. 39817, but the subjects are generally the same design with differences in detail.[1]

The Oxford borders are even more delicate than those of the British Museum edition, and a certain wiry quality of line gives it almost the character of metal even if such be not actually the case. The Caillaut edition reprints some blocks from IA. 39817, and replaces others, which may have passed into other hands (such as the *Dives and Lazarus*). In one case, that of *Les Trois Vifs et les Trois Morts*, the subject represented in two blocks in the British Museum (fig. 416) and Oxford issues is combined by Caillaut on a single block.

[1] E.g. the *Dives and Lazarus* of B.M., IA. 39817 shows a single serving-man at the table and no bed in the background; the same subject in the Oxford edition shows two serving-men and a bed in the background.

In subtle draughtsmanship, charm of decoration and harmony of page, these editions are the most perfect little books of their kind.

This pocket-book Caillaut edition must not be confused with another *Horae* of somewhat larger form (woodcut surface about $5\frac{7}{8} \times 3\frac{1}{2}$ inches) issued by Caillaut about 1490 (British Museum, Proctor 7963, IA. 39507). The borders are narrow as in the case of the copper-plate Dupré (B.M., IA. 39821). In the calendar section they are in the style of the pocket-book Caillaut, but in the rest of the book are for the most part divided into panels with figures, largely busts and half-lengths. Most of the work is in black line, but its upper and outer corner-pieces are designed on a plain black ground. The larger subjects are partly the same as in the pocket-book edition, including the *Dives and Lazarus* from the British Museum issue of Dupré, IA. 39817.

Fig. 426. The Annunciation to the Shepherds, from *Horae* (Grandes Heures), Paris (Vérard), about 1490.

Nearly related to the Dupré-Caillaut pocket-book group is another *Horae*, printed by Dupré for DENIS MESLIER, 14th February 1489/90, of which the only copy known to me is that of the Pierpont Morgan Library, New York, No. 565 (from the Ashburnham, No. 2023, and Bennett Collections). The borders are of similar type, delicate outline designs, chiefly of branch, bird and beast, with occasional figures; some in a single piece (e.g. round the *Annunciation* and *Crucifixion*), but mostly in four pieces. It has already been noted that seven of the little subjects, measuring about $2\frac{7}{8} \times 1\frac{7}{8}$ inches, are from the same blocks as the set of ten *Horae* subjects in the second volume of Le Rouge's *Mer des Hystoires* of the preceding year (February 1488/89).[1] The borders,

---

[1] See p. 634. The subjects which correspond are the *Visitation, Nativity, Annunciation to Shepherds, Adoration of the Kings, Pietà, Coronation of the Virgin* and *St. John the Evangelist*.

however, are different from the *Mer des Hystoires* series, and eight different subjects also occur, of which one is here reproduced (fig. 418).

Denis Meslier also issued a certain larger *Horae*, one in the *Roman Use*

Fig. 427. Printer's mark of Philippe Pigouchet, Paris.

of about 1490 (almanac 1488–1508), with woodcut surface about 6⅛ × 4 inches (B.M., IA. 40274). This at least is the attribution of the British Museum Short-title Catalogue. Its borders are partly branch and scroll and partly divided into regular compartments with figures as in the larger Caillaut and in the Pigouchet edition of 1st December 1491,[1] and it is all in black line. Among the larger subjects *Les Trois Vifs et les Trois Morts* is represented on one block as in the pocket-book Caillaut, but in a different version.

Another, of the *Bourges Use*, with almanac 1488–1508, was published by Denis Meslier under the date 8th May without year, but is placed by Claudin about

1491–92 (Cl. ii. 106, Paris).[2] It is of the same size as the former, and contains some of the same subjects (e.g. *Les Trois Vifs et les Trois Morts*), but its borders include pieces of very different character, scroll-work on dotted ground such as one meets later in a *Paris Horae* printed by Jehannot, with almanac 1493–1508.[3] Very nearly related to the latter, if not largely from the same blocks, is the *Sarum Horae* in the British Museum, with woodcut surface of about 4⅝ × 3⅛ inches (IA. 40910), which has been variously attributed to Jean Philippe, about 1495 (Duff 187, STC. 15881), and to J. Poitevin, about 1499 (H. Thomas, Short-title Catalogue of French Books in the B.M.). This *Sarum Horae* is a most attractive book, and contains at the end the autograph of Arthur, Prince of Wales, eldest son of Henry VII., dedicating it as a gift to Sir Thomas Poyntz (fig. 419).

[1] See p. 691.   [2] Lacombe dates it 1488 with a query.
[3] Bohatta, Parma Collection, Vienna 1909, No. 182; Sale Catalogue, Duc Robert de Parme, Paris (Giraud-Badin) 1932, No. 122.

Very different from his smallest *Horae* is Dupré's edition of 4th February 1488/89 (B.M., IA. 39821), to which I have already alluded as printed from copper plates (plate surface about 5⅝ × 3⅝ inches). Most of the border-pieces are narrower than in the smaller Dupré *Horae*; there is little of the branch, bird and beast pattern, and many borders divide into three rectangular panels. Many of the larger subjects are made up with head- and side-pieces of irregular shape as in the attractive page with *David and Bathsheba* (fig. 420). There are many good designs among its larger subjects, that of *Death* at sig. h. 6 being one of the most striking. A subject with the *Printer* (or *publisher*) *adoring the Virgin and Child* occurs at the beginning of the *Oratio devotissima ad beatissimam Virginem Mariam*, sig. l. 3, verso (fig. 421). A similar subject occurs in Vérard's *Grandes Heures* of about 1490 (B.M., IB. 41116). In the latter example, which is more roughly cut, it is

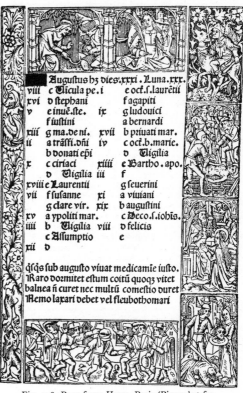

Fig. 428. Page from *Horae*, Paris (Pigouchet for Vostre) 1496/97.

practically certain that Vérard is represented with his large nose and mouth. The face in the Dupré edition is similar, but the mouth is smaller, and it seems probable that it offers a portrait of Jean Dupré.[1] There is an earlier edition of the Dupré *Horae* dated 10th May 1488, largely from the same copper plates, though the use of copper is not mentioned in the text (Cl. i. 240). The plate surface is somewhat larger, about 6 inches in height.

---

[1] The same woodcut with shield altered to contain the initials of Nicolas Le Rouge occurs in that printer's edition of *La Grande Danse Macabre*, Troyes, about 1496 (see above, p. 622).

Many of the same plates (border and subject) were used in another unique edition of Dupré, issued in 1490 and printed in three colours, red, blue and green, in addition to the black type (B.M., Proctor 8047,

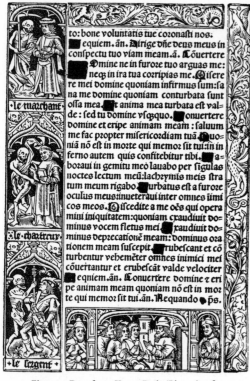

IA. 39829). No page shows more than two colours, but as each of these would require separate printing from the black type, there is little wonder that it appears to have remained an experiment. It is without the complete borders, and the pages are made up in various combinations between the larger subjects, the side-panels with three subjects, and little upright panels of initial letter size. Some fifteen new subjects are added, chiefly from the Bible, corresponding in size to the *Death*, *Annunciation* and *Zodiac Man*, in the edition of 4th February 1488/89 (about $4\frac{3}{8} \times 3\frac{1}{8}$ inches). They are among the best subject illustrations in contemporary *Horae*, with

Fig. 429. Page from *Horae*, Paris (Pigouchet for Vostre) 1496/97.

the characteristic finesse of well-engraved metal-cuts, and I have not found them in any other editions (see the page with the *Annunciation to the Shepherds*, which also includes a border-piece with a Siren, not known to me elsewhere; fig. 422). Another border-piece, remarkable for its vivid draughtsmanship, as if from the life, is the small lower panel with four half-figures in profile (see fig. 423). Dupré's beautiful *Printer's mark with the Two Swans* occurs in both these metal-cut editions, though my reproduction is made from a copy of Bonnor, *L'Arbre des Batailles*, of 1493 (fig. 424).[1]

[1] See p. 635.

Another slightly larger *Horae* printed by Dupré (woodcut surface about 6 × 3¾ inches) was published by Vérard, 10th April 1489/90,[1] with the woodcut title *Les Figures de la Bible*, the L being a characteristic initial with a woman's head (B.M., Proctor 8046, IA. 39825). It carries on the style of Dupré's *Horae*, IA. 39817, with its marginal decoration of branch, bird and beast, but has new features in its designs of bare tree-trunks, and many other new subjects, religious and genre, in its borders. The borders, which are entirely in black line, are made up of pieces of various sizes and shapes, chiefly of subjects and figures in rectangular compartments. A characteristic page, sig. f. 1, verso, is reproduced in fig. 425, and in its clear and strong woodcut forms an immediate comparison with the metal-cuts reproduced in figs. 421-24. Many of the subjects, especially those in the L-shaped corner-pieces, show very vivid characteristics of face and figure, as if done from the life (e.g. sig. h. 2, verso).

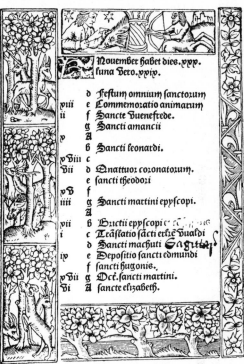

Fig. 430. Page from *Sarum Horae*, Paris (Pigouchet for Jean Richard) 1494.

Another of Vérard's *Horae*, issued 8th February 1489/90 (Macf. 199, Paris), with woodcut surface about 6½ × 4¼ inches, has attractive black-line borders, in Dupré's manner. Moreover, its Bible and other subjects in the text are for the most part the small uprights (about 3 × 1⅞ inches) which appeared in the earlier Dupré (IA. 39817), so that the same printer was probably responsible for this edition as well. The borders and other

---

[1] An edition 3rd April 1488/89 (Macf. 198, Toulouse) appears to be the earliest of the *Horae* published by Vérard with complete borders.

cuts of this edition were reprinted by Laurens Philippe, 1493 (B.M., IA. 40633).

I have already spoken of the *Grandes Heures* of Vérard, but would

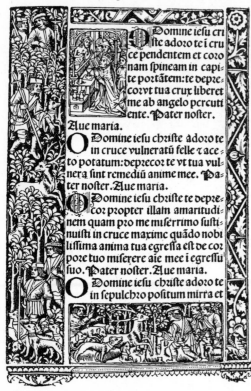

add a few further notes about the British Museum copy of about 1490 (Macf. 204, IB. 41116). In style of work its borders are near the smaller *Horae* printed by Dupré for Vérard, 10th April 1489/90, (B.M., IA. 39825), and entirely in black line, but it is less delicately cut and lacks sensitiveness in quality. It is not far removed from the harder characteristics of the later cuts of Vérard's chief designer. There is a good series of large cuts, about $4\frac{1}{2} \times 3$ inches in size, many of which had also appeared in the Dupré-Vérard *Horae* just mentioned (IA. 39825). The *Annunciation to the Shepherds, with a Country Dance* (fig. 426), and a contemporary *Funeral Service* are particularly interesting.

Fig. 431. Page from *Horae*, Paris (Pigouchet for Vostre) n.d.

These cuts are near in size and style to four which had appeared in the early Dupré-Caillaut group, but the latter generally had rectangular cartouches for inscriptions in the middle of the subject (e.g. *Dives and Lazarus*, fig. 417).

Most of the woodcuts in this edition reappeared in several other *Grandes Heures* of about the same date, e.g. one example of the *Rouen Use*[1] in the

---

[1] The *Horae* quoted may be assumed to be of the *Roman Use* (*ad usum Romanum*), and in Latin, unless otherwise described. The printer's notes and colophon are generally in French, even in the Latin *Horae*.

British Museum (IB. 41119). In general the Paris printers seem to have bestowed less care on their local *Horae* than on those of the *Roman Use*, the latter being much more frequently printed on vellum and often illuminated, no doubt on account of a richer clientèle.

I would mention one other local *Horae* published by Vérard, that of the *Sarum Use* of about 1505, with woodcut surface of about $7\frac{7}{8} \times 5\frac{1}{8}$ inches (B.M., C. 35. e. 4). There is considerable variety in quality as in all the later books of Vérard, cruder cuts of saints being mixed with some of the finer early cuts. It contains a series of *Tourneys of the Virtues and Vices* (oblong panels at the foot of page) copied from a finer set in Gringore's *Chasteau de Labour*, printed by Pigouchet for Vostre, 1499 and 1500/1501,[1] which in their turn were probably used in other *Horae*.

The combination of the printer PIGOUCHET with the publisher SIMON VOSTRE [2]

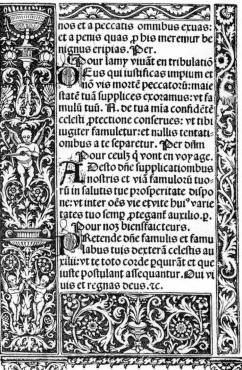

Fig. 432. Page from *Horae*, Paris (Pigouchet for Vostre) n.d.

produced the most numerous and most typical of xv-century French Books of Hours. The earliest *Horae* printed by Pigouchet were entirely in black line in a style nearly related to the earlier issues of Vérard, and in their comparative weakness more on a level with such a book as one attributed to Denis Meslier in the British Museum (IA. 40274).[3] I refer in particular to the edition of 1st December 1491 in the British

---

[1] See pp. 674, 675.
[2] See J. Renouvier, *Des gravures sur bois dans les livres de Simon Vostre*, Paris 1862.
[3] See p. 686.

Museum, with woodcut surface measuring about $6\frac{1}{8} \times 4\frac{1}{4}$ inches, the side borders mostly in upright rectangular compartments, little figures of prophets and sibyls, etc., in the lower borders (IA. 40287). A second copy in the British Museum of the same date bears the device of Marnef (IA. 40288), and most of the same blocks occur (with text set up in single instead of double column) in an edition by Geoffroi de Marnef, 20th June 1493 (B.M., IA. 40277), and in an edition of the *Troyes Use*, issued by the same publisher, 13th August 1493 (B.M., IA. 40277). Brunet described a *Horae* printed by Pigouchet for Vostre on 16th September 1488, but Claudin was unable to locate it, and the earliest Pigouchet known to him is that of 1st December 1491 just described.

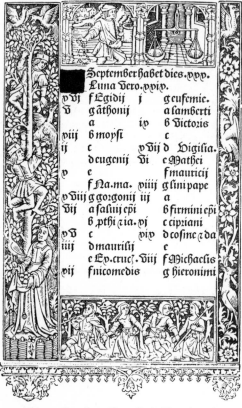

Fig. 433. Page from *Horae*, Paris (Kerver) 1506.

Of the actual combination of Pigouchet and Vostre the earliest *Horae* which I have examined is that of 8th May 1492, of pocket size (woodcut surface about $4\frac{1}{2} \times 3\frac{1}{4}$ inches) and with black-line borders of branch, bird and beast, near in style to Dupré, though hardly so good (B.M., IA. 40302). The only cut on black ground is a little *Mass of St. Gregory*, near the end. Editions dated 2nd August 1493 and 22nd August 1493 (B.M., IA. 40306 and 40308) show the same style of border decoration, but the form is larger (woodcut surface about 6×4 inches).

Pigouchet's most characteristic work for Vostre appears after the

middle of the 'nineties, e.g. in editions of 23rd January 1496/97 (B.M.,
IA. 40318) and of 20th March and 17th April 1496/97 (B.M., IA.

Fig. 434. Page from *Horae*, Paris (J. Pychore and Rémy de Laistre) 1503.

40321). They are both of the same form and size, woodcut surface about
$5\frac{1}{2} \times 3\frac{1}{2}$ inches, the borders of both are frequently made up of several
little upright panels, and both have a portion of the work (though the

lesser part) on a dotted ground, notably in the borders with the *Dance of Death*. The chief difference between the two editions lies in the calendar. In the earlier issue the lower borders contain little subjects, partly on

dotted ground: in the later issue these lower pieces contain a delightful series of children's games. These black-line woodcuts of contemporary genre are more subtle and delicate in cutting than anything in Vérard's *Horae*, just as his dotted borders, such as those with the *Dance of Death*, show an unrivalled accomplishment and finesse.

A *Sarum Horae* printed by Pigouchet for Jean Richard of Rouen in 1494, of the same size, contains some different material, with attractive border-pieces such as that of unicorns, stags and goats amid trees, here reproduced (B.M., IA. 40311, STC. 15879; fig. 430). A similar series of borders ap-

Fig. 435. Mark of the Publisher Gillet Hardouin, Paris.

pears in an undated edition of the *Roman Use* at Oxford (Proctor 8182, 8° Rawl. 1092), and adapted into larger form, made up with further border-pieces to about 6¼ or 6½ × 4⅜ inches, in another issue of 20th August 1496 (B.M., IA. 40315).

The smaller form was continued in various issues in the following years. One of 8th August 1497 (B.M., IA. 40338) has a delightful addition in the border with the *Apple Harvest*; another in the British Museum, with Calendar 1502–20 (C. 29. h. 18), has additional subjects of *Stag-hunts* (fig. 431).[1] This issue has additional ornamentation in decorated bases below the lower borders, and there is considerably more decoration in the style of the Italian Renaissance (see fig. 432).

In addition to the ornate bases further frills are added at the top of the page in certain later editions, of which the British Museum possesses a handsome example with almanac covering the years 1508–28, and probably issued near the beginning of that cycle (C. 41. e. 7; complete woodcut surface about 7½ × 4½ inches).

Besides the *Horae* in the *Roman Use*, a very large number of the local books were issued by Pigouchet and Vostre. The *Sarum Horae* of 16th May 1498, with woodcut surface 5½ × 3½ inches, occurs in a good uncoloured example in the British Museum (IA. 40335), similar in material to IA. 40321 of 1496/97, and put together with more care than was often accorded to the local *Horae*.

[1] These appeared as early as 22nd August 1498 in the larger form (B.M., IA. 40340).

THIELMANN KERVER was both printer and publisher of *Horae*, and only less prolific than Pigouchet and Vostre. But he was far from attaining their distinction, and constantly repeated their motives in his borders, with

Fig. 436. The Rape of Deianeira: Mark of the Publishers Gillet and Germain Hardouin, Paris.

considerable loss in quality. He also divided his work fairly equally between black-line cuts and blocks with dotted backgrounds, made considerable use of Italian renaissance ornament, of frills at the top of page and ornamental bases. He is seen at his best in an edition of 22nd June 1506 in

the British Museum (C. 29. f. 8), and his versions of Pigouchet's *Apple Harvest, with a Country Dance* (fig. 433) are as strong if not as delicate as the originals. Pigouchet's hunting scenes are also repeated. One of his earliest *Horae* is that of the *Sarum Use*, printed for Jean Richard, Rouen 1497 (B.M., IA. 40487). He used an excellent device of *Two Unicorns* (fig. 413).

Among the most elaborate of the *Horae* is the edition printed by J. PYCHORE and RÉMY DE LAISTRE, 5th April 1503, with woodcut surface of about $8\frac{1}{2} \times 5$ inches (B.M., Print Room, and C. 29. k. 21; see fig. 434). The whole-page subjects, in elaborate architectural frames, exceed the space of the borders. Many of the subjects of contemporary genre are repeated from Pigouchet, but classical ornament predominates.

Fig. 437. Adoration of the Kings, from *Horae*, Paris (Tory) 1525/26.

With the publishers of the family of HARDOUIN we are further into the XVI century, their earliest *Horae* being issued in 1504/05. The edition printed by Antoine Chappiel for Gillet Hardouin, 9th January 1504/05, with woodcut surface $7\frac{1}{2} \times 4\frac{3}{4}$ inches (B.M., C. 41. e. 4), is characteristic and shows his work as inferior to Kerver, not to speak of Pigouchet and Vostre. The page is made up of a great variety of blocks, and in the foot-pieces little blocks are regularly turned sideways merely to make up space.

One of their most interesting *Horae* is the edition of a narrow upright form, commonly called the *Agenda* form, printed by Antoine Chappiel for Gillet Hardouin, 19th January 1504–05 (B.M., C. 29. k. 24). Its woodcut surface is about $8\frac{1}{8} \times 3$ inches; the cuts are largely on dotted ground, and the copy, the only one known, is an excellent uncoloured impression. Hardouin's small device of woodmen on the title-page is one of its most attractive features (fig. 435).

A larger device used by the firm, with the *Rape of Deianeira* (fig. 436), is another of their most attractive cuts, and it is here reproduced from an edition printed by G. Anabat for Gillet & Germain Hardouin, with almanac 1507–20 (B.M., C. 29. h. 8), one of their finest and most richly ornamented issues. Both in style of work, and in motives used, the cuts derive largely from Pigouchet and Vostre.

Though lying well beyond my period of the xv century, I would reproduce two pages from *Horae* published by GEOFFROY TORY[1] to illustrate the last phase of which I

Fig. 438. Death, from *Horae*, Paris (Tory) 1527.

have spoken in describing the general development of French *Horae*.

The edition printed by Simon de Colines for Geoffroy Tory, 16th January 1525/26, is the more severely classic of the two specimens in the British

[1] See Auguste Bernard, *Geoffroy Tory*, Paris 1857, 2nd ed., 1865 (English translation by G. B. Ives, Boston and New York 1909); A. W. Pollard, *The Books of Hours of Geoffroy Tory*, Bibliographica, i. (1895), 114; A. F. Johnson, *Geoffroy Tory*, The Fleuron, No. vi. (1928), p. 37. The mark of the double (Lorraine) Cross which appears on many of the cuts has recently been interpreted as referring to the woodcutter Jacquemin Woeiriot (see Albert Ohl des Marais, Byblis, x. (1931), p. 13), and it is probable that Tory himself was only the designer. A monogram with a small S within a large G surmounted by the Lorraine Cross, which appears, e.g., on a series of woodcuts of the *Labours of Hercules*, has sometimes been attributed to Geoffroy Tory, but it has recently been shown to be the mark of Gabriel Salmon, another woodcutter of Lorraine (see Albert Ohl des Marais, Byblis, x. (1931), p. 139).

Museum (C. 27. k. 15). Its line is of extraordinarily delicate quality, and looks as if it were printed from metal blocks. The scroll and candelabra are in the purest North Italian style. Occasional black surfaces and white line are used with great effect, as in the negro figure in the *Adoration of the Magi* (fig. 437).

Fig. 439. Border-piece from *Horae*, Lyon 1499/1500.

The edition of the 22nd October 1527, printed for Geoffroy Tory by Simon du Bois, is broader in its line, and certainly printed from wood (C. 27. h. 17). Moreover, in this later *Book of Hours* he preserves a thoroughly French flavour in the border designs, with their isolated birds and flowers, in the manner of illumination of the school of Jean Bourdichon.[1] The page illustrated again shows a most effective use of white line in the design of *Death on a Black Horse* (fig. 438).

Paris was not only the centre of production of provincial French *Horae*, but supplied several foreign countries with their *Books of Hours*. A Spanish example may be cited in the edition issued by Kerver, 30th April 1502 (B.M., C. 24. a. 42), and a Dutch edition, *Ghetiden van onser lieuer Vrouwen*, was printed in Paris by J. Higman for sale by W. Houtmaert at Antwerp about 1497 (B.M., C. 29. f. 9), the latter with borders in the style of the *Sarum Horae* of about 1495.[2]

There is very little of interest in the woodcut *Horae* produced in France outside Paris during the xv century, and the only edition to which I would refer is that printed by BONINUS DE BONINIS at Lyon, 20th March 1499/1500, with woodcut surface of about $5\frac{3}{8} \times 3\frac{5}{8}$ inches (B.M., IA. 42127). In its form it follows the earlier Paris model, and is largely in black line, the chief exceptions being as usual the *Dance of Death* on dotted ground. The designs are good, and probably by an Italian designer brought by the printer from Italy, for they reflect the North Italian style both in figure and landscape (fig. 439). Occasional subjects like the *Death of Goliath* show an accomplished designer, seconded by an accomplished cutter, but in general the cuts, in spite of their delicate line, are carelessly executed.

---

[1] Cf. MS. *Horae* in the British Museum (Add. MSS. 18855 and 35318).
[2] B.M., IA. 40910. See p. 686 and fig. 419.

CONTEMPORARY SINGLE CUTS

In earlier chapters mention has been made of various French single cuts up to about 1470,[1] and some attention devoted to the production of Playing-cards in France throughout the xv century.[2] I would now add short notes on a few single cuts of the last quarter of the xv century.

After the introduction of illustrated books, book-illustration engrossed by far the larger share of the woodcutters' activity, so that the present section does not present anything comparable in importance or interest.

A woodcut of *St. Francis of Assisi and St. Anthony of Padua* at Manchester[3] is a large oblong with the Arms of Pope Innocent VIII. on the right portion of the block. The date is therefore limited to the years 1484–92. On account of its shape, Mr. Dodgson suggests that it might have formed the head-piece of a broadside connected with the Franciscan order. In style, with its thin line, straight folds with pot-hook ends, pointed noses and black pupils to the eyes, it carries on the tradition of the *Twelve Apostles* (S. 1759, Paris)[4] to a point near to the illustrations in *La Cité de Dieu*, printed by Dupré and Gérard at Abbeville, 1486–87.[5]

One actual broadside may be mentioned, amusing for its subject, but crude enough in its woodcut illustration, i.e. the *Ballade des Hauts Bonnets* (Bouchot 187, S. 1973, Paris), a skit on the fashion of top-hats, which were in vogue during the reign of Louis XI. (1461–83).

One of the most remarkable of French woodcuts of about 1500, both in character and size, is a *Christ on the Cross between the Virgin and St. John*, printed from four blocks, and measuring some $41\frac{1}{2} \times 30$ inches (S. 370 i). There is a complete uncoloured impression at Nice (fig. 440), and a coloured impression, considerably cut at each side, in the British Museum.[6] The subject is framed in a handsome border, and has a background imitating tapestry pattern. It is conceivable that it might have been intended, like certain earlier cuts, as a textile pattern, but it is more probable that its intention was church or house decoration, and that it was merely influenced in style by tapestry. The uncoloured impression came from a church at Luceram, near Nice, while that of the British Museum, which is a later

---

[1] See p. 154.   [2] See p. 86.

[3] Reproduced, No. VIII., in C. Dodgson, *Woodcuts of the xv Century in the John Rylands Library, Manchester*, 1915.   [4] See p. 156.   [5] See p. 622.

[6] See C. Dodgson, *Two Early French Woodcuts*, Burlington Magazine, lix. (1931), 225. Schreiber refers to the original blocks being at Nice, but this appears to be based on a misreading of the reference to *planches* in Pierre Gusman, *La Gravure sur bois*, 1916, p. 79.

state, with a blank tablet in place of a plant beneath the skull, was found at Toulouse. With it a companion print of similar character and size, and equally cut at the sides, was also acquired for the British Museum, a *Death and Assumption of the Virgin*. These two cut impressions had been folded to be used as the lining of a burse, a stiff flat case of silk used to cover the Eucharistic vessels when carried to the altar for celebration of the Mass. In a certain dignity of style I feel Italian influence, and Schreiber noted the same influence in details such as the slanting nimbus of the Christ. Considering this and the provenance of the impressions, I should be inclined to regard both subjects as productions of the South of France.

The British Museum possesses another large woodcut of *Christ on the Cross between the Virgin and St. John*, of about the same period, and measuring about $15\frac{1}{2} \times 10\frac{3}{4}$ inches, within a four-piece border of branch and flower pattern, with the name of the publisher, printer, designer or cutter *adrien de liures* in the lower piece. There are three lines of text in Gothic type between the subject and the border. The background shows a town rather like that in the *Francis receiving the Stigmata*, in Paris (see p. 702). Though large, it is not too large to have been used, at least without its border, in some Missal, but I have failed to identify it.

Another of the largest French woodcuts is a single sheet with the *Passion of Christ*, measuring about $19\frac{1}{2} \times 14$ inches (Paris, Bouchot 191; Lemoisne cxxviii.). The work is nearly related in style to illustrations in certain of Vérard's books about the end of the century, e.g. of *Ogier Le Danois*, 1498, and *Terence* of about 1500,[1] and might well be by the same hand.

A considerable number of French single cuts of about 1490–1500 are preserved, pasted in deed- and travelling-boxes.[2] An interesting example is the subject of the *Two Saints Roch, Pilgrim and Bishop, with small Votive Figures*, crudely designed and cut, but attractive in its border of branch, flower and fruit (S. 1669 m, Vienna). It was found in an alms-box with a companion print of *St. John the Baptist and St. John the Evangelist*, with a border of diamond pattern with fleur-de-lis (1518 g, Paris). The French inscriptions appear to be in the dialect of Savoy, which is probably the locality of its production.[3]

---

[1] See pp. 667, 669.

[2] For a general study describing and reproducing most of such prints which are known, see W. L. Schreiber, *Kassetten-Holzschnitte*, Einblattdrucke 76, Strassburg 1931. The Bibliothèque Nationale, Paris, is particularly rich in these boxes. See p. 76.

[3] Another somewhat similar print, also found in an alms-box, a *St. Anthony of Padua* (S. 1216 a = 1233 a, Oxford), has also been attributed to the same region, but I think it is more likely to be Portuguese or Spanish, and refer to it in that relation (see p. 758).

Fig. 440. Christ on the Cross between the Virgin and St. John. S. 370 i.

Perhaps the most attractive of all the woodcuts used in this way is the *Virgin and Child in a Glory, with the Signs of the Evangelists*, of which impressions occur at Paris (S. 1129 a, Lemoisne cvii.) and in the Historisches

Fig. 441. The Virgin and Child in a Glory. S. 1129 a.

Museum, Basle (fig. 441). Another of comparable style and beauty, also at Paris, is a *Virgin and Child with Angels beneath a Canopy* (Kassetten-Holzschnitte 16). Harder in quality is the *St. Francis receiving the Stigmata* (*ibid.* 23), to which the *Man of Sorrows* (Lemoisne cix.) is closely related, though not actually found in a box. Both of the latter show backgrounds of town views, as in the *Virgin beneath a Canopy*.

Then there is a series of somewhat smaller size than the four preceding examples and measuring about 9 × 6½ inches, e.g. the *Nativity* (Met. Museum, New York), the *Last Supper* (Paris), the *Agony in the Garden* (Paris), the *Taking of Christ* (Paris) the *Resurrection* (Berlin), *Christ appearing to the Magdalene* (Paris), and *St. Margaret* (Paris) (Kassetten-Holzschnitte 2, 3, 4, 5, 7, 9 and 25), while a *Christ carrying the Cross* (Paris, Lemoisne cxviii.), though not preserved in a box, evidently belongs to the same set.

Another cut of similar character, nearest perhaps in its more gracious qualities to the *Christ appearing to the Magdalene*, and to the larger *Virgin and Child in a Glory* and *Virgin and Child under a Canopy*, is the *Annunciation* from the McGuire Collection, now in the Metropolitan Museum, New York (S. 31 m; Kassetten-Holzschnitte 1 a; fig. 442). It was found with its pendant, a *Virgin and Child enthroned with Angels* (S. 1044 m; Einblattdrucke 72, pl. 10), in the cover of a copy of the *Missale Strigonense*, printed by Georg Stuchs, Nuremberg 1490, but they are both evidently French productions. The text at the foot had been described as in the type of Jean Bellot of Geneva, but the more recent research of the Inkunabel-Kommission at Berlin relates it rather to Jean Dupré of Paris. Though several of the earliest boxes found came from the regions of Lyon, Savoy and Geneva, it would now appear more likely that Paris was the centre of the production of these works.

As certain of these cuts appear in several boxes, it seems probable that the box-makers had special sets of woodcuts which they pasted in their boxes before sale.

In one or two instances there are variant versions, e.g. *Christ appearing to the Magdalene* (Dresden and Paris, Kassetten-Holzschnitte 8 and 9), the *Annunciation* (Rosenthal, and New York, *ibid.* 1 and 1 a), while the various impressions of the *Nativity* described by Schreiber under one number (*ibid.* 2) may, I think, be found to be from more than one block.

Another of these box-lid cuts, the *Monograms of Christ and the Virgin Mary* (Paris, Kassetten-Holzschnitte 31), is of interest for its signature *Jehan bezart*, Bezart being a family of which there are various printers, illuminators and draughtsmen recorded in the early xvi century.

Very different in character is a *Vierge Protectrice*, a roundel within a decorative border (once in the Schreiber Collection, S. 1012 a),[1] which Schreiber suggests might have been intended for pasting in a medicine-box. This is

[1] Heitz, *Pestblätter*, 5.

more German in style, and might be a work of the region of Alsace, possibly of the early years of the xvi century.

Finally, I would mention a print of *St. Bathilde kneeling in a Gothic*

Fig. 442. The Annunciation. S. 31 m.

Church, known in two impressions on vellum (Paris, Bouchot 189, and the second in the Schreiber Sale, 1909, No. 48). It is evidently printed from metal, and is described by Schreiber in his volume devoted to metal-cuts and *criblée* prints (No. 2564), but as a line-block it falls into more natural relation with the work on copper which is found in French book-illustration. It contrasts with Dupré's work on copper, in being broad and coarse in line, but as a design it possesses both refinement and charm.

BIBLIOGRAPHY

SILVESTRE, L. C. Marques Typographiques des imprimeurs en France de 1470 jusqu'à la fin du xvie siècle. Paris 1853.

RENOUARD, Philippe. Imprimeurs Parisiens depuis l'introduction de l'Imprimerie à Paris (1470) jusqu'à la fin du xvi siècle. Paris 1898 (new edition in progress in the *Revue des Bibliothèques*, Paris, from 1922).

RENOUARD, Philippe. Les Marques typographiques parisiennes des xv et xvi siècles. Paris 1926, 1928 (*Revue des Bibliothèques*, Supplement 13*).

CLAUDIN, Anatole, and LACOMBE, Paul. Histoire de l'imprimerie en France au xve et au xvie siècles. 4 vols. Paris 1900–14. Vols. i. and ii. (Paris printers); Vols. iii. and iv. (Lyon printers).

CLAUDIN, Anatole, and RICCI, Seymour de. Documents sur la typographie et la gravure en France aux xve et xvie siècles. London 1926 (700 facsimiles, with short bibliographical notes by Seymour de Ricci, from Claudin's posthumous material, relating to French printers outside Paris and Lyon).

FAIRFAX MURRAY, C. Catalogue of a Collection of Early French Books in the library of C.F.M. by Hugh W. Davies. 2 vols. London (privately printed) 1910 (the record of an extraordinarily rich collection).

BRITISH MUSEUM. Short-title Catalogue of Books printed in France and of French books printed in other countries 1470–1600, now in the British Museum. Edited by Henry Thomas. London 1924.

MEYER, Wilhelm Jos. Die französischen Drucker- und Verlegerzeichen des xv Jahrhunderts. Munich 1926.

BLUM, André. Les Origines du livre à gravures en France: Les Incunables typographiques. Paris and Brussels 1928.

MARTIN, André. Le Livre français illustré du xve siècle. Paris 1931.

CHAPTER IX

BOOK-ILLUSTRATION AND CONTEMPORARY SINGLE CUTS
IN ENGLAND

THE revolution of methods implied by the introduction of printing inevitably attracted men of enterprise and ability, and among them not the least distinguished was WILLIAM CAXTON.[1] Born in Kent, apprenticed in 1438 to a mercer in the City of London, he went abroad about 1441, and was engaged in the cloth trade on the Continent for more than thirty years before his literary interests turned him to the idea of printing.

He had lived chiefly at Bruges, and attained a leading position among his fellow-countrymen in the Netherlands. Between 1465 and 1469 he acted as Governor of the English Merchant Adventurers in the Low Countries, and was engaged in negotiating commercial treaties with Philip the Good and Charles the Bold, Duke of Burgundy, in 1464 and 1468.

It was as early as 1469 that Caxton began his translation of Raoul Le Fèvre's *Recueil des Histoires de Troye*, and he was encouraged in the work and helped to amend his 'rude English' by the Duchess of Burgundy, Margaret of York, sister of Edward IV. of England, to whose household he was attached between 1471 and 1476. He completed his translation when staying at Cologne in 1471, but whether it was here or at Bruges that he issued this first book printed in the English language is still a matter of controversy. A stanza in some verses appended to Wynkyn de Worde's English edition of Bartholomaeus Anglicus, *De Proprietatibus Rerum*, 1495,[2] refers quite definitely to the first Latin edition of this work as printed by Caxton at Cologne, and such a statement from one who

---

[1] See William Blades, *Life and Typography of William Caxton*, 2 vols., London 1861, 1863; W. Blades, *Biography and Typography of William Caxton*, London 1877 (2nd ed., 1882); E. Gordon Duff, *William Caxton*, Chicago (Caxton Club) 1905; Seymour de Ricci, *A Census of Caxtons*, Bibliographical Society Illustrated Monographs, xv., London 1909; H. R. Plomer, *William Caxton*, London 1925; Nellie S. Aurner, *Caxton*, London 1926; Rudolf Hittmair, *William Caxton*, Innsbruck 1931.

[2] The verses are entitled 'Prohemium Bartholomei' and the passage runs:

And also of your charytie call to remembraunce
The soule of William Caxton first prynter of this boke
In laten tonge at Coleyn hymselfe to avaunce.

had been Caxton's foreman naturally demands credence. He very probably helped (and may partly have financed) the anonymous printer who issued the first edition of 'Bartholomew the Englishman' described by Proctor under his No. 1105 (Hain 2498), the printer responsible for the *Dialogi decem Auctorum* in 1473 and the undated *Flores Sancti Augustini*.

But this still leaves unsolved the place of publication of the *Recuyell*, which is printed in type used later by Colard Mansion. Blades and Gordon Duff, followed by Pollard and Redgrave, conjecturally place the printing of Caxton's *Recuyell of the Histories of Troye*,[1] at Bruges, about 1475, in collaboration with Colard Mansion (Blades 1, Duff 242, STC. 15375), while Plomer considers Cologne, about 1472–73, as the more probable place and date.

A plate representing *Caxton presenting his Book to Margaret of York*[2] is found in only one of the few known copies of the book, that of the Huntington Library, San Marino, California, acquired with the complete Caxton collection of the Duke of Devonshire at Chatsworth. The print is merely inlaid in the first blank leaf, and may have been inserted at a later date than the first publication, but there is every reason to think that it had been originally designed to illustrate the book. It is an engraving on copper done in a style closely related to the line-engravings[3] in Colard Mansion's French edition of Boccaccio, *De Casibus virorum et foeminarum illustrium*, Bruges 1476, and might be by the same hand. No woodcuts appear in any of the books with which Caxton might have been associated with Colard Mansion in Bruges.

In the autumn of 1476 Caxton returned to England, and established his press within the precincts at Westminster, issuing some eighty books, many being his own translations from French originals, between 1477 and his death in 1491.

English woodcut illustration in the xv century lags far behind contemporary work on the continent of Europe both in extent and quality, and its interest is for the most part literary and antiquarian rather than artistic.

---

[1] Caxton's translation from the French of Raoul Le Fèvre.

[2] Reproduced as frontispiece to Seymour de Ricci, *A Census of Caxtons*, 1909, and at p. 1 of A. W. Pollard, *Fine Books*, London 1912.

[3] Only known in two copies of the book, one at Göttingen and the other in the Boston Museum of Fine Arts from the library of the Marquis of Lothian (Sale, American Art Association, New York, 27th January 1932, Lot 46). See my *History of Engraving and Etching*, 3rd ed., 1923, pp. 32 and 33. For Colard Mansion and his only other illustrated work, the *Metamorphoses* of Ovid, 1484, see p. 591.

The earliest illustrated book printed in England is generally supposed
to be the *Mirrour of the World*, Caxton's version of the famous *Speculum
Historiale* of Vincent de Beauvais, issued about 1481 (Blades 31, Duff

401, STC. 24762).[1] There are
numerous little subjects and
diagrams (some with figures in
circles), in thin outline and open
shading, drawn and cut by a
manifestly unpractised hand, no
doubt in Caxton's workshop.
The woodcuts of a *Master and
Pupils* at sigg. a 4, c 4 and
c 4 verso (fig. 443) and of a
*Woman singing to the accom-
paniment of a man playing the
flageolet* (sig. c 6) are among the
more entertaining. The two

Fig. 443. Master and Pupils, from the *Mirrour of the
World*, Westminster, about 1481.

versions of *Master and Pupils* which occur at sig. c 4 and c 4 verso also
appear in the third edition of Caxton's *Cato parvus et magnus*, which has
likewise been conjecturally dated about 1481, and is placed by Pollard
Redgrave in 1480 (Blades 30, Duff 78, STC. 4852). Blades also inferred
from the condition of the blocks that it was earlier than the *Mirrour*. The
woodcuts in the copies of the *Cato* in the British Museum, St. John's
College, Oxford, and the John Rylands Library, Manchester, are more
heavily inked than the impressions in the *Mirrour*, but I find no evidence
of priority of impression, and the impressions in the St. John's College
copy of the *Cato* are in certain details more akin to those in the Exeter
College copy of the second edition of the *Mirrour* of about 1490 (Duff
402, STC. 24763). Moreover, as the first two editions of the *Cato* were
without illustration, it is more probable that the woodcuts were borrowed
from the *Mirrour* series, rather than done in the first instance for the
Cato. So that on the whole I would give the *Mirrour* priority in date.

Stronger in line, but equally poor in execution, are the sixteen blocks
(repeated to make twenty-four figures) in Caxton's second edition of
Jacobus de Cessolis, *Game of Chesse*, of about 1483 (Blades 34, Duff 82,
STC. 4921; see fig. 444). It opens with a frontispiece representing King

[1] The work was finished 8th March 1480/81; 2nd ed., about 1490 (e.g. Cambridge). Many
of the original blocks were reprinted, amid a variety of other illustrations, in an undated edition
issued by Lawrence Andrewe, about 1527.

Evilmerodach, son of Nebuchadnezzar, 'a jolly man without justice who did do hew his father his body into three hundred pieces', and follows with the usual type of subject illustrating the various ranks and occupations of

Fig. 444. From Jacobus de Cessolis, *Game of Chesse*, Westminster, about 1483.

mankind. In style the woodcuts show Netherlandish influence, but there is no reason to think that they were not cut in England.

The *Aesop* woodcuts in the *Subtyl hystoryes and Fables of Esope*, issued 26th March 1484 (Blades 55, Duff 4, STC. 175, GW. 376), are derived either directly or indirectly, like nearly all fifteenth-century Aesops, from Johann Zainer's Ulm edition of about 1476–77.[1] Not only in style, but in details of design, they are much further removed from the Ulm originals than Knoblochtzer's Strassburg edition of about 1480,[2] or the first French edition, that of Philippi and Reinhard, Lyon 1480,[3] which are among the earliest series of copies. In their crude drawing and broad handling they are not far removed from the style of the woodcuts in the Oxford *Festial* of 1486.[4] Caxton states that he made his translation from the French, and he might well have used the Lyon edition of 1480, but I find no definite clue on the side of the woodcuts. The full-page frontispiece representing *Aesop* is only known in the Windsor copy (Blades, pl. xxxiv.).

[1] See p. 306. [2] See p. 336.
[3] See p. 602. [4] See p. 723.

In or about the same year, 1484, Caxton issued his second edition of
Chaucer's *Canterbury Tales* (Blades 57, Duff 88, STC. 5083), the first to
contain woodcuts (see fig. 445). The woodcuts are of the same broad line

and crude execution as
the *Aesop*, but these
mounted figures of the
pilgrims illustrating the
characters as they ap-
pear in the Prologue,
and repeated at the
head of the respective
Tales, have at least the
virtue of originality.
There is also an amus-
ing cut in the Prologue
of the *Pilgrims at Table*
(fig. 446), which was
used later by Wynkyn
de Worde for a feast

Fig. 445. The Wife of Bath, from the *Canterbury Tales*,
Westminster, about 1484.

of the immortals in John Lydgate, *Assembly of the Gods*, 1498 (Duff 253,
STC. 17005).

It is noteworthy that a copy of Caxton's edition of Chaucer's *Troilus and
Cressid* of about 1482 (Duff 94, STC. 5094) in St. John's College, Oxford,
which is bound with the *Canterbury Tales*, contains an illuminated frontispiece on vellum drawn very much in a woodcutter's manner. Outline
and shading are done with the pen in brown and blue, and the colour is in
transparent washes of blue, green, brown and rose. If not a copy of some
French or Netherlandish woodcut, it is certainly drawn in the manner of
woodcutters of the Netherlands or North France, and might be by the
designer responsible for Caxton's *Golden Legend*.

Caxton's English version of the *Golden Legend* was completed, according
to his colophon, on the 20th November 1483, and this seems only to refer
to the translation, and not to the printing, which may be assumed to have
been carried through about 1484–85 (Blades 53, Duff 408, STC. 24873).
It is the most extensive of his works both in text and illustration. The
introductory section, which opens with an oblong heraldic design of a *Horse
by a Tree* with the motto 'my truste is', the badge of William Fitzalan,
Earl of Arundel (1417–1487), at whose request the translation was made,
and with a full-page cut of the *Trinity adored by Saints*, contains a series of

some fourteen oblong cuts (about $4\frac{3}{8} \times 6\frac{3}{4}$ inches), chiefly illustrating the life of the Virgin and of Christ. This introductory section differentiates Caxton's *Golden Legend* at once from foreign editions, which deal more exclusively with the Lives of the Saints. At a time when Lollardry was still suspect, and when the printing of Wycliffe's English Bible would have been forbidden by the Church, Caxton's short paraphrase of parts of Scripture is at least a sign of coming freedom. To judge from certain blind translations of misprints, Caxton's version of the main part

Fig. 446. The Pilgrims at Table, from the *Canterbury Tales,* Westminster, about 1484.

of the work appears to have been based on an anonymous edition, which was probably printed in North France about 1475 (B.M., Proctor 8802, IC. 46325).[1]

Then the bulk of the work is illustrated by some sixty-two column-cuts (about $4 \times 2\frac{7}{8}$ inches), with a few of the larger oblongs interspersed. Whether the author (designer or cutter) is English or not, he was at least chiefly inspired by Netherlandish woodcut in the manner of the earlier illustrations produced at Gouda (e.g. the *Liden ons Heren* of 1482)[2] and doing work comparable with the Antwerp and Delft *Ludolphus* of 1487 and 1488,[3] and the Delft *Passionael* of 1487.[4]

I am unable to identify the immediate sources used by Caxton's designer, in any of the German editions, from that of Günther Zainer of Augsburg (1472) onwards, or in the two French editions that certainly precede him, the Lyon editions, of Philippi and Reinhard of about 1480, and of Hus and Petrus of Hungary, 1483.[5] In scriptural illustration of his introductory

---

[1] See F. S. Ellis, *Memoranda* at end of Kelmscott Press edition of Caxton's *Golden Legend,* 1892, vol. iii. p. 1282.

[2] See p. 566.   [3] See pp. 568-572.   [4] See p. 573.   [5] See p. 603.

section he may have had recourse to the great Cologne Bible of about 1478–79, but here again the reminiscences are too general to establish any definite link. Moreover, none of the Netherlandish editions of the *Golden Legend (Passionael)* is illustrated.

The most interesting parts of the text concern English saints, whose

Fig. 447. The Murder of Thomas à Becket, from the *Golden Legend*, Westminster, about 1484–85.

lives do not appear in the foreign editions of Jacob de Voragine's work, and in illustrations such as the *Murder of Thomas à Becket* (fig. 447). That this woodcut has often been mutilated, or removed from copies of the book, is no doubt due to the suppression of Becket's shrine and cult in the reign of Henry VIII. The column-cuts are for the most part cruder in execution (though this seems to come from lack of care rather than difference of style), and many appear as if printed from worn blocks, though I am unable to trace their use in any earlier edition.

The British Museum copy is made up partly of the first edition and partly of a variant issue with head-lines in larger type, probably printed about 1487 (Blades 66, Duff 409, STC. 24874).[1] In both these issues initial letters are supplied by hand.

---

[1] This variant issue has not been found complete, so it may only have been printed to make up deficiencies.

Of a very different type, and more refined in character and more delicate in line, are the small upright cuts, measuring about $3\frac{1}{2} \times 2\frac{3}{4}$ inches, mostly within double border, in Bonaventura, *Speculum Vite Cristi*, first printed about 1486 (Blades 70, Duff 48, STC. 3259, Cambridge) and reprinted with only slight differences (e.g. *Capitulum* written in full in place of the earlier *Ca.* in the head-lines) about 1490 (Blades 71, Duff 49, STC. 3260). The lighter touch shown in these cuts is reminiscent of the work of Bellaert's chief woodcutter at Haarlem. Some of the series were not used in the *Speculum*, but appear in various books printed by Wynkyn de Worde.

Fig. 448. Christ at Emmaus, from the *Speculum Vite Cristi*, Westminster, about 1486.

Caxton's large and decorative mark appears to have been originally made for the *Sarum Missal* printed for him by Maynyal at Paris in 1487 (Duff 322, STC. 16164, Lord Newton, and Corpus Christi College, Cambridge), but is here reproduced from the second edition of the *Speculum* (fig. 449).

The *Royal Book*, Caxton's translation of the *Livre des Vices et des Vertus* [1] (Blades 67, Duff 366, STC. 21429), which appeared about 1486 or soon after, contains one cut from the *Golden Legend* (*Moses and the Tables of the Law*) and six of the *Speculum* series. Odd cuts from the *Speculum* also occur in Guy de Roye, *Doctrinal of Sapyence*, after 7th May 1489 (Blades 71, Duff 127, STC. 21431), and in the *Book of Divers Ghostly Matters*, of about 1491 (Blades 85, Duff 55, STC. 3305).

Of Caxton's woodcut initials there is an isolated rustic A (fig. 450) which occurs in the *Aesop* of 26th March 1484, and in the *Book of the Order of Chivalry* of about the same date (Blades 56, Duff 58, STC. 3326), and in Wynkyn de Worde's 1498 edition of the *Golden Legend*. Apart from certain smaller series of initials, he also used several letters of the design with leaf and flower, which figured more completely in de Worde's books (see fig. 453). Examples of this series appeared in the *Royal Book*, about 1486 (Blades 67, Duff 366, STC. 21429), in the *Governayle of Helthe* about 1489

---

[1] An undated edition in the British Museum, catalogued under the Italian title *Fiore di Virtù*, is conjecturally dated about 1485 (IA. 46385).

(Blades 76, Duff 165, STC. 12138, Oxford), in Virgil, *Eneydos*, after 22nd June 1490 (Blades 81, Duff 404, STC. 24796), in the *Fifteen Oes* about 1491 (Blades 82, Duff 150, STC. 20195), and the *Book of Divers Ghostly Matters* about 1491 (Blades 85, Duff 55, STC. 3305).

Fig. 449. Printer's mark of William Caxton, Westminster.

Caxton printed various editions of the *Hours of the Virgin* (*Horae Beatae Mariae Virginis ad usum Sarum*), the 'Primer' as it was commonly called in English. But these books of private devotion are exceedingly rare, and several editions are only known from fragments found in the linings of book-covers.

The two earliest editions known, that of about 1477–78 in the Pierpont Morgan Library, New York (62 leaves, vellum, covering the third part of the Primer, 'Vigils of the Dead', etc., Duff 174, STC. 15867),[1] and that of about 1480 (4 leaves, Duff 175, STC. 15868), are without cuts in the portions that remain. The fragment of a third edition of about 1490, preserved, like the second, in the British Museum (8 leaves, Duff 178, STC. 15871), contains two small cuts, an *Image of Pity* (*Christ in the Tomb, with the signs of the Passion*, 52 × 57 mm.) and a *Christ on the Cross with the Virgin and St. John* (54 × 39 mm.). A further fragment of a fourth edition, of about 1490, also in the British Museum (4 leaves, Duff 179, STC. 15872), has no woodcuts.

Even if there were no cuts in the first and second editions, when complete, it is more than probable that the third and fourth editions and others, which may have been issued during the 'eighties, contained more cuts than the two preserved. There are numerous cuts of initial size corresponding in style and dimensions with the *Christ on the Cross* of the third edition, in later *Horae* of Wynkyn de Worde,[2] and in de Worde's edition of Caxton's *Golden Legend*, and these almost certainly came from lost *Horae* printed by Caxton. I shall speak later in more detail of Wynkyn's *Primers* of 1494 with

---

[1] See E. Gordon Duff, *The First Edition of the Sarum Primer, printed on vellum at Westminster by William Caxton*, c. 1477. 1908.

[2] E.g. in his 4to *Horae* of 1494 (see p. 719).

Fig. 450. Initial A, from *Aesop*, Westminster 1484.

woodcut borders, but I would add here note of his other *Horae* which merely contain isolated cuts, i.e. Duff 185, STC. 15878 (6 leaves, 8vo, about 1494, with two small illustrations, the *Martyrdom of St. Erasmus* and *St. Roch and an Angel*, well designed and cut, and probably by the master responsible for his edition of Bartholomaeus;[1] Corpus Christi College, Oxford); STC. 15898, 8vo, 1502 (Oxford); STC. 15899, 4to, 1503 (B.M.); STC. 15908, 8vo, 1508? (4 leaves, Cambridge); STC. 15914, 4to, 1513, *Matyns of Our Lady* (B.M.); STC. 15922, 4to, 1519, *Matyns of Our Lady* (B.M.).

The earliest English Primer known with a series of borders was printed by WILLIAM DE MACHLINIA, about 1485 (Duff 176, STC. 15869).[2] Until recently this was only known from fragments in the British Museum and various other libraries, but in 1928 a copy, bound early in the XVII century, was discovered by Mr. George Smith of the firm of Ellis, New Bond Street. It contains 100 leaves out of the complement of 108, covering the three parts of the Primer: (1) the Hours of the Virgin, (2) the Penitential Psalms and (3) the Vigils of the Dead, etc.

A considerable number of its pages are enclosed in floral scroll borders, of which there are two varieties, one of which is always used round text, the other to enclose the woodcut subjects, eight in number (see fig. 451). The impression is on vellum, the woodcut borders and subjects being lightly coloured, a few borders and initial letters being added by hand. Both borders were used later by Pynson.[3] Two other borders of similar dimensions and design appeared in books issued by Wynkyn de Worde in the early XVI century (McKerrow and Ferguson, plates 3 and 5), while a third border used by de Worde in the *Lamentacyon of Our Lady* (STC. 17537, Cambridge, McKerrow and Ferguson, pl. 6) is also near in type, but includes birds in its design and is slightly larger.

In character of design these borders are most nearly related to the work

[1] See p. 726.
[2] See *William de Machlinia, the Primer on vellum printed by him in London about 1484. Newly found and described by George Smith. With facsimiles of the Woodcuts.* London (Ellis, New Bond St.) 1929.
[3] See R. B. McKerrow and F. S. Ferguson, *Title-page borders used in England and Scotland, 1485-1640.* Bibliographical Society Illustrated Monographs, xxi., London 1932 (for 1931), plates 1 and 2.

of Jean Dupré, particularly in the borders of his *Horae* of about 1488 (B.M., IA. 39817) and the related group.[1] The earliest of the French *Horae* known with borders of this character is the one published by Vérard, 6th February 1485/86 (Cl. ii. 388-89), so that Machlinia's *Primer* is all the more remarkable as being among the very first examples of its kind. Machlinia's borders compare well in charm of invention (if not in precision of cutting) with contemporary French work, but the woodcut subjects are much cruder and rather Flemish or German than French in character. The designer and cutter may be the same for both border and subject, but it is evident that his talent was fully equal to decorative design, but limited in more naturalistic forms of expression. But all in all Machlinia's *Primer* is a fascinating little book, and among the most interesting monuments of English xv-century illustration.

A more important, but hardly more attractive, achievement is the *Book of Prayers*, printed by Caxton about 1491, called the *Fifteen Oes*, from the fifteen prayers each beginning with O (Blades 82, Duff 150, STC. 20195). It is an octavo of twenty-two leaves, two gatherings of eight leaves and one of six, with signatures *a, b* and *c*. The first page is blank, the remainder are surrounded with four-piece borders of branch, flower, bird and beast, in the manner of Jean Dupré. The second page forms a frontispiece with the subject of *Calvary* (fig. 452). The third page, the first of the text, opens with a woodcut initial O (fig. 453) of the leaf and flower series which we have already described,[2] the later initial letters in the book belonging to smaller series.

These *Prayers*, printed, as the colophon states, by the command of Elizabeth of York (Queen of Henry VII.) and of the king's mother, Margaret Beaufort, constitute a complete work in themselves, but they may have formed the supplement to a lost Primer, like the Wynkyn de Worde edition about to be described. The designer of the *Calvary* is easily the most spirited artist engaged in book-illustration in England in the xv century. He shows an individual sense of curving lines, and an incisive power of expression.

Except for a fragment of four leaves in the Baptist College at Bristol,[3] the book is only known from the British Museum copy. In several instances border-pieces are printed upside-down (e.g. f. 2), a common form of carelessness by no means confined to Caxton.

The same borders were used in the *Horae* printed by Wynkyn de Worde, in and about 1494 (Duff 182, STC. 15875, Lambeth Palace; Duff 183, STC. 15876, British Museum). The Lambeth copy, on vellum, is the more complete, and its last page, which contains the *Annunciation* from Caxton's *Speculum*, includes in its colophon the title applied to Caxton's

Fig. 451. The Nativity, from *Horae*, London (Machlinia), about 1485.

prayers, *These forsayd prayers as the XV Oes in Englysshe and ye other follow-yng*, also repeats Caxton's statement that they were printed by the command of Elizabeth, Queen of Henry VII., and of Margaret Beaufort. It contains the *Calvary*, and four other cuts of the same size, the *Three Rioters and the Three Skeletons* (fig. 454), the *Tree of Jesse with the Virgin and Child*, *Dives and Lazarus*, and *David (with Goliath above and Bath-*

sheba below).[1] The *Three Rioters and the Three Skeletons* is based on the story of *Les Trois Vifs et les Trois Morts*, which appears in most of the French *Horae*, and the design may have been adapted from one or

Fig. 452. Calvary, from the *Fifteen Oes*, Westminster, about 1491.

another of those in the Dupré-Caillaut group, corresponding to the Caillaut edition in showing the subject on one block.[2] But the com-

---

[1] Several of these blocks were used in other books of Wynkyn de Worde: The *Calvary* in his 'Golden Legend', 1493, John Alcock, *Mons Perfectionis*, 1497, and in the 'Three Kynges of Coleyn', about 1499 (Duff 398, STC. 5572, Edinburgh); both the *Calvary* and the *Tree of Jesse* in his 'Golden Legend' of 1498; the *Three Rioters and the Three Skeletons* in Richard Rolle, 'Contemplacyons', 1506 (STC. 21259); the *Dives and Lazarus* in Cordiale, 'Memorare novissima', n.d. (Duff 110, STC. 5759, Oxford), and both *Dives and Lazarus* and the *David* in Wynkyn's *Sarum Horae* of 1513.   [2] See p. 684. The Caillaut subject is reproduced in Claudin i. p. 257.

position is treated with considerable variation, so that it might be drawn from another source. The *Dives and Lazarus* is also nearly related to woodcuts in the Dupré-Caillaut group, while the *David* is a modified

rendering of the same combination of motives seen in a woodcut in Pierre Gringore, *Casteau d'Amours,* issued by Michel le Noir, Paris 1500,[1] which may have been done earlier for some *Horae.* These quarto *Horae* of Wynkyn de Worde also contain a considerable number of the small cuts of initial letter size (about 2 to 2⅝ by 1½ to 1¾ inches) to which we have already alluded as probably coming from lost *Primers* of Caxton,[2] the most attractive being a *St. George and the Dragon,* on sig. h. v. of the Lambeth and British Museum copies. There are no woodcut initials, these being added by hand.

Fig. 453. Initial O, from the *Fifteen Oes,* Westminster, about 1491.

The only other English xv-century *Horae* with complete borders to which I can refer is that of RICHARD PYNSON, printed about 1497 (Duff 192, STC. 15886, Oxford; see fig. 455). It is French in style, and except for two small border-pieces of Prophet and Sibyl, entirely in black line. Its outer and lower borders are largely divided into rectangular subjects, and the woodcut surface measures about 6¼ × 4¼ inches. I have not identified the blocks in any French edition, and they may have been cut specially for Pynson's Primer. It contains a series of subject cuts in various sizes, from nearly full-page to the size of initial letters. Of Pynson's other *Primers* of the xv century, there are only fragments left, and only two of these, of about 1498 and 1500, contain woodcuts (Duff 197, STC. 15891, Cambridge; and Duff 199, STC. 15893, Durham).

A considerable number of *Horae* and Missals in the Sarum Use were printed abroad during the xv century, and I have already alluded to one or two issued at Rouen and Paris.[3] Their study should be illuminating in relation to the development of English woodcut, as it is to be expected that the decoration of foreign books produced for English use would have most influence on artists working in England.

It is an important fact that most of these imported *Horae* date before 1491, by which time both Machlinia and Caxton had issued their *Horae* with borders, and the only Sarum Missal printed abroad before the same date is the edition printed by Guillaume Maynyal for Caxton in 1487. After the *Sarum Horae* printed by Gerard Leeuw at Antwerp, about

---

[1] See p. 676.   [2] See p. 714.

[3] See pp. 625, 626, 629.

1491–92, of which there is only a single quire and single woodcut, at Brasenose College, Oxford (Duff 180, STC. 15873), the most important work is the Missal printed at Rouen by Martin Morin, in 1492.[1] The

Fig. 454. The Three Rioters and the Three Skeletons, from *Horae*, Westminster (Wynkyn de Worde), about 1494.

four-piece border, with branch and bird motives, is entirely in the style of Dupré, and perhaps came from his Paris workshop.

Then come the octavo and folio Missals printed in 1494 for the London booksellers FREDERICK EGMONT and GERARDUS BARREVELT, by Johannes Hamman at Venice: the splendid folio with a fine outline border (Essling, *Les Missels vénitiens*, p. 270, No. 215, Duff 324, STC. 16167,

Cambridge; the British Museum copy being very imperfect); the octavo edition with little outline initials and small *Canon* cut, but no borders (Duff 325, STC. 16168, fragments only, e.g. in B.M.), and the small *Sarum Horae* of the same printer and same year, with most attractive

Fig. 455. The Nativity, from *Horae*, London (Pynson), about 1497.

outline borders (Duff 181, STC. 15874; fragments in B.M., etc.).[1] But this Venetian art finds no reflection on English soil.

Most of the cuts in the English Missals of the late xv and early xvi centuries are based on French originals, if indeed French blocks are not used.

The *Christ on the Cross* in the *Sarum Missal* printed for Wynkyn de

Worde by JULIAN NOTARY and JEAN BARBIER in 1498 (Duff 328, STC. 16172) is based on the *Canon* cut which appeared first in Pierre Le Rouge's *Toul Missal* of 1492,[1] and later in the *Sarum Missal* printed by Jean Dupré, 30th September 1500 (Duff 331, STC. 16175, complete with *Canon* cut at Ely), and by Dupré's successors in 1504 (STC. 16178).[2]

The same original design is followed in another version, again without the border, in Pynson's *Sarum Missal* of 1512 (STC. 16190), a Missal which also reprints Vérard's original block of *Les Joyes de Paradis* from his *Art de bien Vivre et de bien Mourir*. The *Resurrection*, which occurs at f. 81, is a very close copy of the block in Dupré's *Sarum Missal*, Paris 1500, and in the edition of Dupré's successors, 1504.

In his earlier *Sarum Missal* of 10th January 1500/1501, the so-called *Morton Missal*, printed at the expense of Cardinal Morton, Archbishop of Canterbury, and decorated with his arms and a rebus on his name in the borders and initials (Duff 329, STC. 16173, Oxford, etc.), Pynson had used a different model for his *Christ on the Cross*, which shows the Apostle John with his hand to his face as in the *Canon* cuts in Gering and Rembolt's *Paris Missal* of 1497 (Cl. i. 107) and Wolfgang Hopyl's *Sarum Missals* of 1500 (Duff 330, STC. 16174, Oxford) and 1504 (B.M., C. 36. l. 8).

The *Morton Missal* is perhaps the finest missal printed in England at the period. The four-piece border, which is used at the head of various sections, is well designed and cut, the side-pieces in black line, the upper and lower members (each from two blocks fitted together) on dotted ground, all being in the French style of branch and bird, etc., and there are several handsome woodcut initials printed in red (see fig. 456).

Most of the English books printed abroad, and English editions of foreign books printed in England, have already been described in the sections dealing with the original editions. Apart from liturgical works, few borders with woodcuts were printed abroad for the English market during the xv century, the only one to which I can here refer being the *Cronycles of the Londe of Englonde*, printed by Gerard Leeuw at Antwerp, 1493 (Duff 100, and pl. li.; STC. 9994).[3] In the early xvi century there were various editions of the *Shepherds' Calendar*,[4] the *Art of Good Living and Good Dying*,[5] the *Ordinarye of Crysten Men*,[6] and Pierre Gringore's *Castell of Labour*.[7]

---

[1] Monceaux, i. p. 275, No. 28 (with reproduction).
[2] See p. 629.   [3] See p. 580.   [4] See p. 651.
[5] See pp. 662-663.   [6] See p. 673.   [7] See p. 676.

Fig. 456. Initial A, from the *Morton Missal,* London 1500/1501.

Another foreign printer of English books may be mentioned here, i.e. JAN VAN DOESBORGH, who followed Leeuw in his interest in the English book trade at Antwerp,[1] but his work falls entirely in the XVI century (about 1505–30), and the artistic merit of his woodcuts is very slight. Among his earliest books is the *Fifteen Tokens of the Day of Doom,* of about 1505, based on the section of *L'Art de bien Vivre et de bien Mourir* entitled *Les Quinze Signes de l'Antechrist.* He succeeded to the business of Roelant van den Dorpe, as is shown by his use of the same printer's mark of Knight Roland (Juchhoff 13) which occurs in this and other books.[2]

Resuming my survey of books printed in England, I would mention certain works issued at Oxford and St. Albans, contemporaneously with Caxton, before coming to Caxton's successors at Westminster and in the City of London.

The large folio of Lyndewode's *Constitutiones Provinciales* printed at Oxford by THEODORICUS ROOD, about 1483 (Duff 278, STC. 17102), contains a woodcut frontispiece of a *Monk seated writing at a desk beneath an architectural canopy,* with landscape and trees on either side. In style it is entirely Netherlandish, and of good average quality of design and cutting, and there seems reason to believe that it was originally intended to figure as Jacobus de Voragine in a *Golden Legend,* of which no copies are known, if it was ever published.

The other relics of this conjectured *Golden Legend* appear in the woodcuts illustrating John Mirk's *Festial,* printed by Rood at Oxford in 1486 (Duff 300, S.T.C. 17958, Oxford; see fig. 457). It is a series of oblong cuts within double border-lines, the blocks being cut down to fit the page to a width of about five inches, from an original size which was probably nearly that of the *Voragine* portrait ($4\frac{7}{8} \times 7\frac{3}{8}$ inches). They are considerably cruder in execution than the portrait, but greater care was probably spent on the frontispiece cut. Their very crudeness inclines one to accept them as by some native craftsman with little training in his art. The treatment of the blocks, and the nature of the subjects, point indubitably to the assumption of a lost Book of Saints. Two small upright cuts of *St. Andrew*

---

[1] See Robert Proctor, Bibliographical Society, Illustrated Monographs, ii., 1894.

[2] See p. 580.

with his Cross (each about $2\frac{1}{2} \times 1\frac{5}{8}$ inches) were probably done for a Book of Hours, but no Oxford Primer is known.

In addition to these subject cuts, Theodoricus Rood has a set of four large border-pieces, of branch, bird and flower design, which decorate the front page of Alexander de Hales, *Expositio Librorum de Anima* (Aris-

Fig. 457. The Murder of Thomas à Becket, from Mirk, *Festial*, Oxford 1486.

totle), of 1481 (Duff 21, STC. 314), and John Latterbury, *Commentary on the Lamentations of Jeremiah (Super Threnis Ieremiae)*, 1482 (Duff 238, STC. 15297). They are attractive in design, though somewhat weak in execution.

The press of the anonymous schoolmaster at St. Albans issued two books with woodcuts. The earlier of these, the *Chronicles of England* (generally called the *St. Albans Chronicle*), printed about 1485 (Duff 101, STC. 9995), contains a few cuts of little importance, such as a *Tower of Babel* and some diagrams. The second publication, generally known as the *Book of St. Albans*, a book on hawking, hunting and blasing of arms, by Juliana Bernes, issued in 1486 (Duff 56, STC. 3308), is of interest on account of the use of colour blocks in the section on the 'blasyng of armys' in the same manner as the early astronomical woodcuts of Ratdolt at Venice. Most of the coats-of-arms are in single colours: others are in black line with one or two colours from different blocks. In the second edition, printed by Wynkyn de Worde in 1496, the coats-of-arms are newly cut, and coloured by hand.

WYNKYN DE WORDE (Jan van Wynkyn, born at Worth in Alsace) probably came to England with Caxton in 1476, and became his foreman, succeeding to the press at Westminster after his master's death in 1491. In 1500 he removed to Fleet Street, and in 1509 opened a shop in St. Paul's Churchyard, which remained so long the centre of the London publishing and bookselling trades. His activity in the xvi century until his death at the end of 1534 or beginning of 1535[1] is outside our period, and a great deal of his work in the xv century was concerned with new editions of Caxton's books, in which the old woodcuts were largely reprinted.

Fig. 458. Printer's mark of Wynkyn de Worde, London.

One of the earliest of these new editions was his *Golden Legend* of 1493 (Duff 410, STC. 24875). In addition to a proportion of the cuts from the original edition, it contains a certain number of illustrations from other books of Caxton, e.g. an *Annunciation* on f. 112, verso, from the *Speculum Vite Cristi*, the *Calvary*, on the last page, from the *Fifteen Oes*, and numerous little cuts of initial size which no doubt belonged originally to the lost *Horae* of Caxton.[2] Moreover, he added woodcut initials; in the first place a large initial T (fig. 459), on the reverse of the first and last leaves, based on the G of Veldener's *Fasciculus Temporum*, Utrecht 1481.[3]

For his smaller initials he used here and elsewhere a set which had originally belonged to Gotfridus de Os of Gouda,[4] in addition to Caxton's leaf and flower series described and illustrated above.[5] He issued another edition of the *Golden Legend* in 1498 (Duff 411, STC. 24876), in which the *Tree of Jesse* as well as the *Calvary*, from the *Fifteen Oes* series, appeared on the last leaf.

His edition of Bonaventura's *Speculum Vite Cristi*, 1494 (Duff 50, STC. 3261), of which the only complete copy is at Holkham, is practically the same in its woodcut illustration as the original Caxton.

An interesting woodcut of the *Virgin and Child within a floral border* occurs on the title-page of Walter Hylton, *Scala Perfectionis*, 1494 (Duff 203, STC. 14042; fig. 460). The border is on the same block as the subject, and exemplifies how the lack of naturalistic power, evident in the subject, may be no detriment when applied to the decorative elements of

---

[1] His will, dated 5th June 1534, was proved 19th January 1535.
[2] See p. 714.
[3] See p. 560, and fig. 318.
[4] See p. 586, and fig. 341.
[5] See p. 713, and fig. 453.

Fig. 459. Initial T, from the *Golden Legend*, Westminster 1493.

design, a fact noted above in relation to Machlinia's *Primer*.[1] The block is reprinted in his edition of *Dives and Pauper*, 1496.

Wynkyn de Worde's English edition of Bartholomaeus Anglicus, *De Proprietatibus Rerum* (*All the Proprytees of Thynges*), translated by John de Trevisa, 1495 (Duff 40, STC. 1536), is perhaps Wynkyn's masterpiece in illustration. The designs prefixed to each book are derived partly from Bellaert's Haarlem edition of 1485,[2] especially in the earlier part of the book, and partly from the Lyon edition of 1482, or one of the other Lyon editions closely related to it;[3] but they are in some cases adapted with such freedom as to justify our regarding them as original. Such may be said of the *Landscape* at Book XIV., *De Terra* (fig. 461), with its excellent use of white line in the trees, and of the *Workers in Field and River*, prefixed to Book XVI. (*De Lapidibus et Metallis*), in which Wynkyn's designer adds a third figure to the Lyon original. Wynkyn certainly had a competent designer and cutter, and not a fumbler, in this and a few of his other works. In this book, as in others, during the xv century, he continued to use Caxton's printer's mark. The title is cut on wood in white letters on black ground.

In his *Lyff of the olde Auncyent Holy Faders*, 1495 (Duff 235, STC. 14507), Wynkyn published the first edition of the translation of St. Jerome's *Vitas Patrum*, completed by Caxton on his deathbed. Prefixed to each of the five parts and repeated a sixth time at the end, is a full-page cut of *St. Jerome seated before a company of dignitaries of the Church*. It is sufficiently ambitious, but as poor in drawing and as crudely executed as the smaller column-cuts, of which there are some forty varieties (many being repeated) throughout the book. Whether or not the designer borrowed from any earlier edition, I have been unable to establish any direct link between these subjects and the designs in any of the foreign editions, either among the German issues, from those of Strassburg and Augsburg (1477 and 1478) onwards, or among the French from that of Dupré, Paris 1486. None of the Nether-

[1] See p. 716.   [2] See p. 575.   [3] See pp. 604, 605.

landish editions before Wynkyn's have any series of woodcut designs. The title is cut in white on black as in the *Bartholomaeus*.

Wynkyn's 1496 edition of the *Book of St. Albans* (Duff 57, STC. 3309) is a finer production than the original issue of 1486. The woodcut of *Birds* on f. 1 comes from the *Bartholomaeus* of 1495, but the *Gentleman and a*

Fig. 460. The Virgin and Child, from Hylton, *Scala Perfectionis*, Westminster 1494.

Group of his Retainers on the reverse of the same leaf (fig. 462) is a new cut, and one of the best by the same designer. Better known, but somewhat cruder in character, is the *Angler*, prefixed to the *Treatyse of fysshynge with an Angle*, which was added to this edition. The book ends with a handsome full-page woodcut comprising the Royal Badge of Henry VII.

Of the same stolid character as the *Angler* is the title-woodcut in Henry Parker, *Dives and Pauper*, 1496 (Duff 340, STC. 19213). On the reverse of the title is reprinted the *St. Jerome* from the *Lyff of the olde Auncient Holy Faders* of 1495, and on the last leaf the *Virgin and Child* from Hylton's *Scala Perfectionis* of 1494. Pynson's edition of 1493 of the same work (Duff 339, STC. 19212) is without illustration. In 1498 Wynkyn reprinted Caxton's edition of Chaucer's *Canterbury Tales*, with the original

Fig. 461. Landscape, from Bartholomaeus Anglicus, *All the Proprytees of Thynges*, Westminster 1495.

woodcuts, the only perfect copy known being in the Pierpont Morgan Library, New York (Duff 90, STC. 5085).

In the same year also appeared his edition of Malory's *Morte d'Arthur*, of which only one copy is known, that of the John Rylands Library, Manchester (Duff 284, STC. 802).[1] The oblong cuts, which average about 4 × 4⅞ inches in size, crudely cut in thick line, with regular patches of parallel shading, are remarkable and somewhat bizarre in design. The violent motion seen in the illustration of *How Sir Launcelot in his madnes toke a swerde* (Book XII.) is reminiscent of certain plates in Bellaert's *Historie van Jason* and *Historie van Troyen* (Haarlem 1484 and 1485). The

---

[1] See *Le Morte Darthur . . . the original edition of William Caxton reprinted and edited by* H. Oskar Sommer, 2 vols., London 1889, 1892.

Birth of Sir Tristram de Lyonesse (Book VIII.) is characteristic both in its curious figures and in the originality of its landscape background, with woods and village church (fig. 463).

Some of the blocks of the *Morte d'Arthur* were used by Wynkyn in later books, e.g. in his editions of Raoul Le Fèvre, *The Recuyles of ye*

Fig. 462. A Gentleman and his Retainers, from the *Book of St. Albans*, Westminster 1496.

Hystories of Troye, 1502 (STC. 1502, Pepys Library) and about 1503 (STC. 15377).

Much less interesting are the numerous small cuts, about $2\frac{1}{4} \times 3\frac{1}{4}$ inches in size, in the Book of Sir John Mandeville (*A Lytell Treatyse or booke named Johan Maundeuyll*), 1499 (Duff 286, STC. 17247, Cambridge).

Several of the English editions of French books, to which reference has been made in the French section, were printed by Wynkyn de Worde, i.e. the *Kalender of Shepeherdes*, 1508 (see p. 652), the *Arte or Crafte to lyve well and to dye well*, 1505 and about 1506 (see p. 663), and the *Ordinarye of Crysten Men*, 1502 and 1506 (STC. 5198 and 5199; see p. 673). A few of the cuts in the earlier of the editions of the *Ordinarye* are in the same manner as the *Morte d'Arthur*. Each edition has different cuts, partly based on Vérard's *Art de bien Vivre et de bien Mourir*.

I would note here for convenience three other editions which he printed in the early XVI century, in which text or woodcuts are based on foreign books:

(1) Richard Rolle, *Contemplacyons*, 1506 (STC. 21259); with cut on

the reverse of the title copied from *Visio Lamentabilis*, Louvain
(Ravescot), about 1487 (CA. 1745, CN. xxiii. 1).

(2) Sebastian Brant, *Shyppe of Fooles*, translated by Henry Watson,
1509 (STC. 3547, Paris); cuts based on the Basle designs,
either directly or through one of numerous editions of copies.

Fig. 463. The Birth of Tristram, from Malory, *Morte d'Arthur*, Westminster 1494.

(3) *The Seven Wise Masters of Rome*, about 1520 (STC. 21298); cuts
based on those of the edition of Claes Leeuw, Antwerp 1488.[1]

In the various editions of the *Chronicles of England* issued before 1500
there are few woodcuts. The *St. Albans Chronicle* of about 1485,[2] and the
Cronycles of the Londe of England issued by Gerard Leeuw at Antwerp in
1493,[3] have already been mentioned. Ranulphus Higden's *Policronicon*
printed by Wynkyn de Worde, 1495 (Duff 173, STC. 13439), has no
woodcut subject except a repetition of the *St. Jerome* frontispiece from the
Vitas Patrum of the same year,[4] and Wynkyn's edition of the *Chronicles of
England*, 1497–98 (Duff 102, STC. 9996), reprinted in 1502, has only a
Tower of Babel, a few diagrams like the *St. Albans Chronicle* and a view of
Towns and Country from his *Bartholomaeus* to illustrate the *Descrypcyon of
Englonde*. Nor do his later editions add anything of interest but a heraldic
title-cut with Henry VII.'s badge (in two versions), while a *Town on an
Estuary*, from *Bartholomaeus*, replaces the earlier view. A piece of original

[1] See p. 579.   [2] See p. 724.   [3] See p. 580, and p. 722.   [4] See p. 726.

historical illustration, the title-woodcut to Bishop's Fisher's *Funeral Sermon on Henry VII.*, printed by Wynkyn de Worde, 1509, deserves mention (STC. 10900-01, reproduced in A. W. Pollard, *Fine Books*, p. 254). The decoration and illustration of the *Chronicles* issued by Julian Notary in

Fig. 464. The Knight, from the *Canterbury Tales*, London (Pynson), about 1491.

1504 offer material of more variety, and this and Pynson's edition of 1510 will be noticed below.

We have already referred to Pynson's use of the borders from Machlinia's *Primer*, of about 1485,[1] and it is generally believed that he succeeded to Machlinia's stock about 1491. RICHARD PYNSON, who appears to have been a Norman and to have studied at the University of Paris, commissioned the Rouen printer Guillaume Le Tailleur to print him two Law books for sale in England[2] about 1490, before he began printing on his own account. In 1508 he became King's Printer,[3] succeeding William Faques, the first holder of that office. That the foreign craftsman was not entirely popular in these times is shown by the case for assault which he brought to the Star Chamber in 1500 against a certain Henry Squire and his companions, and by his statement that his workmen were so terrorised that they

---

[1] See p. 715.

[2] Sir Thomas Littleton's *Tenores Novelli* (Duff 275, STC. 15721) and Nicolas Statham, *Abridgment of Cases* (Duff 374, STC. 23238).

[3] About the same time Wynkyn de Worde seems to have received some official *consolatium*, for he styled himself 'Printer to the King's Mother', and after the death of Henry VII., 'Printer to the King's Grandmother'.

Fig. 465. Initial W, from the *Speculum Vite Cristi*, London (Pynson), about 1494.

deserted him. Thereafter he removed to within Temple Bar, having perhaps better protection within the bounds of the City of London.

His earliest dated books belong to 1492, but his edition of Chaucer's *Canterbury Tales*, his first illustrated book, almost certainly appeared about 1491 (Duff 89, STC. 5084). Except for the woodcut of the narrator, placed at the head of each tale, the blocks with their figures on horseback are based on Caxton's designs, and even more crudely designed and cut, with broad black borders occasionally patterned with white line. The only subject which has an added decorative quality is the *Knight* (fig. 464), with the calligraphic rendering of the horse's trappings reminiscent of the frontispieces in *Fierabras* (Geneva 1483) and *Livre de Baudoin, Comte de Flandre* (Chambéry 1485).[1]

Not without reason was he dissatisfied with his local craftsmen, and for his next illustrated book, the *Fall of Princes* (John Lydgate's version of Boccaccio), 1494 (Duff 46, STC. 3175), he borrowed the blocks used in Dupré's Paris edition of 1483/84.[2]

To about the same date belongs his edition of Bonaventura, *Speculum Vite Cristi* (Duff 51, STC. 3262), with numerous small upright cuts about $3\frac{1}{4} \times 2\frac{1}{4}$ inches (or slightly larger when with double border-line), probably based on Caxton's series, and distinctly inferior and more variable in quality. Some of the cuts are of the crude and careless workmanship of Wynkyn's *Vitas Patrum*; others more carefully cut, but hard and angular in character. A *Crucifixion* which occurs at sig. n. iiii, verso ($3\frac{3}{4} \times 2\frac{3}{8}$ inches), stands apart from the rest, and is nearer in style to the designer of the Delft *Ludolphus* of 1488.[3] It is reprinted in the *Libellus qui informatio puerorum appellatur*, issued about 1500 (Duff 224, STC. 14079). The initials used in the *Speculum*, leaf, flower and grotesque faces designed in white on black, are attractive (see fig. 465). The *Informatio* also contains a woodcut of *Master and Pupils* ($5 \times 3\frac{5}{8}$ inches).

Pynson's mark (Juchhoff 66; fig. 466), as it occurs in the *Informatio*, shows a deep bend in its lower border-line, which proves its block to be of metal. In later books the indentation developed into a break.

His edition of Sir Thomas Littleton, *Tenores Novelli*, printed about 1496 (Duff 276, STC. 15722), of which the only perfect copy known is in the

---

[1] See pp. 617, 618, 619.   [2] See p. 629.

[3] See p. 571.

Pierpont Morgan Library, New York, contains a frontispiece of *King and Councillors*, of crude cutting but interesting design.[1]

Pynson's and Wynkyn's editions of Pierre Gringore's *Castell of Laboure* (translated by Alexander Barclay) have already been mentioned in the chapter on illustration in France,[2] and Pynson's copies are hardly less expressive than the original series. Here I would merely remark on an attractive little *View of a Town* which occurs at the end of Pynson's edition of about 1505 (STC. 12380, B.M., Huth 29; fig. 467), and is repeated to represent *Rome* in Pynson's *Chronicles of England*, 1510.

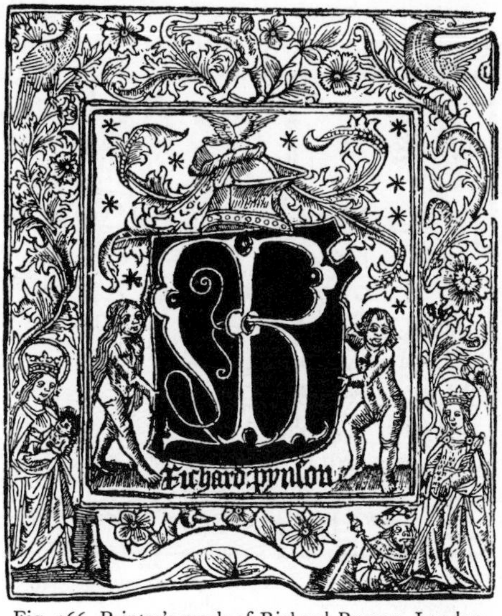

Apart from the usual diagrams, the *Tower of Babel* and the *Town on an Estuary*, from Wynkyn's *Bartholomaeus* (for the *Descrypcyon of Englonde*), Pynson's *Chronicles* of 1510 present no illustration of interest.

Fig. 466. Printer's mark of Richard Pynson, London.

Pynson's finest decorative work is certainly seen in the *Morton Missal* of 1500, which has already been described.[3]

Pynson also published an English edition of Sebastian Brant's *Shyp of Folys*, translated by Alexander Barclay, 1509 (STC. 3545), with copies of the original Basle woodcuts, flanked by border-pieces with dotted ground in four varieties.[4]

WILLIAM FAQUES, whom I have already mentioned as the first holder of the office of King's Printer, and who appears, like Pynson, to have been a native of Normandy, produced one attractive little book with borders and a few woodcuts, i.e. the *Latin Psalter* of 1504 (STC. 16257). The text is surrounded throughout by four-piece borders of chain design, the most interesting of the other cuts being that of *David with his Harp*, and a good

---

[1] Reproduced, L. Olschki, *Le Livre illustré au XV⁺ siècle*, 1926, fig. 131.
[2] See p. 676.   [3] See p. 722.
[4] Pynson also used two other dotted border-pieces in his *Sarum Missal* of 1512.

woodcut initial B with flower design at Psalm i. None of Faques's books is dated except in 1504, but he probably worked until about 1508 when Pynson succeeded to his office.

JULIAN NOTARY (*Julianus Notarii*—Julian the son of a notary—as he first signs himself) was probably an Englishman, though the form *Notaire* used in his *Sarum Missal* of 1498 has been adduced as evidence of French origin.

In company with JEAN BARBIER and I. H. (Jean Huvin?) he printed a *Sarum Horae* for Wynkyn de Worde in 1497, but only four leaves without woodcuts remain (Duff 190, STC. 15884, Oxford). In the following year, also for Wynkyn, and again in partnership with Jean Barbier, he printed the *Sarum Missal*, to which we have already referred.[1]

Apart from this *Missal* he printed no work in the xv century remarkable for woodcut, and thereafter the only two works which concern us are his *Golden Legend* of 16th February

Fig. 467. View of a Town, from Gringore, *Castell of Laboure*, London, about 1505.

1503/04 (STC. 24877) and his *Chronicles of England* of 1504 (STC. 9998). They are chiefly noteworthy for the use of a series of borders with dotted background.

In the *Golden Legend* eighteen of these borders are used to frame the colophon and printer's mark, including a small metal cut of the *Nativity* (fig. 468). The *Nativity* also appears at f. 158. These borders are exactly in the same style as some used by Hopyl at Paris, e.g. in the *Somerstuk* of his *Passionael* (*Golden Legend* in Dutch), Paris 1505, 1507, and, like those of the *Sarum Horae*, attributed to J. Philippe and others (Duff 187, STC. 15881); but I have been unable to identify the actual border-pieces in any French book. Moreover, the large cut of the *Assembly of Saints* (or *Joyes de Paradis*), which occurs on the first page of Notary's *Golden Legend*, was also used by Hopyl in his Paris *Passionael*. This block, which was based on the cut in Vérard's *Art de bien Vivre et de bien Mourir*, has been already noted in the French chapter for its use in various other books.[2]

[1] See pp. 721, 722. [2] See p. 673.

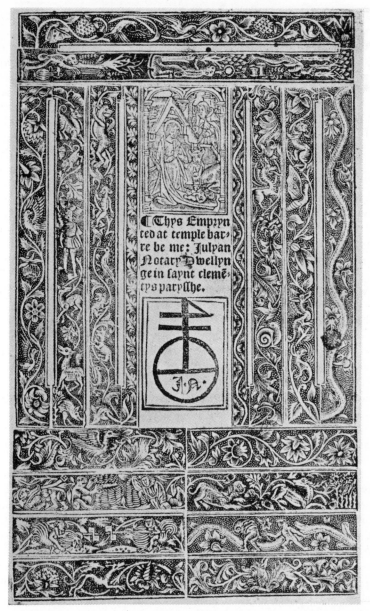

Fig. 468. Border-pieces, and Printer's mark of Julian Notary, from his *Golden Legend*, London 1503/04.

Fig. 469. Initial W, from the *Golden Legend*, London 1503/04.

Apart from the borders the *Golden Legend* contains a series of five dotted prints, somewhat roughly executed (measuring about $2\frac{5}{8} \times 1\frac{7}{8}$ inches), *Adam and Eve*, the *Nativity*, the *Ascension*, *Pentecost* and *Christ before Pilate* (f. 1, verso of table, and ff. 4, 17, 19, verso, and 40). Their designs come from a foreign source, and are seen in prints by the Master of the Berlin Passion and his school, and in various series of dotted prints, e.g. those described by Leidinger, and now in the British Museum.[1]

Then there are a few smaller metal-cuts of initial letter size, e.g. the already-mentioned *Annunciation* (f. 71, verso), the *Nativity*, and certain single figures of Saints (e.g. f. 228, verso).

In black line, apart from the large *Assembly of Saints*, there are various column-cuts, based in part on Caxton's *Golden Legend*, and numerous smaller cuts of initial letter size, including several of the series from Caxton's *Horae* (e.g. the *Adoration of the Magi*, f. 6, verso).

There are two interesting sets of initial letters: (1) A, M and P, from a series with *Dragons*, which appear to have been brought from Paris;[2] (2) L, P, Y, W, in decorative Roman letter on black ground, in some cases flicked with white, like the series of five dotted prints (see fig. 469).

The first page of Notary's *Chronicles of England*, 1504, contains a medley of black-line woodcuts (including *St. George* and *King David*) surrounded by fifteen dotted border-pieces, of which thirteen correspond to those in the *Golden Legend*. Various pieces from the *Golden Legend* set also occur at Part IV. (*Anno Christi*), one of the narrow strips being here cut in two, at the head of the *Descripcion of Englonde* and round the printer's mark on the last page. The combination of cuts and border-pieces at the head of the *Descripcion of Englonde* again includes one of the divided pieces, adds a third new piece and includes four black-line cuts, two being figures from Vérard's *Terence*.

From the *Golden Legend* is also taken the *Adam and Eve* from the series of five dotted prints, and various black-line cuts. New black-line cuts include a *View of a Town* (with little black figures of men), used for London and Rome, and various historical subjects in the style of Vérard's chief designer and probably brought from Paris. Many of the initials of the *Golden Legend* also recur.

---

[1] See p. 190.

[2] They correspond to those belonging to André Bocard (Cl. ii. 146), which Claudin mentions as used also by Michel Toulouse and F. Baligault.

Notary's later edition of the *Chronicles*, 1515 (STC. 10000), has an even more jumbled medley of cuts and border-pieces on its first page, including one of Vérard's *Terence* figures, the *St. George and Dragon* from Wynkyn's *Horae* of 1494 (possibly a cut of Caxton's) and pieces of chain borders. The volume contains miscellaneous material from the earlier edition, but none of the dotted border-pieces, and of the five dotted prints only the *Nativity*, in very bad condition.

CONTEMPORARY SINGLE CUTS

The possibility that the *Grotesque Alphabet* of 1464 was produced in England, on account of English MS. inscriptions, has already been discussed and refuted.[1] And some further reference has also been made to the question as to whether any of the few English single cuts still preserved can belong to a date anterior to Caxton's earliest book-illustrations.[2] This question was also answered in the negative.

The subject has been recently treated in detail by Mr. Campbell Dodgson, partly on the basis of Henry Bradshaw's bibliographical studies.[3]

Most of these early English woodcuts are so-called *Images of Pity* (or *Piety*), figures representing the *Man of Sorrows*, generally shown half-length in the Tomb, with or without the signs of the Passion. They bear inscriptions referring to Indulgences, a purpose for which the *Mass of St. Gregory* was in use abroad. The subject may in fact be considered as a part of the *Mass of St. Gregory*, for in the woodcut of this subject in Wynkyn's *Horae* of about 1494 (Lambeth copy, at sig. r 4) the vision is actually the *Christ half-length in the Tomb*.

The subject also occasionally occurred in English *Horae*, e.g. in the fragment of the third edition of Caxton's *Primer*, preserved in the British Museum,[4] and in another version in Wynkyn's *Horae* of about 1494 (Lambeth copy, at sig. g 6).

The Bodleian Library is richest in these *Images of Pity* which have been preserved in books or manuscripts, one of the earliest being inserted in MS. Bodl. 939 (reproduced with three others in the Walpole Society,

---

[1] See p. 151.   [2] See p. 159.

[3] Henry Bradshaw, *On the earliest English engravings of the Indulgence known as the 'Image of Piety'*, Collected Papers, Cambridge 1889, p. 84; Campbell Dodgson, *Woodcuts of the Fifteenth Century in the Ashmolean Museum, Oxford, with notes on similar prints in the Bodleian Library*, Oxford 1929; Campbell Dodgson, *English Devotional Woodcuts of the late fifteenth century, with special reference to those in the Bodleian Library*, Walpole Society, xvii., 1928–29, 95.

[4] See p. 714.

xvii. pl. xxxv.). Other early examples are in the British Museum (CD. 3, Schreiber 869), and in the Metropolitan Museum, New York (CD. 11 and 12, from the McGuire Collection, reproduced *Einbl*. lxv. pl. 14 and 17).

One indication of the origin of these devotional cuts is offered by the inscription *Arma Beate Birgitte De Syon* at the foot of a large *Last Judgment* (CD. 6, Schreiber 608, Walpole Society, xvii. pl. xxxvi. *a*), which with two *Images of Pity* (S. 858 and 976) occurs in the Bodleian MS. Rawl. D. 403. This must refer to the only house of the Brigittine Order in England, the Convent of Syon, near Isleworth; and the *Last Judgment*, and probably others of these devotional cuts, must have been produced for the Convent, if not within its doors.[1] The type used in the *Last Judgment* has not been definitely assigned to any printer, but has letters which are found in both Wynkyn de Worde and Pynson.[2] The cut has something of the character of the blocks in Wynkyn's Bartholomaeus, *De Proprietatibus Rerum*, 1495.[3] The design is probably original in its foreground details, but the general scheme corresponds with the subject as represented, e.g., in the Lyon *Légende Dorée*, printed by Huss and Petrus of Hungary, 1483, and in Vérard's *Art de bien Vivre et de bien Mourir*, Paris 1492.

A further clue to origin appears in the inscription *Ex domꝛ Jhesu de Betheleem* on two cuts representing the *Arms of Jesus Christ*, or the Emblems of the Passion in heraldic form (CD. 18, 19),[4] now in the Bodleian Library, Arch. G. f. 13, 14, and detached from a *Sarum Horae* printed by Pigouchet, Paris 1495 (Duff 186). It refers to the Carthusian Priory of Sheen (Richmond), and the cuts are more likely to have been made for presentation or sale to visitors as souvenirs than as book-plates.

The same subject of the *Arms of Christ* is also found used as an Indulgence (CD. 20, York Minster), and there is another example of an Indulgence with the *Virgin and Child in Glory with the Signs of the Passion* (CD. 10, S. 1053, Oxford, MS. Bodl. 113; reprod. Walpole Society, xvii. p. 103).

Finally I would mention two large single woodcuts of very different

---

[1] For a line-engraving of about the same period produced for the Convent of Syon see A. M. Hind, *History of Engraving and Etching*, 1923, p. 124, footnote 1.

[2] Lt.-Colonel F. S. Isaac has recently found similar capitals in the *Myroure of our Lady* printed by R. Faques for the Abbess of Syon in 1530 (B.M., C. 11. b. 8). R. Faques succeeded about 1508–09 to the stock of William Faques. No books of William Faques are known before 1504, but as he then styled himself 'King's printer', he must have been in practice some years. The two links, i.e. the relation to the convent of Syon and the identity of capital letters, renders it more likely that the *Last Judgment* cut was printed by him rather than by Wynkyn or Pynson.

[3] See p. 726.

[4] Reproduced, Walpole Society, xvii. pl. xxxvi. b and c.

character. In the first place a sheet, measuring about 3 × 14 inches, with a *Heraldic Lion*, the arms of William Gray (Bishop of Ely from 1454 to 1478), which is pasted on a column near his tomb in Ely Cathedral (CD. 5, S. 2030). Then the *King Henry VI. invoked as a Saint* (fig. 470), inserted in a MS. English Bible on vellum, of the latter part of the xv century, in the Bodleian

Fig. 470. King Henry VI. invoked as a Saint. Fragment. Bodleian Library, Oxford.

Library (CD. 21, MS. Bodl. 277, reprod. Walpole Society, xvii. pl. xxxvii.). It is in fragmentary state, but the main part of the subject, with figures kneeling before the standing king, remains intact. Unfortunately the King's face is removed, and only a few letters of the inscription above and below remain. But from the arms and the *cu* of the lettering above, *Henricus* is evidently intended, and every detail points to the identity of the subject. It forms a most interesting historical record of the veneration paid to Henry VI. under the Tudors, of a short-lived popularity of pilgrimage to his shrine at Windsor, and of the efforts made by Henry VII. about 1490 towards his kinsman's canonisation. In style I can refer to nothing comparable in English book-illustration except the *Arundel badge* on the first page of Caxton's *Golden Legend*. It is most nearly related to the phase of North French woodcut which shows some kinship to the Flemish scheme of cutting with regular series of short lines of parallel shading, of which examples may be noted in books printed by Dupré.

Bibliography

Ames, Joseph. Typographical Antiquities, being an historical account of printing in England. London 1749 (2nd ed., W. Herbert, 1785–90; 3rd ed., T. F. Dibdin, 1810–19).

Bradshaw, Henry. On the Earliest English Engravings of the Indulgence known as the 'Image of Piety', Cambridge Antiquarian Society's *Communications*, iii. (1867), 25th February. Reprinted with revisions in H. Bradshaw, Collected Papers, Cambridge 1889, p. 84. (This deals with book-illustration as well as with single cuts.)

Duff, Edward Gordon. Chapter on England, in A. W. Pollard, Early Illustrated Books. London 1893; 2nd ed., 1917, p. 219.

Duff, Edward Gordon, and others. Hand-lists of English Printers, 1501–1556. 4 vols. London (Bibliographical Society) 1895–1913.

Duff, Edward Gordon. A Century of the English Book Trade. Short notices of all printers, stationers, etc., 1457–1557. London 1905.

Duff, Edward Gordon. The Printers, Stationers and Bookbinders of Westminster and London from 1476 to 1535. Cambridge 1906.

Duff, Edward Gordon. The English Provincial Printers, Stationers and Bookbinders to 1557. Cambridge 1912.

Duff, Edward Gordon. Fifteenth-Century English Books. Bibliographical Society, Illustrated Monographs, xviii. London 1917.

McKerrow, R. B. Printers' and Publishers' Devices in England, 1485–1640. Bibliographical Society, Illustrated Monographs, xvi. London 1913.

McKerrow, R. B. Border-pieces used by English Printers. Paper read before the Bibliographical Society. London 1924.

Plomer, H. R. Short History of English Printing, 1476–1900. London 1915.

Plomer, H. R. English Printers' Ornaments. London 1924.

Plomer, H. R. Wynkyn de Worde and his Contemporaries, from the death of Caxton till 1535. London 1925.

Short-Title Catalogue of books printed in England, Scotland and Ireland and of English books printed abroad, 1475–1640. Compiled by A. W. Pollard, G. R. Redgrave and others. London (Bibliographical Society) 1926.

Juchhoff, Rudolf. Drucker- und Verlegerzeichen des xv Jahrhunderts in den Niederländen, England, Spanien, Böhmen, Mähren und Polen. Munich 1927.

McKerrow, R. B., and Ferguson, F. S. Title-page borders used in England and Scotland 1485–1640. Bibliographical Society, Illustrated Monographs, xxi. London 1932 (for 1931).

Hind, A. M. Studies in English Engraving. 1. Woodcut Illustration in the xv Century. The *Connoisseur*, February 1933.

Hodnett, Edward. English Woodcuts 1480–1535. Bibliographical Society, Illustrated Monographs, xxii. London 1935.

CHAPTER X

BOOK-ILLUSTRATION AND CONTEMPORARY SINGLE CUTS
IN SPAIN AND PORTUGAL

The amount of original work in book-illustration produced in Spain
and Portugal during the xv century is incomparably less than the corresponding production in Italy, Germany, France and the Netherlands.
Many of the early printers in Spain came from abroad, and in many
popular books they would almost be expected to use the earlier and well-
known designs.

Thus the cuts in the first illustrated book issued in Spain,[1] Werner
Rolewinck, *Fasciculus Temporum*, printed at Seville in 1480 by ALFONSO
DEL PUERTO and BARTOLOMÉ SEGURA, was probably based on the Venice
edition, printed by Georgius Walch in 1479.[2] But these woodcuts are of
small artistic interest, repeating the typical subjects such as *Noah's Ark*, the
Tower of Babel, various towns, and the figure of *Christ blessing*, which
appeared in this book from its earliest German editions (about 1473)
onwards.

Then PABLO and JUAN HURUS, immigrants from Constance who became the chief printers at Saragossa, issued copies of the Ulm originals
in their *Aesop* of 1489 (K. 21, Haebler 6, Escorial) and Boccaccio, *Mujeres
Illustres*, of 1494 (K. 69, Haebler 52, Berlin, Pierpont Morgan, etc.),
while in their Rodericus Zamorensis, *Spejo de la Vida humana* (*Speculum
Vitae Humanae*) of 1491 (K. 320, Haebler 579, Cambridge, Madrid,
etc.) they used blocks from Philippi and Reinhard's Lyon edition of
1482 which were in part Zainer's original Augsburg blocks and in
part copies from the same.[3] Other copies of foreign works issued by the
same firm were Franciscus de Retza, *Defensorium inviolatae virginitatis
Mariae*, about 1488 (K. 165, Haebler 190 [10]), based on a German
block-book of 1470,[4] various small editions of the *Ars Moriendi*, with
copies after the block-book, between about 1483 and 1493 (about 1483,
K. 53, Haebler 36 bis, Escorial; about 1489, K. 54, Haebler 37, Oxford;
about 1493, K. 55, Haebler 37 [5], Barcelona), Ketham, *Compendio de la*

---

[1] But cf. 748.   [2] See pp. 456 and 357.   [3] See p. 602.

[4] See W. L. Schreiber, *Defensorium ... aus der Druckerei des Hurus in Saragossa*, in Facsimile-
Reproduktion. Weimar (Gesellschaft der Bibliophilen) 1910.

Salud humana (*Fasciculus Medicinae*), 1494 (K. 220, Haebler 160, Madrid), with copies after the Venetian originals, and Andres de Lí, *Tesoro de la Pasión*, 1494 (K. 40, Haebler 200, Berlin Print Room, Escorial), containing copies after the Netherlandish Delbecq-Schreiber Passion.[1]

An edition of Breydenbach, *Viaje a Tierra Santa*, Pablo Hurus, 1498 (K. 77, Haebler 75), was printed from the original Mainz blocks of 1486,[2] made up with material from other books by Hurus (e.g. from the *Tesoro de la Pasión*), and from the stock of Matthias Huss of Lyon. Other printers to use copies of well-known foreign illustrations were FRIEDRICH BIEL of Basle, in his *Aesop*, printed at Burgos, 1496 (K. 22, Haebler 7, Paris), and JUAN DE BURGOS in his Spanish edition of Ketham's *Fasciculus Medicinae* (*Epilogo en medicina y cirurgia*), printed at Burgos, 1495 (K. 221, Haebler 246, Madrid, Paris, New York Hisp. Soc.). A third series of copies of Ketham was printed at Pamplona, by Arnao Guillen de Brocar, 1495 (K. 222, Haebler 27, Paris, Madrid).

In his edition of Jodocus Badius, *Stultifera Navis*, printed by Friedrich Biel at Burgos soon after 1500 (Haebler 39), the cuts are based on the Paris edition of Kerver for de Marnef of February 1500/1501.[3]

And not infrequently woodcut illustrations are found based on line-engravings by the German Master E.S.[4] and Martin Schongauer, who must have been well known to craftsmen in Spain and in Italy in the late xv century.

Spanish and Portuguese books are particularly notable for their decorative character, in type, borders, initials and illustrative material. The quality of Spanish type-founders is evidenced in the well-known excellence of their Greek type in the early xvi century, which has never been surpassed and remains the pattern of the most modern founts.[5]

Even on the side of decoration a good deal of the earliest work is based on foreign models, and it is only from about 1490 that a genuine Spanish style may be said to emerge.

Of the borders inspired by foreign work there are in the first place a few jn black-line scroll-work nearly related to the Southern German styles of Augsburg and Strassburg, e.g. those in Turrecremata, *Expositio*

---

[1] See p. 582.   [2] See pp. 352-356.   [3] See p. 674.

[4] E.g. the *Canon* cut in the Lisbon Ludolphus, *Vita Christi*, 1495, after E.S., Lehrs 31.

[5] The fount of Arnao Guillen de Brocar, first used in the great Polyglot Bible of Cardinal Francisco Ximenes, at Alcalá, 1514 (reproduced in the more developed form used in the undated *Musaeus*, in Victor Scholderer, *Greek Printing Types, 1465–1927, Facsimiles from an Exhibition*, British Museum, 1927, fig. 24).

Fig. 471. Initial D, from Diaz de Montalvo, *Compilación de Leyes*, Huete 1484.

in Psalmos, printed by Hurus at Saragossa, 12th November 1482 (Haebler 651, K. 224 b, Madrid, etc.),[1] in a *Horae* (*Officium B.M.V.*) issued by the same printer about 1490 (K. 286, Haebler 490 (5), Hispanic Society, New York), in Felip de Malla, *Pecador remut*, printed by ROSENBACH at Barcelona, about 1495 (K. 242, H. 390), and in Ludolphus de Saxonia, *Vita Christi*, printed by VALENTIN FERNANDEZ, Lisbon 1495 (K. 237, Haebler 373, Don Manuel 5). Other black-line borders which may be mentioned occur in Domenico Cavalca, *Espejo de la Cruz*, printed by ANTONIO MARTINEZ at Seville, 1486 (K. 88, Haebler 144, Madrid), in Bonaventura, *Meditationes Vitae Christi*, printed by PERE MIQUEL, Barcelona 1493 (K. 75, Haebler 67), and in Donatus, *De Octo Partibus Orationis*, printed by Friedrich Biel, Burgos 1498 (K. 126; Haebler 236 [5], present locality unknown, once Rosenthal; reprod. Lyell, fig. 60). The last is a very attractive example, representing *Children hunting and climbing a tree*, evidently inspired by subjects in

Fig. 472. Lower Border-piece, from Diaz de Montalvo, *Compilación de Leyes*, Huete 1484.

Paris *Horae*. Then a chain-work border on black ground, copied from one of Ratdolt's Venetian borders (used in his Johann Müller, *Calendarium*, 1482),[2] was used at Barcelona, e.g. by PEDRO POSA in his *Imitacio Christi*, 1482 (K. 176, Haebler 293, Paris), and Phocas, *De Partibus Orationis*, 1488 (K. 303, Haebler 549, Madrid), and by Pere Miquel in St. Jerome, *Vida e transit*, 1493 (K. 199, Haebler 682, Barcelona, Stuttgart).

Very remarkable in design is the two-sided metal-cut border-piece, partly executed in punch-work (see fig. 472), which occurs at the

---

[1] Cf. E. P. Goldschmidt, Catalogue viii. No. 96, London.

[2] See p. 460.

beginning of each of the six blocks in Alfonso Diaz de Montalvo, *Compilación de leyes y ordenanzas reales*, printed by ALVARO DE CASTRO at Huete, 1484 and 1485 (K. 109, 110, Haebler 214, 216). The six pictorial initials which occur in the same place are equally interesting. From their subjects the initials appear to have been made for the book,

Fig. 473. Page and Border, from Moses ben Nachman, *Perusch ha-Tora*, Lisbon 1489.

but it is curious that the initial reproduced in fig. 471, which from its form can be hardly other than D, is used for B(uena).

Most delicate of all the Iberian borders on black ground is that reproduced in fig. 473. It was first used by ALFONSO FERNÁNDEZ de Córdoba in his *Manuale Caesaraugustanum*, printed at Hijar, about 1487 (K. 244, Haebler 394 (5), Berlin), and later in the Hebrew books printed by the

Fig. 474. Page with border, from *Tirant lo Blanch*, Valencia 1490.

Fig. 475. Initial A, from Juan de Mena, *La Coronación*, Seville 1499.

RABBI ELIEZER at Lisbon, i.e. Moses ben Nachman, *Perusch ha-Tora* (*Nuevas de la ley o comentario sobre el pentateuco*), July 1489 (K. 278, Don Manuel 3), and David Abu-Derahim, *Comentario sobre el orden de las oraciones*, November 1489 (K. 102, Don Manuel 4). In its combination of delicate tendril and scroll, with animals and conventional grotesque, it shows definite Islamic influence, and is characteristic of Hispano-Mauresque design. It is comparable with Rat-dolt's work (especially with his border to Cepio, *Gesta Mocenici*, 1477), but the style is carried to an extraordinary finesse in technique.

Bolder and even more characteristic Spanish work is the four-piece border first used by NICOLAUS SPINDELER at Valencia in his *Tirant lo Blanch* (by Juan Martorell?), 1490 (K. 252, Haebler 639; fig. 474). The page also includes a narrow fifth panel to divide the columns of text, and two initial letters. The book is only known in three copies, those of the British Museum (the finest of the three), Valencia and the Hispanic Society, New York. The border-pieces were used later (without the fifth panel) by J. Rosenbach, e.g. in his *Constitucións de Cataluña*, 1494 (K. 148 and 149, Haebler 167 and 168), and by Pere Miquel and Diego de Gumiel in their *Usatges de Barcelona e Constitucións de Cataluña*, 1495 (K. 98, Haebler 652). In Spindeler's border the character of the animals is Gothic rather than Islamic. Both of the borders reproduced (figs. 473 and 474) are undoubtedly cut on metal.

Another border of indigenous character, of bold and handsome design, with scroll-work and heraldic animals, and again certainly cut in metal, appeared in Jacob ben Ascher, *Tur Orach Chajim*, printed by ABRAHAM BEN SAMUEL D'ORTAS, at Leiria (Portugal), 1495 (K. 211, Haebler 331, Frankfurt, Valladolid). The animals show more relation to Islamic style than those of *Tirant lo Blanch*.

Initial letters on black ground are used by most of the good Spanish printers, some of the best series belonging to UNGUT and STANISLAUS POLONUS at Seville (fig. 475), SPINDELER at Valencia, ROSENBACH at Barcelona, ARNAO GUILLEN DE BROCAR at Pamplona, and FRIEDRICH BIEL at Burgos.

The Spanish craftsman of the XV century was usually happy in the execution of heraldic designs, and the *Arms of Ferdinand and Isabella*, which so constantly occur, offered a most decorative pattern (fig. 476). The title-designs to the *Flors de Vertuts*, printed by DIEGO DE GUMIEL, Barcelona 1495 (K. 180, Haebler 275), and to Bernardus de Gordonio, *Lilio de Medicina*, printed by UNGUT and STANISLAUS POLONUS, Seville 1495 (K. 64, Haebler 300), are characteristic examples. And the most attractive of the printer's marks is certainly that of Ungut and Stanislaus Polonus (fig. 477).

Fig. 476. The Arms of Ferdinand and Isabella, from Garcia, *Peregrina*, Seville 1498.

I have already referred to the use of metal in certain of the borders and initials, and in white-line work it was fairly common in Spanish book-illustration. Crude metal-cuts occur in the first Spanish illustrated book, the *Fasciculus Temporum* of 1480, already mentioned (see p. 741), i.e. in the *Signs of the Evangelists* used as corner-pieces of the subject of *Christ blessing*. Apart from borders and initials perhaps the most interesting series in this manner occurs in Enrique de Villena, *Trabajos de Hércules*, printed by JUAN DE BURGOS, Burgos 1499 (K. 368, Haebler 689). If, as seems probable, these cuts are in metal, it cannot be said that the method is very aptly used, for though here and there the white-line serves some purpose, in general the style is black-line, with a dull regularity of shading, and the series of short lines laid in parallel series for the ground, as in Netherlandish woodcuts.

Isolated examples on metal will be mentioned in dealing with the work of various printers.

I would now offer a short survey of the chief woodcut illustrations in Spain and Portugal, apart from those already mentioned, to some extent in order of the various printers.

Fig. 477. Mark of the Printers Ungut and Stanislaus Polonus, Seville.

SEVILLE—VALLADOLID—ZAMORA

I have spoken of the *Fasciculus Temporum* printed by PUERTO and SEGURA at Seville in 1480 as the first Spanish illustrated book.

If any woodcut illustration precedes this it is only in the unimportant representations of seals (with little figures of the Man of Sorrows, Saints, etc.) on papal bulls. The earliest of these with certain date is the *Bulla de indulgencias en favor de la iglesia de S. Salvador de Avila*, printed at Valladolid, 1481 (K. 28, Haebler 111 [2], Lyell Collection), but a date as early as about 1477 has been conjectured for another bull in Mr. Lyell's Collection, *Bulla de indulgencias en favor de la christianisación de Guinea*, printed by Puerto and Segura at Seville (K. 13, Haebler 111, 6), though both Haebler and Kurz only venture to date it 'about 1480'.[1]

There are few subject illustrations during the eighties of the xv century, except those based on foreign models. The earliest which may be considered characteristically Spanish are those in Enrique de Villena, *Doze Trabajos de Hércules*, printed by ANTONIO DE CENTENERA at Zamora, 15th January 1483 (K. 367, Haebler 688; see fig. 478). In their free outline and open shading they are comparable with certain of the earliest Lyon woodcut illustrations, but might derive their style equally from a source such as that of the Ulm Boccaccio. Apart from these technical relationships, they show a combination of decorative and bizarre qualities which characterise much Spanish work.

I have already spoken of the decorative work of the printers UNGUT and STANISLAUS POLONUS at Seville, and I would mention one or two of their illustrations. The most excellent is that of a *King enthroned* (fig. 479), the title-cut to Egidio Colonna, *Regimiento de los Principes*, 1494 (K. 94, Haebler 156). The style is to some extent Netherlandish, but the shading

---

[1] See Lyell, pp. 5-7, and figs. 3 and 4.

is somewhat freer and more functional than usual, and the cutting shows individual quality.

Among other books printed by Ungut and Stanislaus Polonus, Gaspar Gorricio de Novaria, *Contemplaciones sobre el Rosario*, 1495 (K. 179, Haebler 301), has two full-page illustrations and various smaller subjects, rendered

Fig. 478. Hercules and Cerberus, from Villena, *Doze Trabajos de Hércules*, Zamora 1483.

more decorative by the variety of their border designs. They are cut more lightly and with a freer hand than most Spanish blocks.

Far poorer in artistic quality than the *King enthroned*, but more typical of the run of Spanish illustration, stiff in its line and regular in shading, is the woodcut of a *Man preaching to Turks* in Ricoldus de Montecrucis, *Improbatio Alcorani*, 1500 (K. 319, Haebler 577). By the same hand is the subject of *Master and Pupils* which occurs in an edition of Juan Infante, *Forma libellandi*, probably printed by Stanislaus Polonus about 1498–1500, which I do not find recorded in Haebler or Kurz (B.M., IA. 52875 [1], fig. 480).

Among other illustrated books printed at Seville, the *Historia di Vespasiano*, printed by PEDRO BRUN, 1499 (K. 360, Haebler 674), has an interesting series of cuts, which shows both French and Netherlandish influence.

VALENCIA

The most important work done at Valencia, the border to *Tirant lo Blanch*, printed by NICOLAUS SPINDELER in 1490, has already been described. Of an

Fig. 479. King enthroned, from Colonna, *Regimiento de los Principes*, Seville 1494.

earlier Valencia printer, in fact one of the first printers in Spain,[1] LAMBERT

[1] He has until recently been regarded as the printer of the earliest book in Spain (1474), but there is now some question of his having worked at first under the direction of Jacob or Philipp Vizlant (see Haebler, *Geschichte der Spanischen Frühdruckes*, p. 21).

PALMART, I would only mention a rough metal-cut in the *criblée* manner, the *Virgin and Child in Glory, with Four Dominican Saints*, which occurs in Jerònim Fuster, *Omelia sobre lo psalm De Profundis*, 1490 (K. 166, Haebler 285). Metal-cuts may also be noted in S. Bernardus, *Epistola de Regimine Domus*, printed by Spindeler about 1498 (K. 61, Haebler 47, Cagliari),

Fig. 480. Master and Pupils, from Juan Infante, *Forma Libellandi*, Seville, about 1498–1500.

and in the *Obra allaors de Sant Cristofol*, printed by PEDRO TRINCHER, 1498 (K. 283, Haebler 487). The latter book also contains a *St. Christopher*, a black-line cut within a border on black ground, which is thoroughly Venetian in inspiration.

Entirely Spanish in its style, stiff in handling but decorative in character, is the frontispiece of *Figures before a Town Gate* in Francisco Ximenez, *Regiment de la Cosa Publica*, printed by CRISTOBAL COFMAN at Valencia, 28th January 1499 (K. 134, Haebler 708).

BARCELONA

AND MISCELLANEOUS WOODCUTS BY, OR RELATED TO, THE MASTER ID

At Barcelona, PEDRO POSA, JOHANN ROSENBACH, PERE MIQUEL and DIEGO DE GUMIEL are all responsible for interesting work, and several decorative pieces have already been mentioned. I would here add some further notes of subject woodcuts in books by Rosenbach and Pere Miquel.

An interesting series of cuts appeared in Diego de San Pedro, *Cárcel de*

Amor, printed by Rosenbach, 1493 (K. 331, Haebler 606; fig. 481).[1] The subject reproduced certainly shows knowledge of the engravings after Botticelli, with its reminiscence of the illustration to Canto I. in Landino's Dante (Florence 1481).

Fig. 481. The Author meets the Wild Man, from Diego de San Pedro, *Cárcel de Amor*, Barcelona 1493.

Remarkable in style is the large title-cut with the *Author and eight women pupils* in Francisco Ximenez, *Libre de les dones*, printed by Rosenbach, 1495 (K. 132, Haebler 706, Madrid; Widener Library, Harvard; Hispanic Society, New York, reprod. Lyell, p. 47). Though cruder in character, it is similar in style to the work of the Master ID, whose signed cuts, about 1489–90, have already been described above in the chapter on France,[2] and I would refer to that place for the general discussion of his artistic personality. Of greater quality and interest, and equally near to the style of ID, is the *King in Council (Jaime I. and the Cortes of Lleida)* which appeared in the *Usatges de Barcelona e Constitucións de Cataluña*, printed by Pere Miquel and Diego de Gumiel, 20th February 1495 (K. 98, Haebler 652, Madrid, Paris, Boston; fig. 482).[3] The block, which is certainly of metal, is probably by the same cutter as the border in the same book, which first appeared in 1490 in Spindeler's *Tirant lo Blanch*.[4] Other cuts not unlike ID in character are the *David kneeling in prayer at the head of his Army*, which appeared in Narcis Vinyoles, *Omelia sobre lo psalm del Miserere*,

---

[1] Good copies were printed by Friedrich Biel, Burgos 1496 (K. 332, Haebler 604).

[2] See pp. 614-616.

[3] Kristeller (*Kupferstich und Holzschnitt*, 1922, p. 124) refers to an edition of 1480, with the cuts, and told me personally that he had noted a copy in the Archivio Municipal, Barcelona, but Haebler does not recognise any edition before 1493 (Haebler 166, Barcelona, Univ. Library), and that one without the illustrations. Cf. Olschki, Bibliofilia, Florence 1903, p. 127.

[4] See p. 746 and fig. 474.

Fig. 482. Jaime I. of Aragon in council, from *Usatges de Barcelona*, Barcelona 1495.

printed by Spindeler at Valencia, 1499 (K. 370, Haebler 692, reprod. Lyell, p. 25), and the *Author writing*, in Livy, *Las Decadas*, printed anonymously at Salamanca, 1497 (K. 231, Haebler 365, Paris, Madrid, reprod. Lyell, p. 71).

Whether the Master ID is responsible for any of these cuts or not, one signed woodcut by him is known in a Spanish book, the large *Christ on the Cross between the Virgin and St. John*, which appeared in Fernandez Perez de Guzman, *La Cronica del Rey don Juan II.*, printed by ARNAO GUILLEN DE BROCAR at Logroño, 1517 (reprod. Lyell, p. 287). Though not known in any earlier book it was probably done between 1490 and 1500. There is also a smaller woodcut, the *Last Judgment*, signed ID (in monogram form) in Gomez Garcia, *Carro de dos Vidas*, printed by JOHANN PEGNITZER and MAGNUS HERBST at Seville, 1500 (K. 174, Haebler 288, Madrid), but I have not seen the print, and the monogram form renders it likely that it is by another hand.

SALAMANCA

At Salamanca a long series of cuts, fairly crude in execution, appeared in Guillermus, *Postilla super Epistolas et Evangelia* (in Spanish), issued by an anonymous press in 1493, of which the only known copy is at Upsala (K. 190, Haebler 250 [3]).[1] An earlier edition is recorded, that of Pablo Hurus, Saragossa, 20th February 1485 (K. 189, Haebler 250), but cannot now be traced, so that the relation of the blocks is uncertain. Probably both editions were based on that issued by Philippi at Lyon about 1483–84 (Cl. iii. 141), which in its turn may have derived from one or another of the numerous German *Plenarien*.[2] Later editions, with similar cuts, were issued by Ungut and Stanislaus Polonus, Seville, 28th February 1497 (K. 191, Haebler 309, Madrid), and by Rodrigo Alvarez at Porto, 25th October 1497 (K. 192, Lisbon). More attractive is the vivacious design on the title to Boccaccio, *La Fiammetta* (in Spanish), printed anonymously, 1497 (K. 68, Haebler 55, Pierpont Morgan, New York; Huntington, San Marino; reprod. Lyell, p. 54). In its open line it is near in character to early Lyon woodcut (e.g. to *L'Abusé en Court*).[3] Interesting also, and not without decorative value, is the series of illustrations of chess in Luis Ramirez de Lucena, *Repetición de Amores y arte de Ajedres*, printed by Leonhard Hutz and Lope Sanz, about 1497 (K. 234, Haebler 371).

[1] See Isak Collijn, *Notas sobre un incunable español desconocido*, Madrid 1906.
[2] See pp. 604 and 290.   [3] See p. 600.

SARAGOSSA

The work of PABLO and JEAN HURUS at Saragossa[1] consisted largely of copies of foreign work, which we have already mentioned. German in character, and showing the influence of the school of Wolgemut, is the frontispiece of the *Author* (or *translator*) *presenting his book to a king*, in Aristotle, *Ethica*, in the Latin translation of Leonardo Bruni (Aretino), 1492 (K. 52, Haebler 29). More characteristic of Spanish work, in their stiff outline and regular shading, are the illustrations in the *Expositio Aurea Hymnorum*, printed by Pablo Hurus, 1499 (K. 139, Haebler 254, Stuttgart) and the several versions of Hurus's printer's mark, a design with two heraldic lions, sometimes accompanied by side-pieces of St. James and St. Sebastian (Juchhoff 110-113).

BURGOS

At Burgos also we have found various copies of foreign woodcuts, in the illustrated books printed by FRIEDRICH BIEL and JUAN DE BURGOS. I would mention a few other works issued by these printers.

Well designed and cut is the *Author writing in a Study*, somewhat in the manner of the Lyon *Terence* of 1493, in the *Libro del Anticristo*, printed by Biel, 1497 (K. 42, Haebler 17, Paris, reprod. Lyell, fig. 59), a cut which re-appeared in the same printer's Donatus, *De octo partibus Orationis*, 1498 (K. 126, Haebler 236 (5), present locality unknown, once in Rosenthal's possession). A border which appeared in the latter work has already been described.[2] In David Aubert, *Oliveros de Castilla y Artus dalgarbe*, 1499 (K. 57, Haebler 494, Hispanic Society, New York), Biel issued numerous cuts again showing a blurred reflection of the style of the woodcuts in the Lyon *Terence*.

In the Netherlandish style, but heavier in character, is the subject of a *Knight kneeling before a King* in Alfonso de Cartagena, *Doctrinal de los Caballeros*, printed by Juan de Burgos, 1497 (K. 27, Haebler 126, Madrid, Hispanic Society, New York). And again under Lyon or Netherlandish influence are the numerous column cuts in Voragine, *La Leyenda de los Santos*, printed without date (probably about 1500) by Juan de Burgos (Haebler 698), some in broadly cut lines, others in a finer technique nearer to the quality of metal-cut. The only other illustrated Spanish *Golden Legend* of the xv century to which I can refer is the *Flos sanctorum Romançat*,

---

[1] See J. M. Sánchez, *Bibliografía zaragózana del siglo xv*, Madrid 1908. For P. and J. Hurus, cf. above, p. 602.   [2] See p. 743.

printed by Rosenbach at Barcelona, 1494 (K. 208, Haebler 297, Barcelona, Madrid).

PAMPLONA—TOLEDO

At Pamplona a typical cut of Spanish character is that of the *Preacher* (within a black-ground border of branches, leaves, and flowers), on the title of Gulielmus Peraldus, *Doctrina de los religiosos en romançe*, printed by ARNAO GUILLEN DE BROCAR, 1499 (K. 188, Haebler 533, Oxford, reprod. Lyell, fig. 75). At Toledo appeared, printed by PEDRO HAGENBACH, a Spanish translation of Julius Caesar, *Los Comentarios*, 1498 (K. 82, Haebler 113, Escorial; Hispanic Society, New York) with a good title-page containing the arms of Ferdinand and Isabella, and the handsome *Mozarabic Missal* (*Missale mixtum secundum regulam beati Isidori dictum Mozarabes*), handsomely printed by Pedro Hagenbach, 9th January 1500 (K. 273, Haebler 446), with a *Canon* cut of *Christ on the Cross with the Virgin and St. John*, clearly influenced by, if not baséd on, French models.

MONTSERRAT

Characteristic metal-cuts are the *Standing Madonna of Montserrat* (in the form of a seal), which appeared in Bonaventura, *Meditationes vitae Christi*, printed by LUSCHNER at Montserrat, 1499 (K. 76, Haebler 69, Madrid; Paris; Hispanic Society, New York; Manchester), and the *Seated Madonna of Montserrat* which Luschner used as his printer's mark (Juchhoff 87), e.g. in Bonaventura, *De Instructione Novitiorum*, 1499 (K. 74, Haebler 63, Madrid, Paris, Huntington).

The number of illustrated books printed in Portugal during the xv century is small, and they are described in detail in the late Don Manuel's fine work on the Portuguese books in his own library. Apart from the Jewish books with borders and initials printed at Lisbon by the Rabbi Eliezer, and at Leiria by Abraham ben Samuel d' Ortas, to which reference has already been made,[1] there only remains the production of VALENTIN FERNANDEZ, of Moravia, who printed at Lisbon between 1493 and 1516.

His most important work, done in collaboration with NICOLAO DE SAXONIA, is an edition of Ludolphus de Saxonia, *Vita Christi*, 1495 (Don

[1] See pp. 744 and 746.

Manuel 5, K. 237, Haebler 373, Lisbon, Porto, Evora, Don Manuel Collection).[1]

Beside the handsome border of scroll work, with vine branch and squirrels, which has already been mentioned,[2] there are woodcuts of a *King and Queen at Prayer* (fig. 483), a *Christ on the Cross between the Virgin and*

Fig. 483. King and Queen at Prayer, from Ludolphus, *Vita Christi*, Lisbon 1495.

St. John (copied from the Master E.S., Lehrs 31), some heraldic cuts, and a good series of capital letters (copied from Israhel van Meckenem).

The most elaborate of the woodcut initals, the letter A, is an isolated example from a set of which various other letters appeared in Fernandez's edition of Marco Polo's book of travels, 1502 (Don Manuel 8, Lisbon; Paris; Don Manuel Collection). The border of the first page, which encloses an illustration of the traveller's ship, is partly made up from the Ludolphus border. Pieces of the same border, and initials from the Ludolphus, also reappear in *Os Autos dos Apostolos*, 1505 (Don Manuel 11, Evora; Don Manuel Collection).

The only other woodcut illustration in Fernandez's books during the xv century which might be mentioned is that of the *Author adoring the Virgin and Child* in Kaminto, *Regimento contra ha Pestenença*, n.d., about 1496? (Don Manuel 7, K. 228, Haebler 346, Madrid; Don Manuel collection).

[1] Apart from the copy in the collection of the late Don Manuel, the only other copy known outside Portugal was recently in the possession of Maggs Bros. (Catalogue 416).

[2] See p. 743

Contemporary Single Cuts

Practically nothing is known to me of xv century single woodcuts produced in Spain or Portugal. The only example to which I would refer is a *St. Anthony of Padua* of about the end of the century (Schreiber 1216 a and 1233 a), once in the Schreiber Collection, and presented to the Ashmolean Museum, Oxford, by Mr. C. W. Dyson Perrins in 1917.[1] A long inscription at the foot begins *O proles hyspanie*, and the cut also contains the arms of Portugal. The heavy outline, the stiff drawing, and regular shading are all in keeping with Spanish and Portuguese work, and the inscription and arms both tell in favour of Iberian origin. The cut shows kinship to certain French woodcuts already described, and was found, like them, in a box-lid, but neither consideration justifies, in my opinion, the attribution of the cut to France or Savoy.[2]

Bibliography

Haebler, Conrad. Early Printers of Spain and Portugal. Bibliographical Society, Illustrated Monographs, iv. London 1897 (for 1896).

Haebler, Conrad. Spanische und portuguesische Bücherzeichen. Strassburg 1898.

Haebler, Conrad. Bibliografía ibérica del siglo xv. 2 vols. The Hague 1903, 1917.

Haebler, Conrad. Geschichte der spanischen Frühdruckes in Stammbäumen. Leipzig 1923 ('in Stammbäumen' refers to the classification of printers in genealogical trees, or groups).

Bibliofilia. Publicat per R. Miguel'y Planas. Barcelona 1914, etc. (a periodical containing much material and illustration of early Spanish book-illustration).

British Museum. Short-title Catalogue of books printed in Spain, and of Spanish books printed elsewhere in Europe before 1601, now in the British Museum. Edited by Henry Thomas. London 1921.

Lyell, J. P. R. Early Book Illustration in Spain. London 1926.

Manuel II., King of Portugal. Early Portuguese Books 1489–1600 in the Library of H.M. the King of Portugal. I. 1489–1539. London 1929. II. 1540–1569. London 1932. III. 1570–1600, and supplement, 1500–1569. London 1934.
    The late Don Manuel (†1932) left his library to the Portuguese nation.

Kurz, Martin. Handbuch der iberischen Bilddrucke des xv Jahrhunderts. Leipzig 1931.

[1] Schreiber sale, 1909, No. 26 (with reproduction).
[2] Cf. p. 700 and see Schreiber, *Manuel* and *Handbuch*, and Dodgson, *Woodcuts of the xv Century in the Ashmolean Museum, Oxford*. Oxford 1929, No. 42. St. Anthony was actually born at Lisbon.

INDEXES

INDEX I

DESIGNERS AND ENGRAVERS OF WOODCUT

In the above title *engraver* is used for *cutter* or *engraver*. As far as possible indication is given as to whether an artist was designer, cutter (with knife) or engraver (with graver or burin). These categories are abbreviated as wood-d., wood-c., and wood-en. Metal-c. is used to denote both the cutter in white line on metal and the engraver in the dotted manner. The distinction between designer and cutter is often very obscure in xv-century work. A certain number of printers of books have been admitted who seem to have been woodcutters, but a query is added after the description in cases of uncertainty. It also includes names recorded as of *printers* in early documents, before the discovery of movable type, no doubt of craftsmen engaged in the printing and colouring of early woodcuts, even if they were not actually cutters. Their titles as recorded are quoted in italics. Printers of block-books are given in this index, not with printers of books.

Masters known by monograms, initials and descriptive titles are indexed in the alphabet under *Master*.

The first page reference generally indicates the principal passage dealing with the designer or engraver in question.

b. = born; d. = died; w. = worked.

INDEX II

PRINTERS AND PUBLISHERS OF BOOKS

THIS list has been made from many bibliographical sources. Though it cannot claim to be authoritative, it will probably be a useful guide to the student of woodcut illustration.

A certain number of craftsmen known in early documents, before the discovery of movable type as *printers*, i.e. printers and possibly cutters of wood blocks, are given in the Index of Designers and Engravers of Woodcut. Known or presumed printers or producers of block-books are also given in the Index of Designers and Engravers.

The first page reference generally indicates the principal passage dealing with the printer's or publisher's books.

b. = born; d. = died; w. = worked.

INDEX III

BOOKS ILLUSTRATED WITH WOODCUTS

The books are indexed under author when such is known; otherwise under title.
The first title quoted is usually the original.
The omission of date may generally be assumed to indicate an undated edition, *n.d.* only being added to distinguish an edition from dated issues in the same reference.
The first page quoted generally indicates the principal reference to each book.

The first group, entitled *Horae* with no further qualification, includes for the most part General *Horae* (Roman Use), whether in Latin or French. I add 'for the most part', as the conditions under which the index has been made render it probable that I have not avoided inconsistencies. Arrangement is by town, printer and date. Then follow (1) *Horae* according to the use of different dioceses and in various languages; (2) Latin editions printed in Italy and Spain, mostly under the title *Officium Beatae Virginis Mariae*; (3) editions in Dutch, German and Spanish under various titles.

INDEX IV

PRINTS MENTIONED OR REPRODUCED

No attempt is made to classify subjects systematically. Thus many events in the Life of the Virgin and of Christ are indexed under the first word of their most familiar title, e.g. *Death of the Virgin*. There may be many inconsistencies, but it is hoped that the sacrifice of a more rigid system in favour of familiar headings will facilitate reference. Occasionally the same subject may be quoted under various titles, *e.g. Virgin and Child* and *Madonna*.

The *Crucifixion* subject is for the most part divided in the index between *Calvary* (i.e. the Three Crosses), and the more symbolic subject *Christ on the Cross* (generally *with the Virgin and St. John*), which is the usual *Canon* cut in Missals. *Crucifixion* may have occasionally been used in the text for either subject. It would be necessary to have three lives to clear up such inconsistencies in description.

INDEX V

SUBJECTS DISCUSSED IN THE TEXT

INCLUDING ARTISTS OTHER THAN DESIGNERS
OR ENGRAVERS OF WOODCUT

A CATALOGUE OF SELECTED DOVER BOOKS
IN ALL FIELDS OF INTEREST

A CATALOGUE OF SELECTED DOVER BOOKS
IN ALL FIELDS OF INTEREST

LEATHER TOOLING AND CARVING, Chris H. Groneman. One of few books concentrating on tooling and carving, with complete instructions and grid designs for 39 projects ranging from bookmarks to bags. 148 illustrations. 111pp. 7⅞ x 10.
23061-9 Pa. $2.50

THE CODEX NUTTALL, A PICTURE MANUSCRIPT FROM ANCIENT MEXICO, as first edited by Zelia Nuttall. Only inexpensive edition, in full color, of a pre-Columbian Mexican (Mixtec) book. 88 color plates show kings, gods, heroes, temples, sacrifices. New explanatory, historical introduction by Arthur G. Miller. 96pp. 11⅜ x 8½.
23168-2 Pa. $7.50

AMERICAN PRIMITIVE PAINTING, Jean Lipman. Classic collection of an enduring American tradition. 109 plates, 8 in full color—portraits, landscapes, Biblical and historical scenes, etc., showing family groups, farm life, and so on. 80pp. of lucid text. 8⅜ x 11¼.
22815-0 Pa. $4.00

WILL BRADLEY: HIS GRAPHIC ART, edited by Clarence P. Hornung. Striking collection of work by foremost practitioner of Art Nouveau in America: posters, cover designs, sample pages, advertisements, other illustrations. 97 plates, including 8 in full color and 19 in two colors. 97pp. 9⅜ x 12¼.
20701-3 Pa. $4.00
22120-2 Clothbd. $10.00

THE UNDERGROUND SKETCHBOOK OF JAN FAUST, Jan Faust. 101 bitter, horrifying, black-humorous, penetrating sketches on sex, war, greed, various liberations, etc. Sometimes sexual, but not pornographic. Not for prudish. 101pp. 6½ x 9¼.
22740-5 Pa. $1.50

THE GIBSON GIRL AND HER AMERICA, Charles Dana Gibson. 155 finest drawings of effervescent world of 1900-1910: the Gibson Girl and her loves, amusements, adventures, Mr. Pipp, etc. Selected by E. Gillon; introduction by Henry Pitz. 144pp. 8¼ x 11⅜.
21986-0 Pa. $3.50

STAINED GLASS CRAFT, J.A.F. Divine, G. Blachford. One of the very few books that tell the beginner exactly what he needs to know: planning cuts, making shapes, avoiding design weaknesses, fitting glass, etc. 93 illustrations. 115pp.
22812-6 Pa. $1.50

DRIED FLOWERS, Sarah Whitlock and Martha Rankin. Concise, clear, practical guide to dehydration, glycerinizing, pressing plant material, and more. Covers use of silica gel. 12 drawings. Originally titled "New Techniques with Dried Flowers." 32pp. 21802-3 Pa. $1.00

ABC OF POULTRY RAISING, J.H. Florea. Poultry expert, editor tells how to raise chickens on home or small business basis. Breeds, feeding, housing, laying, etc. Very concrete, practical. 50 illustrations. 256pp. 23201-8 Pa. $3.00

HOW INDIANS USE WILD PLANTS FOR FOOD, MEDICINE & CRAFTS, Frances Densmore. Smithsonian, Bureau of American Ethnology report presents wealth of material on nearly 200 plants used by Chippewas of Minnesota and Wisconsin. 33 plates plus 122pp. of text. 6⅛ x 9¼. 23019-8 Pa. $2.50

THE HERBAL OR GENERAL HISTORY OF PLANTS, John Gerard. The 1633 edition revised and enlarged by Thomas Johnson. Containing almost 2850 plant descriptions and 2705 superb illustrations, Gerard's Herbal is a monumental work, the book all modern English herbals are derived from, and the one herbal every serious enthusiast should have in its entirety. Original editions are worth perhaps $750. 1678pp. 8½ x 12¼. 23147-X Clothbd..$50.00

A MODERN HERBAL, Margaret Grieve. Much the fullest, most exact, most useful compilation of herbal material. Gigantic alphabetical encyclopedia, from aconite to zedoary, gives botanical information, medical properties, folklore, economic uses, and much else. Indispensable to serious reader. 161 illustrations. 888pp. 6½ x 9¼. USO 22798-7, 22799-5 Pa., Two vol. set $10.00

HOW TO KNOW THE FERNS, Frances T. Parsons. Delightful classic. Identification, fern lore, for Eastern and Central U.S.A. Has introduced thousands to interesting life form. 99 illustrations. 215pp. 20740-4 Pa. $2.50

THE MUSHROOM HANDBOOK, Louis C.C. Krieger. Still the best popular handbook. Full descriptions of 259 species, extremely thorough text, habitats, luminescence, poisons, folklore, etc. 32 color plates; 126 other illustrations. 560pp. 21861-9 Pa. $4.50

HOW TO KNOW THE WILD FRUITS, Maude G. Peterson. Classic guide covers nearly 200 trees, shrubs, smaller plants of the U.S. arranged by color of fruit and then by family. Full text provides names, descriptions, edibility, uses. 80 illustrations. 400pp. 22943-2 Pa. $3.00

COMMON WEEDS OF THE UNITED STATES, U.S. Department of Agriculture. Covers 220 important weeds with illustration, maps, botanical information, plant lore for each. Over 225 illustrations. 463pp. 6⅛ x 9¼. 20504-5 Pa. $4.50

HOW TO KNOW THE WILD FLOWERS, Mrs. William S. Dana. Still best popular book for East and Central USA. Over 500 plants easily identified, with plant lore; arranged according to color and flowering time. 174 plates. 459pp. 20332-8 Pa. $3.50

CREATIVE LITHOGRAPHY AND HOW TO DO IT, Grant Arnold. Lithography as art form: working directly on stone, transfer of drawings, lithotint, mezzotint, color printing; also metal plates. Detailed, thorough. 27 illustrations. 214pp.
21208-4 Pa. $3.00

DESIGN MOTIFS OF ANCIENT MEXICO, Jorge Enciso. Vigorous, powerful ceramic stamp impressions — Maya, Aztec, Toltec, Olmec. Serpents, gods, priests, dancers, etc. 153pp. 6⅛ x 9¼.
20084-1 Pa. $2.50

AMERICAN INDIAN DESIGN AND DECORATION, Leroy Appleton. Full text, plus more than 700 precise drawings of Inca, Maya, Aztec, Pueblo, Plains, NW Coast basketry, sculpture, painting, pottery, sand paintings, metal, etc. 4 plates in color. 279pp. 8⅜ x 11¼.
22704-9 Pa. $4.50

CHINESE LATTICE DESIGNS, Daniel S. Dye. Incredibly beautiful geometric designs: circles, voluted, simple dissections, etc. Inexhaustible source of ideas, motifs. 1239 illustrations. 469pp. 6⅛ x 9¼.
23096-1 Pa. $5.00

JAPANESE DESIGN MOTIFS, Matsuya Co. Mon, or heraldic designs. Over 4000 typical, beautiful designs: birds, animals, flowers, swords, fans, geometric; all beautifully stylized. 213pp. 11⅜ x 8¼.
22874-6 Pa. $4.95

PERSPECTIVE, Jan Vredeman de Vries. 73 perspective plates from 1604 edition; buildings, townscapes, stairways, fantastic scenes. Remarkable for beauty, surrealistic atmosphere; real eye-catchers. Introduction by Adolf Placzek. 74pp. 11⅜ x 8¼.
20186-4 Pa. $2.75

EARLY AMERICAN DESIGN MOTIFS, Suzanne E. Chapman. 497 motifs, designs, from painting on wood, ceramics, appliqué, glassware, samplers, metal work, etc. Florals, landscapes, birds and animals, geometrics, letters, etc. Inexhaustible. Enlarged edition. 138pp. 8⅜ x 11¼.
22985-8 Pa. $3.50
23084-8 Clothbd. $7.95

VICTORIAN STENCILS FOR DESIGN AND DECORATION, edited by E.V. Gillon, Jr. 113 wonderful ornate Victorian pieces from German sources; florals, geometrics; borders, corner pieces; bird motifs, etc. 64pp. 9⅜ x 12¼.
21995-X Pa. $2.50

ART NOUVEAU: AN ANTHOLOGY OF DESIGN AND ILLUSTRATION FROM THE STUDIO, edited by E.V. Gillon, Jr. Graphic arts: book jackets, posters, engravings, illustrations, decorations; Crane, Beardsley, Bradley and many others. Inexhaustible. 92pp. 8⅛ x 11.
22388-4 Pa. $2.50

ORIGINAL ART DECO DESIGNS, William Rowe. First-rate, highly imaginative modern Art Deco frames, borders, compositions, alphabets, florals, insectals, Wurlitzer-types, etc. Much finest modern Art Deco. 80 plates, 8 in color. 8⅜ x 11¼.
22567-4 Pa. $3.00

HANDBOOK OF DESIGNS AND DEVICES, Clarence P. Hornung. Over 1800 basic geometric designs based on circle, triangle, square, scroll, cross, etc. Largest such collection in existence. 261pp.
20125-2 Pa. $2.50

THE JOURNAL OF HENRY D. THOREAU, edited by Bradford Torrey, F.H. Allen. Complete reprinting of 14 volumes, 1837-1861, over two million words; the sourcebooks for Walden, etc. Definitive. All original sketches, plus 75 photographs. Introduction by Walter Harding. Total of 1804pp. 8½ x 12¼.
20312-3, 20313-1 Clothbd., Two vol. set $50.00

MASTERS OF THE DRAMA, John Gassner. Most comprehensive history of the drama, every tradition from Greeks to modern Europe and America, including Orient. Covers 800 dramatists, 2000 plays; biography, plot summaries, criticism, theatre history, etc. 77 illustrations. 890pp. 20100-7 Clothbd. $10.00

GHOST AND HORROR STORIES OF AMBROSE BIERCE, Ambrose Bierce. 23 modern horror stories: The Eyes of the Panther, The Damned Thing, etc., plus the dream-essay Visions of the Night. Edited by E.F. Bleiler. 199pp. 20767-6 Pa. $2.00

BEST GHOST STORIES, Algernon Blackwood. 13 great stories by foremost British 20th century supernaturalist. The Willows, The Wendigo, Ancient Sorceries, others. Edited by E.F. Bleiler. 366pp. USO 22977-7 Pa. $3.00

THE BEST TALES OF HOFFMANN, E.T.A. Hoffmann. 10 of Hoffmann's most important stories, in modern re-editings of standard translations: Nutcracker and the King of Mice, The Golden Flowerpot, etc. 7 illustrations by Hoffmann. Edited by E.F. Bleiler. 458pp. 21793-0 Pa. $3.95

BEST GHOST STORIES OF J.S. LEFANU, J. Sheridan LeFanu. 16 stories by greatest Victorian master: Green Tea, Carmilla, Haunted Baronet, The Familiar, etc. Mostly unavailable elsewhere. Edited by E.F. Bleiler. 8 illustrations. 467pp.
20415-4 Pa. $4.00

SUPERNATURAL HORROR IN LITERATURE, H.P. Lovecraft. Great modern American supernaturalist brilliantly surveys history of genre to 1930's, summarizing, evaluating scores of books. Necessary for every student, lover of form. Introduction by E.F. Bleiler. 111pp. 20105-8 Pa. $1.50

THREE GOTHIC NOVELS, ed. by E.F. Bleiler. Full texts Castle of Otranto, Walpole; Vathek, Beckford; The Vampyre, Polidori; Fragment of a Novel, Lord Byron. 331pp. 21232-7 Pa. $3.00

SEVEN SCIENCE FICTION NOVELS, H.G. Wells. Full novels. First Men in the Moon, Island of Dr. Moreau, War of the Worlds, Food of the Gods, Invisible Man, Time Machine, In the Days of the Comet. A basic science-fiction library. 1015pp.
USO 20264-X Clothbd. $6.00

LADY AUDLEY'S SECRET, Mary E. Braddon. Great Victorian mystery classic, beautifully plotted, suspenseful; praised by Thackeray, Boucher, Starrett, others. What happened to beautiful, vicious Lady Audley's husband? Introduction by Norman Donaldson. 286pp. 23011-2 Pa. $3.00

150 MASTERPIECES OF DRAWING, edited by Anthony Toney. 150 plates, early 15th century to end of 18th century; Rembrandt, Michelangelo, Dürer, Fragonard, Watteau, Wouwerman, many others. 150pp. 8⅜ x 11¼. 21032-4 Pa. $3.50

THE GOLDEN AGE OF THE POSTER, Hayward and Blanche Cirker. 70 extraordinary posters in full colors, from Maîtres de l'Affiche, Mucha, Lautrec, Bradley, Cheret, Beardsley, many others. 9⅜ x 12¼. 22753-7 Pa. $4.95
21718-3 Clothbd. $7.95

SIMPLICISSIMUS, selection, translations and text by Stanley Appelbaum. 180 satirical drawings, 16 in full color, from the famous German weekly magazine in the years 1896 to 1926. 24 artists included: Grosz, Kley, Pascin, Kubin, Kollwitz, plus Heine, Thöny, Bruno Paul, others. 172pp. 8½ x 12¼. 23098-8 Pa. $5.00
23099-6 Clothbd. $10.00

THE EARLY WORK OF AUBREY BEARDSLEY, Aubrey Beardsley. 157 plates, 2 in color: Manon Lescaut, Madame Bovary, Morte d'Arthur, Salome, other. Introduction by H. Marillier. 175pp. 8½ x 11. 21816-3 Pa. $3.50

THE LATER WORK OF AUBREY BEARDSLEY, Aubrey Beardsley. Exotic masterpieces of full maturity: Venus and Tannhäuser, Lysistrata, Rape of the Lock, Volpone, Savoy material, etc. 174 plates, 2 in color. 176pp. 8½ x 11. 21817-1 Pa. $3.75

DRAWINGS OF WILLIAM BLAKE, William Blake. 92 plates from Book of Job, Divine Comedy, Paradise Lost, visionary heads, mythological figures, Laocoön, etc. Selection, introduction, commentary by Sir Geoffrey Keynes. 178pp. 8½ x 11. 22303-5 Pa. $3.50

LONDON: A PILGRIMAGE, Gustave Doré, Blanchard Jerrold. Squalor, riches, misery, beauty of mid-Victorian metropolis; 55 wonderful plates, 125 other illustrations, full social, cultural text by Jerrold. 191pp. of text. 8⅛ x 11. 22306-X Pa. $5.00

THE COMPLETE WOODCUTS OF ALBRECHT DÜRER, edited by Dr. W. Kurth. 346 in all: Old Testament, St. Jerome, Passion, Life of Virgin, Apocalypse, many others. Introduction by Campbell Dodgson. 285pp. 8½ x 12¼. 21097-9 Pa. $6.00

THE DISASTERS OF WAR, Francisco Goya. 83 etchings record horrors of Napoleonic wars in Spain and war in general. Reprint of 1st edition, plus 3 additional plates. Introduction by Philip Hofer. 97pp. 9⅜ x 8¼. 21872-4 Pa. $2.50

ENGRAVINGS OF HOGARTH, William Hogarth. 101 of Hogarth's greatest works: Rake's Progress, Harlot's Progress, Illustrations for Hudibras, Midnight Modern Conversation, Before and After, Beer Street and Gin Lane, many more. Full commentary. 256pp. 11 x 14. 22479-1 Pa. $6.00
23023-6 Clothbd. $13.50

PRIMITIVE ART, Franz Boas. Great anthropologist on ceramics, textiles, wood, stone, metal, etc.; patterns, technology, symbols, styles. All areas, but fullest on Northwest Coast Indians. 350 illustrations. 378pp. 20025-6 Pa. $3.50

DECORATIVE ALPHABETS AND INITIALS, edited by Alexander Nesbitt. 91 complete alphabets (medieval to modern), 3924 decorative initials, including Victorian novelty and Art Nouveau. 192pp. 7¾ x 10¾.   20544-4 Pa. $3.50

CALLIGRAPHY, Arthur Baker. Over 100 original alphabets from the hand of our greatest living calligrapher: simple, bold, fine-line, richly ornamented, etc. — all strikingly original and different, a fusion of many influences and styles. 155pp. 11⅜ x 8¼.   22895-9 Pa. $4.00

MONOGRAMS AND ALPHABETIC DEVICES, edited by Hayward and Blanche Cirker. Over 2500 combinations, names, crests in very varied styles: script engraving, ornate Victorian, simple Roman, and many others. 226pp. 8⅛ x 11.
        22330-2 Pa. $4.00

THE BOOK OF SIGNS, Rudolf Koch. Famed German type designer renders 493 symbols: religious, alchemical, imperial, runes, property marks, etc. Timeless. 104pp. 6⅛ x 9¼.   20162-7 Pa. $1.50

200 DECORATIVE TITLE PAGES, edited by Alexander Nesbitt. 1478 to late 1920's. Baskerville, Dürer, Beardsley, W. Morris, Pyle, many others in most varied techniques. For posters, programs, other uses. 222pp. 8⅜ x 11¼.   21264-5 Pa. $3.50

DICTIONARY OF AMERICAN PORTRAITS, edited by Hayward and Blanche Cirker. 4000 important Americans, earliest times to 1905, mostly in clear line. Politicians, writers, soldiers, scientists, inventors, industrialists, Indians, Blacks, women, outlaws, etc. Identificatory information. 756pp. 9¼ x 12¾. 21823-6 Clothbd. $30.00

ART FORMS IN NATURE, Ernst Haeckel. Multitude of strangely beautiful natural forms: Radiolaria, Foraminifera, jellyfishes, fungi, turtles, bats, etc. All 100 plates of the 19th century evolutionist's Kunstformen der Natur (1904). 100pp. 9⅜ x 12¼.   22987-4 Pa. $4.00

DECOUPAGE: THE BIG PICTURE SOURCEBOOK, Eleanor Rawlings. Make hundreds of beautiful objects, over 550 florals, animals, letters, shells, period costumes, frames, etc. selected by foremost practitioner. Printed on one side of page. 8 color plates. Instructions. 176pp. 9³/₁₆ x 12¼.   23182-8 Pa. $5.00

AMERICAN FOLK DECORATION, Jean Lipman, Eve Meulendyke. Thorough coverage of all aspects of wood, tin, leather, paper, cloth decoration — scapes, humans, trees, flowers, geometrics — and how to make them. Full instructions. 233 illustrations, 5 in color. 163pp. 8⅜ x 11¼.   22217-9 Pa. $3.95

WHITTLING AND WOODCARVING, E.J. Tangerman. Best book on market; clear, full. If you can cut a potato, you can carve toys, puzzles, chains, caricatures, masks, patterns, frames, decorate surfaces, etc. Also covers serious wood sculpture. Over 200 photos. 293pp.   20965-2 Pa. $2.50

EARLY NEW ENGLAND GRAVESTONE RUBBINGS, Edmund V. Gillon, Jr. 43 photographs, 226 rubbings show heavily symbolic, macabre, sometimes humorous primitive American art. Up to early 19th century. 207pp. 8⅜ x 11¼.
21380-3 Pa. $4.00

L.J.M. DAGUERRE: THE HISTORY OF THE DIORAMA AND THE DAGUERREOTYPE, Helmut and Alison Gernsheim. Definitive account. Early history, life and work of Daguerre; discovery of daguerreotype process; diffusion abroad; other early photography. 124 illustrations. 226pp. 6⅙ x 9¼.
22290-X Pa. $4.00

PHOTOGRAPHY AND THE AMERICAN SCENE, Robert Taft. The basic book on American photography as art, recording form, 1839-1889. Development, influence on society, great photographers, types (portraits, war, frontier, etc.), whatever else needed. Inexhaustible. Illustrated with 322 early photos, daguerreotypes, tintypes, stereo slides, etc. 546pp. 6⅛ x 9¼.
21201-7 Pa. $5.00

PHOTOGRAPHIC SKETCHBOOK OF THE CIVIL WAR, Alexander Gardner. Reproduction of 1866 volume with 100 on-the-field photographs: Manassas, Lincoln on battlefield, slave pens, etc. Introduction by E.F. Bleiler. 224pp. 10¾ x 9.
22731-6 Pa. $4.50

THE MOVIES: A PICTURE QUIZ BOOK, Stanley Appelbaum & Hayward Cirker. Match stars with their movies, name actors and actresses, test your movie skill with 241 stills from 236 great movies, 1902-1959. Indexes of performers and films. 128pp. 8⅜ x 9¼.
20222-4 Pa. $2.50

THE TALKIES, Richard Griffith. Anthology of features, articles from Photoplay, 1928-1940, reproduced complete. Stars, famous movies, technical features, fabulous ads, etc.; Garbo, Chaplin, King Kong, Lubitsch, etc. 4 color plates, scores of illustrations. 327pp. 8⅜ x 11¼.
22762-6 Pa. $5.95

THE MOVIE MUSICAL FROM VITAPHONE TO "42ND STREET," edited by Miles Kreuger. Relive the rise of the movie musical as reported in the pages of Photoplay magazine (1926-1933): every movie review, cast list, ad, and record review; every significant feature article, production still, biography, forecast, and gossip story. Profusely illustrated. 367pp. 8⅜ x 11¼.
23154-2 Pa. $6.95

JOHANN SEBASTIAN BACH, Philipp Spitta. Great classic of biography, musical commentary, with hundreds of pieces analyzed. Also good for Bach's contemporaries. 450 musical examples. Total of 1799pp.
EUK 22278-0, 22279-9 Clothbd., Two vol. set $25.00

BEETHOVEN AND HIS NINE SYMPHONIES, Sir George Grove. Thorough history, analysis, commentary on symphonies and some related pieces. For either beginner or advanced student. 436 musical passages. 407pp.
20334-4 Pa. $4.00

MOZART AND HIS PIANO CONCERTOS, Cuthbert Girdlestone. The only full-length study. Detailed analyses of all 21 concertos, sources; 417 musical examples. 509pp.
21271-8 Pa. $4.50

HOUDINI ON MAGIC, Harold Houdini. Edited by Walter Gibson, Morris N. Young. How he escaped; exposés of fake spiritualists; instructions for eye-catching tricks; other fascinating material by and about greatest magician. 155 illustrations. 280pp. 20384-0 Pa. $2.50

HANDBOOK OF THE NUTRITIONAL CONTENTS OF FOOD, U.S. Dept. of Agriculture. Largest, most detailed source of food nutrition information ever prepared. Two mammoth tables: one measuring nutrients in 100 grams of edible portion; the other, in edible portion of 1 pound as purchased. Originally titled Composition of Foods. 190pp. 9 x 12. 21342-0 Pa. $4.00

COMPLETE GUIDE TO HOME CANNING, PRESERVING AND FREEZING, U.S. Dept. of Agriculture. Seven basic manuals with full instructions for jams and jellies; pickles and relishes; canning fruits, vegetables, meat; freezing anything. Really good recipes, exact instructions for optimal results. Save a fortune in food. 156 illustrations. 214pp. 6⅛ x 9¼. 22911-4 Pa. $2.50

THE BREAD TRAY, Louis P. De Gouy. Nearly every bread the cook could buy or make: bread sticks of Italy, fruit breads of Greece, glazed rolls of Vienna, everything from corn pone to croissants. Over 500 recipes altogether. including buns, rolls, muffins, scones, and more. 463pp. 23000-7 Pa. $3.50

CREATIVE HAMBURGER COOKERY, Louis P. De Gouy. 182 unusual recipes for casseroles, meat loaves and hamburgers that turn inexpensive ground meat into memorable main dishes: Arizona chili burgers, burger tamale pie, burger stew, burger corn loaf, burger wine loaf, and more. 120pp. 23001-5 Pa. $1.75

LONG ISLAND SEAFOOD COOKBOOK, J. George Frederick and Jean Joyce. Probably the best American seafood cookbook. Hundreds of recipes. 40 gourmet sauces, 123 recipes using oysters alone! All varieties of fish and seafood amply represented. 324pp. 22677-8 Pa. $3.00

THE EPICUREAN: A COMPLETE TREATISE OF ANALYTICAL AND PRACTICAL STUDIES IN THE CULINARY ART, Charles Ranhofer. Great modern classic. 3,500 recipes from master chef of Delmonico's, turn-of-the-century America's best restaurant. Also explained, many techniques known only to professional chefs. 775 illustrations. 1183pp. 6⅝ x 10. 22680-8 Clothbd. $17.50

THE AMERICAN WINE COOK BOOK, Ted Hatch. Over 700 recipes: old favorites livened up with wine plus many more: Czech fish soup, quince soup, sauce Perigueux, shrimp shortcake, filets Stroganoff, cordon bleu goulash, jambonneau, wine fruit cake, more. 314pp. 22796-0 Pa. $2.50

DELICIOUS VEGETARIAN COOKING, Ivan Baker. Close to 500 delicious and varied recipes: soups, main course dishes (pea, bean, lentil, cheese, vegetable, pasta, and egg dishes), savories, stews, whole-wheat breads and cakes, more. 168pp. USO 22834-7 Pa. $1.75

VICTORIAN HOUSES: A TREASURY OF LESSER-KNOWN EXAMPLES, Edmund Gillon and Clay Lancaster. 116 photographs, excellent commentary illustrate distinct characteristics, many borrowings of local Victorian architecture. Octagonal houses, Americanized chalets, grand country estates, small cottages, etc. Rich heritage often overlooked. 116 plates. 11⅜ x 10. 22966-1 Pa. $4.00

STICKS AND STONES, Lewis Mumford. Great classic of American cultural history; architecture from medieval-inspired earliest forms to 20th century; evolution of structure and style, influence of environment. 21 illustrations. 113pp. 20202-X Pa. $2.00

ON THE LAWS OF JAPANESE PAINTING, Henry P. Bowie. Best substitute for training with genius Oriental master, based on years of study in Kano school. Philosophy, brushes, inks, style, etc. 66 illustrations. 117pp. 6⅛ x 9¼. 20030-2 Pa. $4.00

A HANDBOOK OF ANATOMY FOR ART STUDENTS, Arthur Thomson. Virtually exhaustive. Skeletal structure, muscles, heads, special features. Full text, anatomical figures, undraped photos. Male and female. 337 illustrations. 459pp. 21163-0 Pa. $5.00

AN ATLAS OF ANATOMY FOR ARTISTS, Fritz Schider. Finest text, working book. Full text, plus anatomical illustrations; plates by great artists showing anatomy. 593 illustrations. 192pp. 7⅞ x 10¾. 20241-0 Clothbd. $6.95

THE HUMAN FIGURE IN MOTION, Eadweard Muybridge. More than 4500 stopped-action photos, in action series, showing undraped men, women, children jumping, lying down, throwing, sitting, wrestling, carrying, etc. "Unparalleled dictionary for artists," American Artist. Taken by great 19th century photographer. 390pp. 7⅞ x 10⅝. 20204-6 Clothbd. $12.50

AN ATLAS OF ANIMAL ANATOMY FOR ARTISTS, W. Ellenberger et al. Horses, dogs, cats, lions, cattle, deer, etc. Muscles, skeleton, surface features. The basic work. Enlarged edition. 288 illustrations. 151pp. 9⅜ x 12¼. 20082-5 Pa. $4.00

LETTER FORMS: 110 COMPLETE ALPHABETS, Frederick Lambert. 110 sets of capital letters; 16 lower case alphabets; 70 sets of numbers and other symbols. Edited and expanded by Theodore Menten. 110pp. 8⅛ x 11. 22872-X Pa. $2.50

THE METHODS OF CONSTRUCTION OF CELTIC ART, George Bain. Simple geometric techniques for making wonderful Celtic interlacements, spirals, Kells-type initials, animals, humans, etc. Unique for artists, craftsmen. Over 500 illustrations. 160pp. 9 x 12. USO 22923-8 Pa. $4.00

SCULPTURE, PRINCIPLES AND PRACTICE, Louis Slobodkin. Step by step approach to clay, plaster, metals, stone; classical and modern. 253 drawings, photos. 255pp. 8⅛ x 11. 22960-2 Pa. $4.50

THE ART OF ETCHING, E.S. Lumsden. Clear, detailed instructions for etching, drypoint, softground, aquatint; from 1st sketch to print. Very detailed, thorough. 200 illustrations. 376pp. 20049-3 Pa. $3.50

MANUAL OF THE TREES OF NORTH AMERICA, Charles S. Sargent. The basic survey of every native tree and tree-like shrub, 717 species in all. Extremely full descriptions, information on habitat, growth, locales, economics, etc. Necessary to every serious tree lover. Over 100 finding keys. 783 illustrations. Total of 986pp.
20277-1, 20278-X Pa., Two vol. set $8.00

BIRDS OF THE NEW YORK AREA, John Bull. Indispensable guide to more than 400 species within a hundred-mile radius of Manhattan. Information on range, status, breeding, migration, distribution trends, etc. Foreword by Roger Tory Peterson. 17 drawings; maps. 540pp.
23222-0 Pa. $6.00

THE SEA-BEACH AT EBB-TIDE, Augusta Foote Arnold. Identify hundreds of marine plants and animals: algae, seaweeds, squids, crabs, corals, etc. Descriptions cover food, life cycle, size, shape, habitat. Over 600 drawings. 490pp.
21949-6 Pa. $4.00

THE MOTH BOOK, William J. Holland. Identify more than 2,000 moths of North America. General information, precise species descriptions. 623 illustrations plus 48 color plates show almost all species, full size. 1968 edition. Still the basic book. Total of 551pp. 6½ x 9¼.
21948-8 Pa. $6.00

AN INTRODUCTION TO THE REPTILES AND AMPHIBIANS OF THE UNITED STATES, Percy A. Morris. All lizards, crocodiles, turtles, snakes, toads, frogs; life history, identification, habits, suitability as pets, etc. Non-technical, but sound and broad. 130 photos. 253pp.
22982-3 Pa. $3.00

OLD NEW YORK IN EARLY PHOTOGRAPHS, edited by Mary Black. Your only chance to see New York City as it was 1853-1906, through 196 wonderful photographs from N.Y. Historical Society. Great Blizzard, Lincoln's funeral procession, great buildings. 228pp. 9 x 12.
22907-6 Pa. $6.00

THE AMERICAN REVOLUTION, A PICTURE SOURCEBOOK, John Grafton. Wonderful Bicentennial picture source, with 411 illustrations (contemporary and 19th century) showing battles, personalities, maps, events, flags, posters, soldier's life, ships, etc. all captioned and explained. A wonderful browsing book, supplement to other historical reading. 160pp. 9 x 12.
23226-3 Pa. $4.00

PERSONAL NARRATIVE OF A PILGRIMAGE TO AL-MADINAH AND MECCAH, Richard Burton. Great travel classic by remarkably colorful personality. Burton, disguised as a Moroccan, visited sacred shrines of Islam, narrowly escaping death. Wonderful observations of Islamic life, customs, personalities. 47 illustrations. Total of 959pp.
21217-3, 21218-1 Pa., Two vol. set $7.00

INCIDENTS OF TRAVEL IN CENTRAL AMERICA, CHIAPAS, AND YUCATAN, John L. Stephens. Almost single-handed discovery of Maya culture; exploration of ruined cities, monuments, temples; customs of Indians. 115 drawings. 892pp.
22404-X, 22405-8 Pa., Two vol. set $8.00

THE STYLE OF PALESTRINA AND THE DISSONANCE, Knud Jeppesen. Standard analysis of rhythm, line, harmony, accented and unaccented dissonances. Also pre-Palestrina dissonances. 306pp. 22386-8 Pa. $3.00

DOVER OPERA GUIDE AND LIBRETTO SERIES prepared by Ellen H. Bleiler. Each volume contains everything needed for background, complete enjoyment: complete libretto, new English translation with all repeats, biography of composer and librettist, early performance history, musical lore, much else. All volumes lavishly illustrated with performance photos, portraits, similar material. Do not confuse with skimpy performance booklets.

CARMEN, Georges Bizet. 66 illustrations. 222pp. 22111-3 Pa. $2.00
DON GIOVANNI, Wolfgang A. Mozart. 92 illustrations. 209pp. 21134-7 Pa. $2.50
LA BOHÈME, Giacomo Puccini. 73 illustrations. 124pp. USO 20404-9 Pa. $1.75
ÄIDA, Giuseppe Verdi. 76 illustrations. 181pp. 20405-7 Pa. $2.00
LUCIA DI LAMMERMOOR, Gaetano Donizetti. 44 illustrations. 186pp.
22110-5 Pa. $2.00

ANTONIO STRADIVARI: HIS LIFE AND WORK, W. H. Hill, et al. Great work of musicology. Construction methods, woods, varnishes, known instruments, types of instruments, life, special features. Introduction by Sydney Beck. 98 illustrations, plus 4 color plates. 315pp. 20425-1 Pa. $3.00

MUSIC FOR THE PIANO, James Friskin, Irwin Freundlich. Both famous, little-known compositions; 1500 to 1950's. Listing, description, classification, technical aspects for student, teacher, performer. Indispensable for enlarging repertory. 448pp.
22918-1 Pa. $4.00

PIANOS AND THEIR MAKERS, Alfred Dolge. Leading inventor offers full history of piano technology, earliest models to 1910. Types, makers, components, mechanisms, musical aspects. Very strong on offtrail models, inventions; also player pianos. 300 illustrations. 581pp. 22856-8 Pa. $5.00

KEYBOARD MUSIC, J.S. Bach. Bach-Gesellschaft edition. For harpsichord, piano, other keyboard instruments. English Suites, French Suites, Six Partitas, Goldberg Variations, Two-Part Inventions, Three-Part Sinfonias. 312pp. 8⅛ x 11.
22360-4 Pa. $5.00

COMPLETE STRING QUARTETS, Ludwig van Beethoven. Breitkopf and Härtel edition. 6 quartets of Opus 18; 3 quartets of Opus 59; Opera 74, 95, 127, 130, 131, 132, 135 and Grosse Fuge. Study score. 434pp. 9⅜ x 12¼. 22361-2 Pa. $7.95

COMPLETE PIANO SONATAS AND VARIATIONS FOR SOLO PIANO, Johannes Brahms. All sonatas, five variations on themes from Schumann, Paganini, Handel, etc. Vienna Gesellschaft der Musikfreunde edition. 178pp. 9 x 12. 22650-6 Pa. $4.00

PIANO MUSIC 1888-1905, Claude Debussy. Deux Arabesques, Suite Bergamesque, Masques, 1st series of Images, etc. 9 others, in corrected editions. 175pp. 9⅜ x 12¼. 22771-5 Pa. $4.00

HOW TO SOLVE CHESS PROBLEMS, Kenneth S. Howard. Practical suggestions on problem solving for very beginners. 58 two-move problems, 46 3-movers, 8 4-movers for practice, plus hints. 171pp. 20748-X Pa. $2.00

A GUIDE TO FAIRY CHESS, Anthony Dickins. 3-D chess, 4-D chess, chess on a cylindrical board, reflecting pieces that bounce off edges, cooperative chess, retrograde chess, maximummers, much more. Most based on work of great Dawson. Full handbook, 100 problems. 66pp. 7⅞ x 10¾. 22687-5 Pa. $2.00

WIN AT BACKGAMMON, Millard Hopper. Best opening moves, running game, blocking game, back game, tables of odds, etc. Hopper makes the game clear enough for anyone to play, and win. 43 diagrams. 111pp. 22894-0 Pa. $1.50

BIDDING A BRIDGE HAND, Terence Reese. Master player "thinks out loud" the binding of 75 hands that defy point count systems. Organized by bidding problem—no-fit situations, overbidding, underbidding, cueing your defense, etc. 254pp. EBE 22830-4 Pa. $2.50

THE PRECISION BIDDING SYSTEM IN BRIDGE, C.C. Wei, edited by Alan Truscott. Inventor of precision bidding presents average hands and hands from actual play, including games from 1969 Bermuda Bowl where system emerged. 114 exercises. 116pp. 21171-1 Pa. $1.75

LEARN MAGIC, Henry Hay. 20 simple, easy-to-follow lessons on magic for the new magician: illusions, card tricks, silks, sleights of hand, coin manipulations, escapes, and more —all with a minimum amount of equipment. Final chapter explains the great stage illusions. 92 illustrations. 285pp. 21238-6 Pa. $2.95

THE NEW MAGICIAN'S MANUAL, Walter B. Gibson. Step-by-step instructions and clear illustrations guide the novice in mastering 36 tricks; much equipment supplied on 16 pages of cut-out materials. 36 additional tricks. 64 illustrations. 159pp. 6⅝ x 10. 23113-5 Pa. $3.00

PROFESSIONAL MAGIC FOR AMATEURS, Walter B. Gibson. 50 easy, effective tricks used by professionals —cards, string, tumblers, handkerchiefs, mental magic, etc. 63 illustrations. 223pp. 23012-0 Pa. $2.50

CARD MANIPULATIONS, Jean Hugard. Very rich collection of manipulations; has taught thousands of fine magicians tricks that are really workable, eye-catching. Easily followed, serious work. Over 200 illustrations. 163pp. 20539-8 Pa. $2.00

ABBOTT'S ENCYCLOPEDIA OF ROPE TRICKS FOR MAGICIANS, Stewart James. Complete reference book for amateur and professional magicians containing more than 150 tricks involving knots, penetrations, cut and restored rope, etc. 510 illustrations. Reprint of 3rd edition. 400pp. 23206-9 Pa. $3.50

THE SECRETS OF HOUDINI, J.C. Cannell. Classic study of Houdini's incredible magic, exposing closely-kept professional secrets and revealing, in general terms, the whole art of stage magic. 67 illustrations. 279pp. 22913-0 Pa. $2.50

THE MAGIC MOVING PICTURE BOOK, Bliss, Sands & Co. The pictures in this book move! Volcanoes erupt, a house burns, a serpentine dancer wiggles her way through a number. By using a specially ruled acetate screen provided, you can obtain these and 15 other startling effects. Originally "The Motograph Moving Picture Book." 32pp. 8¼ x 11.   23224-7 Pa. $1.75

STRING FIGURES AND HOW TO MAKE THEM, Caroline F. Jayne. Fullest, clearest instructions on string figures from around world: Eskimo, Navajo, Lapp, Europe, more. Cats cradle, moving spear, lightning, stars. Introduction by A.C. Haddon. 950 illustrations. 407pp.   20152-X Pa. $3.00

PAPER FOLDING FOR BEGINNERS, William D. Murray and Francis J. Rigney. Clearest book on market for making origami sail boats, roosters, frogs that move legs, cups, bonbon boxes. 40 projects. More than 275 illustrations. Photographs. 94pp.
20713-7 Pa. $1.25

INDIAN SIGN LANGUAGE, William Tomkins. Over 525 signs developed by Sioux, Blackfoot, Cheyenne, Arapahoe and other tribes. Written instructions and diagrams: how to make words, construct sentences. Also 290 pictographs of Sioux and Ojibway tribes. 111pp. 6⅛ x 9¼.   22029-X Pa. $1.50

BOOMERANGS: HOW TO MAKE AND THROW THEM, Bernard S. Mason. Easy to make and throw, dozens of designs: cross-stick, pinwheel, boomabird, tumblestick, Australian curved stick boomerang. Complete throwing instructions. All safe. 99pp.   23028-7 Pa. $1.50

25 KITES THAT FLY, Leslie Hunt. Full, easy to follow instructions for kites made from inexpensive materials. Many novelties. Reeling, raising, designing your own. 70 illustrations. 110pp.   22550-X Pa. $1.25

TRICKS AND GAMES ON THE POOL TABLE, Fred Herrmann. 79 tricks and games, some solitaires, some for 2 or more players, some competitive; mystifying shots and throws, unusual carom, tricks involving cork, coins, a hat, more. 77 figures. 95pp.   21814-7 Pa. $1.25

WOODCRAFT AND CAMPING, Bernard S. Mason. How to make a quick emergency shelter, select woods that will burn immediately, make do with limited supplies, etc. Also making many things out of wood, rawhide, bark, at camp. Formerly titled Woodcraft. 295 illustrations. 580pp.   21951-8 Pa. $4.00

AN INTRODUCTION TO CHESS MOVES AND TACTICS SIMPLY EXPLAINED, Leonard Barden. Informal intermediate introduction: reasons for moves, tactics, openings, traps, positional play, endgame. Isolates patterns. 102pp. USO 21210-6 Pa. $1.35

LASKER'S MANUAL OF CHESS, Dr. Emanuel Lasker. Great world champion offers very thorough coverage of all aspects of chess. Combinations, position play, openings, endgame, aesthetics of chess, philosophy of struggle, much more. Filled with analyzed games. 390pp.   20640-8 Pa. $3.50

THE FITZWILLIAM VIRGINAL BOOK, edited by J. Fuller Maitland, W.B. Squire. Famous early 17th century collection of keyboard music, 300 works by Morley, Byrd, Bull, Gibbons, etc. Modern notation. Total of 938pp. $8\frac{3}{8}$ x 11.
ECE 21068-5, 21069-3 Pa., Two vol. set $12.00

COMPLETE STRING QUARTETS, Wolfgang A. Mozart. Breitkopf and Härtel edition. All 23 string quartets plus alternate slow movement to K156. Study score. 277pp. $9\frac{3}{8}$ x $12\frac{1}{4}$.
22372-8 Pa. $6.00

COMPLETE SONG CYCLES, Franz Schubert. Complete piano, vocal music of Die Schöne Müllerin, Die Winterreise, Schwanengesang. Also Drinker English singing translations. Breitkopf and Härtel edition. 217pp. $9\frac{3}{8}$ x $12\frac{1}{4}$.
22649-2 Pa. $4.00

THE COMPLETE PRELUDES AND ETUDES FOR PIANOFORTE SOLO, Alexander Scriabin. All the preludes and etudes including many perfectly spun miniatures. Edited by K.N. Igumnov and Y.I. Mil'shteyn. 250pp. 9 x 12.
22919-X Pa. $5.00

TRISTAN UND ISOLDE, Richard Wagner. Full orchestral score with complete instrumentation. Do not confuse with piano reduction. Commentary by Felix Mottl, great Wagnerian conductor and scholar. Study score. 655pp. $8\frac{1}{8}$ x 11.
22915-7 Pa. $10.00

FAVORITE SONGS OF THE NINETIES, ed. Robert Fremont. Full reproduction, including covers, of 88 favorites: Ta-Ra-Ra-Boom-De-Aye, The Band Played On, Bird in a Gilded Cage, Under the Bamboo Tree, After the Ball, etc. 401pp. 9 x 12.
EBE 21536-9 Pa. $6.95

SOUSA'S GREAT MARCHES IN PIANO TRANSCRIPTION: ORIGINAL SHEET MUSIC OF 23 WORKS, John Philip Sousa. Selected by Lester S. Levy. Playing edition includes: The Stars and Stripes Forever, The Thunderer, The Gladiator, King Cotton, Washington Post, much more. 24 illustrations. 111pp. 9 x 12.
USO 23132-1 Pa. $3.50

CLASSIC PIANO RAGS, selected with an introduction by Rudi Blesh. Best ragtime music (1897-1922) by Scott Joplin, James Scott, Joseph F. Lamb, Tom Turpin, 9 others. Printed from best original sheet music, plus covers. 364pp. 9 x 12.
EBE 20469-3 Pa. $6.95

ANALYSIS OF CHINESE CHARACTERS, C.D. Wilder, J.H. Ingram. 1000 most important characters analyzed according to primitives, phonetics, historical development. Traditional method offers mnemonic aid to beginner, intermediate student of Chinese, Japanese. 365pp.
23045-7 Pa. $4.00

MODERN CHINESE: A BASIC COURSE, Faculty of Peking University. Self study, classroom course in modern Mandarin. Records contain phonetics, vocabulary, sentences, lessons. 249 page book contains all recorded text, translations, grammar, vocabulary, exercises. Best course on market. 3 12" $33\frac{1}{3}$ monaural records, book, album.
98832-5 Set $12.50

CONSTRUCTION OF AMERICAN FURNITURE TREASURES, Lester Margon. 344 detail drawings, complete text on constructing exact reproductions of 38 early American masterpieces: Hepplewhite sideboard, Duncan Phyfe drop-leaf table, mantel clock, gate-leg dining table, Pa. German cupboard, more. 38 plates. 54 photographs. 168pp. 8⅜ x 11¼. 23056-2 Pa. $4.00

JEWELRY MAKING AND DESIGN, Augustus F. Rose, Antonio Cirino. Professional secrets revealed in thorough, practical guide: tools, materials, processes; rings, brooches, chains, cast pieces, enamelling, setting stones, etc. Do not confuse with skimpy introductions: beginner can use, professional can learn from it. Over 200 illustrations. 306pp. 21750-7 Pa. $3.00

METALWORK AND ENAMELLING, Herbert Maryon. Generally conceded best all-around book. Countless trade secrets: materials, tools, soldering, filigree, setting, inlay, niello, repoussé, casting, polishing, etc. For beginner or expert. Author was foremost British expert. 330 illustrations. 335pp. 22702-2 Pa. $3.50

WEAVING WITH FOOT-POWER LOOMS, Edward F. Worst. Setting up a loom, beginning to weave, constructing equipment, using dyes, more, plus over 285 drafts of traditional patterns including Colonial and Swedish weaves. More than 200 other figures. For beginning and advanced. 275pp. 8¾ x 6⅜. 23064-3 Pa. $4.00

WEAVING A NAVAJO BLANKET, Gladys A. Reichard. Foremost anthropologist studied under Navajo women, reveals every step in process from wool, dyeing, spinning, setting up loom, designing, weaving. Much history, symbolism. With this book you could make one yourself. 97 illustrations. 222pp. 22992-0 Pa. $3.00

NATURAL DYES AND HOME DYEING, Rita J. Adrosko. Use natural ingredients: bark, flowers, leaves, lichens, insects etc. Over 135 specific recipes from historical sources for cotton, wool, other fabrics. Genuine premodern handicrafts. 12 illustrations. 160pp. 22688-3 Pa. $2.00

THE HAND DECORATION OF FABRICS, Francis J. Kafka. Outstanding, profusely illustrated guide to stenciling, batik, block printing, tie dyeing, freehand painting, silk screen printing, and novelty decoration. 356 illustrations. 198pp. 6 x 9. 21401-X Pa. $3.00

THOMAS NAST: CARTOONS AND ILLUSTRATIONS, with text by Thomas Nast St. Hill. Father of American political cartooning. Cartoons that destroyed Tweed Ring; inflation, free love, church and state; original Republican elephant and Democratic donkey; Santa Claus; more. 117 illustrations. 146pp. 9 x 12.
22983-1 Pa. $4.00
23067-8 Clothbd. $8.50

FREDERIC REMINGTON: 173 DRAWINGS AND ILLUSTRATIONS. Most famous of the Western artists, most responsible for our myths about the American West in its untamed days. Complete reprinting of *Drawings of Frederic Remington* (1897), plus other selections. 4 additional drawings in color on covers. 140pp. 9 x 12. 20714-5 Pa. $3.95

AUSTRIAN COOKING AND BAKING, Gretel Beer. Authentic thick soups, wiener schnitzel, veal goulash, more, plus dumplings, puff pastries, nut cakes, sacher tortes, other great Austrian desserts. 224pp. USO 23220-4 Pa. $2.50

CHEESES OF THE WORLD, U.S.D.A. Dictionary of cheeses containing descriptions of over 400 varieties of cheese from common Cheddar to exotic Surati. Up to two pages are given to important cheeses like Camembert, Cottage, Edam, etc. 151pp. 22831-2 Pa. $1.50

TRITTON'S GUIDE TO BETTER WINE AND BEER MAKING FOR BEGINNERS, S.M. Tritton. All you need to know to make family-sized quantities of over 100 types of grape, fruit, herb, vegetable wines; plus beers, mead, cider, more. 11 illustrations. 157pp. USO 22528-3 Pa. $2.00

DECORATIVE LABELS FOR HOME CANNING, PRESERVING, AND OTHER HOUSEHOLD AND GIFT USES, Theodore Menten. 128 gummed, perforated labels, beautifully printed in 2 colors. 12 versions in traditional, Art Nouveau, Art Deco styles. Adhere to metal, glass, wood, most plastics. 24pp. 8¼ x 11. 23219-0 Pa. $2.00

FIVE ACRES AND INDEPENDENCE, Maurice G. Kains. Great back-to-the-land classic explains basics of self-sufficient farming: economics, plants, crops, animals, orchards, soils, land selection, host of other necessary things. Do not confuse with skimpy faddist literature; Kains was one of America's greatest agriculturalists. 95 illustrations. 397pp. 20974-1 Pa. $2.95

GROWING VEGETABLES IN THE HOME GARDEN, U.S. Dept. of Agriculture. Basic information on site, soil conditions, selection of vegetables, planting, cultivation, gathering. Up-to-date, concise, authoritative. Covers 60 vegetables. 30 illustrations. 123pp. 23167-4 Pa. $1.35

FRUITS FOR THE HOME GARDEN, Dr. U.P. Hedrick. A chapter covering each type of garden fruit, advice on plant care, soils, grafting, pruning, sprays, transplanting, and much more! Very full. 53 illustrations. 175pp. 22944-0 Pa. $2.50

GARDENING ON SANDY SOIL IN NORTH TEMPERATE AREAS, Christine Kelway. Is your soil too light, too sandy? Improve your soil, select plants that survive under such conditions. Both vegetables and flowers. 42 photos. 148pp. USO 23199-2 Pa. $2.50

THE FRAGRANT GARDEN: A BOOK ABOUT SWEET SCENTED FLOWERS AND LEAVES, Louise Beebe Wilder. Fullest, best book on growing plants for their fragrances. Descriptions of hundreds of plants, both well-known and overlooked. 407pp. 23071-6 Pa. $3.50

EASY GARDENING WITH DROUGHT-RESISTANT PLANTS, Arno and Irene Nehrling. Authoritative guide to gardening with plants that require a minimum of water: seashore, desert, and rock gardens; house plants; annuals and perennials; much more. 190 illustrations. 320pp. 23230-1 Pa. $3.50

THE BEST DR. THORNDYKE DETECTIVE STORIES, R. Austin Freeman. The Case of Oscar Brodski, The Moabite Cipher, and 5 other favorites featuring the great scientific detective, plus his long-believed-lost first adventure — 31 New Inn — reprinted here for the first time. Edited by E.F. Bleiler. USO 20388-3 Pa. $3.00

BEST "THINKING MACHINE" DETECTIVE STORIES, Jacques Futrelle. The Problem of Cell 13 and 11 other stories about Prof. Augustus S.F.X. Van Dusen, including two "lost" stories. First reprinting of several. Edited by E.F. Bleiler. 241pp.
20537-1 Pa. $3.00

UNCLE SILAS, J. Sheridan LeFanu. Victorian Gothic mystery novel, considered by many best of period, even better than Collins or Dickens. Wonderful psychological terror. Introduction by Frederick Shroyer. 436pp. 21715-9 Pa. $4.00

BEST DR. POGGIOLI DETECTIVE STORIES, T.S. Stribling. 15 best stories from EQMM and The Saint offer new adventures in Mexico, Florida, Tennessee hills as Poggioli unravels mysteries and combats Count Jalacki. 217pp. 23227-1 Pa. $3.00

EIGHT DIME NOVELS, selected with an introduction by E.F. Bleiler. Adventures of Old King Brady, Frank James, Nick Carter, Deadwood Dick, Buffalo Bill, The Steam Man, Frank Merriwell, and Horatio Alger — 1877 to 1905. Important, entertaining popular literature in facsimile reprint, with original covers. 190pp. 9 x 12. 22975-0 Pa. $3.50

ALICE'S ADVENTURES UNDER GROUND, Lewis Carroll. Facsimile of ms. Carroll gave Alice Liddell in 1864. Different in many ways from final Alice. Handlettered, illustrated by Carroll. Introduction by Martin Gardner. 128pp. 21482-6 Pa. $1.50

ALICE IN WONDERLAND COLORING BOOK, Lewis Carroll. Pictures by John Tenniel. Large-size versions of the famous illustrations of Alice, Cheshire Cat, Mad Hatter and all the others, waiting for your crayons. Abridged text. 36 illustrations. 64pp. 8¼ x 11. 22853-3 Pa. $1.50

AVENTURES D'ALICE AU PAYS DES MERVEILLES, Lewis Carroll. Bué's translation of "Alice" into French, supervised by Carroll himself. Novel way to learn language. (No English text.) 42 Tenniel illustrations. 196pp. 22836-3 Pa. $2.00

MYTHS AND FOLK TALES OF IRELAND, Jeremiah Curtin. 11 stories that are Irish versions of European fairy tales and 9 stories from the Fenian cycle — 20 tales of legend and magic that comprise an essential work in the history of folklore. 256pp. 22430-9 Pa. $3.00

EAST O' THE SUN AND WEST O' THE MOON, George W. Dasent. Only full edition of favorite, wonderful Norwegian fairytales — Why the Sea is Salt, Boots and the Troll, etc. — with 77 illustrations by Kittelsen & Werenskiöld. 418pp.
22521-6 Pa. $3.50

PERRAULT'S FAIRY TALES, Charles Perrault and Gustave Doré. Original versions of Cinderella, Sleeping Beauty, Little Red Riding Hood, etc. in best translation, with 34 wonderful illustrations by Gustave Doré. 117pp. 8⅛ x 11. 22311-6 Pa. $2.50

SLEEPING BEAUTY, illustrated by Arthur Rackham. Perhaps the fullest, most delightful version ever, told by C.S. Evans. Rackham's best work. 49 illustrations. 110pp. 7⅞ x 10¾. 22756-1 Pa. $2.00

THE WONDERFUL WIZARD OF OZ, L. Frank Baum. Facsimile in full color of America's finest children's classic. Introduction by Martin Gardner. 143 illustrations by W.W. Denslow. 267pp. 20691-2 Pa. $2.50

GOOPS AND HOW TO BE THEM, Gelett Burgess. Classic tongue-in-cheek masquerading as etiquette book. 87 verses, 170 cartoons as Goops demonstrate virtues of table manners, neatness, courtesy, more. 88pp. 6½ x 9¼. 22233-0 Pa. $1.50

THE BROWNIES, THEIR BOOK, Palmer Cox. Small as mice, cunning as foxes, exuberant, mischievous, Brownies go to zoo, toy shop, seashore, circus, more. 24 verse adventures. 266 illustrations. 144pp. 6⅝ x 9¼. 21265-3 Pa. $1.75

BILLY WHISKERS: THE AUTOBIOGRAPHY OF A GOAT, Frances Trego Montgomery. Escapades of that rambunctious goat. Favorite from turn of the century America. 24 illustrations. 259pp. 22345-0 Pa. $2.75

THE ROCKET BOOK, Peter Newell. Fritz, janitor's kid, sets off rocket in basement of apartment house; an ingenious hole punched through every page traces course of rocket. 22 duotone drawings, verses. 48pp. 6⅞ x 8⅜. 22044-3 Pa. $1.50

PECK'S BAD BOY AND HIS PA, George W. Peck. Complete double-volume of great American childhood classic. Hennery's ingenious pranks against outraged pomposity of pa and the grocery man. 97 illustrations. Introduction by E.F. Bleiler. 347pp. 20497-9 Pa. $2.50

THE TALE OF PETER RABBIT, Beatrix Potter. The inimitable Peter's terrifying adventure in Mr. McGregor's garden, with all 27 wonderful, full-color Potter illustrations. 55pp. 4¼ x 5½. USO 22827-4 Pa. $1.00

THE TALE OF MRS. TIGGY-WINKLE, Beatrix Potter. Your child will love this story about a very special hedgehog and all 27 wonderful, full-color Potter illustrations. 57pp. 4¼ x 5½. USO 20546-0 Pa. $1.00

THE TALE OF BENJAMIN BUNNY, Beatrix Potter. Peter Rabbit's cousin coaxes him back into Mr. McGregor's garden for a whole new set of adventures. A favorite with children. All 27 full-color illustrations. 59pp. 4¼ x 5½. USO 21102-9 Pa. $1.00

THE MERRY ADVENTURES OF ROBIN HOOD, Howard Pyle. Facsimile of original (1883) edition, finest modern version of English outlaw's adventures. 23 illustrations by Pyle. 296pp. 6½ x 9¼. 22043-5 Pa. $2.75

TWO LITTLE SAVAGES, Ernest Thompson Seton. Adventures of two boys who lived as Indians; explaining Indian ways, woodlore, pioneer methods. 293 illustrations. 286pp. 20985-7 Pa. $3.00

MOTHER GOOSE'S MELODIES. Facsimile of fabulously rare Munroe and Francis "copyright 1833" Boston edition. Familiar and unusual rhymes, wonderful old woodcut illustrations. Edited by E.F. Bleiler. 128pp. 4½ x 6⅜. 22577-1 Pa. $1.00

MOTHER GOOSE IN HIEROGLYPHICS. Favorite nursery rhymes presented in rebus form for children. Fascinating 1849 edition reproduced in toto, with key. Introduction by E.F. Bleiler. About 400 woodcuts. 64pp. 6⅞ x 5¼. 20745-5 Pa. $1.00

PETER PIPER'S PRACTICAL PRINCIPLES OF PLAIN & PERFECT PRONUNCIATION. Alliterative jingles and tongue-twisters. Reproduction in full of 1830 first American edition. 25 spirited woodcuts. 32pp. 4½ x 6⅜. 22560-7 Pa. $1.00

MARMADUKE MULTIPLY'S MERRY METHOD OF MAKING MINOR MATHEMATICIANS. Fellow to Peter Piper, it teaches multiplication table by catchy rhymes and woodcuts. 1841 Munroe & Francis edition. Edited by E.F. Bleiler. 103pp. 4⅝ x 6.
22773-1 Pa. $1.25
20171-6 Clothbd. $3.00

THE NIGHT BEFORE CHRISTMAS, Clement Moore. Full text, and woodcuts from original 1848 book. Also critical, historical material. 19 illustrations. 40pp. 4⅝ x 6. 22797-9 Pa. $1.00

THE KING OF THE GOLDEN RIVER, John Ruskin. Victorian children's classic of three brothers, their attempts to reach the Golden River, what becomes of them. Facsimile of original 1889 edition. 22 illustrations. 56pp. 4⅝ x 6⅜.
20066-3 Pa. $1.25

DREAMS OF THE RAREBIT FIEND, Winsor McCay. Pioneer cartoon strip, unexcelled for beauty, imagination, in 60 full sequences. Incredible technical virtuosity, wonderful visual wit. Historical introduction. 62pp. 8⅜ x 11¼. 21347-1 Pa. $2.00

THE KATZENJAMMER KIDS, Rudolf Dirks. In full color, 14 strips from 1906-7; full of imagination, characteristic humor. Classic of great historical importance. Introduction by August Derleth. 32pp. 9¼ x 12¼. 23005-8 Pa. $2.00

LITTLE ORPHAN ANNIE AND LITTLE ORPHAN ANNIE IN COSMIC CITY, Harold Gray. Two great sequences from the early strips: our curly-haired heroine defends the Warbucks' financial empire and, then, takes on meanie Phineas P. Pinchpenny. Leapin' lizards! 178pp. 6⅛ x 8⅜. 23107-0 Pa. $2.00

WHEN A FELLER NEEDS A FRIEND, Clare Briggs. 122 cartoons by one of the greatest newspaper cartoonists of the early 20th century — about growing up, making a living, family life, daily frustrations and occasional triumphs. 121pp. 8½ x 9½.
23148-8 Pa. $2.50

THE BEST OF GLUYAS WILLIAMS. 100 drawings by one of America's finest cartoonists: The Day a Cake of Ivory Soap Sank at Proctor & Gamble's, At the Life Insurance Agents' Banquet, and many other gems from the 20's and 30's. 118pp. 8⅜ x 11¼. 22737-5 Pa. $2.50

JEWISH GREETING CARDS, Ed Sibbett, Jr. 16 cards to cut and color. Three say "Happy Chanukah," one "Happy New Year," others have no message, show stars of David, Torahs, wine cups, other traditional themes. 16 envelopes. 8¼ x 11.
23225-5 Pa. $2.00

AUBREY BEARDSLEY GREETING CARD BOOK, Aubrey Beardsley. Edited by Theodore Menten. 16 elegant yet inexpensive greeting cards let you combine your own sentiments with subtle Art Nouveau lines. 16 different Aubrey Beardsley designs that you can color or not, as you wish. 16 envelopes. 64pp. 8¼ x 11.
23173-9 Pa. $2.00

RECREATIONS IN THE THEORY OF NUMBERS, Albert Beiler. Number theory, an inexhaustible source of puzzles, recreations, for beginners and advanced. Divisors, perfect numbers. scales of notation, etc. 349pp.
21096-0 Pa. $2.50

AMUSEMENTS IN MATHEMATICS, Henry E. Dudeney. One of largest puzzle collections, based on algebra, arithmetic, permutations, probability, plane figure dissection, properties of numbers, by one of world's foremost puzzlists. Solutions. 450 illustrations. 258pp.
20473-1 Pa. $2.75

MATHEMATICS, MAGIC AND MYSTERY, Martin Gardner. Puzzle editor for Scientific American explains math behind: card tricks, stage mind reading, coin and match tricks, counting out games, geometric dissections. Probability, sets, theory of numbers, clearly explained. Plus more than 400 tricks, guaranteed to work. 135 illustrations. 176pp.
20335-2 Pa. $2.00

BEST MATHEMATICAL PUZZLES OF SAM LOYD, edited by Martin Gardner. Bizarre, original, whimsical puzzles by America's greatest puzzler. From fabulously rare Cyclopedia, including famous 14-15 puzzles, the Horse of a Different Color, 115 more. Elementary math. 150 illustrations. 167pp.
20498-7 Pa. $2.00

MATHEMATICAL PUZZLES FOR BEGINNERS AND ENTHUSIASTS, Geoffrey Mott-Smith. 189 puzzles from easy to difficult involving arithmetic, logic, algebra, properties of digits, probability. Explanation of math behind puzzles. 135 illustrations. 248pp.
20198-8 Pa. $2.00

BIG BOOK OF MAZES AND LABYRINTHS, Walter Shepherd. Classical, solid, and ripple mazes; short path and avoidance labyrinths; more —50 mazes and labyrinths in all. 12 other figures. Full solutions. 112pp. 8⅛ x 11.
22951-3 Pa. $2.00

COIN GAMES AND PUZZLES, Maxey Brooke. 60 puzzles, games and stunts —from Japan, Korea, Africa and the ancient world, by Dudeney and the other great puzzlers, as well as Maxey Brooke's own creations. Full solutions. 67 illustrations. 94pp.
22893-2 Pa. $1.25

HAND SHADOWS TO BE THROWN UPON THE WALL, Henry Bursill. Wonderful Victorian novelty tells how to make flying birds, dog, goose, deer, and 14 others. 32pp. 6½ x 9¼.
21779-5 Pa. $1.00

BUILD YOUR OWN LOW-COST HOME, L.O. Anderson, H.F. Zornig. U.S. Dept. of Agriculture sets of plans, full, detailed, for 11 houses: A-Frame, circular, conventional. Also construction manual. Save hundreds of dollars. 204pp. 11 x 16.
21525-3 Pa. $5.95

HOW TO BUILD A WOOD-FRAME HOUSE, L.O. Anderson. Comprehensive, easy to follow U.S. Government manual: placement, foundations, framing, sheathing, roof, insulation, plaster, finishing — almost everything else. 179 illustrations. 223pp. 7⅞ x 10¾.
22954-8 Pa. $3.50

CONCRETE, MASONRY AND BRICKWORK, U.S. Department of the Army. Practical handbook for the home owner and small builder, manual contains basic principles, techniques, and important background information on construction with concrete, concrete blocks, and brick. 177 figures, 37 tables. 200pp. 6½ x 9¼.
23203-4 Pa. $4.00

THE STANDARD BOOK OF QUILT MAKING AND COLLECTING, Marguerite Ickis. Full information, full-sized patterns for making 46 traditional quilts, also 150 other patterns. Quilted cloths, lamé, satin quilts, etc. 483 illustrations. 273pp. 6⅞ x 9⅝.
20582-7 Pa. $3.50

101 PATCHWORK PATTERNS, Ruby S. McKim. 101 beautiful, immediately useable patterns, full-size, modern and traditional. Also general information, estimating, quilt lore. 124pp. 7⅞ x 10¾.
20773-0 Pa. $2.50

KNIT YOUR OWN NORWEGIAN SWEATERS, Dale Yarn Company. Complete instructions for 50 authentic sweaters, hats, mittens, gloves, caps, etc. Thoroughly modern designs that command high prices in stores. 24 patterns, 24 color photographs. Nearly 100 charts and other illustrations. 58pp. 8⅜ x 11¼.
23031-7 Pa. $2.50

IRON-ON TRANSFER PATTERNS FOR CREWEL AND EMBROIDERY FROM EARLY AMERICAN SOURCES, edited by Rita Weiss. 75 designs, borders, alphabets, from traditional American sources printed on translucent paper in transfer ink. Reuseable. Instructions. Test patterns. 24pp. 8¼ x 11.
23162-3 Pa. $1.50

AMERICAN INDIAN NEEDLEPOINT DESIGNS FOR PILLOWS, BELTS, HANDBAGS AND OTHER PROJECTS, Roslyn Epstein. 37 authentic American Indian designs adapted for modern needlepoint projects. Grid backing makes designs easily transferable to canvas. 48pp. 8¼ x 11.
22973-4 Pa. $1.50

CHARTED FOLK DESIGNS FOR CROSS-STITCH EMBROIDERY, Maria Foris & Andreas Foris. 278 charted folk designs, most in 2 colors, from Danube region: florals, fantastic beasts, geometrics, traditional symbols, more. Border and central patterns. 77pp. 8¼ x 11.
USO 23191-7 Pa. $2.00

Prices subject to change without notice.
Available at your book dealer or write for free catalogue to Dept. GI, Dover Publications, Inc., 180 Varick St., N.Y., N.Y. 10014. Dover publishes more than 150 books each year on science, elementary and advanced mathematics, biology, music, art, literary history, social sciences and other areas.